Crime
Classification
Manual

Crime Classification Manual

John E. Douglas
Federal Bureau of Investigation
Ann W. Burgess
University of Pennsylvania
Allen G. Burgess
Northeastern University
Robert K. Ressler
Federal Bureau of Investigation (Retired)

WITH CHAPTERS BY
John E. Douglas and Corinne M. Munn
Peter A. Smerick   Gregory M. Cooper
Corinne M. Munn

JOSSEY-BASS
A Wiley Company
www.josseybass.com

Published by

JOSSEY-BASS
A Wiley Company
989 Market Street
San Francisco, CA 94103-1741

www.josseybass.com

364.012
C929
1997

FIRST JOSSEY-BASS PAPERBACK EDITION 1997.
FIRST LEXINGTON BOOKS PAPERBACK EDITION 1995.

Jossey-Bass books and products are available through most bookstores. To contact Jossey-Bass directly, call (888) 378-2537, fax to (800) 605-2665, or visit our website at www.josseybass.com.

Substantial discounts on bulk quantities of Jossey-Bass books are available to corporations, professional associations, and other organizations. For details and discount information, contact the special sales department at Jossey-Bass.

We at Jossey-Bass strive to use the most environmentally sensitive paper stocks available to us. Our publications are printed on acid-free recycled stock whenever possible, and our paper always meets or exceeds minimum GPO and EPA requirements.

Library of Congress Cataloging-in-Publication Data

Crime classification manual / [edited by] John E. Douglas ... [et
   al.].
         p.   cm.
      Originally published: New York : Lexington Books, c1992.
      Includes bibliographical references and index.
      ISBN 0-7879-3885-8
      1. Crime—Classification—Handbooks, manuals, etc.   2. Crime—
   United States—Classification—Handbooks, manuals, etc.
   I. Douglas, John E.
   HV6253.C75   1997
   364'.01'2—dc21   91-17809

The definitions and classifications of crimes in this manual are not necessarily consistent with state or Federal law and are for purposes of crime classification only.

Readers are further reminded that the subsections of the manual and their contents are not meant to be all-inclusive.

The contents of this manual are the product of the National Center for the Analysis of Violent Crime but may not represent the views of all law enforcement agencies.

PB Printing 10 9 8 7 6

Contents

Preface

This book is about classifying crime. Professions develop and advance their science as they are able to organize and classify their work. The nature of science began when organisms began to generalize, to see similarities between themselves and members of their own species or to see differences and other similarities between other species and themselves (Boring 1957). Thus, the nature of science requires that one first observe and then attempt to categorize, compare, and classify observations. Classification is a process in data collection and analysis in which data are grouped according to previously determined characteristics (Mosby 1987).

The 1980s witnessed major advancement in investigative science. A series of FBI studies conducted in the 1980s on sexual murderers, rapists, child molesters and abductors, and arsonists described and identified critical characteristics of these crimes. These characteristics initially were used for profiling techniques. An additional use of the research findings has now been compiled into this crime classification manual.

This is the first edition of the *Crime Classification Manual*, better known simply as CCM. The development of this manual over the last six years has begun to receive notice from FBI investigative profilers, law enforcement officers, corrections and parole staff, and mental health staff.

The purpose of this manual is fourfold:

1. To standardize terminology within the criminal justice field
2. To facilitate communication within the criminal justice field and between criminal justice and mental health

3. To educate the criminal justice system and the public at large to the types of crimes being committed

4. To develop a data base for investigative research

In the development of the manual, a decision was made to base the classification on the primary intent of the criminal. The intent categories include: (1) criminal enterprise, (2) personal cause, (3) sexual intent, and (4) group cause.

Task Force

Task force groups chaired by supervisory Special Agents at the FBI's National Center for the Analysis of Violent Crime (NCAVC) worked on refining the crime categories. The preliminary draft of the manual was presented to an advisory committee, which provided additional comments and suggestions for refinement of the manual.

Definitions

For the purposes of this book, the crime definitions are taken from the FBI's Uniform Crime Reporting Program and are as follows:

Murder is the willful and unlawful killing of one human being by another. The classification of this offense, as for all other crime index offenses, is based solely on police investigation as opposed to the determination of a court, medical examiner, coroner, jury, or other judicial body. Not included in this classification are deaths caused by negligence, suicide, or accident; justifiable homicides; and attempts to murder or assaults to murder, which are scored as aggravated assaults.

Sexual assault includes forcible rape, as defined by the FBI's Uniform Crime Reports: the carnal knowledge of a female forcibly and against her will. In addition, assaults and attempts to commit rape by force or threat of force against females and males are included, as well as crimes of noncontact, commonly called nuisance offenses. All ages, child, adolescent, and adult, are included in this category.

Arson, as defined by the Uniform Crime Reports, is any willful or malicious burning or attempt to burn, with or without intent to defraud, a dwelling house, public building, motor vehicle or aircraft, or personal property of another.

Organization of the Manual

This manual is divided into two major parts. The first part contains the three major crime categories that are classified to date. These categories contain defining characteristics, victimology, crime scene indicators, forensics, and investigative considerations where applicable. Case illustrations accompany each classification.

The second part presents a review of the study of crime. It also addresses key concepts in the decision process for classifying a crime, the detection of staging and personation at the crime scene, the modus operandi and the signature aspects of violent crime, crime scene photography, prescriptive interviewing, and the role of the FBI Academy's Investigative Support Unit in assisting law enforcement.

Our results have implications not only for law enforcement personnel who are responsible for the investigation of a crime, but also for professionals in other disciplines that address the crime problem. These groups include criminal justice professionals directly involved with the legal aspects of crime; correctional institution administrators and staff personnel, who not only have custody of criminals, but also are responsible for decisions regarding these individuals' return to society; for mental health professionals, both those involved with offender treatment and those assisting victims and families affected by these crimes; for social service personnel working with juveniles, as they detect early signs and characteristics of violent individuals and seek to divert these individuals from criminal activity; for criminologists who study the problem of violent crime; and for public policymakers who attempt to address the problem through their decisions. It is our hope that this book will advance the knowledge base of these professionals as they seek increased understanding of the nature of crime and of the individuals who commit such crime.

Acknowledgments

Many people have helped with this project. We wish to acknowledge past FBI Director William H. Webster and Executive Assistant Director John E. Otto for their early support of the criminal investigative research project efforts of the Behavioral Science Unit, as well as current FBI Director William S. Sessions for his continuing support.

We also wish to acknowledge Anthony E. Daniels, Assistant Director, FBI Academy, Quantico; John J. Burke, Inspector–Deputy Assistant Director, Training and Administration; Vernon D. Kohl, Inspector–Deputy Assistant Director, Instruction and Operations; Lawrence J. Monroe, Section Chief, Instruction and Operations Section; and Jon J. Wehmeyer, Assistant Section Chief for their encouragement of the crime classification project.

We are especially appreciative for the grant monies received from the Department of Justice. We are indebted to many Department of Justice officials, including Robert W. Sweet, Jr., Administrator, Office of Juvenile Justice and Delinquency Prevention, for the release of monies to study serial child molesters, abductors, and murderers of children; Robert O. Heck for his belief in the criminal profiling concept and the Violent Criminal Apprehension Program, and Jane Nady Burnley and John Dawson from Office for Victims of Crime for the monies to extend data collection on the victim to victimizer linkage.

This manual represents over a decade of work by the Special Agents (SA) in the Investigative Support Unit, the Behavioral Science Unit, and the Forensic Science Research Training Center at the FBI Academy, Quantico,

Virginia. We wish to acknowledge the Special Agent authors of this manual who are individually identified by work group in this book's contributors section and to the Classification Committee Chairmen SA John E. Douglas, SA Robert R. Hazelwood, Dr. David J. Icove, SA Kenneth V. Lanning, SA Gregg O. McCrary, SA Judson M. Ray, Robert K. Ressler and SA James A. Wright. We also wish to acknowledge the superb work of Classification Coordinator and Research Associate Corinne Munn, who as a summer 1990 intern met tirelessly with the work groups to detail the defining characteristics of each crime classification. She handled the communications between Boston and Quantico, researched crime case examples, and typed drafts of the manual. She is entitled to a large measure of gratitude for her efforts. Thanks also are extended to Regina C. Caddy, Bernadette Cloniger, and Cynthia Lent for easing the transition over the years from idea to final project.

The national wire services, national magazines, and local newspapers provided direction for our search of case studies used in this manual. We wish to take this opportunity to thank those newswriters for their excellent work in crime reporting.

Contributors

COEDITORS

John E. Douglas
Allen G. Burgess

Ann W. Burgess
Robert K. Ressler

CLASSIFICATION COORDINATOR/RESEARCH ASSOCIATE

Corinne M. Munn

CLASSIFICATION COMMITTEES

Group Cause Homicide

Committee Chairmen:
SA James A. Wright and SA Judson M. Ray

SA Larry G. Ankrom
SA Joseph M. Conley
SA Gregory M. Cooper
SA John E. Douglas
SA Stephen E. Etter
SA David C. Gomez
Terence J. Green
SA William Hagmaier III

SA Gregg O. McCrary
SA R. Stephen Mardigian
SA Jana D. Monroe
Winston C. Norman
SA Thomas F. Salp
SA Peter A. Smerick
SA Clinton R. VanZandt
Eric W. Witzig

Personal Cause Homicide

Committee Chairman:
SA Judson M. Ray

SA Larry G. Ankrom
SA Alan C. Brantley
SA Gregory M. Cooper
SA John E. Douglas
SA Stephen E. Etter
SA David C. Gomez
Terence J. Green
SA William Hagmaier III
SA Gregg O. McCrary

SA R. Stephen Mardigian
SA Jana D. Monroe
Winston C. Norman
SA Thomas F. Salp
SA Peter A. Smerick
SA Clinton R. VanZandt
Eric W. Witzig
SA James A. Wright

Criminal Enterprise Homicide

Committee Chairman:
SA Gregg O. McCrary

SA Larry G. Ankrom
SA Alan C. Brantley
SA Gregory M. Cooper
SA John E. Douglas
SA Stephen E. Etter
SA David C. Gomez
Terence J. Green
SA William Hagmaier III
SA R. Stephen Mardigian

SA Jana D. Monroe
Winston C. Norman
SA Judson M. Ray
SA Thomas F. Salp
SA Peter A. Smerick
SA Clinton R. VanZandt
Eric W. Witzig
SA James A. Wright

Sexual Homicide

Committee Cochairmen:
SA John E. Douglas and Robert K. Ressler

SA Larry G. Ankrom
SA Gregory M. Cooper
SA Stephen E. Etter
SA David C. Gomez
SA William Hagmaier III
SA Robert R. Hazelwood
SA Kenneth V. Lanning

SA Gregg O. McCrary
SA R. Stephen Mardigian
SA Jana D. Monroe
SA Judson M. Ray
SA Thomas F. Salp
SA Peter A. Smerick
SA James A. Wright

Rape and Sexual Assault

Committee Cochairmen:
SA Robert R. Hazelwood and SA Kenneth V. Lanning

Allen G. Burgess
Ann W. Burgess
SA John E. Douglas

Raymond Knight
Robert A. Prentky

Arson

Committee Chairman:
David J. Icove

SA John E. Douglas
SA Gus Gary

Timothy G. Huff
SA Peter A. Smerick

OTHER CONTRIBUTORS

Randy Blackmon, Sheriff, Homicide, Jasper County, Ridgeland, South Carolina

Skip Coile, Sergeant, Criminal Enterprise Homicide, Bureau of Drug Enforcement, Alaska Department of Public Safety, Anchorage, Alaska

Harold Duke, Detective, Rock Hill Police Department, South Carolina

James Elvins, Captain, Criminal Enterprise Homicide, Sedgwick County Sheriff's Department, Wichita, Kansas

Robert Friis, Sargeant, Investigation Unit, Fridley Police Department, Minnesota

SA Faye Greenlee, Criminal Enterprise Homicide, FBI, Seattle, Washington

SA Harold W. Head, Criminal Enterprise, FBI, Portland, Oregon

SA Lou Ann Henderson, Criminal Enterprise Homicide, FBI, Anchorage, Alaska

Richard Henry, Chief of Investigations, Homicide, Gloucester County Prosecutor's Office, New Jersey

Robert Hole, Deputy District Attorney, Search Warrant Consultant, Contra Costa County District Attorney's Office, California

Sgt. Joseph Holmes, Gang Murder, Operation Safe Streets, Los Angeles County Sheriff's Department, California

Hedy Immoos, Criminal Intelligence Specialist, Gang Murder, Gangs/Criminal Extremists Unit, California Bureau of Organized Crime and Criminal Intelligence, Sacramento, California

R. E. MacKay, Inspector, Criminal Profile Unit, Royal Canadian Mounted Police, Ottawa, Ontario, Canada

Jim McCormick, Detective, Major Crime Unit, New Jersey State Police, Trenton, New Jersey

SA James J. McNamara, Criminal Enterprise, FBI, Honolulu, Hawaii

Robert Moran, Detective Captain, Vice and Intelligence, Homicide, Waterbury Police Department, Waterbury, Connecticut

Lt. Tim O'Brien, Contract Killing, Daytona Beach Police Department, Florida

Victoria O'Brien, Attorney, Special Projects Division, Office for Victims of Crime, Department of Justice, Washington, D.C.

Michael J. Prodan, Supervisory Special Agent, California Bureau of Investigation, Sacramento, California

Michael Ratcliff, Captain, Homicide, Victoria County Sheriff's Department, Victoria, Texas

Ruben Sanchez, Homicide, Metropolitan Police Department, Washington, D.C.

Dominick Steo, Executive Officer, Deputy Inspector, Group Cause Homicide, Suffolk County Police Department,

SA William Tobin, Product Tampering, FBI Laboratory Division, Washington, D.C.

Arthur Westveer, Major Case Specialist, Homicide Forensics, Criminalist Death Investigation, FBI Academy, Quantico, Virginia

CONSULTANTS

Abuobieda Badi, Colonel, Police of Sudan, Khartoum, Sudan

William Bertrand, Sergeant/Pilot, Florida Highway Patrol, Tallahassee, Florida

Walter Bruckshaw, Sergeant, Detective Bureau, Providence Police Department, Rhode Island

Donald "Lucky" DeLouche, Assistant Chief of Detectives, Calcasieu Parish Sheriff Department, Louisiana

Joseph DeMarchis, Lieutenant, Jeannette Police Department, Pennsylvania

James Dougherty, Detective, Conshohocken Police Department, Pennsylvania

Huston Eads, Sergeant/District Commander, West Virginia Department of Public Safety, Wheeling, West Virginia

Joseph Ellis, Captain, United States Marine Corps

Alfred Finchman III, Lieutenant, City of Grosse Point, Michigan Department of Public Safety

Christopher Galetti, Detective, Plymouth Township Police Department, Norristown, Pennsylvania

Bernard Hart, Lieutenant, Fort Lee Police Department, New Jersey

Richard Holden, Chief, Nassau Bay Police Department, Texas

Renaldo Levy, Inspector, Policia Tecnica Judicial, Panama

Pablo Lopez, Lieutenant, Criminal Investigations, Pinal County Sheriff Department, Arizona

Jim Mays, Detective, Columbus Police Department, Georgia

Eddie Rhodes, Sergeant, Pueblo Police Department, Colorado

Ramon Rosario, Investigator, Policia de Puerto Rico, Hato Rey, Puerto Rico

William Shovlin, Inspector, Pennsylvania State Police, Harrisburg, Pennsylvania

Alvaro Tejeira, Inspector, Policia Tecnica Judicial, Panama

CRIME CLASSIFICATION MANUAL ADVISORY BOARD

Karen Babich, Violence and Traumatic Stress Section, National Institute of Mental Health, Rockville, Maryland

Christy Bisher, National Institute of Justice, US Department of Justice, Washington, D.C.

James Breiling, Violence and Traumatic Stress Section, National Institute of Mental Health, Rockville, Maryland

John Campbell, Unit Chief, Behavioral Science Services Unit, FBI Academy, Quantico, Virginia

Major General Eugene Cromartie (ret.), Deputy Executive Director and Chief of Staff, International Association of Chiefs of Police, Arlington, Virginia

Edward F. Davis, National Training Representative, Uniform Crime Reports, FBI, Washington, D.C.

John E. Dawson, Director, Special Project Division, Office for Victims of Crime, US Department of Justice, Washington, D.C.

Roger L. Depue, President, The Academy Group, Inc., Manassas, Virginia

Michael First, DSM-IV Consultant, New York Psychiatric Institute, New York, New York

Richard Goldberg, Department of Psychiatry, Georgetown University Medical Center, Washington, D.C.

Robert O. Heck, Office of Juvenile Justice, US Department of Justice, Washington, D.C.

Raymond Knight, Brandeis University, Waltham, Massachusetts

Cynthia Lent, Research Specialist, Behavioral Science Services Unit, FBI Academy, Quantico, Virginia

James L. Luke, Forensic Pathologist, Consultant to the NCAVC, FBI Academy, Quantico, Virginia

Robert A. Prentky, Massachusetts Treatment Center, Bridgewater, Massachusetts

John B. Rabun, Jr., Vice President, Chief Operating Officer, National Center for Missing and Exploited Children, US Department of Justice, Washington, D.C.

Richard Rau, Program Manager, National Institute of Justice, US Department of Justice, Washington, D.C.

Robert Simon, Potomac, Maryland

Robert W. Sweet, Jr., Administrator, Office of Juvenile and Delinquency Prevention, US Department of Justice, Washington, D.C.

Ecford Voit, Violence and Traumatic Stress Section, National Institute of Mental Health, Rockville, Maryland

Marvin Wolfgang, Department of Criminology, University of Pennsylvania, Philadelphia, Pennsylvania

POLICE FELLOWSHIP PROGRAM, FBI ACADEMY

SA Steven Amico, United States Secret Service, Washington, D.C.

Sgt. Carlos Avila, Los Angeles County Sheriff's Department (Retired)

ATSAIC Kenneth P. Baker, United States Secret Service (Retired)

Thomas P. Brennan, Pennsylvania State Police (Retired)

Lt. Sam Bowerman, Baltimore County Police Department, Maryland

SA David Caldwell, South Carolina Law Enforcement Division, Columbia, South Carolina

Kathryn Cavanagh, Criminal Investigation Branch, Ontario Provincial Police, Ontario, Canada

SA Joseph J. Chisholm, Alcohol, Tobacco, and Firearms, Department of the Treasury, Washington, D.C.

SA Steven Conlon, Iowa Division of Criminal Investigation, Des Moines, Iowa

SA Gus Gary, Alcohol, Tobacco, and Firearms, Department of the Treasury, Washington, D.C.

SA Paul Gebicke, United States Secret Service, Washington, D.C.

Det. Robert Gebo, Seattle Police Department, Washington, D.C.

Lt. John Grant, New York State Police, Albany, New York

SA Dayle Hinman, Florida Department of Law Enforcement, Tallahassee, Florida

SA Phil Horbert, Alcohol, Tobacco, and Firearms, Department of the Treasury, Washington, D.C.

Sr. Sgt. Bronwyn Killmier, South Australia Police, Australia

SA Joel Kohout, Minnesota Bureau of Criminal Apprehension, St. Paul, Minnesota

Larry McCann, Virginia Department of State Police, Richmond, Virginia

Det. James McCormick, New Jersey State Police, Trenton, New Jersey

Insp. Ronald MacKay, Royal Canadian Mounted Police, Ottowa, Ontario, Canada

Det. Claudio Minisini, Victoria Police, Australia

Sgt. Kevin Mullen, Boston Police Department, Massachusetts

Sgt. Jon Perry, Kansas City Police Department, Missouri

Det. II Ray Pierce, New York City Police Department, New York

Det. Gary L. Plank, Nebraska State Patrol, Lincoln, Nebraska

SA Michael Prodan, California Department of Justice, Sacramento, California

Lt. Ed Richards, Texas Department of Public Safety, Austin, Texas

Carlo Schippers, National Criminal Intelligence Service, The Hague, Netherlands

Sgt. Diana Sievers, Illinois State Police, Springfield, Illinois

SA Ralph Stone, Georgia Bureau of Investigation, Decatur, Georgia

Eric Witzig, Violent Criminal Apprehension Program, FBI Academy Quantico, Virginia

Introduction

THE STUDY OF CRIME

Crime and the criminal have always fascinated society. Violent crime is of increasing concern in our society. Murder, arson, and sexual assault represent serious interpersonal violent behaviors, and law enforcement officials feel public pressure to apprehend the perpetrators as quickly as possible.

Scope of the Problem

Murder. The total number of murders in the United States during 1989 was estimated at 21,500, or 1 percent of the violent crimes reported. More persons were murdered in July of that year than during any other month, while the fewest were killed during February.

Geographically, the South, the most populous region, accounted for 43 percent of the murders. The Western states reported 20 percent; the Midwest, 19 percent; and the Northeast, 18 percent.

The murder volume increased 4 percent nationwide in 1989 over 1988. The nation's cities overall experienced an increase of 6 percent, with upward trends recorded in all but two city population groupings. Of the cities, those with populations of 25,000 to 49,999 registered the greatest increase, 14 percent. Suburban counties recorded a 1 percent rise, while the rural counties registered a 3 percent decline.

All regions experienced more murders during 1989 than in 1988. The

1

number of murders was up 6 percent in the South; 4 percent in both the Northeast and Midwest; and 1 percent in the West.

The largest group of murder victims, 76 percent, was made up of males, and 90 percent was persons eighteen years of age or older. Of victims, 49 percent were between ages twenty and thirty-four. Of victims for whom race was known, an average of fifty of every one hundred were black, forty-nine were white, and the remainder were persons of other races.

The clearance rates for murder continued to be higher than for any other crime index offense. Law enforcement agencies nationwide, as well as in the cities, were successful in clearing 68 percent of the murders occurring in their jurisdictions during 1989. Of all murder arrestees in 1989, 49 percent were under twenty-five years of age. The eighteen-to-twenty-four-year age group accounted for 36 percent of the total. Of those arrested, 88 percent were males and 12 percent were females. Blacks constituted 56 percent of the total arrestees for murder in 1989. Whites made up 42 percent, and the remainder were of other races (Uniform Crime Report, 1989).

Arson. A total of 99,599 arson offenses was reported in 1989 by 12,750 law enforcement agencies across the country. The number of arson offenses reported nationally declined 1 percent in 1989 as compared to the 1988 total. Counts for the nation's cities and suburban counties dropped 1 percent and 4 percent, respectively, while the rural counties registered a 4 percent increase. Geographically, arson decreases were experienced in the Midwest, 5 percent; in the Northeast, 3 percent; and in the South, 1 percent. A 3 percent increase was recorded in the West.

The 1989 clearance rate was 15 percent. The estimated number of arrests for arson during 1989 totaled 18,600. Of the estimated actual arson arrests for 1990, 44 percent were under eighteen years of age, and 64 percent were under age twenty-five. Males comprised 87 percent of all arson arrestees. Of those arrested, 75 percent were white, 23 percent were black, and the remainder were of other races (Uniform Crime Report, 1989).

Rape. During 1989 there were an estimated 94,504 forcible rapes of women in the United States. Rape offenses made up 6 percent of the total violent crimes. Geographically, the Southern states, the region with the largest population, accounted for 37 percent of the forcible rapes reported to law enforcement. Following were the Midwest, with 15 percent; the West, with 23 percent; and the Northeast, with 15 percent. Compared to the previous year, the 1989 forcible rape volume increased 2 percent nationwide.

Nationwide and in the cities, 52 percent of the forcible rapes reported to law enforcement were cleared by arrest or exceptional means in 1989. Of the forcible rape arrestees in 1989, 44 percent were persons under the age of twenty-five, with 28 percent of the total being in the eighteen- to twenty-four-year age group. Of those arrested, 52 percent were white, 47 percent were black, and the remainder were other races (Uniform Crime Report, 1989).

Historical Perspective

Understanding behavior and methodology has been a challenge to the civilized world. The term *dangerous classes* has been used throughout history to describe individuals who are deemed a threat to law and order. Initially, the term described the environment in which one lived or was found to be living in versus the reality of any type of crime being committed. An example of this occurred in England at the end of the Hundred Years' War with France. The demobilization of thousands of soldiers coupled with the changing economic trade market saw the displacement of farmers increase the homeless population nationwide (Rennie 1977). During the reign of England's King Henry VIII, 72,000 major and minor thieves were hanged. Under his daughter Queen Elizabeth I, vagabonds were strung up in rows, as many as 300 and 400 at a time (Rennie 1977).

Categorizing these individuals began to change in 1838, when the winning entry at the French Académie des Sciences Morales et Politiques was titled, "The Dangerous Classes of the Population in the Great Cities, and the Means of Making Them Better" (Rennie 1977, 3). Dangerous class was then used to describe individuals who were criminals or who had such potential. Initially, these included the poor, homeless, and unemployed of the large cities.

Beginning classification of offenders began in the work of statistics. These early works permitted a comparison of the incidence of crime with factors such as race, age, sex, education, and geography (Rennie 1977). Cesare Lombrosos, the famed Italian physician, generally is credited with launching the scientific era in criminology. In 1872 he differentiated five types of criminals: the born criminal, the insane criminal, the criminal by passion, the habitual criminal, and the occasional criminal (Lindesmith & Dunham 1941).

This early classification system was based on Darwin's theory of evolution. Operational definitions for the five groups were developed, which allowed for subsequent investigators to test Lombrosos's formulations empirically. A majority of his hypotheses and theories proved to be invalid, but the fact that they were testable was an advancement for the science (Megargee & Bohn 1979).

Englishman Charles Goring refuted the Lombrosian theory of the degenerate criminal man in 1913. The English studies concluded that "the one vital mental constitutional factor in the etiology of crime is defective intelligence" (Goring 1913, 369). This concept persisted in the literature and in the social mind for several decades. Henry Goddard, who did his early work on feeblemindedness in 1914, reported that 50 percent of all offenders were defective (Goddard 1914). V. V. Anderson reported 28 percent to 50 percent defective in 1919, while Healy and Bronner, working with juvenile delinquents, found 13.5 percent feebleminded and 9 percent subnormal in 1926 (Bromberg 1965). Overholser stated that 16.9 percent of all prisoners examined in Massachusetts showed suggestive or obvious mental abnormality (Overholser 1935).

As psychometric techniques improved, the finding of mental deficiency changed. Thus Murchison in 1928 concluded that those in the criminal group are superior in intelligence to the white draft group of WWII (Bromberg 1965). As studies progressed, it became obvious that a disordered personality organization (including psychoses, neuroses, and personality problems) was a more significant factor in crime than feeblemindedness.

With increasing rapidity from the late 1930s to the World War II years to the present, interest has shifted away from insanity and mental defectiveness to personality disturbances in analyzing the genesis of crime. In the decades before the report of Bernard Glueck from Sing Sing Prison in New York State (1918), the accent in crime study was on subnormal mentality.

In 1932 the Psychiatric Clinic of the Court of General Sessions in New York State began to classify each offender according to a personality evaluation, thus combining the insights of psychoanalysis, descriptive psychiatry, and behavioral phenomenology. Each convicted offender presented was analyzed in relation to four categories: (1) presence or absence of psychosis, (2) intellectual level, (3) presence of psychopathic or neurotic features and/or personality diagnosis, and (4) physical condition.

Typologies of crime traditionally have been developed addressing the criminal offense. The psychiatric perspective to understanding crime has utilized two approaches: scrutiny of the inner (mental and moral) world of the criminal offender and examination of the external (social) world in which the offender lives (Bromberg 1965).

A project at the Bellevue Psychiatric Hospital, spanning 1932 to 1965 (Bromberg 1965), found that the personality patterns of criminals far overshadowed the significance of psychotic or defective diagnoses in terms of analyzing criminal behavior and in assisting the court and probation department in estimating the potentials or deficits of the individual offender. Fifteen personality diagnoses were established by this project.

The investigation of the psychological motivations and social stresses that underlie crime has proved that those behavior patterns involved in criminal acts are not far removed from those of normal behavior. Studies indicate that criminal behavior, as true of all behavior, is responsive to inner and outer stresses. The external realities of mental life—social pressures, cultural emphases, physical needs, subcultural patterns of life—precipitate criminal action. The inner realities of behavior—neurotic reactions, impulses, unconscious motivations, preconscious striving, eruption of infantile aggressions—represent a precondition to criminal acts. Crime is part of the human condition; the forces that make for crime are difficult to grasp or to control, but although they are widespread, elusive, and seemingly outside the scope of social coexistence, they are not beyond our conception. Criminal behavior is suggested to derive from three behavioral areas: (1) the aggressive tendency, both destructive and acquisitive; (2) passive, or subverted, aggression; and (3) psychological needs (Bromberg 1965).

Several research-based classification typologies for offenders have been developed. Julian Roebuck in 1967 provided rules to classify offenders based upon the frequency and recency of said offense during the criminal career. This system allows for an offender to be classified into a single offense pattern. The function of his typology was in terms of explanatory theory, rather than in terms of diagnostic systems used in treatment (Roebuck 1967). Investigation into the offender's arrest history, regardless of length, was the primary tool utilized in developing a classification system. The total of known arrests, included with behavior, allowed for the observance of a pattern, if one existed. One basic assumption used was that the arrest pattern would indicate a particular pattern of behavior or criminal career. The most frequent charge or charges in the offender's history was the basis for classification (Roebuck 1967, 100). An obvious weakness of this theory is that not all criminals have accurate arrest histories.

Classification of criminal offenders has been and is currently an important component in correctional facilities throughout this country. In 1973 the National Advisory Commission called for criminal classification programs to be initiated throughout the criminal justice system (Megargee & Bohn 1979). This has not been an easy task to undertake. The correctional system is a complex, expanding, expensive operation that has accountability to society, individual communities, correctional staff, and the inmates themselves. The current trend within the correctional system has been growth of the inmate population with a modest growth in facilities. As the population within the system is faced with economic and now medical issues (such as AIDS), classification is a cost-effective and efficient management and treatment tool.

Megargee and Bohn (1979) found during their research project that a comprehensive classification system must take into account many different components of the criminal population. They stressed that an important element in any classification system is the personality and behavior pattern of the individual offender (Megargee & Bohn 1979).

In the 1980s a research team at the Massachusetts Treatment Center in Bridgewater, Massachusetts, began a program of research to classify sexual offenders (Knight, Rosenberg & Schneider 1985). Their application of a programmatic approach to typology construction and validation has produced taxonomic systems for both child molesters and rapists. The former has demonstrated reasonable reliability and consistent ties to distinctive developmental antecedents. In addition, preliminary results of a twenty-five-year recidivism study of child molesters indicate that aspects of the model have important prognostic implications (Knight & Prentky 1990).

Crime Characteristics and Crime Classifications Today

The National Crime Survey (NCS) program is based on findings from a continuous survey of a representative sample of housing units across the United States. Approximately 46,000 housing units, inhabited by about 93,000 individuals age twelve or older, take part in the survey. The participation rate for 1987 was 96 percent of all eligible housing units (*Criminal Victimization in the United States* 1988).

The NCS focuses on certain criminal offenses, whether completed or attempted, that are of major concern to the general public and law enforcement authorities. These are the personal crimes of rape, robbery, assault, and larceny and the household crimes of burglary, larceny, and motor vehicle theft. Definitions of the measured crimes generally are compatible with conventional usage and with the definitions used by the FBI in its annual publication, *Crime in the United States: Uniform Crime Reports*. The NCS reports on characteristics of personal crime victims, victim-offender relationships, offender characteristics in personal crimes of violence, and crime characteristics.

The work of investigative analysts at the FBI Academy with the large number of cases seen weekly has led to an expansion of these traditional crime categories. The *Crime Classification Manual* (CCM) is the first step to make explicit crime categories that have been utilized informally.

CRIME CLASSIFICATION: THE DECISION PROCESS

To classify a crime using the CCM, an investigator needs to ask questions about the victim, the crime scene, and the nature of the victim-offender exchange. The answers to these questions will guide the investigator toward making a decision on how best to classify the offense. However, the optimum use of this manual depends on the quality of information the investigator has concerning the crime.

Defining Characteristics

The defining characteristics of each offense need to be as comprehensive and complete as possible. Victimology is an essential step in arriving at a possible motive. If investigators fail to obtain complete victim histories, they may be overlooking information that could quickly direct their investigations to motives and to suspects.

As one looks through the classification sections, it becomes apparent that a blend of motivations inspire many violent crimes. This is especially true when multiple offenders are involved. One may find as many different reasons for the crime as there are offenders.

The approach taken in the CCM for multiple motives is to classify the offense according to the predominant motive. An example of this would be if a husband kills his wife for insurance money. He then attempts to cover the murder with a fire. In addition, he was having an affair and his wife would not give him a divorce. This homicide has criminal enterprise (financial gain) and personal cause (domestic) motives. It also can be classified as crime concealment under the arson section. The financial considerations should be the primary criteria for classifying this crime. The other applicable categories would be subclassifications. So once classified, this homicide would appear as follows:

107.01: Individual Profit Murder

122.02: Staged Domestic Homicide

231.00: Murder Concealment-Motivated Arson

The investigator will now be able to consult the investigative considerations and search warrant suggestions for each of these categories for possible guidance. Prosecutors also will benefit from having all aspects of the crime detailed. Later on, other investigators working cases with one or more elements of this offense can use this case or any others with the applicable heading for reference.

The main rule when several of the categories apply (e.g., sexual assault and murder, or sexual assault and arson) is that the main classification is the appropriate homicide category. Homicide takes precedence. Next comes arson/bombing, and then sexual assault, if applicable.

The following sections describe each of the key elements in categorizing a crime. These defining characteristics in categorizing a crime are victimology, crime scene indicators, staging, forensic findings, and investigative considerations.

Victimology

Victimology is often one of the most beneficial investigative tools in classifying and solving a violent crime. It is also a crucial part of crime analysis. Through it, the investigator tries to evaluate why this particular person was targeted for a violent crime. Very often, just answering this question will lead the investigator to the motive, which will lead to the offender.

Was the victim known to the offender? What were the victim's chances of becoming a target for violent crime? What risk did the offender take in perpetrating this crime? These are some of the important questions investigators should keep in mind as they analyze the crime.

One of the most important aspects of classifying an offense and determining the motive is a thorough understanding of all offender activity with the victim (or targeted property). With a sexual assault, this exchange between the victim and offender includes verbal interchange as well as physical and sexual activity.

The tone of exchange between an offender and a victim of sexual assault is extremely helpful in directing the investigator to an appropriate classification. Excessively vulgar or abusive language, scripting, or apologetic language are each common to a certain type of rapist.

Victimology is the complete history of the victim. (If the crime is an arson, than victimology includes targeted property.) A comprehensive victimology should include as much as possible of the information on the victim listed in the sample worksheet that appears near the end of this introduction.

Crime Scene Indicators

There are many elements that constitute the crime scene. Not all of these factors will be present or recognizable with every offense. The following sections describe the major points an investigator should consider when looking at the crime scene, especially as it pertains to crime classification. The modus operandi (MO) as it relates to the crime scene and forensics is covered in chapter 5.

How Many Crime Scenes? How many crime scenes are involved with the offense? There may be one site, as in group excitement homicide. In contrast, the product tamperer may taint the product at one location and then put it on shelves in several stores. The victim may consume the product in one location but die in another location. In such a case, there are at least four crime scenes involved.

The use of several locales during the commission of an offense frequently gives the investigator significant insight into the nature of the offender. One example is the disorganized sexual killer who may confront, assault, kill, and leave the body, all in the same location. In contrast, the organized killer may abduct, assault, kill, and dispose of the victim using separate locations for each event.

Environment/Place/Time. The environment of a crime scene refers to the conditions or circumstances in which the offense occurs. Is it indoors or outside? Was it during daylight hours or in the middle of the night? Did it happen on a busy street or on a deserted country road? Answering these questions not only assists in defining the classification of an offense, but also provides an assessment of the offender risk. Gauging these risk factors usually offers insight into an offender's motivations and behavior patterns.

With some offenses, location may have more obvious bearing on the motive classification than others. An example is street gang murder, in which the homicide is commonly a so-called drive-by in an area of known gang conflict. In other offenses, like arson for excitement, the investigator may not know that the typical location of this crime scene is residential property, as opposed to vandalism arson, which usually involves educational facilities. Adding this information to other characteristics of the arson will often lead the investigator to the classification and, most important, possible motives.

How long did the offender stay at the scene? Generally, the amount of time the offender spends at the scene is usually proportional to the degree of comfort that offender feels committing the offense at that particular location. Evidence of a lingering offender often will assist the investigation by directing it toward a subject who lives or works near the crime scene, knows the neighborhood, and consequently feels at ease there.

How Many Offenders? The answer to this question will help the investigator determine whether to place the offense into either the criminal enterprise category or the group cause category. The offenses included in these two groupings involve multiple offenders.

Organized or Disorganized/Physical Evidence/Weapon. The general condition of the crime scene is very important in classifying a crime. Is it like a group excitement killing, spontaneous and disarrayed with a great deal of physical evidence at the scene? Or does the crime scene reflect a methodical, well-organized subject who did not leave a single print or piece of physical evidence behind? The latter may be seen with an organized crime hit, as in the criminal competition category.

The amount of organization or disorganization at the crime scene will tell much about the offender's level of criminal sophistication. It also will demonstrate how well the offender was able to control the victim and how much premeditation was involved with the crime. It should be emphasized that *the crime scene rarely will be completely organized or disorganized.* It is more likely to be somewhere on a continuum between the two extremes of the orderly, neat crime scene and the disarrayed, sloppy one.

Another aspect of crime scene examination concerns the weapon. Questions the investigator needs to answer about the weapon include the following: Was it a weapon of choice, brought to the crime scene by the offender? Or was it a weapon of opportunity, acquired at the scene? (With arson, did the fire start from materials at hand, or did the offender bring accelerants to the scene?) Is the weapon absent from the crime scene, or has it been left behind? Was there evidence of multiple weapons and ammunition? Multiple weaponry does not always signify multiple offenders. Authority killing and Nonspecific-motive killing are examples of offenses that often involve the use of multiple firearms and ammunition by a lone offender.

Body Disposition. Was the body openly displayed or otherwise placed in a deliberate manner to ensure discovery? Or was the body concealed or buried to prevent discovery? Did the offender seem to have no concern as to whether the body would be discovered or not? These are some questions whose answers will further aid the classification of a homicide. Certain homicides (disorganized sexual homicide, for example) may involve the *intentional* arranging of the body in an unnatural or unusual position. (See chapter 4 for a discussion of personation.) In some homicides, like cult murder or drug murder, the body may be left in a degrading position or in a location to convey a message.

Items Left/Missing. The addition or absence of items at the crime scene often will assist the investigator in classifying the offense. The presence of unusual artifacts, drawings, graffiti, or other items may be seen with offenses such as extremist murder or street gang murder. Offender communication (e.g., a ransom demand or extortion note) frequently will be associated with the crime scene of a kidnap murder or product tampering.

Items taken from the scene as a crime scene indicator is found in felony murder, breaking and entering arson for crime concealment, and felony sexual assault. A victim's personal belongings may be taken from the scene of a sexual homicide. These so-called souvenirs (i.e., photos, driver's license, costume jewelry; all belonging to victim) often may not be monetarily valuable.

Other Crime Scene Indicators. There are other crime scene indicators common to certain offenses that will help the investigator to classify the crime and motive. Examples of these indicators are wounded victims, no escape plan, and the probability of witnesses. The nature of the confrontation between the victim and offender is also important in determining the motive/classification. How did the offender control the victim? Are restraints present at the scene, or did the offender immediately blitz attack and incapacitate the victim?

Staging

Staging is the purposeful alteration of a crime scene. The detection and characteristics of staging are covered in chapter 4.

Forensic Findings

Forensic findings include the analysis of physical evidence pertaining to a crime, evidence that is used toward legal proof that a crime occurred. This evidence is often called a silent witness, offering objective facts specific to the commission of a crime. The primary sources of physical evidence are the victim, the suspect, and the crime scene. Secondary sources include the home or work environment of a suspect; however, search warrants are necessary for the collection of such evidence (Moreau 1987).

Medical reports provide important evidence. These reports include toxicological results, X-ray films, and autopsy findings. In homicide cases, the forensic pathologist identifies and documents the postmortem findings present and interprets the findings within the context of the circumstances of death (Luke 1988).

Cause of Death. The mechanism of death is often a determining factor when investigators attempt to classify a homicide. The victim of a street gang murder almost always dies from gunshot wounds. Explosive trauma is a frequent forensic finding with many criminal competition and extremist murders. Strangulation is common to the more personal crimes, such as domestic murder and sexual homicide.

Trauma. The type, extent, and focus of injury sustained by the victim are additional critical factors the investigator uses when classifying a crime. Overkill, facial battery, torture, bite marks, and mutilation are examples of forensic findings that often will lead the investigator to a specific homicide category and thus a possible motive for the offense.

Sexual Assault. Evidence of assault to the victim's sexual organs or body cavities has great bearing on motive and classification. The type and sequence of the assault is important, as well as the timing of the assault (before, during, or after death).

The investigator should remember that the apparent absence of penetration with the penis does not mean the victim was not sexually assaulted. Sexual assault also includes insertion of foreign objects, regressive necrophilia, and many activities that target the breasts, buttocks, and genitals.

Investigative Considerations and Search Warrant Suggestions

Once the investigator has classified the offense (and thus, the motive), the investigative considerations and search warrant suggestions can be used to give direction and assistance to the investigation. It should be emphasized that these considerations are general suggestions and are not absolutes that apply in every case.

Moreau (1987) outlines ten basic steps to a crime scene search. These basic steps are approach scene; secure and protect; preliminary survey; narrative description; photograph scene; sketch scene; evaluation of latent fingerprint evidence and other forms of evidence; detailed search for evidence and collection, preservation, and documentation of evidence; final survey; and release of scene. The forensic analysis of physical evidence of hair and fibers, blood, semen, and saliva can provide the basis for critical testimony in court.

Classification by Type, Style, and Number of Victims

Crimes may be classified by type, style, and number of victims. Using the homicide classification as an example, a single homicide is one victim, one homicidal event. A double homicide is two victims, one event, and in one location. A triple homicide has three victims in one location during one event. Anything beyond three victims is classified as a mass murder—that is, a homicide involving four or more victims in one location and within one event.

Two additional types of multiple murder are spree murder and serial murder. A spree murder involves killing at two or more locations with no emotional cooling-off period between murders. The killings are all the result of a single event, which can be of short or long duration. Serial murders involve three or more separate events, with an emotional cooling-off period between homicides.

Crime Classification Sample Worksheet

The following sample worksheet is an outline of the defining characteristics of each of the categories. Under each characteristic are some of the aspects that will assist the investigator in classifying the offense.

   I. Victimology
Why did this person become the victim of a violent crime?
     A. About the victim
       Life-style
       Employment
       Personality
       Friends (type, number)
       Income (amount, source)
       Family
       Alcohol/drug use or abuse
       Normal dress
       Handicaps
       Transportation used
       Reputation, habits, fears
       Marital status
       Dating habits
       Leisure activities
       Criminal history
       Assertiveness
       Likes and dislikes
       Significant events prior to the crime
       Activities prior to the crime
     B. Sexual assault: verbal interaction
       Excessively vulgar or abusive

Scripting
Apologetic
C. Arson: targeted property
Residential
Commercial
Educational
Mobile, vehicle
Forest, fields
II. Crime Scene
How many?
Environment, time, place
How many offenders?
Organized, disorganized
Physical evidence
Weapon
Body disposition
Items left/missing
Other (i.e., witnesses, escape plan, wounded victims, etc.)
III. Staging
Natural death
Accidental
Suicide
Criminal activity (i.e., robbery, rape/homicide)
IV. Forensic findings
A. Forensic analysis
Hair/fibers
Blood
Semen
Saliva
Other
B. Autopsy results
Cause of death
Trauma (type, extent, location on body)
Overkill
Torture
Facial battery (depersonalization)
Bite marks

Mutilation

Sexual assault (when, sequence, to where, insertion, insertional necrophilia)

Toxicological results

V. Investigative considerations

A. Search warrents

Home

Work

Car

Other

B. Locating and interviewing witnesses

Crime Classification Numbering System

The numbering system used to classify crimes was developed with some memory-assist features. The basic code uses three digits, with the first digit representing the major crime category. All possible codes are not currently assigned in anticipation of future editions. There are three major crime categories in this edition: homicide, arson, and sexual assault. The homicide category is identified by the number 1 (codes 100 to 199), arson is designated by the number 2 (codes 200 to 299), and sexual assault is indicated with the number 3 (codes 300 to 399). As other major crime categories are classified, such as threat assessment, they will be assigned appropriate identification codes.

The second digit of the code represents a further grouping of the major crimes. For example, homicides are divided into four groups: criminal enterprise (100 to 108), personal cause (120 to 129), sexual (130 to 134), and group cause (140 to 143). There are unassigned numbers that allow for future editions within specific categories and additional groups within a major category. Specific classifications within these groups are represented by the third digit of the code.

Individual classifications within these groups are further divided into subgroups using two additional digits following a decimal point after the code. The division into subgroups occurs when there are unique characteristics within a factor that clearly identify a major difference within the group. For example, domestic homicide (code 122) has two subgroups: spontaneous domestic homicide (122.01) and staged domestic homicide (122.02).

The Classifications

1

Homicide

100: Criminal enterprise homicide
  101: Contract (third party) killing
  102: Gang-motivated murder
  103: Criminal competition homicide
  104: Kidnap murder
  105: Product tampering homicide
  106: Drug murder
  107: Insurance inheritance-related death
    107.01: Individual profit murder
    107.02: Commercial profit murder
  108: Felony murder
    108.01: Indiscriminate felony murder
    108.02: Situational felony murder
120: Personal cause homicide
  121: Erotomania-motivated killing
  122: Domestic homicide
    122.01: Spontaneous domestic homicide
    122.02: Staged domestic homicide
  123: Argument/conflict murder
    123.01: Argument murder
    123.02: Conflict murder

124: Authority killing

125: Revenge killing

126: Nonspecific-motive killing

127: Extremist homicide

    127.01: Political extremist homicide

    127.02: Religious extremist homicide

    127.03: Socioeconomic extremist homicide

128: Mercy/hero homicide

    128.01: Mercy homicide

    128.02: Hero homicide

129 Hostage murder

130: Sexual homicide

    131: Organized sexual homicide

    132: Disorganized sexual homicide

    133: Mixed sexual homicide

    134: Sadistic murder

140: Group cause homicide

    141: Cult murder

    142: Extremist murder

        142.01: Paramilitary extremist murder

        142.02: Hostage extremist murder

    143: Group excitement homicide

Murder is the unlawful taking of human life. It is a behavioral act that terminates life in the context of power, personal gain, brutality, and sometimes sexuality. Murder is a subcategory of homicide, which also includes the taking of human life (e.g., manslaughter, deaths resulting from criminal and noncriminal negligence, unpremeditated vehicular deaths, and the like) (Megargee 1982). Although a distinction is made in the literature among homicide, murder, and killing, for the purpose of this manual, the terms are used interchangably.

THE UNIFORM CRIME REPORTING PROGRAM

The earliest system for classification of homicide is the Uniform Crime Reports (UCR). The UCR, prepared by the FBI in conjunction with the U.S. Department of Justice, presents statistics for crimes committed in the United States within a given year. Recognizing a need for national crime statistics, the International Association of Chiefs of Police formed the Committee on Uniform Crime Records in the 1920s to develop a system of uniform police statistics. Seven offenses were chosen to serve as an index for gauging fluctuations in the overall volume and rate of crime. Known collectively as the crime index, these offenses included the violent crimes of murder and nonnegligent manslaughter, forcible rape, robbery, and aggravated assault and the property crimes of burglary, larceny theft, and motor vehicle theft. By congressional mandate, arson was added as the eighth index offense in 1979.

A survey of the figures reported in the UCR for all murders committed in the period between 1976 through 1989 shows that the number of murders in the United States has fluctuated from 16,605 in 1976 to a peak of 21,860 in 1980, dropping to 20,613 in 1986 and up to 21,500 in 1989 (Uniform Crime Reports 1977, 1981, 1987, 1989). The UCR also cites information about age, race, and sex of victims and offenders, about types of weapons used, and about situations in which killings took place.

The current UCR classifies murders as follows:

1. Felony murder (occurs during commission of a felony)
2. Suspected felony murder (elements of felony are present)
3. Argument-motivated murder (noncriminally motivated)
4. Miscellaneous or nonfelony types (any *known* motivation not included in previous categories)
5. Unknown motives (motive fits into none of the above categories)

Percentages for all categories of murders except the unknown motives category have remained relatively stable over the past decade. For example, felony-connected murders represented 17.7 percent of all murders in 1976, 17.2 percent in 1981, 18.0 percent in 1984, 19.4 percent in 1986, and 21.4 percent in 1989. The percentages for those murders placed in the miscellaneous category are as follows: 1976, 18.6 percent; 1981, 17.1 percent; 1984, 17.6 percent; 1986, 18.6 percent; and 18.9 percent in 1989 (Uniform Crime Reports 1977, 1982, 1985, 1989).

The number of murders classified in the unknown motive category, however, has risen dramatically. These murders represented 8.5 percent of all murders in 1976, 17.8 percent in 1981, 22.1 percent in 1984, 22.5 percent in 1986, and 23.7 percent in 1989. This trend is particularly noteworthy in that it suggests both the heterogeneity of motives that give rise to murder and the clear inadequacy of a system that partitions murder essentially into three categories: felony, noncriminal, and miscellaneous. The miscellaneous and unknown motives categories represent, of course, wastebasket classifications. A classification system that fails to capture 40 percent to 50 percent of the cases (*other* and *unknown*) clearly is suboptimal in its ability to explain the universe of behavior.

HOMICIDE CLASSIFICATION BY VICTIMS, TYPE, AND STYLE

The FBI Academy's Behavioral Science Unit at Quantico, Virginia, began contributing to the literature on the classification of homicide with the Hazelwood and Douglas (1980) publication on typing lust murderers. The classifying of homicides by number of victims, type, and style was published by Douglas and colleagues in 1986. A *single homicide* is defined as one victim and one homicidal event. A *double homicide* is defined as two victims who are killed at one time in one location. A *triple homicide* is defined as three victims who are killed at one time in one location. Any single event, single location homicide involving four or more victims is classified as *mass murder.*

There are two subcategories of mass murder: *classic mass murder* and *family mass murder.* A classic mass murder involves one person operating in one location at one period of time. The time period could be minutes or hours or even days. The prototype of a classic mass murderer is a mentally disordered individual whose problems have increased to the point that he acts out against groups of people who are unrelated to him or his problems, unleashing his hostility through shootings and stabbings. One classic mass murderer was Charles Whitman, who in 1966 armed himself with boxes of ammunition, weapons, ropes, a radio, and food, barricaded himself in a tower at the University of Texas at Austin, and opened fire for ninety minutes, killing sixteen people and wounding more than thirty others. He was stopped only when he was killed during an assault on the tower (Ressler, Burgess & Douglas 1988).

The second type of mass murder is family mass murder. If four or more family members are killed and the perpetrator takes his own life, it is classified as a mass murder/suicide. Without the suicide and with four or more victims, the murder is classified as family mass murder. An example is John List, an insurance salesman who killed his entire family in 1972. List disappeared after the crime, and his car was found at an airport parking lot. He was located seventeen years later following a television program describing the murders.

A *spree murder* is defined as a single event with two or more locations and no emotional cooling-off period between murders. The single event in a spree murder can be of short or long duration. On 6 September 1949 spree murderer Howard Unruh of Camden, New Jersey, took a loaded German lugar with extra ammunition and randomly fired the handgun while walking through his neighborhood, killing thirteen people and wounding three in about twenty minutes. Even though Unruh's killing took a short length of time, it was not classified as a mass murder because he moved to different locations (Ressler, Burgess & Douglas 1988).

Serial murder is defined as three or more separate events in three or more separate locations with an emotional cooling-off period between homicides. The serial murder is hypothesized to be premeditated, involving offense-related fantasy and detailed planning. When the time is right for him and he has cooled off from his last homicide, the serial killer selects his next victim and proceeds with his plan. The cooling-off period can last for days, weeks, or months and is the key feature that distinguishes the serial killer from other multiple killers. Ted Bundy is an example of a serial murderer. Bundy killed thirty or more times over a period of many years in at least five different states.

There are other differences that are hypothesized to distinguish the mass, spree, and serial murderers. In addition to the number of events and locations and the presence or absence of a cooling-off period, the classic mass murderer and the spree murderer are not concerned with who their victims are; they will kill anyone who comes in contact with them. In contrast, the serial murderer usually selects a type of victim. He thinks he will never be caught, and sometimes he is right. A serial murderer carefully monitors his behaviors to avoid detection, whereas a spree murderer, who often has been identified and is being closely pursued by law enforcement, is usually unable to control the course of events. The serial killer, by contrast, will plan and choose victim and location, sometimes stopping the act of murder if it is not meeting his requirements. With a sexually motivated murderer, the offense may be classified as any of the aforementioned types.

INVESTIGATIVE PROFILING

Crime classification assists investigative profiling, a step within investigative considerations. Investigative profiling is best viewed as a strategy enabling law enforcement to narrow the field of options and generate educated guesses about the perpetrator. It has been described as a collection of leads (Rossi 1982), as an informed attempt to provide detailed information about a certain type of criminal (Geberth 1981), and as a biological sketch of behavioral patterns, trends, and tendencies (Vorpagel 1982). Geberth (1981) has noted that the investigative profile is particularly useful when the criminal has demonstrated some clearly identifiable form of psychopathology. In such a case, the crime scene is presumed to reflect the murderer's behavior and personality in much the same way as furnishings reveal the homeowner's character.

Profiling is, in fact, a form of retroclassification, or classification that works backward. Typically, we classify a *known* entity into a discrete category, based upon presenting characteristics that translate into criteria for assignment to that category. In the case of homicide investigation, we have neither the entity (e.g., the offender) nor the victim. It is thus necessary to rely upon the only source of information that typically is available, the crime scene. This information is used to profile, or classify, an individual. In essense, we are forced to bootstrap, using crime-scene-related data, to make our classifications. This bootstrapping process is referred to as profiling. At present, there have been no systematic efforts to validate these profile-derived classifications.

CCM: A MOTIVATIONAL MODEL FOR CLASSIFICATION OF HOMICIDE

The first published FBI Behavioral Science Unit system for typing lust murder (Hazelwood and Douglas 1980), which Megargee (1982) properly described as a syndrome rather than a typology, delineated two categories, the organized nonsocial category and the disorganized asocial category, that were not intended to embrace all cases of sexual homicides. This early work on lust murder evolved into a programmatic effort to devise a classification system for serial sexual murder (Ressler, Burgess & Douglas 1988). In the late 1980s, the agents from the Investigative Support Unit at the FBI Academy joined with the Behavioral Science Unit to begin working on a crime classification manual, using as a guide the Diagnostic and Statistical Manual (DSM) of the American Psychiatric Association. Work groups were assigned to the major crime categories of murder, arson, and sexual assault. An advisory committee representing federal and private associations was formed.

Although many of the conceptual and theoretical underpinnings of this model derive from earlier writings on the subject, this is the first attempt of which we are aware to operationalize a decision-making process based on a well-defined set of criteria. We want to emphasize at the outset that this rationally derived system has not yet been implemented or tested. Although we are in the rudimentary stage of model development, we have progressed to the stage of advancing a testable system. Presentation of the system at this point should provide the reader with a general overview of the presumptively important dimensions that have been incorporated into this hypothetical model.

In the CCM, classification of homicide by motive includes four major categories. The *criminal enterprise* category includes eight subcategories: contract killing (third party), gang-motivated murder, criminal competition, kidnap murder, product tampering, drug murder, insurance-motivated murder (individual profit or commercial profit), and felony murder (indiscriminate or situational). The *personal cause* category includes eleven subcategories: erotomania-motivated killing, domestic killing (spontaneous or staged), argument murder, conflict murder, authority killing, revenge killing, nonspecific motive killing, extremist murder (political, religious, or socioeconomic), mercy killers, hero killers, and hostage murder. The *sexual homicide* category includes four subcategories: organized crime-scene murder, disorganized crime-scene murder, mixed crime-scene murder, and sadistic murder. The *group cause* category includes three subcategories: cult murder, extremists (political, religious, or socioeconomic murder [paramilitary or hostage]), and group excitement.

100: CRIMINAL ENTERPRISE HOMICIDE

Criminal enterprise homicide entails murder committed for material gain. This material gain takes many forms (e.g., money, goods, territory, or favors).

101: CONTRACT (THIRD PARTY) KILLING

A contract killer is one who kills by secret assault or surprise. He is a murderer who agrees to take the life of another person for profit (e.g., a hit man). There is usually an absence of relationship (personal, familial, or business) between killer and victim.

Defining Characteristics

Victimology. The victim of a contract killer is perceived by the person hiring the killer as an obstruction or hindrance to the attainment of a goal. This goal could be a financial one (collecting life insurance or controlling a business), or it could be personal (an extramarital affair, a refusal of divorce, etc.)

The victim's risk is situational. It is the offender's perception of the victim as an obstacle that puts the victim at risk. The risk for the offenders (contractor and killer) is dependent on their relationship with each other and the experience and expertise of the offender(s) committing the murder.

Crime Scene Indicators Frequently Noted. The offender usually spends a minimum amount of time at the scene. In light of this, a quick, fast killing is usually opted for.

There are several factors at the scene that are indicative of offender sophistication. One index of this professionalism is the weapon that is used: customized suppressors, handguns, or other instruments of death often indicate a specialist who is comfortable with killing. The crime scene may reflect this in other ways, including little or no physical evidence left at the scene, effective staging, elaborate body disposal, and a crime scene that shows a systematic, orderly approach before, during, and after the crime.

The weapon may be chosen based on its availability, lack of traceability, and/or difficulty in making ballistic comparisons. The offender often will drop the weapon, possibly at the crime scene with the body to lessen the possibility of being apprehended with it in his possession. Firearms often are stolen or not registered when used for a contract killing.

Arson is sometimes used to conceal the contract murder. Refer to section 231: Murder Arson for further information.

Staging. If staging is absent, there will be no other crime indicators: for example, nothing will be missing, there will be no sexual assault. Secondary criminal activity may mean that the offender is youthful, amateur, or of lower intelligence.

The counter to this is a crime scene that involves complex staging (e.g., cut brake lines or aircraft malfunction) to make the death look accidental. Secondary criminal activity to confuse the primary motive of murder may include the appearance of a robbery or breaking and entering that went wrong, or a kidnapping. The body may be positioned to infer that a sexually motivated homicide occurred (actual sexual assault is a variable depending primarily on offender professionalism).

Common Forensic Findings. Just as staging and other crime scene indicators reflect the offender's level of experience, forensic findings also can offer distinguishing features. The veteran professional killer, for example, may chose a weapon that is difficult to trace and may focus the area of injury on the victim's vital organs, especially the head. Usually there are few wounds, and overkill is rare. A blitz or ambush style of attack also is common to this type of killing.

Investigative Considerations

Most contract killings will have some evidence of premeditation. The killer may stalk the victim. An individual with preexisting, intact criminal connections will be able to contract a murder more easily and with less of a conspiratorial trail than an individual without established criminal connections. While the latter individual's conspiratorial trail may be more easily detected, the nature of the crime ensures the existence of a conspiracy for all offenders. Scrutiny of a suspect's preoffense contacts, discussions, and communications may provide evidence of the conspiracy (telephone and financial records should be reviewed for such evidence).

The contractor (the party engaging the killer) will have a history of personal conflict or business competition with the victim. However, he or she may exhibit a preoffense behavior change that frequently includes an apparent improvement in relationship with the victim. This improvement is often deliberately made apparent to relatives, friends, and business associates. The offender's motivation for projecting an image of caring and concern toward the victim is to lure the victim into a false sense of security while convincing those around him that he is above suspicion once the investigation has begun. Interviews with those close to the offender and victim may reveal this type of preoffense behavior. Additional preoffense behavior that others may observe is a nervousness or preoccupation on the part of the contractor.

Postoffense behavior of the offender (contractor) will often demonstrate selective recall. He or she will have a uncharacteristically detailed, precise, airtight alibi for the time period during which the homicide occurs. Exact times and activities (supported by receipts, etc.) will be known, but actions during time periods preceding and following the offense will be far less precisely remembered. The contractor will most likely be highly visible during the time of the offense (public place, party, etc.).

Search Warrant Suggestions

Telephone records and other communications, financial records showing transfers of money, travel records and receipts (rental cars, motels, etc.), and weapons are all important search warrant suggestions. (See also the indicators of financial difficulty in appendix B.)

CASE STUDY: 101: CONTRACT (THIRD PARTY) KILLING

Background Victimology

U.S. District Court Judge John Wood was known as Maximum John to members of the legal and law enforcement society in Texas. His reputation of handing out the stiffest penalties possible for drug offenders had brought him to the attention of the criminal community as well. Judge Wood had made serious inroads into the organized drug trade of the southern and western areas of Texas, where drug flow from across the Mexican border had made trafficking a lucrative business.

Jamiel Charga (known as Jimmy) especially seemed to be benefiting from the drug business as evidenced by his life-style; he had lost $1.1 million during one three-day Las Vegas gambling trip. Jimmy's brother, Lee, who also had been implicated in drug trafficking (and who was murdered on 23 December 1978), had often expressed feelings of persecution at the hands of federal representatives like Judge Wood and Assistant U.S. Attorney James Kerr, Jr. (Kerr was the object of an attempted assassination in November 1978.)

Jimmy Charga shared his brother's animosity toward Judge Wood, imagining that he was the object of the judge's personal vendetta. He also was convinced that he would be given a life sentence by Judge Wood if he was convicted of the five counts of drug trafficking he faced in Wood's court.

At approximately 8:40 A.M. on 29 May 1979, Judge Wood told his wife good-bye as he walked out the front door of their apartment. Ten to fifteen seconds later, as he walked from the brick condominium to his green Chevrolet, he was struck in the back by a single gunshot. Mrs. Wood came out of the apartment after hearing the noise she had immediately identified as a gunshot. She found the judge lying near his car and attempted to help him. Judge Wood was transported to Northeast Baptist Hospital, San Antonio, where he was pronounced dead on arrival at 9:30 A.M.

Judge Wood was at high risk because of the stance he took when sentencing drug traffickers. Typically, he would not have been considered a high-risk victim in view of other factors that rate a victim's risk level (life-style, income, etc.). However, his occupation and his intolerance toward drug offenders, in addition to his flippant attitude toward the threats against his life (he had ended the protection given him by federal marshals and had stopped carrying the gun they had given him) elevated his risk.

Relating Judge Wood to the victimology of a contract killing shows that his risk was situational. He was viewed as an obstruction to Jimmy Charga's freedom and drug enterprise.*

Crime Scene Indicators

Judge Wood's body was lying 3.5 feet from his car at a 45-degree angle with the feet pointing northwest, the head southeast, and the arms outstretched to the side.

The witnesses who saw the judge struck by the bullet and fall to the ground never saw the gunman. There was no physical evidence (no shell casings, fingerprints, etc.). The exact location of the sniper was not even known. There were reports of several different strangers at the apartment around the time of the murder, but none led to any substantial suspect information.

The fast method of killing meant a minimum of time at the crime scene for the offender. The apparent ease of the killer to slip in, shoot the judge, and escape undetected (especially with a police patrol within two blocks responding at 8:41 A.M.) are all indicators of careful premeditation by an experienced hit man.

Forensic Findings

The bullet entry point was to the lower back, left of the center, with a trajectory through the body of less than 15 degrees. It immediately im-

---

*As in many cases, this homicide can be classified under another classification, 106: Drug Murder. It was placed here due to its illustration of the sophisticated hit, especially when compared with the amateurish job illustrated for drug murders.

pacted with the spine, causing fragmentation of the bullet and its disintegra-
tion. These bullet fragments resulted in wounds throughout the abdomen
and internal organs.

Ballistics revealed that the bullet was .243 caliber or 6mm. Based on the
rifling marks, it was concluded that two kinds of common rifles could have
fired the bullet: the Browning Lever-Action and the Interarms Mark X.

The ambush, the sniper-style of attack on Judge Wood, and the one shot
required to kill almost instantly are forensics information typical of the
more experienced contract killer.†

Investigation

The investigation of Judge Wood's murder became the largest federal investigation since John F. Kennedy's assassination, as it was the only killing of a
federal judge in the twentieth century. Due to the professionalism of the
killer (as evidenced by the lack of forensics and witnesses), the direction of
the investigation depended greatly on the history of conflict between Judge
Wood and Jimmy Charga. In addition, the conspiratorial trail was less
visible due to Charga's criminal contacts. This minimalized the effort to
seek a hit man, therefore minimalizing the number of conspirators who
could later become damaging witnesses.

The extensive investigation involving Charga's business associates, family, and friends, combined with intelligence derived from informants, began
to focus attention on Charles Voyde Harrelson. On 24 June 1979, Charga's
wife, Elizabeth, paid $150,000 to Harrelson's stepdaughter in Las Vegas for
the completed contract killing. Harrelson acknowledged receiving the
money, but said it was for a drug deal. The conspiratorial trail finally began
to emerge after examination of phone bills that linked Harrelson with
Charga through family members.

Charga's wife was audiotaped while visiting her husband in Leavenworth
Prison. "Yeah, go ahead and do it," she said, when the couple discussed
plans to kill Judge Wood. They were repeating a previous conversation that
had taken place before Judge Wood was murdered. Elizabeth Charga also
wrote a letter to Mrs. Wood in which she acknowledged making the payoff
but denied involvement in the conspiracy.

Mrs. Harrelson admitted buying the .240-caliber Weatherby Mark V, the
murder weapon, using a false name, and giving it to her husband. The rifle
butt with the Weatherby trademark was the only part recovered, making a
ballistic match impossible (another indicator of criminal sophistication),
Harrelson's placement near the crime scene, in repudiation to his claim of
being 250 miles away the day of the killing, was solidified when a series of
witnesses testified he was at a nearby motel the night before the murder.

---

†The investigation finally led to a man who had served time for a 1968 hired killing.

Outcome

Charles Harrelson was convicted of murder and conspiracy to murder and was sentenced to two consecutive life sentences without parole. Jimmy Charga was convicted of obstructing justice in the Wood investigation. He was also convicted of conspiracy to commit murder in relation to the attempt made on Assistant U.S. Attorney James Kerr. Kerr, who often had tried drug cases in Wood's court, barely escaped injury from a barrage of bullets by ducking under his car dashboard in November 1978. Charga also was convicted of continuing criminal enterprise, conspiring to import marijuana, and tax fraud.

Elizabeth Charga originally was charged with murder conspiracy, convicted, and sentenced to thirty years. This was later overturned because the judge had not instructed the jury that her guilt had to be based on joining the conspiracy with malicious intent. She also was convicted of obstructing justice and of tax fraud and received a five-year sentence.

Jo Ann Harrelson was convicted of perjury before the grand jury, during her own trial, and to FBI agents. Also convicted for their part in the assassination were Joe Charga, Jimmy's brother, and Theresa Jasper, Harrelson's stepdaughter (United Press International 1981, 1983, 1984, 1985, 1986).

102: GANG MOTIVATED MURDER

A street gang is an organization, association, or group of three or more people, whether formal or informal, that has as one of its primary activities the commission of antisocial behavior and criminal acts, including homicide. Subculture groups (bikers) are also included within this group.

Street gangs were first formed in response to territorial struggles with rival neighborhoods. Fatalities that were associated with gang activity were largely based on these territorial conflicts. Contemporary gangs are demonstrating signs of evolution from loosely knit gangs to more established, organized crime groups. The flourishing cocaine market has been the propelling force behind this evolutionary process. Because the drug enterprise is now the heart of gang existence, drug-related homicide and street gang murder are becoming synonymous.

Defining Characteristics

Victimology. The victims of street gang homicide are usually members and/or associates of a gang. Innocent bystanders are peripheral victims in some drive-by shootings. Local businessmen being extorted by gangs also become homicide victims, but this is usually restricted to Asian gangs. Filipino gangs in Hawaii use firearms as a currency in the drug trade;

therefore, these gangs target victims to obtain guns, victims who include military and law enforcement personnel. Violence involving street gangs most often includes minority, male victims and offenders.

Crime Scene Indicators Frequently Noted. The homicide scene is usually an open, public place within gang territory. Frequently the site of the killing is in front of or near the victim's residence. Drive-by killings are the most frequent tactic employed by gangs. This mobile, public clash has a much greater prevalence over the one-on-one confrontation. Drive-by killings often involve more than one car.

The crime scene is disarrayed, with no concern for the body. It is not concealed and may even be displayed and positioned in a specific manner if a message is intended by the killing. Symbolic items may be left, such as the colors representing a gang or graffiti messages. Sometimes gang members involved with the offense will yell another gang name at the scene to misdirect law enforcement and focus retaliation on another gang.

The weapon is brought to the scene and often is concealed. Frequently, there are additional victims injured and associated offenses related to the homicide.

Staging. Staging is generally absent.

Common Forensic Findings. A firearm is the weapon of choice with most gangs. The typical gang arsenal includes assault rifles, fully automatic weapons, semiautomatic handguns, and shotguns. Knife attacks are rare.

Multiple wounds from multiple-round weapons characterize a common forensic finding of the gang homicide. The offender often empties the gun's magazine into the victim. Such wounds usually are manifested in two different ways:

1. Optimum lethality: the offender targets the victim's head and chest
2. Ritualistic attack (especially prevalent with a retaliatory killing): methodical shooting of arms, knees, groin, and legs first, then chest and head

An execution style of shooting is another method typical of gang murder. There are isolated incidents of insertion and torture, but these are rare and usually occur only in cases of intragang conflict.

The victims who had gang involvement often will have tattoos. Hispanic gangs especially tend to have many intricate tattoos.

Investigative Considerations

"Intelligence is the basis for success of the entire investigation"[1] Known gang conflicts also may give direction to the investigation. Geographic

[1]Sergeant Joe Holmes, Investigative Operation Safe Streets, Los Angeles Sheriff Lynwood Gang Unit.

considerations quickly will help classify a homicide (i.e., an area of concentrated gang activity will increase the likelihood that the killing was gang motivated). Because gang killings are usually public, there are frequently witnesses.

The type of homicide perpctrated by street gangs reflects their emergence as more organized criminal operants. An example of this is that some gangs currently are functioning as contract killers. The largest percentage of gang killings is motivated by drugs, with territory disputes and retaliatory killings the second and third most common motives. One other motive for gang homicide is the intermingling of a female from one gang or territory with the male of another.

The typical gang member is black and is between the ages of 13 and 40, with a median age of 22.5. (The typical gang offender age is 19.4.) He usually wears heavy gold chains; national sports-team shirts, jackets, and hats; brand-name jogging suits; British Knights or Troop tennis shoes; pagers; and colors (e.g., red or blue rubber bands at the end of braids). Signifying one's gang identity can take many forms: a verbal proclamation, a hand sign, an unusual body posture, a display of colors, or even a style of dress, such as wearing a hat tilted to the right or to the left (Chicago Police Department, pers. com. 1990).

Gang members frequently drive small to midsize vehicles that are registered to a family member. Two men and a juvenile or a black man and a white woman are often grouped together to carry out drug business. One ploy used as a diversionary tactic is for a gang member to call 911 and divert police away from the area where a drive-by shooting is scheduled to occur (California Bureau of Organized Crime and Criminal Intelligence, pers. com. 1990). Drive-by shootings can also involve the use of a bicycle.

The law enforcement officer should attempt to keep a log of the addresses of gang members frequently seen together. Gang members often exchange stolen goods, guns, and clothing that may connect them to an offense. If possible, the officer should keep Field Information Cards (FIC) and have the gang member sign the back of the information with his moniker (gang nickname) and logo. Usually, gang members are proud of this and will volunteer to do so. The investigator also should require the gang member to initial, sign, and/or draw his gang graffiti on the back of the rights card when being interviewed. This can prove helpful during prosecution for establishing the subject's membership or involvement with a gang.

Known gang conflicts also may give the investigator direction. Some generalizations about gang conflict are:

1. Bloods do not fight each other
2. Crips will fight each other
3. The beginning of black vs. Hispanic conflict is becoming more prevalent; the two groups used to coexist peacefully

Search Warrant Suggestions

Search warrant suggestions for gang-motivated murder include the following:

- Firearms, ammunition
- Graffiti: walls, garage, books, papers, anywhere in house
- Pictures with guns and gang members, photo albums
- Other items of gang association: clothing with colors, insignias, monikers, pagers, nice cars, jewelry (especially gold)

Multiple addresses should be listed on the search warrant, including gang members recently seen with the offender, due to the frequent exchange of stolen property, guns, and clothing among gang members.

CASE STUDY: 102: GANG-MOTIVATED MURDER

Background

As a group of friends from a Los Angeles neighborhood were piling into their cars to go to a movie, someone shouted, "Get down, get down!" Everyone scrambled for safety as gunfire filled the air. The shots were being fired from a car filled with black males. When the attack was over, two Hispanic males, ages seventeen and eighteen, were dead. In addition, a four-year-old child died several hours later at the hospital.

Victimology

Both teenage victims had an extensive history of gang involvement common to the victims of street-gang homicide. The eighteen-year-old had been jailed several times as a juvenile for assault with a deadly weapon and drug possession charges. The seventeen-year-old also was involved with the same gang for over three years. He, too, was well known to police for being involved with gang conflicts. He had been implicated in a recent drive-by shooting of a rival member, but no action had been taken.

The child victim was typical of many victims of street-gang killings. He was an innocent bystander who happened to be playing on his porch at the wrong time.

Crime Scene Indicators

The area of the shooting had a reputation for being the location of many gang-related conflicts. The crime scene was in an open public place, in front of the child's house and next to the house of the eighteen-year-old.

The killing involved a drive-by assault in which the offenders brought their weapons with them to the crime scene. The bodies were left where they fell until paramedics responded. There were witnesses, but most were gang members who preferred to exact their own form of justice, so they were not cooperative with police.

Forensic Findings

All three victims sustained lethal wounds to the chest area and died of massive blood loss. The seventeen-year-old also had gunshot wounds to the left arm and left side of his neck. Investigators determined from the forensics that at least two different weapons had been involved: a 9mm handgun and a shotgun. The 18-year-old was killed from a shotgun blast. The targeting of vital organs and the presence of multiple gunshot wounds are both forensic findings common to gang murder.

Investigation

Through the use of informants, investigators learned that, indeed, the seventeen-year-old had been involved in the earlier, fatal attack on some rival gang members. He had been recognized and targeted by that gang for retaliation. Investigators were able to come up with three suspects of the four or five gang members believed to be involved. A search warrant produced one of the murder weapons, a 9mm fully automatic MAC-10. Two subjects were charged with murder and a third was charged with his part of the killings, driving the car.

Outcome

The three offenders have been convicted of their respective charges. One of the offenders has been sentenced to twenty years to life; the other two are awaiting sentencing.

103: CRIMINAL COMPETITION HOMICIDE

Death in this type of homicide is a result of *organized crime* conflict over control of territory.

Defining Characteristics

Victimology. Generally, the victim is a prominent or known organized-crime figure or member of the hierarchy. Both intragroup and intergroup conflicts are prevalent prior to the homicide, with the victim reflecting this conflict. Innocent bystanders may become unintentional victims.

Crime Scene Indicators Frequently Noted. The crime scene represents a well-planned crime and reflects the evidence consciousness of the offender. The scene may appear to pose a high risk to the offender, but because there are built-in safeguards (like an escape plan), the risk is considerably lowered. An example of this escape plan is the use of a decoy car that runs interference by blocking traffic, feigning car trouble, or causing an accident while the offender escapes.

The killing is done expeditiously, which keeps the time spent at the scene to a minimum. The offender usually is experienced and will bring a weapon of choice to the scene.

Body disposal tends to be at opposite ends of the spectrum. The offender(s) will either go to great lengths to conceal and dispose of the body or leave it wantonly displayed at the murder scene.

Staging. Staging is usually not present.

Common Forensic Findings. Weaponry or the method of killing depends on the intent of the offender(s). If he is sending a message or making a statement, a bombing, a public killing, or an execution-style shooting (head wounds) will be seen. If the murder is one of elimination, then a small-caliber, untraceable weapon will be more prevalent. Vital organs are targeted in either case.

Investigative Considerations

The use of intelligence obtained from gangland informants is a fundamental consideration that is especially appropriate with this homicide. Intelligence regarding such matters as rival groups and internal power struggles should be explored.

Search Warrant Suggestions

Search warrant suggestions for the suspect's residence include weapons, guns, spent cartridges, clothing similar to that reported by witnesses, communication records (telephone, letters, tapes), and financial records.

CASE STUDY: 103: CRIMINAL COMPETITION HOMICIDE

Background

John T. Scalish was the last great don of the Cleveland Mafia. On 26 May 1976, at the age of sixty-three, he faced heart bypass surgery. The man who had possessed the power to decide the fate of others with the nod of his head was now helpless to control his own. Despite the benefit of Cleveland's best heart specialists, Scalish died a few hours after surgery.

The untimely death of Scalish created a crucial hole in mob leadership because he had not picked a successor. The battle that was ignited by those struggling to fill that void became one of the bloodiest in fifty years of Cleveland's Mafia history.

Victimology

One of the casualties of the mob's leadership transition was Daniel Greene. Born to Irish-American parents in 1929, he was placed in an orphanage as a young child when his father either left or died. Danny Greene was schooled in a tough Italian neighborhood that spawned a life-long hatred of the people who would play a central role in his life.

Greene did a stint in the Marines, where he boxed and became an expert marksman. During the early 1960s, he worked on the Cleveland docks and took over the leadership of the International Longshoreman's Union. He exercised his authority by skimming union funds, extorting money from workers through beatings and threats, and attempting routine shakedowns of employees.

Greene was forced out of the union and convicted in federal court of embezzlement, which was overturned on appeal. He pleaded guilty to a lesser charge of falsifying union records and was fined. He never paid the fine and never saw any prison time for this offense.

Greene started his own business, Emerald Industrial Relations, with which he would have union friends stall or cause trouble on a construction site. He would then offer to settle the dispute for a fee. In addition, he started a business of waste removal by consolidating rubbish haulers, forcing any of the reluctant to join through bombing, burning, and pouring acid on their equipment. Newspaper exposure eventually forced him out of the Solid Waste Guild.

It was during this period that Greene began to make connections with Cleveland's organized crime scene. In 1971 he was implicated in what became the first of a long line of bombings to eliminate threats and further his delusions of a Cleveland-based Celtic crime organization.

At the time of Danny Greene's death, he fit the victimology of being a prominent organized-crime figure and representative of one at odds with those in power. He also had a history of being an FBI informant.

Crime Scene Indicators

After John Scalish died, James Licavoli (alias Jack White) reluctantly took charge of the Cleveland Mafia. Danny Greene began methodically to kill White's associates in an attempt to overthrow him. Cleveland was in the throes of a full-scale bombing war as a result of Greene's ambitions and White's retaliations.

There were several unsuccessful attempts on Greene's life; he walked away from one bombing that demolished his apartment with only a few broken ribs. Because Scalish had bequeathed White such a weak organization, he had no single hit man that could eliminate Greene. To compensate for this deficit, White contacted every thug he knew for the job.

On 16 October 1977 as Greene entered his car after a dentist appointment, Ronald Carabbia sat nervously clutching an airplane transmitter 50 yards away as his accomplice, Ray Ferritto, slowly cruised toward the freeway. The transmitter's target was a platter directional bomb that was planted in the passenger door of a Trojan horse.* Once Greene was between his vehicle and the Trojan horse, Carabbia pushed the button that detonated the directional explosive device. The explosion sent a red ball of fire into the air and blasted debris over the entire parking lot.

Greene's clothing was torn off except his brown zip-up boots and black socks. His left arm landed 100 feet from the bomb site. A blue Adidas duffel bag he was carrying containing a 9mm pistol, two magazines full of bullets, notebooks, and a list of license plates of cars driven by his enemies was found nearly intact.

Traces of the bomb's components (the explosives, the container, and the detonator) were found at the crime scene but were not traceable to their source. No latent prints were found on the Trojan horse.

By noting the fragment patterns and direction and the intensity of damage from the blast and heat/fire, investigators were able to determine where the bomb was (the seat of the blast is where the most damage is).

Forensic Findings

Greene's back was torn apart by the blast. His left arm was severed from his body, as previously mentioned. The cause of death was from massive internal destruction due to both blunt-force trauma and penetrating injury.

Investigation

A woman driving with her husband to an art gallery allowed a blue Plymouth to turn in front of her. For an instant, she and the Plymouth's driver, Ray Ferritto, stared directly at each other. She also noticed a man in the car's back seat staring at the parking lot where Danny Greene was just climbing into his car. The next instant, pieces of Greene's car were flying at the couple, who followed the Plymouth onto the freeway, making note of driver, car, and license plate. The female eyewitness was a commercial artist and was able to sketch a picture of both suspects. In addition, both witnesses later identified Ferritto and Carabbia from photos.

---

*A *Trojan horse* is the name given to a nondescript vehicle that has a bomb planted in it. It is parked next to the target's car and is detonated by remote control when the intended victim comes near it.

The license plates of the Trojan horse played an important role in the investigation. When agents went to the department of motor vehicles to check registrations, they went to the original files, rather than to the computer. Immediately before and after the Trojan horse plates were plates that were registered to the same person. One name was a phony, but the other was the true name. The clerk remembered the man who had filed the tags because he had acquired two sets of plates with different names. The car also was eventually traced to a dealership that was known to be involved with the Cleveland Mafia.

Outcome

Ronald Carabbia was indicted and found guilty of murder. His original sentence was the death penalty, but that later was commuted to life in prison without parole when the state supreme court ruled the death penalty unconstitutional.

Ferritto became a protected government witness and served a five-year term. Another man, Butchy Cisternino, also was convicted for his part in Greene's death by making the bomb.

Jack White was found not guilty during the first state trial. Jury tampering was strongly suspected. At the second state trial, all those involved were found guilty. In federal court, White was convicted for murder, among other charges, and was given a forty-five-year prison sentence. He died in prison around 1986. The first member of the Danny Greene murder conspiracy was scheduled to be released from prison in May 1990.

104: KIDNAP MURDER

Kidnap murder pertains to persons taken against their will and for a variety of motives. It is important to know what designates a kidnapping as opposed to a hostage/barricade situation. A kidnapping involves the seizing and detainment or removal of a person by unlawful force or fraud—often with a demand of ransom. The victim has been taken against his or her will by possibly unknown subject(s) and is detained at a location *unknown* to authorities. Negotiations involving a kidnap situation may include the victim's family, government officials, business leaders, law enforcement authorities, and the offender(s).

A hostage/barricade situation is when a person is held and threatened by an offender to force the fulfillment of substantive demands made on a third party (see also section 129, which deals with hostage murder). The person being held in a hostage situation is at a location *known* to the authorities. This is the major difference between these two situations (Von Zandt 1990).

Defining Characteristics

Victimology. The victim of a kidnap murder has an elevated level of risk due to offender perception. A victim who would be considered low risk due to such factors as life-style and occupation will have this risk elevated due to his or her socioeconomic background or availability of resources to meet possible ransom demands. Resistance and control considerations are also factors affecting risk. Vulnerable victims such as the elderly and the very young would be at higher risk.

Crime Scene Indicators Frequently Noted. There may be multiple crime scenes involved: the location of the abduction, the death scene, and the body disposal site. The victim is usually alone when the abduction occurs. Furniture may be upset; the victim's belongings may be scattered in a way that indicates sudden interruption of activities; doors may be left open. The ransom note may be left at the scene. Future communication from the offender and perhaps the victim is possible. There may be evidence of multiple offenders.

Staging. No staging is present.

Common Forensic Findings. Analysis of the ransom note/recording and/or victim communication is the prime piece of forensic evidence. The technical process called enhancement of recordings should be used to amplify background noise and recording techniques. This information may assist in locating where the recording was made. The method of communication should be analyzed (i.e., typewriter, paper, tape, writing, etc.). The authenticity of both offender and victim communication should be established. Gunshot wounds are often contact or near contact to the head and other vital areas.

Investigative Considerations

Items that should be scrutinized when dealing with a kidnap murder are telephone and financial records. Prior employees should be considered. The possibility that multiple offenders were involved also should be kept in mind. A phone trap and a line trace is usually indicated.

The offender's preoffense surveillance and efforts to trace the victim's movement and routine may help produce witnesses who observed strangers or suspicious persons in the victim's neighborhood or other locations that were part of their routine. Analysis of offender and victim communication using threat assessment also may prove advantageous. Threat assessment is the process of determining validity and potential source of threats received by individuals, groups, or companies. If the threat is determined to be real, countermeasures are developed to protect the potential victim(s). It is the analysis of threat communication, based on the psychology and psychodynamics of the threat, that would denote personality traits of the suspect. Preoffense publicity of the victim or other types of victim visibility may provide leads to victim selection and targeting.

Search Warrant Suggestions

Search warrant suggestions include communication records, such as telephone records. In addition, pictures of the victim, audio or video recordings of the victim, and diaries, journals, and travel-related data, such as airplane tickets, should be considered.

CASE STUDY: 104: KIDNAP MURDER

Background

At 9:50 P.M. on 26 July 1988, the Jackson Police Department of Jackson, Mississippi, received a phone call from Robert Hearin. His wife, Annie, was missing. Hearin had arrived home late that afternoon to an empty house and had become increasingly alarmed after calling friends in an attempt to locate her. A search of the area by police produced a ransom note that had been left in the foyer. The note demanded that Hearin pay twelve people who had fought legal battles with School Pictures of Mississippi Inc., which he owned.

Victimology

Annie Hearin was seventy-two years old at the time of her abduction. She had been married to Robert Hearin for forty-nine years. Annie Hearin was an active part of the Jackson community, patronizing the Jackson symphony and opera. She had held executive positions in the Opera Guild and the Junior League and had co-chaired the Mississippi Arts Festival.

The Hearins had a reputation for being a civic-minded, unpretentious couple who had funded local colleges and universities in addition to contributing to the Jackson art museum. They lived in a posh neighborhood, but their brick home was not considered lavish, especially by Jackson standards.

Robert Hearin was a self-made millionaire who controlled an empire consisting of Mississippi's largest gas-distribution company, its second largest bank, and its second largest insurance company. Hearin also had run School Pictures of Mississippi, the photo-processing operation that had employed the twelve men named on the ransom note as franchisers.

"When corporations are bought and sold, you jerk people's lives around without even knowing it," said one Jackson businessman. This statement illustrates one of the factors that elevated Annie Hearin's risk level as victim: the nature of her husband's business involved making decisions that could be potentially disastrous to some people. Another factor that increased Annie Hearin's risk level is that she was a frail, seventy-two-year-old woman and was not in particularly good health. She would pose minimal resistance to the offender, making her easier to control and minimizing any commotion that would attract unwanted witnesses. Thus, Annie Hearin was a victim whose low risk level became slightly heightened by offender perception.

Crime Scene Indicators

The last one to see Annie Hearin was her maid, who left the Hearin residence around 3:30 P.M. the afternoon of 26 July 1988. Annie Hearin had hosted a bridge game involving several friends that afternoon. Her husband arrived home at 4:30 P.M. He found his wife's car in the driveway and her shoes placed beside a living-room chair. There were no signs of forced entry, and nothing was missing from the home.

At 9:50 P.M. Hearin notified the police. They made a search of the area and discovered a splattering of blood, possibly from nose or lips, on the front door and door frame. A note was found in the foyer.

Forensic Findings

The note was typewritten on a 1920 Vintage Royal manual typewriter. The contents were as follows:

R bert Herrin
    Put these people back in the shape they was in before they got mixed up with School Pictures. Pay them whatever dama ges the y want ant tell them all this so they cank now what your doing b ut dont tell them why. you are doing it. Do this before ten days pass. Don't c all police. [The twelve franchisers were then listed.] If any is dead pay his children.

On 15 August Hearin received a letter dated 10 August and postmarked 12 August from Atlanta, Georgia. This letter was signed by Annie Hearin and later was analyzed to be authentic. Analysis of the letter revealed that she had been directed verbally and mechanically to write it and was under great duress. The note contained the following message:

Bob—
    If you don't do what these people want you to do, they are going to seal me up in the cellar of this house with only a few jugs of water. Please, save me, Annie Laurie.

Blood also was found on this note, but neither this sample or the one found at the crime scene could be definitely linked to the victim.

Investigation

An investigative consideration of great importance in this case was the list of franchisers on the ransom note. A suspect in a kidnapping of this sort, one that was more retaliatory than profit motivated (nonspecific demands in ransom note), would be someone who had been (in his perspective) mistreated by the victim's husband. Careful investigation of the financial status as well as any history of problems precipitating the incident, either domestic or occupational, would be helpful in narrowing down a list of possible suspects.

Another consideration that was of significance in terms of the suspect who finally was charged with Annie Hearin's kidnapping was scrutiny of meetings and travel typical of his routine. His travels had made him familiar with Jackson.

When considering the list of names on the ransom note for a possible suspect who may have had a score to settle with Robert Hearins, investigators found that N. Alfred Winn's name was prominent. A St. Petersburg, Florida, lawyer, Winn had been involved in a court battle with School Pictures in 1983. The company sued him, alleging that he owed them money they had advanced him. Winn countersued, alleging the company had misstated his prospects for making money when it signed him up as a franchisee. In 1983 a district judge in Jackson ordered Winn to pay the company $90,000, and in 1984 he was ordered to pay $153,883. School Pictures, having failed to collect, seized Winn's law office. Winn was quoted as saying he had lost his life's savings.

A neighbor of the Hearins identified Winn from a photo lineup as the man she saw in a white van in the neighborhood a few days before the kidnapping. In addition, a superintendent for a construction crew working at a neighborhood church two blocks from the Hearin residence recalled seeing Winn looking around the neighborhood.

On 5 or 6 August 1988 sometime between 6 A.M. and 9 A.M. at the Quality Inn in DeLand, Florida, Winn met with a woman and asked her to mail the letter in Annie Hearin's handwriting. At Bishop's Planetarium and South Museum in Tampa in late August, Winn again met with this woman to pay her the initial $250 of a $500 promised payment. The rest was paid on 18 February 1989 at about 7:15 A.M., again at the DeLand meeting spot. The woman had agreed to dye her hair and disguise herself as part of the deal.

In a search of Winn's law office and home, the FBI seized a map of Jackson with the Hearin home, businesses, and farm marked; six aerial maps of Jackson; two handguns; and an old Royal typewriter.

Outcome

On 8 February 1990 Winn was convicted of extortion by mail, conspiracy to kidnap, and perjury in connection with Annie Hearin's disappearance. The status of state charges of homicide are as yet uncertain. Annie Hearin's body has not yet been recovered (Fredricksburg Freelance, Kathy Eyre; Clarion-Ledger Staff, Grace Simmons; Associated Press Wire Services; Newsweek, James Baker, Andrew Murr; *USA Today,* Tim Doherty; 1988–90).

105: PRODUCT TAMPERING HOMICIDE

In this type of homicide, death results from contact with a commercial product, sabotaged by the offender usually for achieving financial gain. There are three primary offender strategies used for achieving financial gain: through litigation on behalf of the victim (wrongful death), through extortion, and through business operations. The latter method includes damaging a competing business through sabotage of their product or manipulating the stock market as a result of negative publicity.

Violation of the federal Anti-Tampering Act occurs when any product has been affected by the actions of the perpetrator. With a business attack, tainting or switching labels may happen on a retail level. Elements of this crime include the involvement of a consumer product, such as a drug; the tainting of that product or the switching of product labels to make them materially false; and intent to cause serious injury to the business of a person.

The extortion method also can be tied into the business manipulation approach. An example of this is a crime involving a protection racket, in which the taint is tied into a demand for payments under threat of closing down the store or causing grave damage to the reputation of the business.

Defining Characteristics

Victimology. The victim of product tampering may be random or specific, dependent on the product's distribution, the product's usage, and the offender's strategy. Sabotaged baby food, brake lines, and soft drinks will each involve a particular age group and/or class of people. Some sabotaged products will be distributed only on a local scale, so the victimology will be more confined. The localization of victims can also help establish whether the product is being tampered with at a retail stage or at the manufacturer's level. Random victimology is likely to be seen with extortion or with intent to damage a competitor.

A more specific victim is seen when the offender employs litigation for wrongful death. The victim will be a family member or one closely associated with the offender. Random victims are observed when this type of offender wants to remove suspicion from himself or herself and stages the crime to look like the work of an indiscriminate killer.

Crime Scene Indicators Frequently Noted. Multiple crime scenes usually are involved with this homicide: the site where the product is altered, the location where the product is procured by the victim, the place of use/consumption, and/or the death scene. The location of alteration may offer evidence of the tampering involved. If it is mechanical sabotage, tools particular to that alteration will be present. Chemicals, poisons, and medicines may be found if this type of tampering is employed.

Tampered-product locations and the proximity of victims to sites will aid in deciding the scope and movement of the offender as well as the origin of the product. At the death scene, the proximity of the victim to the altered product can aid the investigator in reconstructing the product's path. In addition, communication from the offender may be found at any of the scenes involved.

Staging. Staging is crucial if the offender is using the litigation strategy. The offender must make it appear as if the family member or close associate was a victim of either a random killer or a company's faulty product. For the first set of circumstances, there could be other random victims selected to give the appearance of an indiscriminate saboteur at work. The other situation may require the death to look like an accident (e.g., a defective automobile part or short-circuited power tool that causes the fatal accident). Fire started by apparently faulty wiring that burns a house down with the victim inside is another illustration of a staged product tampering. The initial impression derived from the crime scene of a staged tampering homicide ranges from violent death to a medical emergency of some kind, without any obvious indicators of a homicide.

Common Forensic Findings. Examination of the product is one of the fundamental considerations of product tampering. There may be visible signs of tampering, such as clearly discolored capsules. The type of analysis done on the product and victim will depend on the instrument of death.

Suspicion of poisoning requires toxicological and chemical analysis of the product and victim to determine if products of the same lot were involved. Because toxicological analysis is not routine in postmortem examination, exhumation of the victim may be necessary to detect poisoning. This, along with the distribution of victims, will help decide if the source of tampering is at the retail or manufacturer level. Type of poison and consistent or varying levels of poison in each tainted product reflect the resources and sophistication of the offender. The packaging of the product also will be revealing of offender sophistication: this includes absence/presence of fingerprints, repackaging, and the physical appearance of the tainted items.

The analysis of offender communication would be approached in the same manner as in kidnap murders (see section 104). If the communication is verbal, the verbatim set of the caller's comments and information about speech patterns and accent are vital to threat assessment.

Investigative Considerations

Threat assessment of offender communication may be helpful. If there is no extortion demand associated with the death and civil litigation has been initiated, the litigant should be scrutinized. The litigant's financial status (beneficiary to insurance claims or inheritance, along with problems such as outstanding debts, etc.), relationship with victim (problems, extramarital affairs), and preoffense and postoffense behavior should be examined.

Although the primary motivation is financial gain, the offender who targets a family member for death often has concurrent secondary motivations or goals that will be equally well served by the victim's death. Conflicts such as domestic problems and extramarital affairs should be explored. Because product tampering deaths are relatively rare, early allegations of such by anyone who stands to benefit from the victim's death should be viewed cautiously and evaluated carefully.

Cyanide is often the poison of choice because it is easily available at chemical and photographic supply houses and in college and high-school laboratories. It can even be ordered through the mail. One ounce can kill 250 people, so its potency makes it a popular choice with product-tampering offenders. An important investigative tool in cases of an offender who has used cyanide is a complex instrument in use at the FDA's Cincinnati district laboratory. It can track down the source of the cyanide and identify the supplier, who can find the geographic customer list rather quickly. This may help narrow the list of typical suspects (chemical firms, grocery clerks, enemies of deceased victims, or a store's terminated personnel) and further isolate the offender.

Search Warrant Considerations

Search warrant considerations for this type of crime include financial records (see also appendix B), materials specific to the tampering (tools, electronic devices, chemicals, drugs, literature pertaining to drugs, manuals, etc.), and any related products (other analgesics, empty capsules). Evidence of tampering practice and other tainted products should also be considered.

CASE STUDY: 105: PRODUCT TAMPERING HOMICIDE

Background

Stella Maudine Nickell's husband, Bruce, came home from work with a headache. After he had given his wife of ten years a kiss, he went into their kitchen and reached for a bottle of Extra-Strength Excedrin. He swallowed four capsules and sat down to watch TV. Stella remembers that Bruce then decided to go for a walk out on the patio. Suddenly she heard Bruce call to her that he felt like he was going to pass out. Within the next minute, he collapsed and was unable to speak. Stella called the paramedics, and Bruce was taken to Harborview Medical Center in Seattle. He died a few hours later, never regaining consciousness.

Six days later on 11 June 1986, Sue Snow started her day by taking two Extra-Strength Excedrin capsules, as was her habit. The caffeine in the capsules was like her morning cup of coffee. Fifteen minutes later, her daughter Hayley found Sue sprawled unconscious on the bathroom floor. By noon, she was dead.

Victimology

At the time of his death, Bruce Nickell was fifty-two. When he married Stella, he was a hard-drinking heavy-equipment operator, which suited Stella because she had a fondness for barhopping. Bruce recently had taken stock of his life and had decided to dry out by attending a rehabilitation program. Stella attended a few sessions with him. Before his death, Bruce was often unemployed, which had begun to grate on Stella's nerves.

Sue Snow was forty years old at the time of her death. She had dropped out of high school to marry but had turned her life around through hard work. She had become the assistant vice-president at a branch of the Puget Sound National Bank and was happily married to Paul Webking. They were rarely apart and were "madly in love," according to Webking.

Both victims were users of the product. Nickell and Snow had never met; Snow was an example of the random victim that is common to many product tampering murders.

Crime Scene Indicators

Five bottles of tainted Extra-Strength Excedrin came from shelves at Johnny's Food Center in Kent, a Seattle suburb, and a Pay 'N Save store in Auburn. Two contaminated containers were found in the Nickell household. Seals on the containers were cut or missing, and the boxes, which had been reglued, demonstrated obvious signs of tampering. The victims lived within 5 miles of each other, a factor that was significant to investigators devising the area of offender operation.

Staging

Sue Snow became a victim because of staging. Stella Nickell had been very disappointed with the medical examiner's initial decision that her husband had died from emphysema and not cyanide poisoning. Her husband's death meant $105,000 to her in addition to the damages she expected to get from

Bristol-Myers. Someone else had to die to alert the authorities that a random cyanide killer was at work in King County. So Stella Nickell poisoned three bottles of Excedrin and slipped them onto the shelves of area stores, one of which was bought by Snow. This set the scene for her to approach officials with her suspicions that her husband had fallen to a cyanide murderer as well as to give her grounds to sue Bristol-Myers.

Forensic Findings

The initial cause of death listed on Bruce Nickell's death certificate was pulmonary emphysema because the coroner had failed to detect the cyanide in his body. It was not until after Snow's death, when Stella Nickell came forward with the hesitant suggestion that her husband also had been the victim of a random cyanide killer, that the true cause of death was determined. At that time, tissue samples demonstrated cyanide poisoning. Sue Snow had levels of cyanide that were easily detected by medical examiners.

After analysis of the tampered bottles, it was established that there had been a random selection of pills poisoned. Some capsules contained more than three times the lethal adult dose of potassium cyanide. Others were not contaminated; Paul Webking took two capsules from the same bottle that proved fatal to Sue Snow twenty minutes later.

The exterior carton and bottle tampering was artless. The boxes were reglued in an amateur manner, exhibiting minimal sophistication on the part of the offender.

Investigation

Stella Nickell had a restless yearning to buy the property the Nickell trailer stood on and open a tropical fish store. Her ambitions were becoming insistent. At the age of forty-four, she had an increasing awareness of the gap between her dreams and reality. To her, the gap seemed to be widening faster as each year passed. Her frequently unemployed husband reinforced her belief that if she did not act soon, her dreams would slip away for good. In addition, she felt her husband was not much fun since he had stopped drinking.

In the fall of 1985, Nickell took out a $40,000 life insurance policy on her husband, naming herself as sole beneficiary. Bruce Nickell also held a state employee policy that paid $31,000, with an additional $107,000 awarded in the event of accidental death. To Nickell, $176,000 could easily make her dreams into reality.

Nickell's daughter, Cynthia, who was living with the Nickells at the time of the murder, eventually came forward and told about the conversations she had had with her mother during the five years leading to the offense. Bruce Nickell's death was a popular topic of conversation with Stella Nickell. Cynthia testified in court that her mother studied library books on poisons and experimented with toxic seeds, either hemlock or foxglove. Bruce Nickell's only reaction was to become lethargic. When Stella Nickell learned that a recovering alcoholic is susceptible to other addictive substances, she discussed the idea of killing her husband with heroin, cocaine, or speed so his death would appear to be an accidental overdose.

According to Cynthia, her mother expressed great interest in the Tylenol murders of Chicago in 1982. Using the same plan, she could not only collect life insurance, but also file suit against the responsible company, Bristol-Myers for wrongful death (which she did). She felt this was a viable alternative to get her fish store and live in the comfort she had always dreamed about.*

These discussions between Cynthia and her mother show how scrutiny of a suspect's preoffense conversations may be helpful in establishing motive and premeditation. There was not enough evidence to bring Stella Nickell in until Cynthia decided to talk.

Outcome

Stella Nickell was convicted of five counts of product tampering and two counts of causing the death of another by product tampering (the first conviction using a federal law enacted in 1983). On 17 June 1988 she was sentenced to ninety years. She will not be eligible for parole until 2018.

---

106 DRUG MURDER

Drug murder is defined as the murder of an individual for which the primary cause is to remove an obstruction and facilitate the operation of an illegal drug business.

Defining Characteristics

Victimology. The victimology of drug-related homicide is dependent on the motive of the offender. The homicides are categorized into five motive groups: discipline, informant, robbery, territory infringement, and anti-drug advocate.

The victim of a discipline-motivated homicide is being punished for breaking the rules of a drug distribution group by which he is employed. Examples of these infringements include skimming money or drugs, steal-

---

*Nickell was not hesitant to try illegal means to achieve her goals, as her criminal history illustrates: in 1968 she was convicted of fraud; in 1969 of felonious beating of Cynthia; and in 1971, forgery.

ing customers, or in some way hindering, obstructing, or impeding the operation. The informant supplies information on the criminal enterprise to law enforcement or competing dealers. A robbery-motivated homicide usually deals with a rip-off of drugs, money, or other goods (especially gold jewelry) related to the sale of drugs from customers, traffickers, and dealers. A drug trafficker who infringes on the territory of another drug dealer also may become the victim of a drug murder. Victims of these four types of murder are commonly known to law enforcement as having a history of association with the drug trade. They may have an arrest record, reflecting a history of drug use, robberies, and assaultive behavior relating to this involvement, or at least an association with known drug offenders.

The last type of victim can be anyone from the neighborhood antidrug crusader to a law enforcement officer. These victims may be social workers or clergy who are offering treatment to drug abusers and thus usurping customers of the dealers. Judges who impose stiff penalties, politicians who vigorously campaign against drugs, and witnesses testifying against drug offenders are other examples of this victimology.

All of these victim types just mentioned are individuals opposed to the drug trade. As such, they are viewed as an obstruction, real or symbolic, that the offender wants removed.

Crime Scene Indicators Frequently Noted. Drug-related homicide often occurs in a public place if the death of the victim is intended to be a message. The body is usually not concealed but is left at the scene with a wanton indifference. Evidence may be removed from the scene (e.g., drugs, money, etc.). The weapon used is frequently one of choice that is brought to the scene and taken from it by the offender. Drugs or drug proceeds removed from the scene or missing from an obvious or known victim trafficker is another indicator that might be apparent at the scene of a drug murder.

Staging. Staging is usually not present.

Common Forensic Findings. The weapon used is predominantly a firearm, often large caliber and semiautomatic. Occasionally knife wounds or blunt-force trauma will be present, but these injuries are not as prevalent.

A high lethality of injury will be seen in which vital organs (chest and head) are targeted. Overkill involving multiple wounds can be seen.

A drug screen done on the victim may help establish possible victim use and connections to the drug business. Sometimes the mode of death might be lethal drug dose, or so-called hotshot, especially if the victim is a user.

The investigator should make certain a latent print process is attempted on the body. Physical contact commonly occurs between the offender and victim of a drug murder before death.

Investigative Considerations

The offender almost always will have a known association with the drug trade as a user, manufacturer, or distributor. This subject commonly will be associated with a street gang, since gangs are immersed in drug trafficking (see section 102).

This homicide appears opportunistic with rip-offs, territory infringements, and some discipline-motivated killings. Informant and antidrug advocate hits usually are set-ups that demonstrate some degree of organization and planning. Although informant use is a fundamental consideration with many investigations, the use of intelligence information is especially valuable with drug-related murder. Use of prison informants might also prove helpful with this type of homicide.

Offenders may exhibit displays of wealth even though they have no legitimate source of money. They have expensive clothing, vehicles, and jewelry, yet they are unemployed or have a job that is inconsistent with their apparent finances.

Search Warrant Considerations

For this type of homicide, search warrant considerations include: large amounts of money, clothing, electronic equipment, and so on reflective of a possible illegitimate money source; drug paraphernalia and items that link the offender to the drug trade; firearms; phone records; rental contracts; address books; financial records and bank records; transaction records, computerized records, and ledgers; packing materials (packaging from drug shipments, processing, lab set-ups, distribution [dividing into smaller parcels for street sale]); and photos (of using, manicuring, and preparing drugs).

Two case examples are given. The first case illustrates a scene where all persons present were killed. The second case illustrates a dual drug murder.

CASE STUDY: 106 DRUG MURDER (A)

Background

On 30 January 1984 FBI agents surrounded a rooming house in Miami's Coconut Grove section. Within a few minutes, they had in custody George Clarence Bridgette, one of the FBI's ten most wanted fugitives. When he was arraigned before a federal magistrate, he continued to claim his name was Odell Davis, the alias he had gone by since he fled Long Beach, California. He was wanted for the drug-related murder of four people and the attempted murder of another.

Bridgette had two accomplices who already had been tried and convicted for their part in the murders. They were Willie ("Chino") Thomas and James Earl Cade.

Victimology

One victim was Pamela Cade, who was an ex-wife of James Earl Cade's uncle. Pamela was thirty years old. Pamela's three-year-old daughter, Chinue Cade, also was killed. Another daughter, fifteen-year-old Carolyn Ferguson, was shot, but she survived to testify against Thomas and Cade. Larry Luther Evans, age thirty-seven, and Crystal Baxter, age twenty-three, were the other two victims.

Crime Scene Indicators

At 10:30 P.M. on September 4, 1977, Cade, Bridgette, and Thomas entered Pamela Cade's Long Beach residence, pulled down the window shades, and immediately killed Baxter. Bridgette carried a shotgun; Cade had a knife; Thomas had a .38-caliber revolver. Thomas then turned his gun on Pamela Cade and shot her. Thomas was first thought to have killed Chinue Cade, but later it was determined that Bridgette tore the child out of her dead mother's arms, held her upside down by the feet, and shot her in the neck. He then tossed the dying child onto the sofa.

Thomas then turned his gun on Ferguson. The fifteen-year-old struggled fiercely for her life as Thomas tried to shoot her in the head. She received a chest wound and feigned death, which enabled her to be the only survivor.

Evans was the target of all three offenders. He was stabbed and shot with both the revolver and the shotgun.

The bodies were left at the scene with no attempt at concealment. The weapons of choice, firearms and a knife, were brought to the scene and removed with the offenders.

Forensic Findings

Crystal Baxter died of multiple head and back wounds. The wounds were caused by a shotgun. Pamela Cade died of a .38-caliber gunshot wound to the head. Chinue Cade died of a gunshot wound to neck. Larry Evans suffered seven stab wounds to the chest, one which penetrated his heart, causing death. He also was shot in the chest with the revolver, and shotgun pellets were retrieved from his legs.

The overkill present for Baxter and Evans is often found in a retaliatory drug killing. Not only were the offenders retaliating against the victims they felt had wronged them, but they also were making a statement to anyone else who might consider ripping them off. Vital areas (head and center chest) that ensure lethality were targeted, another common finding in drug murder.

Investigation

The motive for this multiple murder was a so-called burn on a forty-dollar drug deal between James Cade's cousin and Pamela Cade.

Outcome

Cade and Thomas were convicted on four counts of murder on November 22, 1978 and were sentenced to death. When the state supreme court declared the death penalty unconstitutional, their sentences were commuted to life imprisonment.

CASE STUDY: 106: DRUG MURDER (B)

Background

By the time he was twenty-three, Daniel A. Nicoll had a thriving drug trade that required bimonthly trips to Florida in his 1978 Ford pickup. Even though Nicoll did not live in a mainstream drug trade city, he was important enough to be the target of a unified task force consisting of Drug Enforcement Agency (DEA), state, and local law enforcement.

When he was not making Florida trips or doing business, Nicoll tended bar at the Club California in Buffalo, New York. It is there he met Laura Osborn. As their personal relationship developed, Nicoll began supplying her with cocaine and marijuana for personal use as well as for dealing.

Victimology

Donald and Claire Nicoll referred to their son's drug dealings as "dirty business" and as the reason their son was no longer residing with them. Nicoll was arrested by Buffalo police for possession of methadone, unlawful possession of a controlled substance (PCP), and unlawful possession of marijuana. The case was not disposed of prior to the murder.

Nicoll had experienced some close calls before his death. He returned from one Florida trip with an eye injury, attributing it to a drug rip-off. He also had been threatened with a gun when he was suspected of a drug rip-off on another occasion.

Nicoll demonstrated a fitting picture of the drug murder victim. His history of a drug-related arrest and the fact that his repuation in the drug business had reached a federal level with DEA involvement offered further illustration of his risk as a victim. In addition, Nicoll had a history of previous threatening drug-related confrontations.

Laura Osborn had met Nicoll barhopping in 1975. They had maintained a steady relationship for about four years. Osborn benefited from Nicoll's prosperous drug trade personally as well as financially by dealing drugs herself. She had no arrest record but was under the same DEA investigation as Nicoll.

Osborn paid a price for her involvement with Nicoll. She was the victim of his abuse and was seen on occasion with bruises on her face. Another time, Nicoll explained a head injury of Osborn's as a suicide attempt. However, Osborn claimed that Nicoll had struck her on the head with a bottle. Neighbors had witnessed the assault, but no legal action ever was taken.

Osborn epitomized the drug murder victim for the same reasons Nicoll did. She was known to law enforcement as being associated indirectly (through her relationship with Nicoll) and directly (through her active dealing) with the drug business.

Crime Scene Indicators

There were two crime scenes involved with these homicides. The first was on a back road where the victims were parked, waiting for the offender, who was going to buy drugs from them. The offender, Larry Rendell, pulled up his truck next to Nicoll's truck, facing the opposite direction, so that the two drivers were facing each other. Larry then shot both Nicoll and Osborn from his truck. Nicoll fell over unconscious into Osborn's lap. Osborn was still alert, having been shot in the arm while trying to protect herself.

Rendell climbed into Nicoll's truck and drove it to another road. Osborn pleaded for her life, assuring Rendell she would tell no one about what had happened. She then asked Rendell for some cocaine. It was at this time that Nicoll stopped breathing.

Osborn exited the truck and began to walk away, taking her shoes off as she walked. Rendell felt he could not afford to let Osborn live so he shot her from the truck and then went over to complete the job.

Both bodies were dragged over an embankment and covered with leaves. Rendell then drove Nicoll's truck into a gully off another road nearby.

Forensic Findings

Later, Rendell told his brother that he tore the truck apart to remove any shell casings from the ten to twelve shots he had fired at Osborn and Nicoll. Confiscated at his apartment were clogs and a green jacket with lettering that was worn by the offender at the time of the murder. Both items were soiled with each of the victims' blood.

Cause of death for Daniel Nicoll was multiple gunshot wounds to the head, causing massive cerebral hemorrhage. Osborn also died of massive cerebral hemorrhage from multiple gunshot wounds. She had been struck at least six times by the .22-caliber rifle.

Investigation

Lawrence K. Rendell had several reasons for killing Nicoll and Osborn. He claimed that Nicoll had shorted him on a previous marijuana deal. Nicoll had ignored his protests. He also owed Nicoll anywhere from $450 to $1000 for past drug deals and was constantly hassled by the victim to pay up. Rendell had instructed Nicoll to bring his supply of cocaine the day of the murders because he claimed to have a buyer. Rendell had decided that killing Nicoll served a three-fold purpose of settling his debts, evening the score from the previous rip-off, and providing him with drugs. In addition to the other physical evidence linking Rendell to the crime, two speakers from Nicoll's truck were found in Rendell's apartment during the search.

Outcome

Larry Rendell was convicted of two counts of second-degree murder.

107: INSURANCE/INHERITANCE-RELATED DEATH

The victim is murdered for insurance and/or inheritance purposes. There are two subcategories for this type of homicide: individual profit murder and commercial profit murder.

107.01: INDIVIDUAL PROFIT MURDER

The individual profit murder is defined as one in which the murderer expects to gain financially by the victim's death.

Defining Characteristics

Victimology. The victim of an insurance or inheritance death for individual profit has a close relationship with the offender. This includes family members, business associates, and live-in partners.

Many victims of this category would not typically be characterized as high-risk targets. In fact, their life-styles, occupations, and living circumstances often would classify them as very low risk. However, because of the offender's perception of them as an avenue to his or her financial goals, their risk is greatly elevated.

Crime Scene Indicators Frequently Noted. Usually the body is not concealed but is left in the open or somewhere that discovery is probable. The
nature of the crime scene, or where it falls in the continuum between
organized and disorganized, will depend on the amount of planning and
capcity of the offender.

An example of one extreme of this continuum is the very spontaneous
offense committed by a youthful, impulsive, and/or less intelligent subject.
This crime scene would contain more physical evidence (fingerprints, footprints, etc.). The weapon would be one of opportunity, acquired and left at
the scene. The crime scene would be chaotic, with evidence of sudden
violence to the victim (blitz-style attack.) The body would be left at the
assault site with little or no effort to conceal it.

The other extreme of this crime scene would be the offense committed
by the calculating, proficient offender who has mapped out all aspects of
the crime ahead of time. This methodical approach is represented by an
orderly crime scene in which there is minimal physical evidence present.
The weapon is one of choice, brought to and removed from the scene by
the offender.

Staging. Staging is often employed with this type of homicide. Its com-
plexity can reflect offender capability, resources, and premeditation. The
crime scene will most frequently be staged to give investigators the impression that death resulted from natural or accidental causes or from criminal
activity. Suicide staging is also possible, especially in light of the more
liberal standards of some insurance policies.

Common Forensic Findings. Asphyxial and/or chemical modalities are
common because these deaths often are not considered untimely and therefore not investigated within the medical-legal system. Toxicological studies
of the blood, liver, hair, and so on are essential for determining if poison
was used. Exhumation may be necessary.

The staging used will determine the forensic findings (e.g., a staged
robbery-murder victim might have gunshot wounds, as opposed to the
seemingly accidental drowning victim who has pulmonary edema and
blood-streaked foam present in the nose and mouth). Therefore, the variance of forensic findings is vast.

Investigative Considerations

The mechanisms of money transfer, whether insurance documents or wills,
should be checked to determine authenticity of the victim's signature. Any
recent beneficiary change or increase in insurance premiums and/or new
policy procurement justifies further probing into the victim/beneficiary relationship. Many of the components that are detailed in the discussion of
domestic homicide (see section 122) are pertinent to this investigation,

especially because multiple motives often are involved (extramarital affairs, irreconcilable conflicts, etc.).

Precipitating events may be seen as external stressors (e.g., financial problems; marital discord; dissension with victim due to job, alcohol, or other factors). There may be a change in preoffense behavior toward the victim, very often in the form of apparent relationship improvement. Offender nervousness and/or preoccupation also may be observed by others.

The offender often has an uncommonly detailed, steadfast alibi with selective recall.[2] The offender also may delay reporting the murder, especially if he or she desires a third party to discover the body. A comprehensive examination of the physical and psychological records and history of the victim should be done when the investigator suspects the offender has employed suicide or death-from-natural-cause staging.

Search Warrant Suggestions

Financial records of the victim and offender should be scrutinized. If the death was staged to appear natural, medications, poisons, and drugs of any kind should be looked for. Any indicators that would support the precipitating events (offender in debt, extramarital affairs, etc.) should be sought. (See also appendix B regarding indications of financial difficulty.)

CASE STUDY: 107.01: INDIVIDUAL PROFIT MURDER

Background

Dr. John Dale Cavaness seemed to have the angel of death at his side when it came to his family. In April 1977 his twenty-two-year-old son, Mark Dale Cavaness, was found shot to death, an apparent victim of either a bizarre accidental shooting or a homicide that had remained unsolved. Seven years later, history repeated itself with the shooting death of another son, Sean Dale Cavaness, the apparent victim of an execution-style killing and robbery. When St. Louis homicide detectives arrested Cavaness for Sean's murder, the people of the Little Egypt region in southern Illinois were outraged.

Dr. Dale, as he was affectionately called, was akin to Mother Theresa to his patients and friends. He often did not charge his patients and was not only a tireless and devoted physician, but also a congenial, down-to-earth neighbor who would take time to talk with people despite his overburdened practice.

---

[2]Selective recall entails the offender's ability to remember precise details of his or her actions during the offense, but events removed a few hours or days preoffense or postoffense are vague compared with the time in question.

Cavaness's family and closest office workers, however, knew he had another, darker side. His ex-wife, Marian, had spent some miserable years toward the end of their marriage, the victim of abuse, both physical and verbal. His four sons never had known much from their father besides castigation and torment. The facts of Cavaness's disastrous financial status, the mistreatment of his family, and his history of problems with the law emerged and combined to form a disturbing portrait of a man who was very capable of murdering his own sons for money.

Victimology: Victim 1

At the time of his death, Mark Dale Cavaness was an unsettled twenty-two-year-old with no direction to his life. His parents' divorce and a move to St. Louis had upset him to the point that he had failed his senior year of high school. He had never received his general equivalency diploma (GED) and had drifted around the Midwest, working odd jobs for short periods of time, before returning to Little Egypt in 1977 to work on his father's farm. Marian Cavaness worried about the effect her ex-husband's constant sarcasm and persecution was having on her son. Phone conversations with her ex-husband consisted primarily of his complaints about Mark; he was amounting to nothing and was a no-good pot smoker. Mark's voice often reflected self-belittlement.

Marian Cavaness had decided it was time to persuade Mark to come back to St. Louis, find a job, and get his GED. She and her three other sons were spending the weekend in Little Egypt, so the boys could be near their father and Mark for Easter. She was determined not to return to St. Louis without Mark. On Saturday 9 April, Marian, Sean, and Kevin, another son, set out to find Mark. They were concerned that he had not shown up at the Cavaness house, especially because it had been Mark's idea for the Easter reunion with his mother and brothers. They drove out to the trailer on Dale's farm where Mark was staying.

Fifteen-year-old Sean was the first to find the remains of his oldest brother as he walked through tall grass by Mark's white Jeep pickup truck. Kevin, nineteen at the time, had to take control, calming his hysterical brother and protecting his mother from the sight of Mark's ravished corpse. Scavenger animals had left little; Sean had only known it was Mark by recognizing his belt buckle and his boots sticking out of the grass.

Crime Scene Indicators: Victim 1

Mark's body was positioned on its back, 10 to 12 feet from the truck, with the feet pointing toward the pickup. From the midthigh up, including the arms and hands, were fresh skeletal remains with a few shreds of tissue still intact. The skull was picked clean, with only the left eyeball and the brown hair remaining. Only the lower legs, which were still encased in jeans and laced-up work boots, were intact. Turkey vultures, wild dogs, opossums, and other scavenger animals were responsible for the condition of the body. It was not possible to determine where Mark had been standing or sitting when shot because the animals could have dragged the body into the grass.

A black leather wallet was found in the grass near the body. It carried the identification of Mark Dale Cavaness. A plaid shirt also was found near the truck. A package of Vantage cigarettes and a book of matches were in the left breast pocket. There was a hole about 2½ inches by 4 inches surrounded by dried blood between the left breast pocket and snap buttons.

Buckshot was found under the body site where the rib cage had rested as well as scattered on the floorboard inside the truck. Blood was on the driver's seat, floorboard, inside door panel, and outside just behind the door opening. The blood-spatter pattern and the small, neat hole in Mark's shirt indicated a point-blank shot, either while he was sitting behind the wheel (turned toward the passenger side), getting in or out of the truck, or standing beside it.

The shotgun was a 12-gauge, three-inch Magnum Browning automatic goose gun. It belonged to Dale Cavaness. One round was found in the chamber, and one in the magazine. The safety was off. The gun was lying on the passenger side of the truck with the barrel pointing toward the driver's side. The gun was inside its case, with the front barrel protruding several inches as if the end of the case had been blown off when the gun was fired. The hook end of a metal coat hanger had been wedged into the trigger guard through another hole in the case. Hanging from the coat hanger was a camouflage hunting vest with its lower edge shut in the passenger door. The shotgun had been positioned across an ax handle, which raised the shooting angle.

The shotgun had been rigged in such a way that it looked as if Mark had reached across the driver's side and grabbed the barrel, pulling it toward himself. The coat hanger, hooked on the trigger and anchored on the other side by the vest caught in the passenger door, had pulled the trigger. Mark had taken the shot point-blank in the chest.

Staging: Victim 1

The shooting had been intended to look like an accident or a booby trap. A suicide was unlikely because the gun would have been removed from the case.

Kevin Cavaness was certain his brother, being an experienced hunter, would know better than to grab a gun by its barrel and pull on it. The detective assigned to the case also found this an unlikely sequence of events. The end of the case could have been shot off, but the case also showed signs of wear elsewhere.

The piece of evidence that discounted the attempt to stage an accident or booby trap was the location of the cartridge. If the gun had been in the case when fired by the coat hanger or the murderer's finger, the spent cartridge would have been inside the case.

Only one spent shotgun cartridge was found, on the floorboard of the driver's side. It was reasoned that the offender had fired the gun inside the truck, then returned it to its case. The killer then constructed the phony scene, making the shooting look accidental or booby trapped. No fingerprints or footprints were obtainable from the crime scene because it had been compromised by the initial personnel responding to the call.

Forensic Findings: Victim 1

Mark Dale Cavaness had died from a point-blank shotgun blast through the heart. Time of death was estimated to be fourteen hours before discovery of his remains (Good Friday evening or late afternoon), based on tissue samples taken from the lower legs and feet. He was positively identified through dental records.

Victimology: Victim 2

Sean Dale Cavaness had been through some troubled years as a teenager. He was haunted by the vision of his brother's corpse and healed very slowly from the horrible trauma it had caused. Of all the Cavaness boys, Sean always had hungered most for his father's love and approval. Consequently, he was hurt the deepest by his father's callousness and ridicule. In 1984, at twenty-two, he was struggling to find direction for his life. He had an alcohol problem that had required inpatient treatment, and he was still having problems despite attending Alcoholics Anonymous.

On 14 December Sean was robbed of the chance to find his way through life. His body was found early that morning in a remote part of the county near St. Louis. He had been shot twice in the back of the head. For the second time in seven years, Kevin Cavaness was faced with the appalling task of identifying a dead brother.

Crime Scene Indicators: Victim 2

The body had been discovered by a farmer at 7:45 A.M. on the way to feed his horse. The crime scene was located off a back road that ran along the town of Times Beach. The town had been sealed off and evacuated due to dioxin contamination, therefore offering a location that would seem solitary and rarely traveled to most people.

Sean's body was beside a gate framed by two stone pillars and leading to a pasture. He was lying on his back with his head pointing north, his feet pointing south, and both arms parallel alongside the body. He was dressed in brown corduroy pants, a cream-colored, V-neck, short-sleeved sweater, and blue tennis shoes. A search of the pockets revealed no personal effects and no means of identification.

There were two entrance wounds to the back of the head and one apparent exit wound under the left eye. The body was still warm to the touch.

Sean was identified by fingerprints in the county file. He had been stopped for a traffic misdemeanor one year earlier.

Staging: Victim 2

The staging that is so prevalent in insurance-related murders also was employed with this killing. The execution-style placement of the gun to the back of the head was one element that was intended to give the appearance of drug dealers or similar criminals at work. The absence of the wallet and all personal effects made robbery look like a motive for the murder. These circumstances imply a removed killer with no personal attachments to the victim and motivated by monetary gain to pull the trigger. In actuality, all these implications were true of Sean's murderer.

Forensic Findings: Victim 2

Sean Cavaness had died between 5 A.M. and 7 A.M. that morning, possibly less than one hour before discovery of his body. The cause of death was two .357-caliber Magnum bullets to the head, either of which were lethal.

The shot to the back of the head just to the right of center had traveled upward at angle through the brain and exited at the corner of the left eye. It had been fired from a distance of 1 inch or less but had not been in actual contact, as evidenced by the powder stippling and searing of the flesh. Based on the blood-spatter pattern and flesh fragments found on the left shoulder and in the crook of the left arm, it was evident that Sean had been standing with his left arm slightly raised when he was hit by the first shot.

The second shot was fired from a distance of 12 inches to 18 inches from the head as Sean, already brain-dead from the first wound, lay on the ground. It entered near the right ear and lodged in the brain.

Sean's blood-alcohol level had been .26. This meant he had consumed twelve to thirteen drinks before he died.

Investigation

Although Dale Cavaness was a prime suspect to the DCI detective that had handled Mark's murder, it remained an unsolved homicide. There was never enough evidence to charge Cavaness.

Sean would be a different story. The night before his murder, his father had been seen driving around outside Sean's St. Louis apartment, parking when he spotted Sean walking down the street. The couple who lived on the floor below Sean's apartment not only saw the car, but also wrote down the license plate number on a paper bag because they were alarmed by Dale's hovering around the apartment. Their fears were calmed as they watched Dale embrace Sean under a streetlight. They had met him several weeks before and now recognized him as Sean's father. The couple heard the sounds of boisterous singing and laughing coming from upstairs until 3 A.M., when two distinct sets of footsteps were heard leaving.

Dale's first statement to the homicide detective was that the last time he had seen Sean was nearly four weeks earlier. When he was arrested and interviewed, he denied the encounter at Sean's apartment until confronted with the paper bag with his license number written on it. Cavaness's live-in girlfriend originally supported his alibi, but under pressure she relented and stated that Dale had not been home until late morning on the day of the murder.

Cavaness then came up with the story that he had indeed gone to see Sean that night. They had been out drinking until after 3 A.M. and had then gone for a ride. Cavaness claimed that when they arrived at the crime scene, Sean asked for his gun while the two were standing by the car. "Tell Mom I'm sorry," he said and then shot himself in the head. Dale claimed that after he had determined Sean was dead, he fired another shot and took Sean's belongings to make it appear a robbery/murder. His motive for this was to spare Marian the sorrow and guilt of her son's suicide.

The forensics did not support this version for two reasons. The first shot could not have been the one to the right of the ear as Cavaness claimed, because of the blood and tissue splatter on the left arm. That shot definitely had been fired as Sean lay dead on the ground. Secondly, Sean's greatly elevated blood-alcohol level would have considerably impaired his dexterity, making it nearly impossible for him to reach around behind his head and fire the gun.

The other detail that cast doubt on Dale's veracity was his activities the evening of the day of the murder. He had gone to a big Christmas party attended by most of the people of his town. A number of the party goers were questioned, including several who spent most of the evening with Cavaness. Despite their unwavering belief in Dr. Dale's innocence, each one agreed that he had acted perfectly normal, drinking, laughing, and even staying late. His actions were hardly appropriate for one who supposedly had witnessed the death of his son only hours before (not to mention having to shoot his own son in the head as he lay dying).

Two months before Mark Cavaness was killed, Dale had taken out a $40,000 life insurance policy on him. Dale was named the benefactor. Several months before Sean's murder, Dale had convinced Sean and Kevin to join an investment program that would make them some money in the future. Dale would pay $1,000 each month on each of the policies and claim a tax deduction. The boys had agreed. At the time of Sean's death, Dale claimed that he had let the policies expire. However, the policies were not only paid up, but there were two more policies that Dale had taken out on Sean amounting to another $40,000. There was a total of $140,000 to be made by Cavaness from Sean's death.

Balanced against this was Cavaness's sorry financial state. He was in debt for at least half a million dollars, with assets of about $150,000. He had filed a negative $200,000 income tax return for several years preceding 1984, nullifying any need for the tax write-off he had claimed the investment policies provided.

Outcome:

On 19 November 1985 John Dale Cavaness was convicted of first-degree murder. He was subsequently given the death penalty. On 17 November 1986 a guard found Cavaness hanging from his cell door by three extension cords tied together and looped at one end with a slipknot. After a futile resuscitation attempt, Cavaness was pronounced dead (O'Brien 1989).

107.02: COMMERCIAL PROFIT MURDER

Commercial profit homicide is murder to gain control of a business or to profit from the business.

Defining Characteristics

Victimology. Victimology is the primary point that contrasts this type of murder with individual profit murder (section 107.01). The victim in this type of murder is more likely to have a partner/professional relationship with the offender; however, this does not exclude a familial or personal relationship with the offender.

Crime Scene Indicators Frequently Noted. Crime scene indicators are the same as those for individual profit murder: a continuum from the spontaneous and haphazard murder to the well-executed one.

Staging. Staging also is the same as for individual profit murder. It depends on resources, sophistication, and degree of premeditation of the offender.

Common Forensic Findings. Forensic findings range from violent death to accidental death to natural death.

Investigative Considerations

In a commercially motivated homicide, the business relationships and corporate structure should be checked. As in individual profit murder, the offender's preoffense financial status should be examined. In addition, the victim's preoffense status should be checked, as a motive for the killing could be that the victim was costing the company money (through faulty investments, ineffectual business decisions, alcohol problems, etc.).

The net worth of the victim will be important, as well as will net worth solvency of the business. For example, a business having difficulties may be bailed out by a business partner's life insurance premiums. This may be discovered by looking for a correlation between impending business failure and purchase of the policy.

Search Warrant Suggestions

Business records and the suspect's and the victim's financial records are search warrant suggestions. Additional suggestions are those presented for individual profit murder (section 107.01).

CASE STUDY: 107.02: COMMERCIAL PROFIT MURDER

Background

On the morning of 9 July 1990, thirty-four-year-old Steven Benson surprised everyone by showing up early at his mother's home. He had made arrangements the night before to accompany his family to look at some property that morning. No one really expected him, as it was out of character for him to be up that early. Nevertheless, he appeared at his mother's home at 7:30 A.M. Soon after he arrived, he drove her Chevrolet Suburban to buy some doughnuts and coffee but took almost an hour and a half to return.

After his return, Benson convinced his mother and his brother, Scott, to come along on the outing, despite his mother's brief resistance to the idea. Benson arranged the seating, placing Scott in the driver's seat, the spot Benson usually occupied. He placed his mother in the front passenger seat where his sister, Carol Lynn, usually sat because she had a problem with car sickness. He placed Carol Lynn in the back behind Scott.

Just as Benson ran into the house to get something he had forgotten, the Suburban was engulfed by a thunderous explosion and an orange fireball. Benson ran out the front door, only to return immediately and shut the door behind him as a second explosion rocked the house. Of the car's occupants, sixty-three-year-old tobacco heiress Margaret Benson and her twenty-one-year-old adopted son Scott were killed instantly.* Forty-one-year-old Carol Lynn sustained serious injuries.

Victimology

After Margaret Benson's husband, Edward, died in 1980, her estate was estimated to be around $9 million. This did not include the millions more she would eventually inherit from her father, Harry Hitchcock. By July 1985 Margaret suspected that Steven Benson had squandered at least $2.5 million of her money on his many imprudent business deals. Many times she had bailed Steven out of financial disasters; she now suspected he was embezzling money to support his extravagant life-style.

In part, this extravagance was prompted by the demands of his domineering wife, Debby. Steven lived in fear that if he denied her anything, she would take their three children and leave him, as she had done once before.

By July 1985 Margaret Benson finally had endured enough of Steven's spending. In addition, she had suffered nothing but disrespect and cruelty from both Steven and his wife. The day before her death, she had summoned her lawyer from Pennsylvania to look at the company's books and "finally do something about Steven." She discovered Steven had bought a luxurious home by siphoning money from their joint business (she financed and managed it.) He also had opened up another office in nearby Fort Myers, Florida, that was much more luxurious than the trailer office in Naples. With just one glance at the books, her lawyer was able to tell her that there were many things inappropriate with Steven's bookkeeping.

Once Steven realized what his mother was doing, Margaret Benson's victim risk level skyrocketed. Her life-style and personality would normally have made her at very low risk for becoming the victim of a violent crime, but because of her situation, her risk was considerably elevated.

If Margaret discovered the extent of Steven's embezzlement, she may have either eliminated his inheritance or severely reduced it. In addition, she already was planning to put a lien on his new home and close down his Fort Myers office. The benefits of killing his mother were obvious. By including Scott and Carol Lynn in the fatal explosion, Steven hoped to secure the entire inheritance and family business for himself. Scott's and Carol Lynn's inheritance from Harry Hitchcock would be his. Margaret, Scott, and Carol Lynn became high-risk victims because of their brother's perception of them as obstacles to his absolute control of family business and money.

*In reality, Scott Benson was Margaret Benson's grandson. During Carol Lynn's first year of college, she became pregnant and was convinced by her parents to give the illegitimate child up for adoption. Her parents adopted Scott with the promise that Carol Lynn could have Scott back once she completed college. When that time came, Edward Benson told Carol Lynn that her mother could not bear to give up Scott. Scott went to his death never knowing his mother was Carol.

Crime Scene Indicators

The first blast blew the car's windshield out and both doors open. It also peeled back the top of the car toward the rear. The explosion blasted Margaret and Scott out of the vehicle. Margaret's body landed in the grass alongside the driveway. Scott was thrown away from the house and landed on the driveway.

Carol Lynn survived because her door had been open. She jumped out of the car, which was engulfed in flames, and tried to get her shirt off. Both her shirt and her hair were on fire.

When agents from the Bureau of Alcohol, Tobacco, and Firearms (ATF) examined the crime scene, they noted that the debris was scattered 100 feet in all directions. There were two distinct blast areas in the vehicle, signifying there were probably two devices. Because the floor had been blasted downward, the agents concluded that the devices had been placed inside the vehicle. From the blast pattern, it appeared that one device had been between the two front seats and the other was under the passenger seat directly behind the driver, where Steven had placed Carol Lynn. The injuries on the bodies were also consistent with this placement of the bombs. Fragments from the scene revealed that the devices were pipe bombs.

Forensic Findings

Scott Benson had sustained massive injury to his entire right side. The right side of his trunk was laid open from the waist to the shoulder, with most of the internal organs exposed. A knifelike piece of shrapnel had penetrated his skull.

Margaret Benson's right foot had been destroyed. It appeared she had been resting her left hand on the console over one of the devices, because that hand was completely blown off. Her face had been obliterated from the forehead down. In addition, the left side of her body had sustained heavy damage.

Carol Lynn lost most of her right ear. She sustained gaping shrapnel wounds to the leg and smaller wounds to the arms and shoulder of her right side. Her chin was gashed, and the side of her face was seared. Severe burns covered her right arm and parts of her body. In addition, a neighbor who was running to the scene to help was hit by shrapnel from the second blast, which severed the end of his nose.

Investigation

The investigation focused on Steven Benson when investigators learned from Margaret Benson's lawyer how upset she had been with Steven. Information began surfacing early in the investigation that strengthened the ATF agents and Collier County sheriff's department's suspicion of

Benson. He had the motive and opportunity (being the last person to drive the vehicle) to place the two pipe bombs in the vehicle.

Next, the investigative team needed to determine whether Benson had the ability to make the bombs. Several people were able to answer this. Benson had the reputation of being an electronics whiz. He owned a burglar alarm company, so he was familiar with wiring electrical devices and circuits.

One damaging piece of evidence was in the form of two receipts from a supply company located around the corner from Benson's workplace. One was for four end caps, and one was for two 4-by-12-inch pipes, both components of the two devices recovered from the scene. Both receipts were made out to a construction company spelled differently on each one. Even more damaging were the two palm prints, lifted from the receipts, that matched Benson's.

Outcome

Steven Benson was convicted of two counts of first-degree murder and one count of attempted murder. He was sentenced to serve a minimum of fifty years. He will not be eligible for parole until the year 2036.

108: FELONY MURDER

Property crime (robbery, burglary) is the primary motivation for felony murder, with murder the secondary motivation. During the commission of a violent crime, a homicide occurs. There are two types of felony murder: indiscriminate felony murder and situational felony murder.

108.01: INDISCRIMINATE FELONY MURDER

An indiscriminate felony murder is a homicide that is planned in advance of committing the felony without a specific victim in mind.

Defining Characteristics

Victimology. The victim of an indiscriminate felony murder is a potential witness to the crime. The victim appears to be no apparent threat to the offender. He or she offers no resistance to the offender but is killed anyway. The victim is one of opportunity: walking into a store or house at the wrong time or having a work shift coincide with a robbery.

There are occupations, shifts, and environments that elevate a victim's risk factor. Working the night shift alone at a twenty-four-hour gas station or convenience store is one example. This situation elevates the chance of a person becoming a victim of felony murder (indiscriminate or situational), compared with the department store clerk who works days. Environmental factors that elevate the victim risk factor are being in locations within high crime areas and working in establishments that enhance crime commission (views obstructed by advertising or product shelves, poorly lit, no alarms or intercom systems linking the establishment to local law enforcement stations, one-clerk staffing [especially at night], and establishments with cash readily available [e.g., liquor stores]).

It is also possible for a victim to elevate his or her risk by attitude and behavior. A careless, naive, or flippant approach to personal safety heightens the chance of being targeted for robbery and subsequently felony murder, situational or indiscriminate.

Crime Scene Indicators Frequently Noted. The location of the crime is usually the source of the cash. The weapon is bought to the scene and is most likely removed with the offender. The amount of physical evidence found at the scene is dependent on the offender's mastery and adeptness and on the time available.

This offender tends to spend more time at the crime scene, so there will be signs of interaction between offender and victim. There generally are indications of a completed burglary or robbery. The crime scene commonly is controlled and orderly: the offender is not surprised by the events that surround and include the killing. In most cases, little or no effort is expended to conceal the body.

Staging. If staging is present, arson frequently is used to conceal the felony murder. (See section 230, which discusses crime concealment arson.) If the motive seems to be monetary, investigators should require a sexual assault examination of the victim.

Common Forensic Findings. Most often the manner of death involves the use of firearms. There can be blunt-force trauma and/or battery present. There also may be evidence of restraints used (handcuffs, gags, blindfolds, etc.), evidenced by ligature marks. Sexual assault also may occur.

Investigative Considerations

It is important to focus on this as a robbery and not as a murder. Any known robbery suspects with similar MOs should be scrutinized. The offender of an indiscriminate felony murder is usually a youthful male with a criminal history (history of auto theft appears especially prevalent). This offender often travels on foot to the crime scene and lives in the area of the crime.

Search Warrant Suggestions

The victim's possessions (wallets, watches, jewelry) should be included in any search. Signs of the career criminal, such as stereos, and other expensive possessions that do not appear appropriate in light of the offender's finances based on legitimate sources are also important. Additional search warrant suggestions include possessions common to a burglar, burglary tools, police scanners, robbery items (ski mask, stocking mask, etc.), and drugs or evidence of drug use.

CASE STUDY: 108.01: INDISCRIMINATE FELONY MURDER

Background

On 22 April 1974 airmen Dale Pierre and William Andrews decided to rob a stereo shop in Ogden, Utah. They entered the store and forced the clerks into the basement, tying them up. Over the next few hours, three more people happened into the shop, only to become victims of Pierre and Andrews.

Victimology

The five victims involved in this incident were low-risk victims. The two store clerks had a slightly higher chance of becoming victims of a violent crime because of their jobs. But Ogden did not have much violent crime, so this additional occupational risk was negligible. The other victims fit the victimology of indiscriminate felony murder because they were potential witnesses to the robbery.

All of the victims posed no apparent threat to the offenders because they immediately were tied up and placed face down in the basement. Pierre and Andrews maintained complete control of the victims throughout the entire offense. None of them offered any resistance.

Crime Scene Indicators

Stan Walker and Michelle Ansley were the clerks working at the time of the holdup. Pierre and Andrews tied up Walker and Ansley after forcing them down into the basement. Just then, Cortney Naisbitt, age sixteen, entered the store to thank Walker for allowing him to park by his store. He was also taken to the basement and tied up.

Pierre and Andrews had been loading stereo equipment into their van for about an hour when they heard footsteps approaching the back door. It was Stan Walker's father, Orren. Orren Walker was worried because he knew the stereo shop had been closed for two hours, yet his son had not come home or called. Pierre and Andrews hid in the basement as the sound of Orren Walker's footsteps came closer. As soon as Orren appeared in the basement door, Pierre brandished a gun and forced him down the stairs. Stan Orren moaned aloud and asked his father, "Why did you come down here, Dad?" As soon as Stan spoke, the sound of gunshots rang out. In a sudden frenzy, Pierre had fired two rounds into the basement wall. With the explosion of gunfire, Michelle Ansley and Cortney Naisbitt began to plead with their captors. "I am just nineteen, I don't want to die," Michelle cried out. Stan and Orren Walker kept telling Pierre and Andrews to take the merchandise and leave; they would not identify the offenders.

At Pierre's bidding, Andrews brought in from their van a bottle wrapped in a paper bag. Pierre poured a thick blue liquid from the container into a green plastic cup. He told Orren Walker to give it to the three young people lying on the floor. When Walker refused, Pierre forced him onto his stomach next to Michelle and Stan and bound his hands and feet.

At that moment, Cortney Naisbitt's mother, Carol, entered the store in search of her son. Carol was soon tied hand and foot and lying on the basement floor next to Cortney. Next, Pierre propped Carol into a sitting position and held the cup to her lips. When she questioned him about the blue liquid, Pierre stated it was vodka and a German drug that would make them sleep for a while.

Pierre forced the victims one by one to drink the blue liquid. Each victim violently coughed and choked, spewing liquid from the nose and mouth. Orren Walker was the only one who did not drink the liquid. He feigned swallowing and then imitated the other victims' frantic choking. As Pierre filled Cortney's mouth to overflowing, the liquid spilled down his neck, immediately burning his skin. As he swallowed, he felt the liquid scorching his stomach. He began to retch and vomit, as were the others, who were now being given their second dose of the liquid. Because of the damage the liquid was doing to the victims' stomachs, they all were vomiting. Pierre tried to seal the victims' mouths with tape, but because of the blistering around their mouths, the tape would not stick very well.

After this was done, Pierre went one by one to each victim with his gun. Cortney saw the man lean over his mother and put the muzzle to the back of her head. He heard the bullet enter his mother's head and watched helplessly as her blood spurted onto the carpet a few feet away. He felt the hot muzzle pressed against his own skull, and the air seemed to explode around him as he went limp.

Pierre walked over to Orren Walker and fired a shot that missed his head by inches. He then bent over Stan Walker and fired a bullet into his head. Orren could hear his son say, "I've been shot," in a low but clear voice. Pierre returned to Orren and aimed more carefully. Orren fought to stay lucid as his head rang and his shoulder burned from where the caustic liquid had dripped.

Orren Walker heard Pierre untie Michelle Ansley. She was still pleading for her life as he led her to the far end of the basement. Once there, he forced her to undress and raped her for twenty minutes. When he was done, Pierre brought Michelle back and forced her down on her stomach. All this time, Orren Walker had been pretending to be dead. Pierre returned with a flashlight to check for a pulse on Orren Walker. After he had done this, he shot Michelle in the head.

Before he left, Pierre returned to Orren Walker twice. Once, he attempted to strangle him. Orren expanded the muscles in his neck, giving him enough room to breath once Pierre dropped his body back to the floor. The second time, Pierre inserted a pen into Orren's ear and stomped on it until Orren felt the tip poke through to the inside of his throat. Finally satisfied, Pierre left the basement and joined Andrews outside in the van.

As they were pulling out, Cortney began moving. Orren saw him begin crawling in the darkness toward the stairs. He only made it to the foot of the stairs before lapsing into unconsciousness.

Around 10:30 P.M. police were summoned to the shop by Orren Walker's wife and youngest son. They had begun to worry when Orren had not shown up for dinner.

Pierre and Andrews came to this crime scene well prepared to murder. They had brought the drain cleaner with the intent to kill the victims; they had obtained the idea from a movie.

Forensic Findings

All the victims sustained gunshot wounds to the head. Stan, Michelle, and Carol died from massive brain injury from these wounds. Carol barely lived long enough to make it to the hospital, where she died. Michelle and Stan were dead at the scene. Michelle also had been sexually assaulted.

The blue liquid was drain cleaner containing hydrochloric acid. The mouth, esophagus, and stomach of each victim except Orren Walker had been severely burned. Orren's shoulder and chin were blistered and burned from the drain cleaner. The pen that had been shoved into his ear had penetrated 5 inches and had caused ear damage. Cortney Naisbitt required two hundred sixty-six days of hospitalization due to the combination of brain damage from the gunshot and reconstructive surgeries for the damage from the drain cleaner.

Investigation

The investigation of the robbery and murders was given direction almost immediately by an informant. Several months before the murders, Andrews had told another airman that he and Pierre were planning something big, like a robbery. Andrews had then told the airman, "One of these days

I'm going to rob a hi-fi shop, and if anybody gets in the way, I'm going to kill them."

Within hours of the informant's call, two young boys found purses and wallets belonging to the victims in a dumpster just outside the barracks where Pierre and Andrews lived. After the arrest of the two men, a search warrant produced flyers from the stereo shop and a rental agreement for a commercial storage unit. The search of this storage unit produced stereo equipment worth $25,000 from the shop. In addition to the stolen merchandise, police found a small green drinking cup and a half-full bottle of drain cleaner.

Outcome

Dale Pierre and William Andrews were charged and subsequently convicted for the murders. Both men received the death penalty. Dale Pierre was executed by lethal injection in August 1987. William Andrews came within three days of execution but was granted a stay. He has been on death row fifteen years, longer than anyone in the United States (Kinder 1982; Wilson & Seaman 1985).

108.02: SITUATIONAL FELONY MURDER

Situational felony murder is unplanned prior to commission of the felony. The homicide is committed out of panic, confusion, or impulse.

Defining Characteristics

Victimology. The victim is one of opportunity. All of the victimology features detailed for indiscriminate felony murder apply to this category also. The fundamental difference is that the offender perceives the victim as a threat or an impediment to a successful robbery.

Crime Scene Indicators Frequently Noted. The victim is more often attacked by a blitz-style or surprise assault than in the indiscriminate felony murder. There are less signs of interaction between offender and victim. The victim may have been surprised while going about his or her normal routine. This would be manifested at the crime scene by a spilled purse, by car keys lying on the floor, or by a body that is near a room entrance.

The offender may have made small attempts, like blindfolding the victim, to conceal his identity, but the sequence of events culminates with the triggering event: the surprise or panic of the offender and the subsequent murder.

There are often paradoxical elements present at the crime scene. Entry into the residence or business may be skillful and meticulous, contrasted with a hasty, panicked retreat that leaves physical evidence, such as fingerprints and footprints (often depicting a running retreat). There is evidence of uncompleted acts (e.g., stereos unhooked and pulled out from wall units and jewelry and money on the victim, all left behind).

The situational felony murder tends to offer more evidentiary items, but this is dependent on the level of disorganization or organization of the offender, as well as on the nature of the triggering event.

Staging. If staging is present, arson may be used to conceal this situational felony murder.

Common Forensic Findings. Nonspecific traumatic modalities may be employed, ranging from blunt trauma to sharp instrument use. If firearms are used, the wounds are often contact or near-contact wounds.

Investigative Considerations

The investigative considerations of this homicide are similar to indiscriminate felony murder, with a few exceptions. The perpetrators of this type of crime are usually in the middle stages of their criminal career. They often have a history of alcohol/drug abuse that increases their already volatile nature.

Some outside influence often will trigger the killing (e.g., an alarm sounds, a spouse comes home, a victim screams, etc.). If several offenders are involved, there is a tremendous motivation for the non–trigger puller participant to confess if he is approached properly.

Search Warrant Suggestions

Search warrant suggestions are the same as for indiscriminate felony murder.

CASE STUDY: 108.02: SITUATIONAL FELONY MURDER

Background

On Saturday morning 23 December 1989, New York State Police went to the Harris family residence as the result of a complaint from a neighbor regarding an audible alarm sounding from the victims' residence. The responding officer found a smoldering fire in the upstairs of the residence, along with the bodies of all four of the family members. The fully clothed bodies of the mother, father, and eleven-year-old boy were found in one bedroom. They had been bound to furniture and their heads covered with pillowcases. The nude body of the fifteen-year-old girl was found in another bedroom. All had been shot in the head multiple times. An attempt had been made to burn the crime scene and the bodies. Subsequent medical examination determined that the fifteen-year-old female had been sexually assaulted.

Victimology

The victims could be characterized as a typical upper-middle-class family. The father, Warren Anthony Harris, at age thirty-nine was a corporate computer sales manager. His wife, Delores ("Doty") Harris, age 41, was a housewife who ran a cottage business (The Grey Goose) on the premises of the residence. This business was a small gift boutique dealing primarily in cash sales. She was a socially active, attractive, and pleasant individual well liked in the community.

Marc Anthony Harris was an eleven-year-old boy well integrated in his environment. He was a Boy Scout and was active in sports and other endeavors typical for a boy his age.

Shelby Harris was fifteen years old, a good student, well liked by her peers, and active in social activities.

Crime Scene Indicators

The crime scene indicators were consistent with those frequently noted in this type of homicide. The scene was the family's two-story salt-box colonial home, immediately adjacent to the family business. The business was closed the day of the homicide, making it necessary for the offenders to walk a few yards to the residence and confront the victims there. It is believed the offenders were masked when they entered the residence. They gained and maintained control of the victims by displaying a weapon (.22-caliber firearm). They disabled the telephone in the kitchen and forced the victims upstairs, where they were restrained. The offenders bound the victims and placed the pillowcases over their heads. There was a sexual component to this crime that was secondary to the primary motive of robbery.

It was, in all probability, the sexual assault that led to the murders of the victims. Shelby Harris, the victim of the sexual assault, had been taken to a separate bedroom and sexually assaulted. She was the only victim found who was not bound or blindfolded. During the course of the sexual assault, she saw her attacker(s). The offenders decided they needed to kill Shelby to keep her from identifying them. Once they murdered her, they reasoned they could not leave any victims alive, so the rest of the family was executed.

The offenders tried to destroy evidence by setting fire to the crime scene using gasoline from gas cans found at the residence. Their attempts at arson were only marginally successful, and not all evidence was destroyed.

Within a matter of hours of the crime, the offenders used the Harris's stolen bank and credit cards to obtain cash and purchase various items in different shopping malls within a 50-mile radius of the crime scene.

Investigation

The investigators developed suspects in the case, and on the morning of 7 February 1990, a search warrant was executed at a residence a few miles from the crime scene. One suspect, Michael Kinge, was killed in an exchange of gunfire with police officers. His fifty-four-year-old mother, Shirley, was arrested and charged in connection with the case. A search of that residence resulted in the recovery of a .22-caliber weapon, which was positively identified through ballistics as the murder weapon. Shirley Kinge's fingerprints were on one of the gasoline cans used in the arson at the Harris family residence.

Outcome

Shirley Kinge was convicted in a jury trial for her part in this crime.

120: PERSONAL CAUSE HOMICIDE

Homicide motivated by personal cause is an act ensuing from interpersonal aggression and results in death to person(s) who may not be known to each other. This homicide is not motivated by material gain or sex and is not sanctioned by a group. It is the result of an underlying emotional conflict that propels the offender to kill.

121: EROTOMANIA-MOTIVATED KILLING

In erotomania-related killing, the murder is motivated by an offender-victim relationship that is based on the offender's fixation. This fantasy commonly is expressed in such forms as fusion (the offender blends his personality into the victim's) or erotomania (a fantasy based on idealized romantic love or spiritual union of a person [rather than sexual attraction]). This preoccupation with the victim becomes consuming and ultimately leads to the victim's death. The drive to kill arises from a variety of motives, ranging from rebuffed advances to internal conflicts stemming from the offender's fusion of identity with the victim.

Defining Characteristics

Victimology. The distinguishing characteristic of this type of murder is found in the victimology. The victim targeted is very often a person with high mass media visibility of local, national, or international scope. Through this exposure, the victim comes to the attention of the offender.

In addition to a person with high media visibility, other victims include superiors at work or even complete strangers. The victim almost always is perceived by the offender as someone of higher status.

When erotomania is involved, the victim (usually someone unattainable to the offender) becomes the imagined lover of the offender through hidden messages known only to the offender. The offender builds an elaborate fantasy revolving around this imagined love. Male erotomaniacs tend to act out this fantasy with greater force. When this acting out is rebuffed, the erotomaniac decides to guarantee that no one else will steal his or her imagined lover. If this idealized person will not belong to him, then the offender ensures that the victim will not be given the chance to belong to anyone.

Fusion of identity occurs when an individual identifies so completely with another person that his or her imitation of that person becomes excessive. The person emulated is endangered when the imitator feels his own identity is threatened by the existence of the person he has patterned his life after or when the offender feels the person he has imitated no longer lives up to the offender's ideals. The person this offender chooses to imitate usually is perceived as someone of higher status, just as with erotomania.

Crime Scene Indicators Frequently Noted. The greater the distance between offender and victim at the time of the killing, the more planning and less spontaneous the crime. This will be manifested by the lack of fingerprints and footprints at the scene. A removed location from the victim also signifies that the offender had to take the time to check out the vantage point and must have been familiar with the victim's routine.

The majority of erotomania-motivated murders are close range and confrontational. The offender may even remain at the scene. These close-range assaults tend to be a more spontaneous killing, as reflected by a more haphazard approach to the killing: evidence is left, and there are likely to be witnesses. This does not mean the offender did not fantasize, premeditate, and plan the killing; all of these elements characterize this homicide. It means the actual act is usually an opportunistic one. The offender takes advantage of opportunity to kill as it is presented to him.

Staging. Staging is not usually present.

Common Forensic Findings. Firearms are the most common weapons used, especially with a distance killing. Ballistics and trajectory of projectiles recovered will be of importance. The sophistication and type of weapon and whether it was left at the scene will help establish the degree of offender sophistication.

The vital organs, especially the head and chest, are most frequently targeted. Occasionally, the offender will use a sharp-edged weapon, such as a knife.

Investigative Considerations

The offender almost always surveys and/or stalks the victim preceding the homicide. Therefore, the availability of the victim's itinerary and who may have had access to it is one investigative consideration. There is a likelihood of preoffense attempts by the offender to contact the victim through telephone calls, letters, gifts, and visits to the victim's home or place of employment. There may even be an incident involving law enforcement or security officers having to remove the offender from the victim's residence or workplace.

The offender's conversation often will reflect this preoccupation and/or fantasy life with the victim. When those associated with the offender are interviewed, they will most likely recall that much of the offender's conversation focused on the victim. He or she may have claimed to have had a relationship with the victim and may have invented stories to support this claim.

Search Warrant Suggestions

The primary items to search for are pictures, literature (newspaper articles, books, magazine articles), and recordings concerning the victim. Diaries or journals detailing the offender's preoccupation and/or fantasy life with the victim may also be found.

Other items to look for are evidence of contact or attempted contacts with the victim: telephone records, returned letters or gifts, motel receipts, gas bills, rental agreements, or airline/bus/train tickets implying travel to locations the victim has been. Credit card records also may be helpful in this regard.

CASE STUDY: 121: EROTOMANIA-MOTIVATED KILLING

Background

At 11 P.M. on 8 December 1980, John Lennon, lyricist, lead singer, and composer for the Beatles, was returning home with his wife, Yoko Ono, from a recording studio. As Lennon exited his car, Mark David Chapman, for whom Lennon had autographed an album hours before, stepped out of the darkness and said, "Mr. Lennon?" As Lennon turned, Chapman fired his .38-caliber Charter Arms revolver five times at point-blank range. Although four bullets hit Lennon in the chest, he was able to reach the foyer of the apartment building before collapsing. Lennon died soon after his arrival at the hospital.

Victimology

In the late 1950s John Lennon started the group that was later to become one of the most popular music phenomena of all time. He was a driving force in the group until it disbanded in 1970. Lennon became known as a social and political activist and an especially outspoken proponent of the peace movement. After the Beatles dissolved, he continued to write music until 1975, when he went into retirement. His reentry into the music world was cut short by his assassination at the hands of Chapman. Throughout his career, even during his period of musical inactivity, Lennon's fame and popularity barely waned, which contributed to his high mass media visibility.

Crime Scene Indicators

Although it appeared that Chapman had planned to assassinate Lennon as early as September 1980, he chose to approach Lennon and kill at close range probably because Lennon was not easily accessible for a long-range assassination. Chapman chose the common weapon of assassins, a firearm. The weapon remained at the scene, as did Chapman (calmly reading *Catcher in the Rye* by J. D. Salinger). Chapman had been a security guard at a Honolulu condominium development; therefore, his weapon of choice was one with which he was comfortable: a .38-caliber revolver. Ballistics confirmed his responsibility for Lennon's death.

Forensic Findings

Lennon died from massive blood loss as a result of the chest wounds he sustained.

Investigation

In September 1980 Chapman sold a Norman Rockwell lithograph for $7,500. He paid off a number of debts and kept $5,000 for a "job" he said he had to do. He contacted the FAA to inquire about transporting his gun by plane.

Because Chapman was advised that the change in air pressure that his baggage would be subjected to could damage the bullets, he opted to pack his gun without bullets. When Chapman left his security guard job for the final time, he signed the log "John Lennon."

On 29 October he flew to New York from Honolulu, only to return in frustration on 12 or 13 November. He had been unable to buy bullets for his weapon or gain access to Lennon, who lived in New York City. He made an appointment at the Makiki Mental Health Clinic, but failed to keep it.

On 6 December Chapman returned to New York. Two days later, he waited outside the Dakota apartment building for Lennon. At 4:30 P.M. Lennon and his wife exited the building and were approached by Chapman, who had a copy of Lennon's recent album, *Double Fantasy*. Lennon autographed it as Chapman held it out to him. Chapman then lingered at the apartment entrance. When questioned by the doorman, he said he was waiting to get Yoko Ono's autograph. Chapman was well prepared for his wait in weather much colder than he was accustomed to. He had on two pairs of long underwear, a jacket, an overcoat, and a hat.

Chapman had apparently been building a fantasy life centered on John Lennon for several years. He married a wife of Japanese descent in an attempt to mimic Lennon's Japanese wife. He collected Beatles albums and played in a rock band. Chapman decided to retire from music at the age of twenty-five because Lennon also had been in retirement.

An explanation for his motive may be found in the testimony of a psychiatrist during his trial: the more Chapman imitated Lennon, the more he came to believe he was John Lennon. He eventually began to look upon Lennon as a phony. The fusion of his identity with Lennon became so engulfing that Chapman decided he, too, would become a phony if he didn't stop the process in Lennon.

Outcome

Chapman withdrew an original plea of not guilty by reason of insanity and pleaded guilty to the murder of John Lennon. On 24 August 1981 he was sentenced to twenty years to life, with a recommendation that he receive psychiatric treatment. Under New York State law, he would not be eligible for parole until the year 2001.

When he was given the opportunity to offer a few words in his defense, Chapman simply read a passage from *Catcher in the Rye*. A year later when he was visited in prison by a reporter, he still had it in hand (Wilson & Seaman 1985; Sifakis 1981; Lentz 1988).

122: DOMESTIC HOMICIDE

Domestic homicide occurs when a family or household member kills another member of the household. This definition includes common-law relationships. There are two subcategories for this type of homicide: spontaneous domestic homicide and staged domestic homicide.

122.01: SPONTANEOUS DOMESTIC HOMICIDE

A spontaneous domestic homicide is unstaged and is triggered either by a recent stressful event or by a cumulative buildup of stress.

Defining Characteristics

Victimology. The victim has a familial or common law relationship with the offender in spontaneous domestic homicide. In addition, there is a history of prior abuse or conflict with the offender.

Crime Scene Indicators Frequently Noted. Usually only one crime scene is involved in spontaneous domestic murder, and it is commonly the victim's and/or offender's residence. The crime scene reflects disorder and the impetuous nature of the killing. The weapon will be one of opportunity often obtained and left at the scene. There is no forced entry and no sign of theft. The crime scene also may reflect an escalation of violence (e.g., the confrontation starts as an argument, intensifies into hitting or throwing things, and culminates in the victim's death).

There are often indicators of *undoing*. This is the killer's way of expressing remorse or the desire to undo the murder. Undoing is demonstrated by washing up of the offender and the weapon. The body may be covered up, but this is not for concealment purposes. Washing and/or redressing the body, moving the body from the death scene, and positioning it on a sofa or bed with the head on a pillow are all expressions of undoing.

The attitude and emotional state of the family members present at the crime scene can offer insight into the victim/offender relationship. The offender is often at the scene when law enforcement and/or emergency medical personnel arrive. The offender often will make incriminating statements.

Staging. A spontaneous domestic murder will not involve staging. As mentioned above, personation in the form of undoing (moving and positioning the body) is possible but is for the benefit of the offender and is not intended to mislead law enforcement.[3]

Common Forensic Findings. Alcohol/drugs may be involved. Fingerprints often are present on the murder weapon. There usually are forensic findings consistent with a personal type of assault.

Depersonalization, evidenced by facial battery, overkill, blunt-force trauma, and a focused area of injury are examples of a personal assault. Manual or ligature strangulation is a common cause of death with domestic homicide. Gunshot wounds are also a forensic finding of this type of killing. The victim may show signs of being washed up and/or having wounds cleaned.

Investigative Considerations

If the crime occurs in the victim's residence, domestic murder should be considered. When other family members are contacted, they often describe

[3]See chapter 4 concerning the detection of staging and personation at the crime scene.

a history of domestic violence involving the victim and offender. This is often supported by police reports. A history of conflict due to external sources (financial, vocational, alcohol, etc.) are common elements of domestic homicide. The offender may have delayed reporting the murder, often in order to change clothing and establish a legitimate alibi. Routinely, a third party discovers the body. The offender may have demonstrated personalized aggression in the past as well as a change in attitude after the triggering event.

Search Warrant Suggestions

Although most of the evidence will be left at the crime scene, request financial and medical records to verify the spontaneity of the crime.

CASE STUDY: 122.01: SPONTANEOUS DOMESTIC HOMICIDE

Background

On 5 May 1990 Martha Ann Johnson was convicted of first-degree murder for the smothering death of her eleven-year-old daughter, Jenny Ann Wright. First-degree murder charges are pending in the deaths of her three other children: James William Taylor, Tibitha Jenelle Bowen, and Earl Wayne Wright. The deaths, which occurred between 1977 and 1982, were all within ten days of Johnson's having an argument with her former husband, Earl Bowen.

The first victim was James William Taylor, twenty-three months old. On 23 September 1977 Johnson states that she went in to wake up James from his nap. When she was unable to rouse him, she called for emergency medical personnel, and the child was rushed to the hospital. Attempts to resuscitate James were unsuccessful, and he was pronounced dead at 9:15 A.M. His death was attributed to sudden infant death syndrome (SIDS).

Three years later on 30 November 1980, Johnson bathed, fed, and put three-month-old Tibitha Jenelle Bowen down for her nap. When she checked on the child later, she found the baby had turned blue. Rescue personnel were called and initiated resuscitative measures, which again proved futile. Tibitha was pronounced dead on arrival. Her death also was attributed to SIDS.

Earl Wayne Bowen was a thirty-one-month-old child who had been in excellent health except for an occasional ear infection. On Friday afternoon 23 January 1981, he was found with a package of rodent poison. Although he had some on his hands and mouth, it was not clear if he had ingested any. He was treated and released from the emergency room in satisfactory condition. However, according to his parents, he suffered seizures from that point on, lasting from a few minutes to hours. None of these seizures appeared to be witnessed by medical personnel. Despite the fact that the active ingredient in the poison did not cause seizures, the child was started on medication. While being taken to the hospital on 12 February during a seizure episode, he suffered a cardiopulmonary arrest. He was resuscitated after two hours and placed on life support. Subsequent therapy was ineffective; he was pronounced brain dead, and life support was removed on 15 February.

According to Johnson, her eleven-year-old daughter, Jenny Ann Wright, was complaining of chest pains. She took Jenny to the doctor, who gave her Tylenol and a rib belt. On 21 February 1982 resuce personnel were again summoned to the Johnson residence. They found Jenny Ann face down on her mother's bed with pink foam coming from her nose and mouth and unresponsive to revival attempts.

Victimology

The victims were all children of Johnson by her four husbands and all resided with her at the time of their death.

Crime Scene Indicators

In all cases, the death was staged to appear from natural causes, the crime scene was in the residence, and the weapon was one of opportunity. Johnson weighs 300 pounds, and this certainly was a factor in the smothering death of eleven-year-old Jenny Ann.

Forensic Findings

Autopsy findings when smothering is the suspected cause of death are minimal. One of the forensic indicators of asphyxia, petechial hemorrhage, is rarely seen in children and practically never in infants. This proved to be the case with the three youngest victims. None of them had evidence of petechial hemorrhage; however, the autopsy of eleven-year-old Jenny Ann revealed petechiae on the face around the eyes, face, and conjunctivae. There also were linear abrasions over both cheeks, another forensic indicator of asphyxial death. In three of the four cases, postmortem exams revealed congestion in the lungs and/or airways, evidenced by frothy or foamy liquid coming from the mouth and nose (another finding common to asphyxiation). Earl didn't exhibit this congestion because he had been on a life support system, which allowed for his airways to be suctioned.

Investigation

The investigative consideration of greatest importance in this case is the cycle of domestic conflict that surrounded every incident. Every death was preceded one week to ten days by marital problems that culminated in a separation, the child's death, and then the reunion of Johnson and Earl Bowen, her spouse at the time.

Martha Ann Johnson was reported to have been battered by several of her four husbands. She was completely dependent on her fourth husband, Earl Bowen. Each of the children died within days of an argument and separation between Johnson and Bowen.

Martha Johnson was also highly influenced by her environment and had difficulty dealing with internal impulses, as evidenced by her weight of 300 pounds. She sought life substance from her external environment (e.g., her eating, her relationship with her children, and her husband). When this last crucial crutch was removed from her life, she used her children to draw Earl Bowen back into an active relationship with her. Johnson experienced emotional crises due to her separation from Bowen. Her children's deaths served as a valve for the building internal tensions, which she was ill equipped to handle, in addition to providing the remedy, Bowen's return. It worked every time. The cases were reopened after an *Atlanta Constitution* article in December 1989 questioned Johnson's family tragedies.

Outcome

Martha Ann Johnson was sentenced to life imprisonment for the murder of Jenny Ann Wright and has been indicted for first-degree murder of Tibitha and Earl Bowen.

122.02: STAGED DOMESTIC HOMICIDE

A staged domestic homicide is planned and may be due to the same stresses as in an unstaged domestic homicide. The major difference between these two homicides is seen in their crime scenes.

Defining Characteristics

Victimology. The victimology for staged domestic homicide is the same as for spontaneous domestic homicide.

Crime Scene Indicators Frequently Noted. The crime scene of the well-planned domestic murder reflects a more controlled, organized crime. The weapon, fingerprints, and other evidentiary items often are removed. The body is usually not concealed. The crime scene often involves the victim's and/or offender's residence, but locations of crime scenes outside the home also are possible.

Staging. Staging is frequently noted in the planned murder. Death may be staged to look accidental (e.g., car malfunction, drowning, etc.). Other deaths may appear due to secondary criminal activity, such as robbery or rape. The offender who stages a domestic rape/murder rarely leaves the victim nude; she is almost always partially clothed. Death may be staged to look like suicide (suicide note, guns rigged with string, drug overdose, etc.). Natural causes (slow poisoning, overdose [insulin is a prime example of an overdose that can mimic natural death]) are also examples of staging. Another form of staging the investigator may expect to see more of is the staging of death to appear as a result of occult/satanic activity. This is due to the increasing popularity of this subject with the mass media.

Common Forensic Findings. The forensic findings of a staged domestic homicide are similar to those for spontaneous domestic murder. The exception is when the suspect includes himself as an apparent victim. If the person posing the greatest threat (usually the male) to the alleged intruder receives no or nonlethal injuries while others who pose less of a threat are killed, the investigator should become suspicious that the crime has been staged.

Investigative Considerations

In addition to considerations listed for spontaneous domestic homicide, the offender will demonstrate a change in preoffense behavior toward the victim. Frequently, an improvement in the relationship is seen, and this apparent change in heart will be demonstrated in a highly visible manner to others. Postoffense interviews of close friends or family members often reveal that the victim had expressed concerns or fears regarding his or her safety or even a sense of foreboding. The medical and psychiatric history of the victim becomes important if the investigator suspects the crime has been staged to appear a suicide or death by natural causes.

Search Warrant Suggestions

Search for evidence to corroborate a motive, such as telephone and personal records and travel records of motel and gasoline receipts.

CASE STUDY: 122.02: STAGED DOMESTIC HOMICIDE

Background

Torran Meier was born in 1972 to sixteen-year-old Shirley Meier. Shirley's mother, Joyce, described her daughter's treatment of newborn Torry "as if he were a piece of property." Shirley did not want to hold her son, let alone give him the care and love the child needed. Torry's father, Jon Dennis, was driven away by Shirley Meier's constant insults and belittlement. Dennis tried to maintain contact with his son, but Shirley forbade him to come near them. She told Torran his father was dead.

Throughout the years of mistreatment Torran was to endure, his grandparents tried to intervene on his behalf. Because Shirley became jealous if she saw Torry getting close to them, between his fourth and seventh years his grandparents were allowed to see him only on his birthdays. On his sixth birthday, when they showed up with gifts, Shirley flew into a rage and threatened to call the police if they did not leave. Torry's gifts were returned unopened a few days later because Shirley had decided he was not going to have a birthday party that year.

This incident was characteristic of Torran's life with Shirley. One of his first memories of his mother was climbing into a toy box during a game of hide-and-seek. Shirley sat on the toy box, ignoring his pleas to be let out, until the child had screamed and cried for a half an hour.

Besides being the object of Shirley's cursing and screaming, Torran often suffered public humiliation when she ridiculed him in front of his friends. She would call him a faggot and tell him he would never be a real man. Torry never seemed to do anything that would satisfy Shirley, from his playing high school football to the housecleaning and cooking she demanded of him.

Shirley's erratic and often violent behavior seem to escalate as Torry became older. She also began to direct it toward her younger child, Rory. Torran was encouraged by his friends and grandparents to persist in his situation with Shirley until he graduated from high school, but the years of abuse had burdened him past his endurance. After sixteen years of it, he finally retaliated.

Victimology

Shirley Meier always had been outgoing and lively by her parent's estimation. It was evident at a young age that she was a talented manipulator. She often fabricated elaborate stories for her parents and teachers in order to get her own way.

As an adult, Shirley went through three marriages, none lasting more than a few months, because she did not limit her abusiveness to her children. She became dependent on Valium, attempted suicide twice, and seemed to allow her sense of propriety to slip away. She would often dress provocatively and go out to bars, leaving the two children home alone. On one occasion, she woke Torran up at 2 A.M. to pick her up at a bar 20 miles from their home. Torran was about fifteen years old at the time. An obviously troubled and unhappy person, Shirley never sought the help she so desperately needed; it might have been enough to not only save her life, but also to salvage Torry's as well.

Crime Scene Indicators

About 9:45 P.M. in October 1985, Torran Meier set in motion a plan that he had been brooding over for months. Torry, a high-school friend named Matt Jay, and a twenty-three-year-old transient named Richard Parker whom Torry had befriended finalized a murder scheme.

Torran rode home on his motorcycle, and the other two followed him in a car they parked down the street from his house. Torran entered the house alone and greeted his mother, who was sitting in the dining room. She began to yell at him for coming home so late. Torran offered the excuse of mechanical troubles with his motorcycle. He walked into the kitchen to get some of the dinner that Shirley had left him and then went into his bedroom. He let Jay and Parker into the house through his window, and left them hiding in his room with a noose he had made earlier.

Torran joined his mother, who began complaining about money. After he had finished his meal, he asked her to come into his room so he could show her something. She responded with her typical ire, stating that he was always interrupting her TV programs. Torran told her to wait for a commercial, at which time Shirley rose to follow him into his room.

Torran requested his mother to close her eyes or allow herself to be blindfolded before entering his room, both of which she refused, but she agreed to walk in backward. As she was backing through the door of Torran's room, she saw Jay coming at her from behind the door. Parker approached from the other direction and dropped the noose around her neck before she could react. Torran and Jay knocked her to the floor as Parker pulled on the noose.

The commotion caused by Shirley's kicking and screaming woke eight-year-old Rory and brought him to the doorway in time to witness his mother's death struggle. Torran intercepted Rory and led him to the family room, where he attempted to calm the crying child by watching TV. Over the next twenty minutes, Torran made a circuit between his room to help Jay and Parker and the family room to calm Rory.

When it was apparent that Shirley was finally dead, the three offenders eased off her body. She was bleeding from the nose and mouth, so Jay held a rag under her face to prevent blood stains on the carpet. After Torran closed the garage door to ensure privacy, Shirley's body was stuffed in the trunk of her five-year-old Thunderbird.

At this point, the three offenders discussed the fact that Rory knew what had happened. They concluded that the little boy would be too damaging a witness, so he would have to be killed.

The method of death decided on was rat poison. Jay went to the store and purchased rat and snail poison. Torran laced a peanut butter sandwich and flavored some milk with the poison, but Rory refused both after getting an initial bad taste. After a few minutes of thought, another course of action was decided on.

Ironically, Shirley had helped Torran decide how to stage her death. She had threatened her third husband many times that she was going to drive her car off a cliff someday. Torran also had heard this suicide threat and had made special note of it.

Malibu Canyon Highway contained some of the steepest canyon ledges in Southern California and became the ideal setting to stage Shirley's suicide. The road twists along the face of a sheer rocky cliff. Because there are no guardrails, it is a common sight to see a tow truck hoisting up a car that has gone over the side.

After stopping to fill a gas can at a service station, Torran, Parker, and Rory (sleeping in the back seat) drove out to the canyon and chose a suitable spot. Next, they drove back to the Meier's residence and retrieved Shirley's purse. Once again, they stopped at the service station, where they bought six dollars worth of gas. They proceeded to Jay's house, and he followed them in his father's vehicle.

When they arrived at the preselected spot in the canyon, Torran told Rory he had to be blindfolded and have his hands tied because he did not want Rory to know where Parker lived. Rory did not resist. At this point, Shirley's body was removed from the trunk and propped up in the driver's seat. With the engine running, a rag soaked with gasoline was stuffed in the gas tank opening. Parker then lit the rag while Torran and Jay aimed the car for the cliff and put it into gear. It rolled across the road, over an embankment, and down a hill. As flames spread through the car, it came to rest on a plateau halfway down the gorge. Torran, Jay, and Parker drove away, heading north.

Jay dropped Parker and Torran Meier off at the initial crime scene so any damaging evidence could be removed. Signs of the struggle were cleaned up or removed. The poisons and the towels used to clean the blood from the carpet were dumped in a trash bin. The gas can was dumped, and Torran put the empty can back into the car. Satisfied that any traces of the murder had been removed, Torran Meier headed back to the gas station where he worked with Parker to pick up his bike.

Meanwhile, Rory had felt the car move, smelled the gasoline, and soon after saw the flames through his blindfold. He took off his blindfold and saw his mother's body leaning against the steering wheel with blood all over her face. He managed to free his hand, lower an electric window, and climb out. As the car was enveloped with flames, he climbed a hill, crying for help. A man driving by saw the flames and heard Rory's cry. He helped Rory up to the road and flagged down another car. The heat was too intense for anyone to get close to the car, so by the time the fire department and sheriff arrived, Shirley's body already had been burned beyond recognition.

Investigation

Rory told his story and gave a description of Torran's car to the sheriff who had arrived at the scene. Meanwhile, Torran had suddenly felt like returning to the canyon. He and Parker had driven just far enough to pass the ambulance and sheriff car coming from the scene. Other sheriff units that had been dispatched to the scene recognized his car from Rory's description and pulled him over.

The extensive brutalization that Torran Meier suffered at the hands of his mother obviously fueled his decision to kill her. However, there seemed to be one incident that burdened him beyond his capacity to endure. In March 1985 Shirley informed her mother that Torran no longer wanted to live at home and was not welcome there anymore. She had told Torran that his going to live with his grandparents meant he could never return home. Torry immediately moved in with his grandparents. The warmth and affection he experienced made him feel hopeful that life could be free of the constant harassment and abuse he had known for most his life. Two weeks later, his hope was shattered when the police showed up at Shirley's request. She had sent them there to return her "runaway" son.

From this point on until the murder, everyone noticed the change in Torran's attitude. He began to miss school. His grandmother noticed he now had a blank look in his eyes. The statement that seemed to best describe Torran's state of mind was found on the side of a styrofoam cup holder his grandmother saw him use: "Pardon me, but you've obviously mistaken me for someone who gives a damn."

Torran's conversation reflected his plans. He spoke to classmates and close friends about killing his mother and even showed one friend the noose that he had made. Torran's indiscretion concerning his crime was reflective of his immaturity. Most offenders do not leave quite as obvious a conspiratory trail (Markman 1989).

Outcome

Torran Meier made a complete confession and was found guilty of manslaughter and attempted manslaughter. He was subsequently sentenced to a maximum term of twelve years at the psychiatric facility of the California Youth Authority. He was reunited with his father during his trial. Both his grandparents and father vowed to support him through his trial and incarceration.

Richard Parker and Matthew Jay were found guilty of second-degree murder and were sentenced to fifteen years to life.

123: ARGUMENT/CONFLICT MURDER

Argument/conflict murder is death that results from a dispute between persons, *excluding family or household members.*

Defining Characteristics

Victimology. There is a high incident of young-adult, blue-collar or un-employed, male victims with a lower education level. The offender is known to the victim. The victim commonly has a history of assaultive behavior and of using violence to resolve his problems.

An exception to this victimology is the person who has the misfortune to cross paths and ignite the volatile, impulsive offender, predisposed to vio-lent eruptions. The precipitating event is often a trivial incident (e.g., pulling in front of someone on a freeway).

Crime Scene Indicators Frequently Noted. The crime scene of an argument/conflict murder is often spread out, demonstrating signs of of-fender and victim movement as well as signs of struggle. It is random and sloppy.

The weapon is brought to the scene due to the offender's predisposition to assaultive behavior. In this scene, it becomes a weapon of opportunity based on its ready availability. It may be left at the scene in addition to fingerprints, footprints, and other evidence. The victim is often unarmed. Generally, the body also is left at the crime scene and is not concealed.

Staging. Staging is not present.

Common Forensic Findings. Alcohol/drugs are often involved, and there is no evidence of sexual assault. The mode of death usually is based on weapon availability (i.e., knife, blunt object, or firearm).

Investigative Considerations

The precipitating event (argument or conflict) is the cause of the dispute. The killing can be a spontaneous or delayed reaction to this event. The offender, like the victim, has a history of assaultive behavior and of using violence to resolve problems. Due to the spontaneous nature of the attack, there are usually witnesses, however reluctant and/or inconspicuous. A point to consider is that the suspect lives in the vicinity of the attack and/or victim. Witnesses may know the place of employment, hangouts, and/or residence of the offender.

Search Warrant Suggestions

Search for articles in the location because the crime erupted quickly. Also search for receipts of firearm sales and check the Alcohol, Tobacco, and Firearms registry.

123.01: ARGUMENT MURDER

In an argument murder, death results from verbal dispute. The defining characteristics, investigative considerations, and search warrant suggestions are discussed in section 123 above.

CASE STUDY: 123.01: ARGUMENT MURDER

Background

On a hot July night in 1989, the police of a small, East Coast city received a "shots fired" call. As they arrived at the scene of the incident, they observed a young white male sprawled out in the middle of the street. He had been shot in the chest and was already dead. The officers learned from several witnesses that the victim had started arguing with another man over some money the offender owed the victim. The dispute soon escalated, with the victim punching the offender. The fight spilled out into the street and culminated with the offender pulling a gun out and shooting the victim.

Victimology

The victim was a twenty-two-year-old construction worker who had a history of being thrown out of bars for starting fights. He had a long history of assaultive behavior that included several arrests for aggravated battery and assault on a law enforcement officer. His reputation for solving problems with physical violence was well established at work and after hours in the bars. The victim had been involved in several confrontations with the offender before the night of his death. According to witnesses familiar with both men, they seemed to have a friendship of sorts that periodically was interrupted with brawls.

Crime Scene Indicators

The crime scene was in a tavern district that had a reputation for nightly brawls, especially during the hot summer months. The crime scene was spread out, with indications of the struggle beginning in the bar. Bar stools and several tables were overturned. There were several blood-spatter patterns, indicating both offender and victim had drawn blood before the shooting occurred.

The crime scene was random and sloppy, typical of this type of conflict. The body was left in the open, in the position in which death had occurred. The weapon was brought to the scene and found farther down the street in a garbage can in an alley. There were an abundance of prints in the bar and a few were on the murder weapon, although the offender had hurriedly wiped off the gun before discarding it.

Forensic Findings

The autopsy revealed that the victim had died from a single gunshot wound to the chest that penetrated the heart through the left ventricle, causing immediate death. A .38-caliber bullet was recovered from the body. The victim's serum-alcohol level was .21 percent, well over the .10 percent level of intoxication.

Investigation

Because of the abundance of witnesses and physical evidence, an arrest was made within hours of the shooting. The offender was arrested without incident at his home. His reputation mirrored that of the victim. He, too, had a history of assaultive behavior reflected by an arrest record.

The precipitating event of the dispute was money that the offender had borrowed from the victim three weeks earlier. The offender had vowed repayment several different times but had failed to fulfill his promises. The offender was also very drunk when the victim began yelling at him and declaring his unreliability to the other bar patrons. The exchange became physical and culminated with the shooting.

Outcome

The offender pleaded guilty to manslaughter and was sentenced to fifteen years.

123.02: CONFLICT MURDER

In a conflict murder, death results from personal conflict between the victim and offender. The defining characteristics, investigative considerations, and search warrant suggestions are discussed in section 123.

CASE STUDY: 123.02: CONFLICT MURDER

Background

Life as a teenager for Kristen Costas had been satisfying and agreeable. The fifteen-year-old was a member of her high-school swimming team, soccer team, and community swim team. She had been selected for the varsity cheerleading squad and also belonged to an exclusive volunteer group called the Bobbies. She was very popular at school, having many friends. She seldom dated but was well liked by the male students of her suburban California high school. Words like *pretty* and *vibrant* were used when describing her. Her father was an executive who could afford to give his only daughter the trendy clothes, ski vacations, and cheerleading training-camp trips important to a teenager trying find acceptance from other upper-middle-class peers.

For Bernadette Protti, adolescent life was not so pleasant. She was embarrassed by the modest living imposed by her father's income as a retired public-utilities supervisor. This discomfort was accentuated daily as she went to school, surrounded by the sons and daughters of executives like Costas's father.

Spring of 1984 had not done much to boost her faltering ego. She was cut from the cheerleading squad, rejected from membership to an exclusive club similar to the Bobbies, and denied a place on the yearbook staff. These setbacks probably would have been nothing more than passing disappointments to the typical teenager, but to Protti they confirmed her sense of failure and lack of self-worth. One friend described Protti as never believing she was accepted by her peers, even though she apparently was. She depicted Protti as having an obsession with being liked.

On 22 June 1984 Costas was at cheerleading camp when her mother received a call from an unidentified female around 10 P.M. The caller told Mrs. Costas that Kristen would be picked up for a secret Bobbies initiation dinner the next night. On 23 June Mr. and Mrs. Costas and Kristen's twelve-year-old brother were attending a baseball banquet. At 8:20 P.M. Mrs. Costas phoned Kristen to wish her a good time at the Bobbies dinner. Soon after, Kristen was picked up by a white female in an orange, beat-up Ford Pinto. They drove to the Presbyterian church parking lot and parked. After about thirty minutes, Costas became alarmed at the driver's behavior and exited the car.

Costas rang the doorbell of nearby friends, the Arnolds. When Mrs. Arnold answered the door, Costas explained that she had been with a friend at church who had "gone weird." Arnold described Kristen as being visibly upset but not terrified. She noticed a girl about fifteen years old and with light brown hair on the front sidewalk as she let Costas in to call her parents. When her parents did not answer, Mr. Arnold offered to give Costas a ride home, which she accepted. He noticed the Pinto was following them as he drove Costas home, but Kristen reassured him it was okay.

When Arnold arrived at Costas's home, she noted that her parents were not in yet and told Arnold she was going to go next door. He offered to wait until she was safely inside the house. He watched as Costas walked to the door.

As he prepared to leave, Arnold saw a female figure pass by the right side of his vehicle and enter the porch where Costas stood. At first, Arnold thought he was witnessing a fist fight. The young woman struck at Costas, who fell to the porch screaming. The assailant disappeared seconds later.

Costas staggered to her feet and ran across the street crying for help. A neighbor who had come outside when he heard the scream went to her aid. She collapsed in his arms, still asking for help, and then lost consciousness. He began cardiopulmonary resuscitation while his wife called emergency medical personnel.

Meanwhile, Arnold had started to pursue the Pinto as it squealed away, but decided to return to see if Costas needed help. By this time, the paramedics and police had arrived and were loading Kristen into the ambulance. Mr. and Mrs. Costas arrived home from their son's banquet just in time to see their daughter lying in the ambulance. Kristen Costas was pronounced dead at a nearby hospital at 11:02 P.M.

Victimology

Kristen Costas's chances of becoming a victim of a violent crime were reduced by her warm family relationship, minimal use of alcohol, and self-imposed dating restrictions. Her life-style reinforced this low-risk status. She lived at home, and because of her age and parental control, her socialization was restricted to places that would be considered lower-risk environments (the local hangout [the church parking lot], friends' homes, etc.) as opposed to bars and nightclubs. She had reportedly experimented once with cocaine and once with marijuana, but this isolated usage was not a factor in the attack.

The fact that Costas was well liked and popular would normally have been additional reasons for considering her status as low risk. But because of the nature of the conflict that arose between Protti and Costas, this element elevated her risk to be targeted for a violent crime.

Crime Scene Indicators

In front of the door where the attack took place were multidirectional blood-splatter patterns. A few feet to the left of this area, a trail of blood went down the walkway, the driveway, across the street, to the neighbor's driveway, the sidewalk, and onto the porch.

A butter knife was found at the scene, but this was not the murder weapon. A few latent prints remained unidentified, and one set from the porch post next to the attack site had insufficient detail for evaluation. There was nothing else to aid the investigation from the crime scene.

Forensic Findings

Kristen Costas had been stabbed five times. There was a defensive wound to the right forearm. Two of the wounds were to the back, both 13 centimeters long and puncturing the right lung, diaphragm, and lacerating the liver. Of the two wounds from a frontal assault, one was 15.5 centimeters long and penetrated the left upper arm, chest, and left lung. The other was 4 centimeters long and did minor damage. Any one of the three deeper wounds could have and would have caused death. There was no evidence of any other type of assault, physical or sexual.

Investigation

Over six months, 750 yellow or orange Ford Pintos, including the killer's, were checked by police, but no evidence was found associated with Costas's murder. More than one thousand leads were investigated, and over three hundred people were interviewed, including one hundred girls from Costas's high school. A list of suspects was narrowed down to several dozen people.

The investigators then submitted the victimology, crime scene information, pictures, and autopsy records to the FBI Investigative Support Unit in Quantico, Virginia, for a criminal personality profile. The FBI analysts came up with a profile and sent it back to the sheriff's department in late October. With this profile, the investigators were able to narrow the list to one suspect: Bernadette Protti.

Protti was called in for another extensive interview (she had been interviewed at least four times previously) and another polygraph exam. She failed parts of the polygraph, and other parts were inconclusive. Several days later, Protti returned with her father to the sheriff's department and requested to speak with the FBI agent who had questioned her previously. She then offered a full confession for the murder of Costas.

Protti stated that she had killed Kristen because Costas had rebuffed Protti's attempts at making friends with her. Protti was afraid Costas would tell everyone at school that she was a "weirdo." It was this fear of rejection, Protti claimed, that drove her to kill Costas.

Outcome

Bernadette Protti was convicted of second-degree murder and sentenced to nine years. She will serve four years of that sentence at a California Youth Authority facility before being eligible for parole.

124: AUTHORITY KILLING

An authority killing involves an offender who kills person(s) that have an authority relationship or symbolic authority relationship by which the killer perceives he or she has been wronged. The target of the assault may be a person(s) or a building, structure, or institution symbolizing the authority.

Random victims are often wounded and/or killed during the assault as a result of their actual or perceived association with the authority figure or the institution being attacked.

Defining Characteristics

Victimology. The victimology of an authority killing involves primary and secondary targets. The primary targets are the principal people that the offender perceives as wronging him. The wrong may be actual, such as the offender's being fired, or it may be imagined, such as that based on a psychotic or paranoid delusion (i.e., a conspiracy). The secondary victim(s) become random targets as a result of being in the wrong place at the wrong time because the offender generalizes their immediate presence to symbolize the authority.

Crime Scene Indicators Frequently Noted. The offender is mission oriented, as he is on the scene with his mission having ultimate priority. He has little or no intention to abort his plan and escape from the scene or from responsibility for the act. He may desire to die at the scene, either by suicide or by police bullets and thereby attain martyrdom for his actions and cause. There is always a direct and planned confrontation between the offender and victim(s).

Because of his obsession of being wronged over a period of time, the offender gathers and collects weapons and usually brings multiple weaponry to the scene of his confrontation. Additionally, he often arms himself with an abundance of ammunition and other gear to sustain and support his attack. Weapons used are of optimal lethality (semiautomatic assault weapons, high power, scope sights, etc.), and as a result, the assault often develops into a mass or spree killing.

Staging. Staging is not usually present.

Common Forensic Findings. The forensic finding most prevalent in an authority killing is the use of more than one firearm, and often the weapons selected are of the semiautomatic variety. The weapons often are selected for quick firing and may be of more than one caliber. Therefore, various and numerous shell casings may be found at the scene, which will help establish the number of rounds fired. Wounds usually are severe and numerous. Multiple wounds on a victim may suggest the primary target, and the killing of the primary target may prompt the suicide of the offender. If the primary target is not taken, the offender may commit suicide or surrender when he runs out of ammunition.

Investigative Considerations

The offender will have a history of paranoid behavior and openly voicing dissatisfaction with general or specific circumstances in his life. There are usually long-term precipitating and predisposing factors in the development of this state, and a likely result is emotional or mental illness. The mental disorders commonly found among authority killers are depressive reactions, paranoia, or paranoid psychosis. Another result of this developmental situation is interpersonal failures and conflicts, such as separation, divorce, job loss, failure in school, or other such personal traumatic events that will precipitate the acting out against authority. Frustrations accompanied by the inability to handle or resolve such situations are often precipitating events. Suicide attempts are common.

Search Warrant Suggestions

Investigating officials should be aware of the offender's preparation period for the final event by looking for specific reading material, collections of weaponry, uniforms, paraphernalia, and other items of paramilitary interest. Statements made by the offender just prior to, during, and immediately after the assault should be carefully noted and documented by investigative personnel. Search for diaries, scrap books and computer logs. Also search for prescribed medications to link suspect to psychiatric conditions.

CASE STUDY: 124: AUTHORITY KILLING

Background

Joseph T. Wesbecker, a twice-divorced, forty-seven-year-old, white male, had asked for a transfer from his job as a pressman. He had complained that the job was too stressful, and as his emotional problems worsened during February 1989, his employers responded by placing him on disability leave. Wesbecker felt his employers at Standard Gravure Corporation had inflicted a gross injustice upon him, despite the fact that in reality, his extreme behavior interfered with his duties and the duties of others in his workplace. Nearly every day for seven months, he brooded over how he would repay those in authority who were responsible for his alleged mistreatment.

On the morning of 14 September 1989, Wesbecker walked into the Standard Gravure plant, intent on seeking revenge on those who caused his problems. Using an AK-47 automatic assault rifle and an assortment of other firearms, he killed and wounded over twenty people.

Victimology

Wesbecker's victims were all secondary targets because the primary targets of his aggression were the company's administrators, who were not found in their offices at the time of the assault. His victims were fellow employees, yet Wesbecker considered them to be enemies for that particular day because they symbolized the organizational structure of Standard Gravure.

Crime Scene Indicators

At 8:30 A.M. on 14 September 1989, Wesbecker arrived at the Standard Gravure plant carrying a duffel bag containing an AK-47 semiautomatic assault rifle, two MAC-11 semiautomatic pistols, a 9mm semiautomatic pistol, and a .38-caliber revolver. He carried hundreds of rounds of ammunition. When encountering a friend, John Tingle, who tried to persuade Wesbecker not to enter the plant, Wesbecker ordered Tingle to "get away," stating, "I told them that I'd be back."

After he gained entry to the plant, Wesbecker took the elevator to the third floor, seeking out the executive office complex. He opened fire as the elevator door parted, killing the receptionist and wounding several others of the office staff. He then proceeded down the hallway to the bindery, spraying the area with gunfire and killing and wounding more plant employees. He then moved to the Courier-Journal building, where he shot another employee.

Wesbecker proceeded to the Standard Gravure pressroom, into the basement, and back to the pressroom, firing his weapon all the way until he dropped his AK-47, raised his 9mm pistol under his chin, and killed himself. All events occurred within approximately nine minutes from the firing of the first shot. The police arrived on the scene, finding Wesbecker dead. It was determined that he had fired hundreds of shots during his random murder spree.

This crime is classified as a spree type of authority killing in that it was a confrontational assault spread throughout a large area (several buildings), leaving many dead and wounded in the wake of the assailant.* Wesbecker, during approximately nine minutes, killed seven people and wounded twelve others. He obviously intended to kill all who crossed his path and was intent on revenge, seeking out those of authority in the company for

---

*A spree murder involves multiple killings (two or more) in a single event at two or more locations without any appreciable cooling-off period between murders. It is similar to and an extention of a mass murder episode in that the killer usually suffers from one or more mental disorders (i.e., paranoia, psychosis, depressive disorders, etc.). However, the killer moves from one location to another during his killing spree, rather than barricading himself in one location, as does the mass murderer. The duration of the spree can be brief, as in the case of Wesbecker (nine minutes), or it can be much longer, as in the case of Charles Starkweather or Christopher Wilder (weeks and months). As a rule, the spree is of shorter duration. This type of offender is usually mission oriented and demonstrates no escape plan. He most often is killed by responding police or kills himself in a final act of desperation. Occasionally, he is captured to stand trial. When this occurs, the offender often admits his crimes by pleading guilty or by pleading not guilty by reason of insanity.

which he worked. The offender came to the scene with multiple weapons and an abundance of ammunition. His shots were intended to be lethal, as demonstrated by the death toll and the fact that of the twelve surviving victims, five were critically wounded. Wesbecker was very mission oriented with no escape plan.

Forensic Findings

Seven dead and twelve wounded people were found at the scene by police authorities. Another victim died three days later. Most of the victims died from massive blood loss due to gunshot wounds to the heart and chest area. Most of the twelve wounded workers were in serious to critical condition.

Investigation

The investigation of the shootings at the Standard Gravure plant revealed that Wesbecker had a long history of mental and emotional problems. Two marriages ended in divorce. He had been hospitalized on a voluntarily basis at least three times between 1978 for these problems. He was reported to be withdrawn and troublesome in his workplace and experienced job-related stress problems. He had once declined a promotion and a raise because he could not face the demands the job would place on him. He claimed that his exposure to an industrial chemical had caused memory loss, dizziness, and blackouts. He further attributed to the chemical exposure his bouts of sleeplessness, racing thoughts, anxiety, anger, and confusion.

Wesbecker's feelings and acts of isolation, withdrawal, and depression are all prominent preoffense behavior dynamics of the mass and spree authority killer. Further, he was a single, middle-aged, while male, who harbored a long-term grudge against the management of his employer and had accompanying emotional problems relating to his personal work-related life. Wesbecker often spoke of his deep resentment toward his employer. Fellow employees recalled his conversations surrounding his fantasies of revenge against his company should he be mistreated.

Wesbecker often had articulated his feelings of worthlessness and had attempted suicide on three occasions, once though a drug overdose, another by breathing car exhaust fumes, and a third by hanging. He further articulated a desire to harm others in addition to his suicide attempts. The investigation failed to link Wesbecker with any of his victims in terms of a personal cause or motive for shooting or killing any one or all of the individuals. Therefore, it must be assumed the shootings were random in nature, rather than specific.

125: REVENGE KILLING

Revenge killing involves the murder of another person in retaliation for a perceived wrong, real or imagined, committed against the offender or a significant other.

Defining Characteristics

Victimology. When revenge is the motive for a homicide, the victim may or may not personally know the offender, but something in the victim's life is related directly to the actions of the offender. There is a significant event or interaction that links the offender to the victim. The revenge motive generated by this event may be unknown to the victim or to the victim's family or friends. Multiple victims may be involved, depending on the nature of the event that triggered the act of revenge.

Crime Scene Indicators Frequently Noted. There are often several locations involved with the offense. For example, the precipitating event may happen at one site, but the revenge is acted out later at another location.

An offender who has brooded over the victim's affront very often demonstrates a less spontaneous crime that is reflected by the well-ordered crime scene. However, the mission oriented offender may not be experienced at criminal activity. Some offenders are often in a highly charged emotional state due to extensive fantasizing about the act of vengeance. The crime scene may reflect this inexperience, with a clear shift from an organized to a disorganized behavior: the offense is well planned up to the point of the killing. This may be manifested by a skillful approach to the crime scene (leaving no physical evidence) then a blitz style of attack followed by a rapid exit, with the offender leaving an abundance of physical evidence.[4] The weapon may be left at the scene. Because the act of vengeance was the priority and an end in itself, there may be no escape plan.

The weapon is most often a weapon of choice, brought to the scene. It may be left there, especially with the type of offender described above.

The offense itself can be opportunistic and spontaneous. An example of this is the distraught friend or family member who brings a gun to court and shoots the alleged perpetrator of a crime committed against the offender's loved one. A revenge killing committed in front of the victim's family is another example of the more impulsive form of this killing.

Staging. Staging is not usually present.

Common Forensic Findings. As mentioned, the weapon is one of choice, mostly likely a firearm or knife. The killing is close range and

---

[4]The amount of physical evidence left by the offender is related to the degree of offender sophistication, state of mind, use of alcohol/drugs, and similar factors.

confrontational. The offender derives satisfaction of witnessing "justice" rendered. Contact wounds are prevalent. The presence of defensive wounds are possible and are related in part to the degree of offender skill.

Investigative Considerations

Preoffense behavior by the offender often will follow a pattern in which he or she is at first very verbal about the incident that involves the victim's injustice. Interviews of those close to the offender may reveal that their conversations with the offender often pertained to this incident.

As the offender formulates a plan for vengeance, he or she may become preoccupied and less vocal in general. The offender will seek a weapon, if necessary, at this point.

After the offense, there is often a sense of relief on the part of the offender. The mission has been accomplished. He or she may even stay at the scene to savor the achievement and may make no attempt to conceal his or her identity. The death of the victim is justified in the eyes of the offender; it is restitution. If the offender has this attitude, there are often witnesses to the offense.

The precipitating event that links the victim and offender is the key point of the investigation. However, this event may hold significance only to the offender and may not be obvious to those associated with either the offender or the victim. It may not be obvious to the investigator, either. Also of importance is any significant person in either the offender's and/or the victim's life who may have direct or indirect involvement with the incident.

Search Warrant Suggestions

The offender may have kept the weapon and (bloodied) clothing from the offense as mementos from which renewed satisfaction that justice has been served can be derived. There may be newspapers and other press clippings relating to the significant/precipitating event. A record (written, audio, or videotaped) of the fantasy and feelings leading to the offense also may be present at the offender's residence. There may be mail or other communications with the victim in the offender's possession.

CASE STUDY: 125: REVENGE KILLING

Background

In 1984 a thirty-four-year-old inmate walked away from his work-release detail, intent on a task he had planned for some time. Ten years of incarceration had given him plenty of time to brood over the woman who had put him behind bars. His confinement had provided him with many free hours to plot his vengeance. The relative freedom of the work-release program finally gave him the opportunity.

Victimology

It had taken nearly a decade for the thirty-six-year-old woman to recover from the brutal assault she had suffered in 1975. She had been brutally beaten, sexually assaulted, and sodomized by her attacker. After the assault, she was determined to overcome her fear and sense of humiliation and to face her attacker on the witness stand. It was her unwavering testimony that had put him in jail for what she hoped was a very long time. She did not know that he was already free and searching her out to enact his revenge.

The woman had required counseling and had lived in constant fear for months after the attack. Even ten years later, she would occasionally find herself overcome by an irrational fear, although it was less often compared with the first years after the assault. Much of the healing began with the birth of her only daughter, who was now six. She was a happy child whose cheerful presence was a constant reassurance that life goes on.

The significant event (a key factor of a revenge killing) that linked this offender to these two victims was the testimony of the woman he had assaulted. It had become the focal point of the inmate's life. This event had given his sense of vengeance enough momentum to last ten years. The third victim of this revenge killing was a next-door neighbor who became a victim by being in the wrong place at the wrong time.

Crime Scene Indicators

This offense involved the woman, her daughter, and the neighbor. The offender brought his weapon of choice, a knife, to the scene with him. The offender found the victim's house around mid afternoon. He entered through an unlocked door and immediately attacked the daughter, cutting her throat. He spent more time with the woman because she was his primary target, ruthlessly beating her before he slashed her throat. The unfortunate neighbor stumbled onto the murder scene at this time. She was blitz attacked by the offender as soon as she entered the house.

Although the offender had an immediate escape plan, he was sure he would be apprehended sooner or later because of his preoffense conversations in prison. He was mission oriented in that he knew he would not get away with the revenge killing.

Forensic Findings

The close-range, confrontational assault common to the revenge killing was demonstrated by this case. The woman, her daughter, and the neighbor all died from having their throats slashed. The daughter's throat was slashed so violently that she was nearly decapitated. In addition to having her throat slashed, the woman sustained extensive facial trauma (depersonalization) from being beaten and was sexually assaulted with a blunt instrument.

Investigation

The offender often indulged in preoffense conversation centered on his thoughts of revenge for the woman who put him in prison. Through the use of prison informants, this conversation was substantiated. In addition, his absence from the work-release center coinciding with the murders led police to suspect him immediately.

Outcome

The offender was subsequently apprehended, linked to the crime through physical evidence, and convicted of the murders. He was given the death penalty, and all appeals have been exhausted. At present, he has a stay of execution that expires in 1991.

126: NONSPECIFIC-MOTIVE KILLING

A nonspecific-motive killing pertains to a homicide that appears irrational and is committed for a reason known only to the offender. It subsequently may be defined and categorized after more extensive investigation into the offender's background.

Defining Characteristics

Victimology. The victims of a nonspecific homicide are random, with no direct relationship between victim and offender. Victims can be male, female, adults, or children and demonstrate a disparity of characteristics and life-style.

Crime Scene Indicators Frequently Noted. The crime scene is usually a public place and poses a high risk to the offender. There is nothing missing from it, and it is disorganized, with no effort having been made to conceal the victim(s). A firearm, the weapon of choice for this type of offender, is brought to the crime. This crime often becomes a massacre because it is the offender's goal to kill as many people as possible. This is reflected by use of weapons that offer optimal lethality, by multiple weapons, and by an abundance of ammunition.

Staging. Staging is not present.

Common Forensic Findings. Because nothing is removed from the scene, an abundance of evidence is usually available. This includes shell casings, prints, discarded weapons, and so on. High-powered, high-caliber, and/or high-capacity firearm use will be evident and enables the offender to accomplish his goal of mass killing. Wounds will be concentrated on vital areas (head, neck, and chest).

Investigative Considerations

This crime is almost exclusively committed during daylight in public places because the offender wants the highest death toll possible. Witnesses often are available to identify the offender as he is unconcerned with being identified. The offender has no escape plan and possibly intends to commit suicide or be shot by police. Through a broad neighborhood investigation, preoffense characteristics become evident: the offender usually has a disheveled appearance, is withdrawn, demonstrates an isolated affect, and possibly exhibits erratic behavior.

Search Warrant Suggestions

Search the home of the suspect for weapons, receipts, and records.

CASE STUDY: 126: NONSPECIFIC-MOTIVE KILLING

Background

At age seventeen, Herbert Mullin was voted most likely to succeed by his class. He was engaged to be married and belonged to a group of school athletes, called the Zeros, with his best friend, Dean. He had plans to attend college after high school graduation. He seemed to be a completely normal boy with a bright future.

Then, in 1965 his friend Dean was killed in a motorcycle accident. This seemed to mark the beginning of Mullin's mental deterioration. Mullin arranged his bedroom into a shrine around his friend's picture. When he was called up for military service, he decided to become a conscientious objector and was assigned to work for Goodwill Industries. His girlfriend broke off their engagement because her father's career was in the military.

In 1969 Mullin announced to his family that he was going to India to study religion. A month later, during a family meal, he began repeating all his brother-in-law's actions and words. His family convinced him to seek psychiatric help, which he did for some time. His paranoid schizophrenia became full blown by October 1969, when he shaved his head and burned his penis with a cigarette at the request of voices he claimed to have heard.

By September 1972 after being institutionalized and arrested several times, Mullin allegedly began receiving telepathic messages ordering him to kill. On 13 October 1972 he began to oblige these messages.

Victimology

On 13 October 1972 while driving in a deserted part of the Santa Cruz Mountains in California, Mullin spotted Lawrence White, age fifty-five, walking along the highway. White was an alcoholic transient who had spent much of his time in and out of jails. Mullin pulled over and asked White to look at his engine. As White accommodated him, Mullin produced a baseball bat and beat him to death. There was no apparent motive for the killing.

On 24 October Mullin picked up Mary Guilfoyle, a twenty-two-year-old college student who was hitchhiking home. As they drove toward Santa Cruz, Mullin thrust a hunting knife into her heart, killing her instantly. Her skeletal remains were not found until 11 February 1973.

On 23 November Mullin entered a confessional booth at St. Mary's Church in Los Gatos, California. He stabbed Father Henri Tomei, age sixty-five, to death.

The next five murders occurred on 25 January 1973. On this day, Mullin had set out to look for James Gianera, age twenty-five, who had introduced him to marijuana years before. His search led him to the primitive cabin once owned by Gianera. One of the cabin's occupants, Kathy Francis, age twenty-nine, gave Mullin directions to Gianera's new residence 4 miles away. Mullin drove there, argued with Gianera, and then shot him three times. During the course of the struggle, Gianera ran up the stairs to his twenty-one-year-old wife, Joan, who was taking a shower. Mullin followed, killing Gianera in the bathroom and then turning on Joan Gianera, shooting her five times and stabbing her once. Mullin then returned to the Francis cabin, where he shot and stabbed Kathy and her two sons, Daemon, age four, and David, age nine, killing all three.

On 6 February Mullin went hiking in Santa Cruz State Park. He happened upon a makeshift, one-room cabin occupied by four boys, ages fifteen to nineteen, as they were preparing a meal. As Mullin stood in the doorway, the only escape route, he emptied his .22-caliber pistol, reloaded, and fired again into the victims as they attempted to flee or struggled to take cover.

A week later on 13 February, seventy-two-year-old Fred Perez was out working on his lawn. Suddenly, he fell to the ground, struck by a bullet fired from a station wagon approximately 123 feet away. A neighbor observed a station wagon driving away at normal speed.

The random selection of the nonspecific killer is well illustrated by Mullin's victims. Several of the victims were at high risk due to their habits (i.e., hitchhiking or having a transient life-style). Gianera's past association with the drug trade may have been a factor if his death was a drug murder and he was still actively involved with the drug trade. But because the motive was not drug related, his involvement with drugs, if it still existed, was not consequential to his death. Most of the victims would not be considered likely to become victims of violent crime based on such factors as their life-style, employment, and income.

Except for Gianera, all the victims had no prior contact or relationship with Mullin. They were completely random, selected and murdered for no apparent reason other than to satisfy Mullin's need to kill (and the alleged voices commanding him to kill). The great disparity of ages (four to seventy-four years), physical characteristics, gender, and life-styles all represent the victimology common to the nonspecific motive killing.

Crime Scene Indicators

Many of the crime scenes demonstrated little or no physical evidence. The crime scene involving the priest and the last victim were public places that placed Mullin at higher risk of being apprehended. He eliminated the only damaging witness (Kathy Francis) in the Gianera case. The weapon was one of choice, initially a knife, brought to the scene. Later, after he purchased a gun, Mullin used that almost exclusively.

Mary Guilfoyle's remains were found unclothed in a wooded area in the foothills near Santa Cruz. Her clothing was never recovered. The body was found face up with the legs spread apart and bent under her as if pushed over from a kneeling position.

The crime scene involving Father Tomei had one partial palm print from the confessional booth. This print was later confirmed to be Mullin's. The Gianera crime scene indicated the confrontation occurred in the kitchen, as evidenced by blood splatter on the table and refrigerator. There was also blood on the wall and stairs going up to the second floor. It appeared James Gianera, after being shot three times, ran up the stairs to the bathroom, where he and his wife were killed.

The crime scene of the 10 February homicides involving the four teenagers demonstrated signs of struggle and attempts to flee, but it is apparent that Mullin blocked the entrance. Eight bullets were fired from the same gun. Some empty cartridges were found at the entrance to the cabin. There was a .22-caliber rifle missing from the scene. All other crime scenes demonstrated no physical evidence.

Two of the incidents were spree or mass killings common to this type of offender. No effort was made to conceal any of the bodies. A weapon of choice was brought to the scene. All of the killings were during daylight hours, and several were in public places.

Forensic Findings

The cause of death for most victims was either stabbing and/or gunshot wounds. Only the first victim died from blunt-force trauma. Because Guilfoyle's skeleton was unclothed, it was theorized that she was raped either before or after death.

Father Tomei was stabbed four times, with one thrust penetrating the heart. Kathy Francis was stabbed in the chest, then shot in the head. She also had a defensive gunshot wound to her left arm. Her two sons were each shot in the head, and one was stabbed superficially in the back. Joan Gianera was shot five times and stabbed once in the back. The four teenage boys were shot in the body, with the cause of death being an additional head shot. Fred Perez was killed by a bullet piercing his right arm and continuing through his chest, piercing his aorta.

Nearly all victims sustained multiple wounds to areas containing vital organs. This concentration of attack to vital areas is common to this type of killer. There was also an element of overkill, Mullin's signature, with many of the victims.* Shooting a victim multiple times was not enough; many also were stabbed.

Investigation

Mullin was apprehended ten minutes after the last shooting because witnesses gave police a description of his car. There were witnesses to two of the more public murders, illustrative of Mullin's nonchalance about being identified.

When he was stopped, the .22-caliber rifle stolen from the previous murder scene and responsible for Perez's death was found leaning against the front seat with a paper bag over the muzzle. In a satchel on the front seat was the RG-14 revolver used on nine of the other victims.

Outcome

At his trial, Mullin claimed his motive for killing was to avert natural disasters. He was found legally sane and was convicted on ten of the thirteen second-degree murder counts. He received several life sentences and will be eligible for parole in the year 2020.

---

*See chapter 5, which discusses the signature aspects of violent crime, for a more in-depth explanation of signature crime.

127: EXTREMIST HOMICIDE

Extremist murder is committed on behalf of a body of ideas based upon a particular political, economic, religious, or social system. Although the offender's beliefs may be associated with a particular group, the group does not sanction the actions of the offender.

Extremist Typologies

Classifying an extremist murder poses difficulty whether it is motivated by personal cause or group cause. Even though this category of extremist homicide deals with a lone offender (not acting on behalf of a group), an extremist murder motivated by personal cause often involves the same blending of multiple motives as a group cause killing.

The blending of political belief with religious dogma is found frequently in the motivations of the extremist murder. Religious and socioeconomic doctrines may also fuse and become a catalyst for extremist murder. The following typologies offer a general outline for the motives of an extremist murder.

Political. This type of killing is motivated by doctrines or philosophies in opposition to a current position of a government or its representatives. Assassinations such as Robert Kennedy's would be included in this group. Political extremist homicides are classified as 127.01.

Religious. This homicide is prompted by a fervent devotion to a cause, principle, or system of beliefs based on supernatural or supernormal agencies. Religious extremist homicides are classified as 127.02.

Socioeconomic. This offender kills due to an intense hostility and aversion toward another individual or group that represents a certain ethnic, social, or religious group. Socioeconomic extremist homicide is classified as 127.03.

Defining Characteristics

Victimology. The victim of an extremist murder usually represents the antithesis of the offender's system of beliefs; therefore, victimology depends heavily on offender doctrine. This doctrine is not always readily apparent, so the victim's history becomes an essential step in discerning the motive. This history should include any social, political, or religious activities of the victim as well as a complete life-style description.

Although victimology often will direct the investigator toward possible motives, extremist killings may involve secondary targets. These people become victims through association with the primary target. They may share no political, social, or religious similarities with the primary target. Determining who the primary target was will usually help prevent confusion over the offender's motive.

Crime Scene Indicators Frequently Noted. The crime scene of an extremist murder usually occurs in a public place. The location of the victim often will offer an indication of the motive (e.g., a body left near a gay bar or in a black neighborhood).

The crime scene often will help the investigator to determine whether the offender is acting on his own or on behalf of a group. Group symbols or signs of the offender's attachment to a group left at the scene does not always mean the group is involved. The offender may have demonstrated a knowledge of group MO, but there are usually idiosyncrasies.

The usual signs of multiple offenders will be absent (numerous fibers, footprints, or fingerprints, etc.). The crime scene of a lone offender tends to be less organized than one involving a group effort. The lone offender usually will have more difficulty controlling the victim than multiple offenders. A scene spread beyond the site of confrontation, blood-splatter patterns, and/or defensive wounds on the victim are all indicators of the lone offender having difficulty controlling the victim.

This offender often chooses an ambush or blitz style of attack because of the possibility of a problem with victim control. He may choose a long-range attack as a sniper (long-range attacks may also mean there is a conspiracy involved).

Staging. Staging is not usually present.

Common Forensic Findings. The victims of an extremist attack often will suffer multiple wounds. The weapon of choice is usually a firearm or knife. However, an offender who adopts the MO of a particular group will also adopt their methods of attack. This might mean the offender uses blunt-force trauma or an explosive to kill, methods modeled on the group he identifies with.

Investigative Considerations

Preoffense behavior of the extremist killer often entails surveillance and stalking of the victim. His preoffense conversation often will reflect a preoccupation with the intended target. He may generalize (e.g., making derogatory statements about all blacks or all gays), or he may already have selected an individual who represents the group he despises. Generally, when those associated with him are interviewed, they will especially remember him for this frequently verbalized animosity.

Postoffense conversation may reflect an interest in the homicide. The offender may even express satisfaction, such as stating, "He got what he deserved." The offender often will follow news media reports and even collect newspaper clippings about the incident.

If the investigator receives any communiqués claiming responsibility, especially from an alleged group, the communiqúe should undergo a threat assessment examination to determine authenticity. In some cases, the group identified may issue disclaimers.

Search Warrant Suggestions

The most prevalent sign of an extremist attitude is literature. The investigator should look for reading materials such as pamphlets, recordings, or books pertaining to the offender's belief system. Other items include:

- Physical trappings of the group or belief system (e.g., uniforms, paramilitary paraphernalia, or jewelry [rings, necklaces] containing symbols of the group)
- Diaries, logs, diagrams, sketches, recordings, newspaper clippings concerning the homicide
- Travel records, motel receipts, rental agreements
- Records of any firearm purchases, etc.

CASE STUDY: 127.01: POLITICAL EXTREMIST HOMICIDE

Background

Abuse and neglect during his childhood had conditioned Joseph Paul Franklin to a life of failure and feelings of inadequacy. This inadequacy was reinforced by an accident during early childhood that robbed his left eye of sight. His early years of ridicule, punishment, and criticism shaped him into a disruptive and delinquent teenager who never finished high school despite being average to above average in intelligence.

Franklin initially found direction and acceptance with the Ku Klux Klan, the American Nazi Party, and finally, the fascist National States Rights Party. Soon, however, he formed a purpose for his life that was not sufficiently serviced by these organizations. He felt they lacked the professionalism and commitment required of his mission.

The first expression of the hatred he harbored toward blacks was in 1976, when he wrote a threatening letter to President Jimmy Carter about blacks and assaulted a racially mixed couple with Mace. This targeting of black men accompanied by white women became a characteristic of the victimology for the later, more lethal attacks of which Franklin was suspected.

Victimology

On 7 October 1977 Alphonse Manning and Toni Schwenn, both twenty-three years old, finished an afternoon of shopping at a Madison, Wisconsin, mall. They were pulling out of the parking lot when their car was rammed from behind. The driver of the dark green car then jumped out and began firing a handgun at Manning and Schwenn. Manning was struck twice; Schwenn, four times. Both died as a result of their wounds. Manning was black, and Schwenn was white.

On 22 July 1979 in Doraville, Georgia, Harold McGiver, age twenty-nine, had finished work at the Taco Bell restaurant he managed. As he walked from the front door of the restaurant toward his car, two shots were fired from a wooded area 150 feet away. McGiver was fatally wounded by the sniper.

On 8 August 1979 at a Falls Church, Virginia, Burger King, twenty-eight-year-old Raymond Taylor was sitting at a table eating his dinner. At 9:50 P.M. the sound of breaking glass was heard as a high-velocity rifle bullet passed through a large, plate-glass window on the east side of the building. Taylor was pronounced dead at Arlington County Hospital.

On 21 October 1979 Jesse Taylor and his common-law wife, Marian Besette, were on the way home from a family outing with their three children when they decided to stop at a supermarket for a few groceries. The children stayed in the car while their parents went inside. A short time later, the couple emerged from the store and walked across the parking lot toward their car. As Taylor reached the car, a shot was fired from a clump of shrubbery approximately 195 feet away. Taylor slumped against the car, moaning. Two more shots struck him, driving him to the ground. Marian Besette, who knelt screaming over her dead husband, was then struck once in the chest by the same sniper, dying instantly.

On 12 January 1980 Lawrence Reese, age twenty-two, had just finished eating his meal at Church's Fried Chicken in Indianapolis. It was 11:10 P.M., and he was standing with his back to the front window, waiting for the last customers of the day to leave. Reese was a regular customer at the restaurant, usually coming there before closing to eat chicken in exchange for sweeping. Suddenly, the window behind him was shattered. Reese staggered four or five steps forward and collapsed. He was dead from a single sniper's bullet.

Two days later around 10:50 P.M., Leo Watkins, nineteen, and his father had just arrived at the Qwic Pic Market in a small shopping plaza in Indianapolis. Watkins often assisted his father, who worked as an independent exterminator. Watkins stood facing into the street by the front window while his father mixed the chemicals they would be using that night. They were waiting for the last customers to leave before starting. Watkins had been standing by the window for about five minutes when he was suddenly struck in the center of the chest by a shot that exited his upper right back. The mortally wounded man ran about 30 feet along the front of the store and into an aisle before he fell.

On 29 May 1980 in Fort Wayne, Indiana, Vernon Jordan, the president of the National Urban League, participated in an Urban League meeting at the Marriott Hotel. The day's activities were completed, and Jordan spent the evening with one of the attendees, Martha Coleman. It was around 2:10 A.M. when Coleman brought Jordan back to the hotel. As Jordan exited Coleman's vehicle, he was struck once by a bullet fired from a grassy area approximately 143 feet away. Jordan was one of the few that survived the offender's attack.

Dante Brown, age thirteen, and Darrell Lane, age fourteen, of Cincinnati were not as lucky. On 6 June 1980 the two boys decided to walk to a local convenience market. When they were about 50 feet from a railroad overpass, four shots were fired from the overpass. Each boy was struck twice. Darrell died instantly; Dante lived a few hours longer before he died.

On 15 June 1980 Kathleen Mikula, age sixteen, and Arthur Smothers, age twenty-two, were out for a walk. At 12:14 P.M. they were crossing a bridge on the outskirts of Johnstown, Ohio, when Smothers was struck down by three shots. Mikula was hit twice by the same sniper from a wooded hillside 152 feet away. Both died from their wounds.

David Martin, age eighteen, had just graduated from his Salt Lake City high school at the beginning of the summer of 1980. He had worked full time during the summer in building maintenance for Northwest Pipeline. Despite his plans to begin studies at the University of Utah in several weeks, his employer had offered him continuing employment. It would be part time to accommodate his school schedule, a concession readily made because he had proven himself to be a dependable employee.

Martin had a history of being a hard-working, responsible young man, giving up high school baseball for an after-school job. His friend, Ted Fields, age twenty and also a Northwest Pipeline employee, had the same reputation of being an excellent employee. He had started as a mail-room clerk after high school graduation in 1978 and had already advanced to the position of data-operations clerk. The future looked bright for both these young men.

On 20 August they decided to go for an evening jog through Liberty Park with two young women. At about 10:15 P.M., the joggers emerged from the west side of the park and began crossing an intersection. As they approached the center of the intersection, a loud noise was heard. Fields seemed to stumble and fell to the ground, calling out that he was hit. The rest of the group thought he was joking and told him to stop fooling around. Two more shots hit Fields as Martin and one of the young women tried to drag him across the street. They were almost to the curb when Martin was hit. Martin yelled to the two women to get help, that he had been hit, too. A man driving through the intersection at this time thought the gunfire was coming from the east side of the street and pulled his car around to try to block further attempts by the sniper. More gunfire drove him back into his car as he attempted to come to the aid of Fields and

Martin. He observed several more rounds hitting the men as they lay in the street. Fields and Martin were both dead on arrival at the hospital. One of the young women was struck on the elbow but was not seriously injured. Fields was hit three times; Martin five.

All the male victims of Franklin were black and were predominately young adults. All the female victims were white and were in the company of black men. Vernon Jordan, the only victim with known involvement with civil rights activity, was the only one who survived his injuries.

Each one of these victims became a target because of race or apparent interracial affiliations. The offender had definite criteria in mind as demonstrated by victim similarities in age, race, and companionship. But the victims were victims of opportunity: the person closest to the window, or the one who first crossed the scope of the sniper. He chose areas that offered an abundance of targets, black neighborhoods and businesses that were frequented by blacks.

Crime Scene Indicators

Several crime scene correlations were noted in most of the homicides. Six of the ten shootings clustered between the two-hour span of 9:50 P.M. and 11:30 P.M. The two other episodes were between 6:40 P.M. and 7:00 P.M., and one was at 2:10 A.M. The evening hours played an important role, allowing the sniper, a white man, to slip nearly unnoticed into predominately black neighborhoods and position himself at a vantage point that allowed him to kill with one shot, often from 100 to 150 yards. These vantage points were hills, woods, knolls, and alleys that were often dark in contrast to where the victim was. The shootings were all long distance except for one (the first one). They ranged from 100 feet to 150 yards, with one mid-distance killing of 40 feet.

The shootings all involved very public places that increased offender risk, but this was negated by the distance of the shooting, the lack of pedestrian traffic, and/or the darkness provided by the evening hours and poor lighting. Most of the victims were outside in a parking lot or street. The three victims that were killed inside were sitting or standing next to large windows in well-lit interiors.

The scarcity of physical evidence (one tire track, one footprint, and a handful of cartridge casings out of ten crime scenes) was indicative of offender sophistication. The lack of witnesses despite the public settings of the homicides also indicated the offender's composure and planning.

The general location of each incident near a major interstate highway, which allowed a quick, easy escape from the crime scene, reflected the methodical approach of an organized offender. Not only did this plan allow him to put distance quickly between himself and the homicide, but it also allowed him to fade into the busy traffic of a major highway.

Forensic Findings

The choice of murder weapon served a dual purpose. It allowed the offender to distance himself from the victim, and it also provided optimized lethality with minimal shots. The two murders that did not involve a .30-caliber or .30-06-caliber bullet were the close and midrange murders. In these cases, a choice of large caliber weapon, .357-caliber Magnum and .44-caliber Magnum, inflicted equally fatal injuries.

Most of the injuries were chest wounds that involved damage to the heart, lungs, liver, and large thoracic blood vessels. Several of the victims were killed with one shot. This precise targeting of the vital organs (which, in some cases, necessitated the use of a scope) was another factor that revealed a more proficient and experienced offender. There were a few cases of multiple wounds, especially when racially mixed victims were involved; Franklin kept shooting until they did not move. The accuracy was faultless: thirty-two bullets were fired at these victims without one miss.

Investigation

On 25 September 1980 a police officer was investigating a service-station robbery in Florence, Kentucky. He was walking by a brown Camaro parked at the Scottish Inn Motel when he noticed a handgun on the front seat. A license check revealed that a warrant had been issued in Salt Lake City for the owner of the vehicle, Joseph Paul Franklin. His car had been placed by witnesses as near the vacant lot in which the shells were found from the Fields and Martin shootings.

Shortly after being taken into custody for questioning, Franklin escaped through a window. He left behind a car full of weapons and paraphernalia that left him a suspect not only of the Utah murders, but the series of sniper attacks that had left fourteen dead and two injured. In addition, he was suspected of as many as one dozen bank robberies.

Franklin fled first to Cincinnati but ended up being apprehended at a blood bank in Lakeland, Florida. (He frequented blood banks as a means of obtaining money.) Franklin was interviewed by an FBI agent during the extradition trip back to Utah. He never admitted to his guilt during this interview, but within twenty-four hours he admitted his guilt to his wife and a cell mate for all the shootings except that of Vernon Jordan.

Franklin was connected to many of the cities within the time period that the murders occurred through hotel receipts under aliases in his handwriting, weapons being bought or sold, appearances of a car similar to his near the crime scenes, and/or descriptions of a man that fit him. In addition, he linked himself circumstantially to several of the offenses through his own admissions of familiarity with the actual crime scenes.

The bigotry that gnawed at Franklin was evident during his teen years in a photograph that showed him proudly giving the Nazi salute wearing a swastika armband. His sister recalled that Franklin had always been a believer in Nazism and separation of the races.

Franklin decided that as an adult he would not be deprived of the need to belong and to be special that his childhood had denied him. This lack of attention and the feelings of insignificance it produced required that he take special measures to give his life value and communicate the central theme of his life: "cleaning up America." Franklin decided his message would be taken seriously if it was spelled in blood.

Outcome

Joseph Paul Franklin was convicted in Utah of four counts of violating the civil rights of the victims and two counts of murder. He was sentenced to four life terms.

On 21 August 1990 Franklin was interviewed by a Salt Lake City radio station. An hour into the interview and after refusing to comment about his guilt, he was asked again if had committed the murders. He sighed and answered yes. When prodded by the broadcaster, he responded, "The answer is yes. I won't discuss it any further other than to say yes."

128: MERCY/HERO HOMICIDE

Mercy and hero murders usually are committed on victims who are critically ill. The mercy homicide offender believes inducing death is relieving the victim's suffering. The hero homicide offender is unsuccessful in attempts to save the victim from death.

128.01: MERCY HOMICIDE

Death at the hand of a mercy killer results from the offender's claim/ perception of victim suffering and what the offender believes is his or her duty to relieve it. Most often, the real motivation for mercy killing has little to do with the offender's feelings of compassion and pity for the victim. The sense of power and control the offender derives from killing is usually the real motive. Case studies show that these offenders frequently commit serial murder.

Defining Characteristics

Victimology. The victims of mercy killers are most often the elderly and/ or infirm. They are usually patients in a hospital, nursing home, or other institutional setting. The victim is engaged in a client/caregiver relationship with the offender. The victim is rarely a random victim but is known to the offender. The victim's environment and life-style are low risk, but his or her dependency or state of health elevates risk. Offender risk varies with institutional setting, depending on amount of autonomy/supervision, shift, and quantity of staff.

Crime Scene Indicators Frequently Noted. The instrument of death is one of opportunity, often common to the institutional setting (drugs, syringes, toxic substances, etc.). Signs of struggle are minimal or absent.

Staging. The body is arranged to represent peaceful, natural death. The death is most often staged to look like a natural death, but it is possible that accidental or suicidal death is staged.

Common Forensic Findings. Because the case may not have been reported as suspicious, detailed investigation is mandated. Exhumation may be required for analytical toxicology examination. Many times an autopsy is not performed if the death appears natural, but later scrutiny reveals poisoning, broken ribs, or other signs of suspicious death.

Liver biopsy, thorough blood-chemistry analysis, complete drug screening of blood and urine, and hair analysis for arsenic and drugs (especially digoxin, lidocaine, and smooth-muscle-paralyzing drugs) should be performed. Asphyxiation should be checked for by examining for petechial hemorrhage, taking an X ray for broken ribs, and so on.

Investigative Considerations

A rise in the number of deaths, especially if at all suspicious, should be checked for correlation between suspect's shift and patient assignments. In nine cases of mercy killers cited in an article in the *American Journal of Nursing,* the correlation between suspect presence and a high number of suspicious deaths was deemed sufficient to establish probable cause and to bring indictments by grand juries (Yorker 1988).

Inspection of a suspect's employment history is important: look for frequent job changes with a corresponding increase in mortality associated with the suspect's employment. Other considerations include a significant rise in cardiopulmonary arrests or deaths in a particular patient population, cardiopulmonary arrests or deaths inconsistent with the patient's condition, cardiopulmonary deaths localized to a particular shift, and postmortem examinations revealing toxic levels of an injectable substance (Yorker 1988).

Search Warrant Suggestions

Scrutinize the literature found, checking each page for underlining and modification. Search for diaries and videotapes and analyze for themes of death.

CASE STUDY: 128.01: MERCY HOMICIDE

Background

In early 1987 a Cincinnati medical examiner was performing an autopsy on the victim of a motorcycle crash. As he was examining the stomach cavity, he detected an odor that smelled like almonds. After further testing, the pathologist concluded the victim had been poisoned with cyanide.

The ensuing investigation led to a thirty-five-year-old nurse's assistant, Donald Harvey. After his arrest, Harvey began confessing to numerous other murders, or mercy killings, as he described them. Harvey enjoyed the limelight so much that he continued to add to the list of victims. The toll reached as high as one hundred victims at one point, but Harvey could not supply details for many of the alleged killings. The actual number of victims is still uncertain, and Harvey's later confessions have been held suspect.

Victimology

Harvey claimed his first killings began in the early 1970s in Marymount Hospital in London, Kentucky. He confessed to murdering fifteen patients between 1970 and 1971. Harvey then moved on to Cincinnati and worked in a factory for several years before returning to hospital work.

From 1975 to 1985 Harvey worked in the Cincinnati Veterans Administration (VA) Medical Center. He claimed responsibility for at least fifteen deaths at the VA hospital. Harvey moved on to Drake Memorial Hospital in 1986, where he continued working as a nurse's aid. Harvey killed at least twenty-one patients at Drake Hospital. He was employed there until his arrest in August 1987.

Harvey preyed on the elderly, infirm, or chronically ill. Most victims were involved in a caregiver/client relationship with Harvey. Most of the confirmed deaths took place in an institutional setting, which would have been considered a low-risk environment for the victims. However, the victims' debilitated conditions that necessitated total dependence on a caregiver elevated their risk of becoming victims of violent crime. A few of Harvey's victims were outside of the institutional setting, but he targeted them for revenge and not mercy killing.

Crime Scene Indicators

Most of the crime scenes involved with the mercy killings were in the hospital. There were no signs of struggle or violent death with most of the murders, which was one reason why Harvey was able to kill year after year without being caught. Most of the time, Harvey utilized an instrument of death, one of opportunity, offered by the institutional setting where the offenses occurred. He would use plastic bags and pillows, oxygen tubings, and syringes full of air. When he decided to poison patients, he brought arsenic and cyanide to work and mixed it with their food.

Forensic Findings

Harvey's victims died from a variety of causes. He smothered some by putting a plastic bag over the victim's face and then using a pillow. Harvey killed several patients by cutting their oxygen supply off. One patient died of peritonitis after Harvey punctured his abdomen. Harvey placed another patient face down on his pillow. The patient was unable to move, so he suffocated.

The rest of the victims died of arsenic or cyanide poisoning. The poisoning cases were supported through exhumation, but most of the other cases would have been difficult to prove without Harvey's confession. He was able to provide details on these cases that collaborated his claims.

Investigation

During the initial stages of the investigation, Harvey claimed that he was putting people out of their misery. He described many of the patients as always on their death bed. Many never had any visitors, either because their families had forgotten them or because they had no family. He felt he was releasing these patients from a lonely, pain-filled existence. He hoped someone would do the same for him if he was as sick: "I felt I was doing right."

But after the trial and his convictions, interviews with Harvey began to reveal the true motive for his mercy killings. He began to describe the satisfaction he derived from fooling what he called know-it-all doctors who assumed their patients had died of natural causes. He found murder to be a satisfying outlet for the tensions that built up from personal problems, relationships ending, and living alone. He stated that sometimes he would kill just to relieve the boredom of his job.

Harvey, a homosexual, claims that the killing started two weeks after he was raped by the man from whom he was renting a room. He retaliated by preying on a totally helpless patient who was restrained to his bed because he was disoriented. He took a coat hanger, straightened it out, and rammed it through the man's abdomen, puncturing his intestines. The man lived for two days before dying of peritonitis.

Psychologists described Harvey as a compulsive murderer who killed because it gave him a feeling of power. Yet, Harvey claimed, "I've been portrayed as a cold-blooded murderer, but I don't see myself that way. I think I am a very warm and loving person."

Outcome

Donald Harvey pleaded guilty to twenty-six counts of aggravated murder. His confession was part of a plea bargain that brought him three consecutive life sentences instead of the death penalty. Part of the plea bargain was the agreement that he would cooperate with Kentucky authorities in exchange for a jail term that would run concurrent with his Ohio terms (Helgason 1990).

128.02: HERO HOMICIDE

In a hero homicide, the offender creates a life-threatening condition for the victim and then unsuccessfully attempts to rescue/resuscitate the victim in order to appear valorous. Death is not intentional, but the bulk of cases reviewed have demonstrated that failures do not avert the offender from recidivism.

Defining Characteristics

Victimology. The victimology of this homicide is comparable to that of mercy homicide. It may include the critically ill patient because a medical emergency, such as cardiac arrest, would not appear suspicious. Infants are also included as likely victims of the hero murderer because of their mute vulnerability. When the crime scene is an institutional setting, the victim is one of opportunity with an increased risk factor due to this vulnerability that illness or age imposes. Outside the institutional setting, the victim is a random one who has become a victim of opportunity by being in the building the arsonist torches or in the zone where the emergency medical technician works.

Crime Scene Indicators Frequently Noted. The crime scene demonstrates many similarities to that of a mercy homicide. If the setting is an institutional one, the crisis is usually drug induced. Syringes, medicine vials, and similar items should be collected for analysis of medications or substances peculiar to that patient's particular case or condition. If the suspicious death involves a fire, then the elements of arson may be found.

Staging. In a sense, staging is the central element of this homicide. It is a miscarried attempt to stage a scenario, a life-threatening crisis, in which the offender has the starring role as the hero. The fire fighter or arsonist sets the fire, only to rush back for the rescue. The nurse or emergency medical technician make a timely response to the victim after inducing the state of crisis. The target is made to look like a victim of a natural calamity (e.g., a cardiac arrest), an accident (faulty wiring that starts the fire), or perhaps criminal activity (hit and run, mugging, arson, etc.).

Common Forensic Findings. Forensics findings are the same as for mercy homicide, with special emphasis on postmortem examination for toxic levels of injectable drugs such as digoxin, lidocaine, and potassium hydrochloride.

Investigative Considerations

In addition to the same considerations as for mercy homicide, if the crime scene is within the medical realm and has an unusually high rate of successful cardiopulmonary resuscitations in conjunction with an unusually high death rate, it should be examined. Multiple cardiac or respiratory arrests in the same patient also should raise suspicion. Most unwitnessed cardiopulmonary arrests and/or patients who have had multiple arrests do not respond to resuscitative measures. This could indicate that a hero killer happens to be among the first to the scene and knows the exact measures to remedy the problem.

Interviews of co-workers may reveal that the offender demonstrates an unusually high level of excitement or exhilaration while participating in the rescue or resuscitation efforts. Conversations of the offender may often involve the rescue/resuscitation incidents.

Search Warrant Suggestions

Vials of medications at the residence of the offender and literature concerning drugs beyond the scope of the offender's practice (e.g., the Physician's Desk Reference) are among search warrant suggestions for hero homicide. Other suggestions include diaries, journals, pictures, or newspaper articles commemorating previous rescue efforts and implements of arson.

CASE STUDY: 128.02: HERO HOMICIDE

Background

On 21 September 1981 Susan Maldonado and Pat Alberti reported to work for their usual shift at San Antonio Medical Center's Pediatric Intensive Care Unit (PICU). When they were greeted with the news that two of the unit's four young patients had died that evening, it strengthened a growing suspicion that Maldonado and Alberti recently had been trying to deny. The events of preceding months had made it increasingly more difficult to silence this suspicion.

During their break, the two nurses sat down with the PICU log book that kept track of each patient's name, age, admission diagnosis, admission date, doctor, discharge status, and assigned nurse. The correlation they found between the children that had died in the PICU during the prior months and the one person whose presence was documented during virtually every one of these codes (cardiac and/or respiratory arrest) presented the two nurses with an appalling reality: either the nurse who had been on duty had incredibly bad luck, or she was deliberately killing babies.

The nurse's name was Genene Jones. She had been considered the backbone of her shift at the medical center. She was experienced, cool headed, and seemingly dedicated to her patients. She was more comfortable with pediatric medicine then many physicians. Her nursing skills were superior when caring for critically ill babies, but it was during a crisis that she really seemed to shine.

Jones was a controversial figure. Her supporters described her as level headed, quick, knowledgeable, and extremely competent in a code situation. She was so devoted to her patients that she insisted on carrying the tiny bodies to the morgue herself after unsuccessful resuscitation attempts. It was reported that Jones would often cry and sing to the dead infants as she tenderly cradled them. When the question was raised about the number of babies that seemed to be dying under her care, the response was that she always took care of the most critically ill patients, so naturally she would have a lower recovery rate.

Jones's critics offered quite a different perspective. She bullied her way into any crisis in PICU, becoming argumentative with even the physicians who did not bow to her insistent recommendations. She threw temper tantrums if her authority was challenged and publicly berated the physicians in front of staff and patient families. Jones seemed to crave and relish the pinnacles of emotion that a PICU nurse could experience, working in a place where the stakes were so high. But the theatrics she indulged in were an extreme and unprofessional emotionalism.

When Jones's advisaries started noticing the rising death toll in PICU and her connection with the dying babies, it did not take much to convince them she was the perpetrator. But when Alberti and Maldonado brought their discovery to the attention of several administrators, including the head nurse, they were told to stop backbiting and spreading rumors.

Victimology

The infants who died at the medical center while under the care of Genene Jones ranged between the ages of three weeks to two years. The one exception was a ten-year-old child who was mentally retarded and had the developmental age of an infant. At the clinic in Kerrville, Texas, where Jones worked after leaving San Antonio, all of the children that experienced life-threatening crises in her presence were under age two, with the exception of a seven-year-old severely retarded child. All of these children were involved in a client/caregiver relationship with Jones, either directly, with her as their assigned nurse, or indirectly, with her responding to the code and/or present at the time of the infant's death.

Very general criteria for Jones's victim selection were the inability to talk and physical limitations due to age or developmental handicap. Excepting this, these children would have been considered victims of opportunity. Their chances of becoming a mortality statistic increased significantly if Jones had the opportunity to care for them, however briefly.

Crime Scene Indicators

The crime scenes involved two locations: the PICU and a pediatric clinic in Kerrville Texas, where Jones went after a policy was instituted at San Antonio Medical Center that LVNs could no longer staff the PICU.* One case finally brought Jones to justice.

Chelsea McClellan was a bright, healthy child of fourteen months when she was brought to Dr. Kathleen Holland's office in Kerrville on 24 August 1982. Chelsea was the second child to be seen in the new clinic. She was there because of Petti McClellan's concern over the sniffles her daughter had developed.

While pregnant with Chelsea, Petti McClellan had required an early Caesarean section. Chelsea had experienced respiratory problems due to this premature birth. Despite one bout of pneumonia at six months, from which she fully recovered, Chelsea had been in excellent health.

While Petti was talking with Dr. Holland, the office nurse, Genene Jones, took Chelsea from Petti. Chelsea was becoming impatient with sitting still, so Jones offered to entertain her. Within five minutes, Jones was calling with urgency in her voice for Holland to come into the examining room where she and Chelsea were. When Holland entered the room, she was confronted with the shocking site of the previously energetic, laughing child now draped limply over the treatment table.

Jones claimed that Chelsea suddenly had begun convulsing and stopped breathing. Once Dr. Holland provided Chelsea with oxygen, her blue coloring started to fade. She was transported to the hospital nearby, where she seemed to respond slowly, but her coordination was gone. Her arms would flop when she tried to reach for her face and remove her oxygen mask.

*This measure was taken after a special board of nurses and doctors from around the country reviewed the accumulating allegations that the abnormal rise of deaths in PICU was due to criminal activity. Ironically, the board pinpointed Pat Alberti as a whistle blower and as much of a problem to the PICU as Jones. They felt Jones was simply burned out, therefore the source of many personality conflicts. The panel suggested all LVNs be removed from PICU, therefore eliminating both problem nurses. They would be offered other positions in the hospital or termination with recommendations. Both Jones and Alberti chose termination. Jones went to Kerrville, with no mention on her record of the problems in San Antonio.

Within thirty minutes of admission to the intensive care unit, Chelsea was standing up in her crib, laughing and holding her arms out to the nurses who passed by. She was subjected to exhaustive testing, which revealed no abnormalities that may have caused the seizure episode. She was discharged from the hospital on 2 September. While hospitalized, Chelsea had someone at her bedside constantly. Nothing in addition to the normal movements of a sleeping child were noted by the family and friends who kept the ten-day vigil. Chelsea had no previous history of any seizure activity or apnea (cessation of breathing) before her visit to the Kerrville clinic where Jones worked.

On 17 September Petti McClellan brought Chelsea back to the clinic with her brother, Cameron, who had the flu. While Dr. Holland was looking at Cameron, Jones was to give Chelsea two routine infant immunizations. Jones tried to persuade Petti to leave while she inoculated the child, but Petti insisted it did not bother her to watch her children get shots. In addition, Chelsea had started acting upset when Jones reached for her.

McClellan recalled that Jones became irritated but acquiesced. As Petti held her daughter, Jones dabbed at her thigh with an alcohol swab and injected the first needle into the child's upper left thigh. Within seconds, Petti observed that Chelsea was not acting normally. Petti became extremely alarmed at this point and pleaded with Jones to do something. Jones insisted nothing was wrong, that Chelsea was just angry about getting the shots.

Despite Petti McClellan's telling Jones to stop, that Chelsea was having another seizure, Jones was intent on giving the child the second injection. As soon as she injected the second shot, Chelsea stopped breathing altogether, and her pink cheeks began to turn blue. Petti recalled that Chelsea appeared to try to say Mama and soon after went completely limp.

Again, Jones summoned Dr. Holland, and the scene of less than a month earlier was repeated. The ambulance responded at 10:58 A.M., speeding the child with Jones and an emergency medical technician to the hospital. Holland followed behind in her car. In the emergency room, within twenty-five minutes Chelsea was again thrashing and upset at having in her throat the tube that provided oxygen directly into her lungs.

Dr. Holland decided Chelsea needed to be transferred to San Antonio, where a neurologist could find out what was causing the episodes. Thirty-five minutes later, Chelsea was wheeled from the emergency room to a waiting ambulance. She was resting quietly, breathing with some assistance, and very pink. Holland reassured the frightened McClellans that the emergency had passed.

Jones climbed in the back of the ambulance with Chelsea for the ride to San Antonio. Holland followed in one car, and Chelsea's parents in another. Less than ten minutes out of Kerrville, the heart monitor attached to Chelsea began to sound an alarm. Jones yelled to the driver to pull over because Chelsea was suffering a cardiac arrest. She pulled syringes out of her medical bag and began administering drugs to stimulate the little girl's heart. By this time, Holland was in the ambulance and gave orders for the driver to proceed to the closest hospital.

Thirty-five minutes later, in the Comfort Community Hospital emergency room, Chelsea McClellan was pronounced dead. All attempts to restart her heart had failed, and she was beginning to show the inevitable signs of brain damage. Dr. Holland stated on the death certificate that death was caused by cardiopulmonary arrest due to seizures of undetermined origin.

After taking the dead child from her stunned, weeping mother, Jones accompanied the child back to the hospital in Kerrville. After arrival, she sobbed as she carried the body to the hospital morgue.

Counting the two emergency situations that involved Chelsea, there were six respiratory arrests during the Kerrville clinic's approximately one month of operation. The same day Chelsea died, five-month-old Jacob Evans was brought to the clinic because of an earache. He also experienced a respiratory arrest as a result of seizure activity reported by Jones. He was hospitalized and released six days later, never demonstrating any sign of a seizure disorder. A neurologist in San Antonio failed to uncover any possible source for the seizures after extensively testing Jacob.

The recurrence of life-threatening crises finally had attracted attention from the medical community. Dr. Holland began to entertain suspicions after Jones mentioned that some missing succinylcholine had been found.[†] Holland had never used this drug and wondered why it would even be out of its storage place in the refrigerator. The next day she checked the two bottles of succinylcholine in the refrigerator and discovered that one had its plastic seal removed and had two distinctive needle holes in the vial's rubber stopper. It also had a very slight difference in volume compared with the sealed vial.

When Holland confronted Jones, the nurse first explained the puncture as having been done, during one of the seizure episodes, by another nurse who was there when the emergency occurred. This nurse denied puncturing the stopper when questioned. Jones suggested that Holland just throw the vial away and forget the incident.

Dr. Holland responded that disposing of the vial was legally, medically, and ethically unacceptable to her. That afternoon, she submitted the vial to the Department of Public Safety for analysis after meeting with several doctors and the hospital administrator. While this was unfolding, Jones took a drug overdose and was briefly hospitalized.

[†]Succinylcholine is a drug that chemically blocks nerve transmissions to muscles. This results in a paralysis of all the body muscles, including the diaphragm (the muscle responsible for breathing), and in large doses, the heart is affected.

Jones had staged all of the incidents to appear as medical emergencies arising from the natural course of a physical illness or disorder. If each of the twenty-nine San Antonio PICU deaths that had been linked to Jones's presence were analyzed, this type of staging would emerge. It would also be evident in the six Kerrville emergencies.

Forensic Findings

It was determined that the rubber stopper of the capless vial had two puncture sites that had been used multiple times. When the contents were analyzed, it was discovered the succinylcholine was 80 percent dilute, probably with saline solution.

On 7 May 1983 Chelsea McClellan's body was exhumed, and tissue samples were removed for toxicology studies. Seven days later, the prosecuting attorney received the call that succinylcholine had been found in the gall bladder, urinary bladder, kidneys, liver, and both thighs.

Investigation

The correlation between infant mortality and Jones's presence was best illustrated by the PICU log book. This also demonstrated the localization of deaths to a particular shift. Jones was very often present at the moment of cardiac arrest or was among the first to respond.

Several witnesses to cardiac arrest situations involving Jones described her obvious state of excitement as beyond the usual level at a code situation. One went so far as to depict it as orgasmic.

There were a number of cardiac arrest situations that were successful involving Jones. In addition to the high number of codes, there were many patients who experienced multiple cardiopulmonary arrests (among survivors of the PICU epidemic as well as fatalities.)[‡]

From 9 November 1981 until 7 December 1981, Jones was out of work on sick leave for minor surgery. The PICU chart revealed that during most of the month of November and the first week of December, not a single baby died. In fact, there was not even a single code during the thirty-six day period surrounding Jones's absence.

Isolating some of the deaths into singular incidents allowed reasonable medical explanations for the course of events. But many of the deaths posed enigmas: excessive bleeding of unknown etiology, disruptions of the heart rhythm, seizures in children with no previous history of any seizure activity, and sudden respiratory arrests. Unfortunately, the administration of San Antonio Medical Center never recognized this compilation of facts

---

[‡]A cluster of deaths that is not associated with a change in population characteristics, an infectious disease outbreak, or a change in environment or procedures is termed *epidemic death.*

as worthy of criminal investigation. The medical examiner was never notified for any of these deaths, even when physicians began sharing the suspicion that nursing misadventure was involved. So Jones moved on to Kerrville, to Chelsea McClellan, with the hospital's recommendation.

Evidence presented at the trial showed that Jones had ordered three more bottles of succinylcholine from the Kerrville Pharmacy and had signed Dr. Holland's name to receipts. In addition, Chelsea's baby-sitter testified that she had observed Jones injecting something into the intravenous line as the child was being loaded into the ambulance for the trip to San Antonio. When she questioned Jones about it, Jones replied that it was something to relax Chelsea. This struck the baby-sitter as odd, as Chelsea was already resting quietly. This alleged relaxant had not been ordered by either Dr. Holland or the emergency department physician.

Outcome

Genene Jones was found guilty of first-degree murder and was sentenced to ninety-nine years on 15 February 1984. On 23 October 1984 she was convicted of felony injury to a child for an incident involving an overdose of heparin (a blood thinner) she had given an infant in the PICU. Despite massive bleeding and several cardiac arrests, that child was one of the few who survived (Moore & Reed 1988).

129: HOSTAGE MURDER

A hostage murder is a homicide that takes place within the context of a hostage situation. A *hostage* is defined as a person held and threatened by an offender to force the fulfillment of substantive demands made on a third party. In such situations, the victim clearly is being threatened by the offender, and the threats are used to influence someone else, usually the police. When this situation escalates and the victim is killed, it is hostage murder.

It is important to define what would not constitute a hostage situation and, therefore, a hostage murder. A *homicide-to-be* involves a situation where clear threats or actual injuries are made to victims and no substantive demands are made on a third party. These victims are primary targets of the offender and are not being used as bargaining chips for money or freedom. The offender who kills in this manner usually is impelled by other motivations, such as revenge or an authority conflict; therefore, this offense would be categorized under another, more appropriate classification.

A *pseudohostage situation* is when a person is held, but there are no threats directed toward the victim and no substantive demands are made on a third party. The following is an example of a pseudohostage situation: A husband pulls a gun on his wife during a domestic quarrel. She then leaves the house and summons police. Upon their arrival, the police learn the couple's son is still in the house. When he is contacted, the husband tells the police that he is angry at his wife and that they should leave him alone. Because he makes no demands on the police and does not threaten the child, this is a pseudohostage situation. Because the risk factors are low in this type of incident, the risk to the person held could be considered low. In the unusual event that the victim is killed, the motive, as before, would be categorized under a more suitable homicide classification.

Due to the lack of difficulty in identifying the offender in a hostage murder, this manual includes this category only for classification and definition purposes. The defining characteristics used for other classifications are unnecessary and, therefore, are omitted.

130: SEXUAL HOMICIDE

Sexual homicide involves a sexual element (activity) as the basis for the sequence of acts leading to death. Performance and meaning of this sexual element vary with the offender. The act may range from actual rape involving penetration (either before or after death) to a symbolic sexual assault, such as insertion of foreign objects into a victim's body orifices.

131: ORGANIZED SEXUAL HOMICIDE

The term *organized,* when used to describe a sexual homicide offender, is based on an assessment of the criminal act itself, on a comprehensive analysis of the victim(s) and the crime scene(s) (including any staging), and on an evaluation of forensic reports. These components combine to form traits common to an organized offender: one who appears to plan his murders, who targets his victims, and who displays control at the crime scene. A methodical and ordered approach is reflected through all phases of the crime.

Defining Characteristics

Victimology. The victim of a sexual homicide perpetrated by an organized offender is often female. Adolescent males also are targeted, as demonstrated in the case of John Wayne Gacy.[5] A single, employed person, living alone, is common to this victimology.

---

[5]John Wayne Gacy lured at least thirty-three young men, ranging in age from fourteen to the mid twenties, to their deaths.

The concept of victim risk is an important factor in assessing the victimology. Risk is a two-fold factor. Victim risk is determined by age, lifestyle, occupation, and physical stature. Low-risk types include those whose daily life-styles and occupations do not enhance their chances of being targeted as victims. High-risk victims are ones who are targeted by a killer who knows where to find them (e.g., prostitutes or hitchhikers). Low resistance capabilities, as found in the elderly or the young, elevate the level of victim risk. Risk also can be elevated by locations where the victim becomes more vulnerable, such as isolated areas. A victim's attitude toward safety is also a factor that can raise or lower the risk factor. A naive, overly trusting, or careless stance concerning personal safety can further one's chance of being victimized.

The second facet of victim risk is in the level of gamble the offender takes to commit the crime. Generally, the victim is at a lower risk level if the crime scene is indoors and at a higher risk level if it is outdoors. The time of day that the crime occurs also contributes to the amount of risk the offender takes: an abduction at noon would pose more hazard to the offender that one at midnight.

The victim typically is not known to the offender but is often chosen because he or she meets certain criteria. These criteria are seen especially if multiple victims are involved (i.e., they will share common characteristics, such as age, appearance, occupation, hairstyle, or life-style). The victim is targeted at the location where the killer is staked out; therefore, he or she becomes a victim of opportunity. Consequently, investigators may not observe similarities in the victim characteristics.

Crime Scene Indicators Frequently Noted. There are very often multiple crime scenes involved with the organized killing: the local of initial contact/ assault, the scene of death, and the body disposal site. If the victim is confronted indoors, the first crime scene (confrontation) is commonly the first or second floor of a building or a single-family dwelling. The offender may then transport the victim or body from the site of confrontation, necessitating the use of the offender's or the victim's vehicle.

Weapons generally are brought to the crime scene but are removed by the offender after the completion of the crime. The presence of tape, blindfolds, chains, ropes, clothing, handcuffs, gags, or chemicals indicates the use of restraints. The use of restraints is reflected by the overall controlled, planned appearance of the crime scene. It reflects a methodical approach with a semblance of order existing prior to, during, and after the offense. If the offender has time, evidence such as fingerprints and footprints will be removed.

Also missing from the crime scene may be so-called trophies or souvenirs, which include pictures, jewelry, clothing, or a driver's license belonging to the victim. These items do not necessarily have much extrinsic value, but to the offender they commemorate the successful endeavor and offer proof of his skill. They also serve as a means to fuel the fantasy of the act by serving as a remembrance.

Finally, if the offender has enough time, the victim's corpse will be concealed. The location for disposal is generally an area familiar to the offender.

Staging. Staging may be present at the crime scene(s). The subject may stage the crime to appear careless and disorganized to distract or mislead police. He may stage secondary criminal activity (e.g., a robbery) to cloud the basis for the primary motive of sexual murder.

Common Forensic Findings. The forensic findings of an organized sexual homicide may be bite marks and saliva recovery on the body, semen in body orifices or on body pubic hair, and bruising or cutting of the sex organs. Aggressive acts as well as sexual acts will usually have occurred prior to death. Evidence of restraint devices may also be present.

The act of killing may be eroticized, meaning death comes in a slow, deliberate manner. An asphyxial modality is often noted. An example of this is the deliberate tightening and loosening of a rope around the victim's neck as he or she slips in and out of a conscious state. Sexual activity in which sexual acts are performed in conjunction with the act of killing may also be found.

Investigative Consideration

Because the offender is usually socially adept, he often uses verbal means (the con) to capture the victim. He may strike up a conversation or a pseudorelationship as a prelude to the attack. He may impersonate another role, such as a police officer or security guard, to gain victim confidence. To further gain access to the victim, the offender typically will be dressed neatly, either in business or casual attire.

The methodical approach common to this offender is incorporated into victim selection after he has staked out an area. When neighbors are questioned, particular attention should be paid to any strangers noted lingering around the neighborhood or anyone whose actions or appearance are described above.

The organized sexual murderer often returns for surveillance of any or all of the crime scenes involved (point of abduction, assault, grave site). He may go so far as to interject himself into the investigation in an overly cooperative way or to offer bogus information. This serves the dual purpose of checking on the status of the investigation and/or reliving the crime.

A possible suspect may have a history of prior offenses of lesser notice, escalating to the homicide. His background should be checked for precipitating situational stress, such as financial, employment, or marital/other relationship problems. He may have a history of recent residence or employment change. He may even have left town after the murder. If property is missing, local areas should be checked for burglaries.

Search Warrant Suggestions

Items that should be kept in mind when preparing a search warrant are diaries, calenders, or newspaper clippings that commemorate the murder. Recordings may be found, either audio or videotaped. Photographs of victims are another possible finding. The souvenirs/trophies (victim belongings) mentioned earlier should also be considered when formulating a search warrant. Any law enforcement or similarly related paraphernalia should also be looked for.

CASE STUDY: 131: ORGANIZED SEXUAL HOMICIDE

Background

The local police department of Columbia, South Carolina, received a worried call from the parents of a seventeen-year-old girl. Their daughter had ridden her bike to the end of their driveway to get the mail and had never returned. When the parents went looking for her, they found her bike by the mailbox, along the curb.

After the abduction, the offender made several phone calls to the family and conversed primarily with the victim's older sister. He used an electronic device to disguise his voice because, as he indicated, he was known to the family. These calls continued after the victim's death. The offender made references to a letter, the victim's last will and testament, that he had sent to them. Even though the victim died shortly after her abduction, the offender led the family to believe the victim was still alive until they found her body a week later.

A nine-year-old white female, the second victim, was abducted from her yard one week following the discovery of the first victim's body. The offender contacted the first victim's sister and told her of the abduction and killing of the younger girl as well as the location of the body. During the last telephone conversation, the offender advised the first victim's sister that she would be the next to die.

Victimology

Investigation of both victims revealed that they were low-risk victims. However, the fact that they were not likely to have had the physical strength to fight or resist a strong male assailant increased their risk factor slightly. In the case of the first victim, it appeared the offender was taking pictures of her on her bike as she arrived at the mailbox. She became a victim of opportunity because she crossed the offender's path when he was in search of a victim. The nine-year-old child was taken from her play area. This time, the offender may have been out looking for a victim, or he may have happened upon this victim and decided to act. This abduction was less sophisticated, so it probably was more of an opportunistic incident.

Crime Scene Indicator

The offender had communicated by telephone with the first victim's parents two days after the abduction and then with the victim's sister. With his voice disguised, the offender asked for forgiveness and expressed remorse. He gave the impression the victim was still alive. He told the victim's family he had taken her to a house, where she was tied to a bed. Twelve hours later, the offender gave the victim a choice of the method of her death: strangulation, suffocation, or drowning. The victim chose suffocation, and the offender placed duct tape over her nose and mouth.

The offender appeared to be following a written script. For example, when interrupted over the telephone by family members of the victim, he became upset. This suggested his obsessive-compulsive need to articulate details rigidly to the family. He gave directions to the crime scene that were so detailed that it was obvious he had gone back to the crime scene to measure distances. The victim's body was placed in an area where she was well concealed.

Indicators from the body disposal site suggested that the subject was familiar with the area. There were three locations involved with each crime: the abduction site, the death scene, and the grave site. The offender interacted with his victims, so he needed a place where he could comfortably spend an extended period of time with them. This location, also the murder scene, was discovered to be where the offender was house-sitting. The grave sites were also locations with which he was familiar.

Forensic Findings

The forensic findings indicated both victims had been found with ligatures and duct tape. All bindings had been removed from the bodies before disposal. Duct-tape residue was found on both victims' faces. The offender claimed that the victims had been smothered. The bodies were too decomposed for investigators to determine if they had been sexually assaulted. However, the offender admitted to sexually assaulting both victims. Both victims were fully clothed when their bodies were discovered.

Investigation

The crime was organized in terms of the abduction, murder, and body disposal. A reconstruction of the crime/death scene indicated some offender sophistication in terms of the phone calls to the victims' families, his fantasy, and the degree of planning. He made the first victim write her last will and testament on a legal pad. The will was actually a letter to her family stating that she was ready to die and that she loved them. The offender mailed the letter to the family.

This letter was sent to the state laboratory for analysis, which revealed indented writing not visible to the naked eye. The writing was identified as a phone number with one digit obliterated. By a process of elimination, people with similar phone numbers were interviewed until a list of possible suspects was developed. One telephone number belonged to a house in the abduction locale. When police contacted the person at this number, he told them his parents were not at home but had someone house-sitting for them. His parents had given the house-sitter their son's number to use in case of any problems. The house-sitter's name was Larry Gene Bell.

While this investigation was continuing criminal investigative analysts from the FBI Investigative Support Unit had been consulted. They had generated an offender profile and some investigative techniques for the local police department. When the offender was identified, he matched almost every offender characteristic listed. Larry Gene Bell was a thirty-six-year-old white male who worked doing electrical wiring in homes. At the time of the murders, he was living with his mother and father. He had been married for a short time and had lived away home.

The ISU agents provided an interrogation strategy that would offer a face-saving explanation for Bell. Bell confessed, claiming the "bad Larry Gene Bell did it."

Outcome

Larry Gene Bell was given two death sentences for the murders of the two girls. He is currently under investigation for a third murder.

132: DISORGANIZED SEXUAL HOMICIDE

The term *disorganized,* when used in reference to a sexual homicide, is based on the same factors that defined organized sexual homicide: victim and crime scene analysis, forensic evaluation, and assessment of the act itself. The unplanned, spontaneous nature of the disorganized perpetrator's crime is reflected in each of these factors. This disorganization may be the result of youthfulness of the offender, lack of criminal sophistication, use of drugs and alcohol, and/or mental deficiency.

Defining Characteristics

Victimology. The victim of a disorganized offender may be known to the offender because he often selects a victim of opportunity near his residence or employment. The victim is often from his own geographic area because this offender acts impulsively under stress and also because he derives confidence from familiar surroundings. If there are multiple victims of a disorganized offender, the age, sex, and other victim characteristics show greater variance due to the more random nature of his selection process.

The risk factor of a disorganized sexual homicide victim is situational in the sense that by crossing the path of the offender, the risk of becoming a victim is greatly elevated. The victim essentially becomes a casualty because he or she was in the wrong place at the wrong time. The other considerations when assessing victim and offender risk are the same as detailed for the organized offender.

Crime Scene Indicators Frequently Noted. The crime scene of a disorganized sexual homicide reflects the spontaneous and, in some cases, symbolic quality of the killing. It is random and sloppy with great disarray. The death scene and the crime scene are often the same.

The victim/location is known because it usually is where he or she was going about daily activities when suddenly attacked. There is evidence of sudden violence to the victim, a blitz style of attack. Depersonalization may be present as evidenced by the victim's face being covered by a pillow or towels or by the body being found rolled on the stomach (a more subtle form of depersonalization).

There is no set plan of action by the offender for deterring detection. The weapon is one of opportunity, obtained at the scene and left there. There is little or no effort to remove evidence, such as fingerprints, from the scene. The body is left at the death scene, often in the position in which the victim was killed. There is no attempt or only minimal attempt to conceal the body.

Staging. Secondary criminal activity may be present, but usually it is indicative of a less sophisticated offender (disorganized offenders are often of below-average intelligence) rather than of staging to confuse law enforcement. The body may be positioned or deposited in a way that has special significance for the offender, based on his sexually violent fantasies. Body position may be intended to make a statement or to obscure certain facts about the crime (e.g., to disguise postmortem mutilation he is uncomfortable with). In such positioning, the offender is generating a personal expression (personation) rather than deliberately trying to confuse police.[6]

---

[6]Personation is the investing of characteristics or intimate meaning into the crime scene in the form of body positioning, mutilation, items left, or other symbolic gestures involving the crime scene.

Another example of the disorganized offender's personation of his ritualized sexual fantasies is excessive mutilation of the breasts, genitals, or other areas of sexual association (thighs, abdomen, buttocks, and neck). This overkill is the enactment of his fantasy.

Common Forensic Findings. The disorganized offender is often socially inept and has strong feelings of inadequacy. These feelings of deficiency compel him to assault the victim in an ambush or blitz style of attack that will immediately incapacitate the victim. Injury during a disorganized sexual homicide usually occurs when the offender feels the least intimidated and the most comfortable with the victim. This will be when the victim is unconscious, dying, or dead. In addition, sexual assault will probably occur at this time for the same reasons.

There may be depersonalization that entails mutilation to the face and overkill (excessive amount or severity of wounds or injury) to specific body parts. The face, genitals, and breasts are most often targeted for overkill. Body parts may be missing from the scene.

The blitz style of attack common to this homicide is often manifested by focused blunt trauma to the head and face and by the lack of defensive wounds. There is a prevalence of attacks from behind. Because death is immediate in order for the offender to establish control over the victim, there is minimal use of restraints.

Sexual acts occur after the victim's death and often involve the insertion of foreign objects into body orifices (insertional necrophilia). This is often combined with acts of mutilation (e.g., slashing, stabbing, and biting of the buttocks and breasts). Because these acts often do not coincide with completed acts of sexual penetration, evidence of semen may be found on the victim's clothing and (less frequently) in the victim's wounds. Most often death results from asphyxia, strangulation, blunt force, or the use of a pointed, sharp instrument.

Investigative Considerations

The disorganized offender usually lives alone or with a parental figure. He lives or works within close proximity to the crime scene. He has a history of inconsistent or poor work performance. He also has a past that demonstrates a lack of interpersonal skills, which may be manifested by involvement in relationships with a partner much younger or much older than the offender.

Preoffense circumstances demonstrate minimal situational stress and change in life-style. The offender will be considered odd by those who know him. This offender usually is sloppy and disheveled and has nocturnal habits, such as walking aimlessly around his neighborhood.

Post offense behavior may include a change in eating habits and drinking habits (more alcohol consumption) and nervousness. He also may have an inappropriate interest in the crime, evidenced by his frequently engaging in conversation about it.

Search Warrant Suggestions

The disorganized offender does not concern himself with concealment of bloody clothing, shoes, or other evidentiary items (such as the victim's belongings taken from the crime scene). In addition, souvenirs that serve as remembrances of the event and fuel the fantasy of the act may be found among offender possessions.

CASE STUDY: 132: DISORGANIZED SEXUAL HOMICIDE

Background

Jennifer Sidal, age twelve, and her sister, Elaine, age fourteen, had decided to stop looking for Jenny's bicycle, stolen a few hours earlier.* It was 8:00 P.M. and already dark out, so the two girls headed for home, Jenny on foot and Elaine on her bike. As Elaine rounded the corner of an electric supply store, she glanced back and saw Jenny walking slowly, still a block away. Jenny had a physical problem that often caused her to lag behind the other children. Mentally, Jenny was very bright, with good grades in school. Even though she was somewhat of a loner, she was considered friendly and was always quick to help others. Jenny lived with her mother and sister. Her parents had divorced twelve years earlier, and although her father lived about twelve blocks away, she had not seem him for over a year. Elaine arrived home a little after 8:00 P.M. Jenny never made it home.

Victimology

Jenny's risk for being targeted as a victim of violent crime was minimalized due to her life-style, social habits, and residence in a low-crime neighborhood. However, her young age and physical limitations elevated this risk factor. Because she was slower than other children, it was easier for an offender to single her out and separate her from a group. Her trusting attitude also may have been a factor elevating her risk level.

Crime Scene Indicators

The next day, Jenny's body was discovered by her uncle, who was searching the area along with police and neighbors. The body was approximately halfway down a steep creek bank behind the electrical supply store. The

---

*The names have been changed in this case study because a conviction is pending.

creek had dense, high weeds and trees lining both banks. Although it was fenced off, there was a hole in the fence, near the electrical supply store, that neighborhood youths would use when traveling to the adjacent residential area from local businesses.

The body was found approximately 10 feet down the creek bank path. A small tree had prevented it from falling completely down the embankment. The embankment was quite steep, with an angle of almost 90 degrees, and it was approximately 30 feet from path to creek. The victim's shirt and bra were in place, but the body was nude from the waist down except for the socks. Some of the clothing was scattered along the creek bank, and jeans and underpants were found in the creek. The jeans were slit by a sharp instrument from the bottom cuff to just above both knees.

This crime scene was typical of the disorganized offender. The assault site, death scene, and body recovery site were all the same location. The weapon was one of opportunity: the offender used his fists to gain control initially and then his arm to strangle the victim. The attack was a blitz-style attack in which the offender struck Jenny with enough force to render her unconscious immediately. The body was left at the scene with little or no effort to conceal it. The crime scene portrayed the randomness and sloppiness characteristic of a disorganized offender. There is a high probability that footprints and other physical evidence had been left, but much of it was probably removed by a heavy rainfall before the body was discovered.

Forensic Findings

The autopsy revealed that Jenny had died of strangulation. It was initially thought to be ligature strangulation by something large, such as her jeans. The offender later described using his arm from behind to strangle her.

Focused blunt-force trauma, or depersonalization, was present. Jenny's face had been badly beaten, with numerous cuts, abrasions, and contusions about the mouth and cheekbone areas. There was a lack of defensive wounds, another common forensic finding of this type of offense because the victim most often has little chance to fight back. Restraints were not used. A large amount of semen was found within the vaginal cavity; no seman was found elsewhere.

A more bizarre forensic finding noted with this case (yet routinely observed with the disorganized sexual killer) was the presence of deep postmortem cuts on the victim's wrists and forearms. There were also several hesitation cuts to these same areas. These cuts were almost exploratory in nature, reflecting the offender's curiosity. They were not part of the sexual assault.

Investigation

As result of numerous interviews by the local police, a sketch was prepared and placed on local television and newspapers. In conjunction with this, the FBI Investigative Support Unit provided an offender profile. The offender was profiled as living in the same area as the victim. He would have been known as a troublemaker who liked knives and would have had previous contacts with the police, although not necessarily any arrests.

Outcome

Several neighbors of the victim (and suspect) called police to report that a person who closely resembled the sketch lived in their neighborhood. Further investigation revealed this subject exactly matched the profile. The police again consulted the ISU for interrogation techniques to be used with this subject. As a result, seventeen-year-old Joseph Rogers confessed and then reenacted the crime for investigators. It was discovered that he had several previous contacts with Jenny, talking to her several nights before the attack. He was living several blocks away from her with a sixteen-year-old girlfriend. He had left home to make it on his own. He had drifted around, was unemployed, and was a high school dropout.

133: MIXED SEXUAL HOMICIDE

It is important to note that a crime scene may reflect aspects of both organized and disorganized characteristics for the following reasons:

1. More than one offender may be involved; therefore, differing behavioral patterns will be manifested.
2. The attack may begin as a well-ordered, planned assault but may deteriorate as unanticipated events occur (e.g., an inability to control the victim).
3. The primary motive for the attack may be solely rape, but victim resistance or the offender's emotional state may lead to an escalation. This is especially seen with the hostile/retaliatory type of rapist. The victim selection may reflect an organized offender (i.e., careful selection and stalking of the victim), but the body is not concealed or is poorly concealed. The weapon is one of opportunity (e.g., a rock) that is left at the scene, and the crime scene shows great disarray. Forensic findings show a blitz style of attack, overkill, blunt-force trauma, and often personal weapon use (hands and feet).
4. Inconsistencies in offender behavior manifested during the offense may exhibit varying degrees of organized/disorganized behavior. The youthfulness of the offender and alcohol or drug involvement also contribute to a mixed crime scene.
5. External stressors also may alter the behavior of an offender. Precipi-

tating factors that cause a buildup of tension may lead to an explosive, impetuous assault by a person who would norally approach the crime with planning and control. Ted Bundy is an especially appropriate example of this degeneration of an organized killer into an disorganized one due to external stressors. With all of his abduction-rape murders previous to the Chi Omega murders, he carefully selected, stalked, and abducted his victims and used meticulous body concealment. His discomfort with the fugitive life-style, among other things, led to the explosive homicidal spree in which he bludgeoned random victims of opportunity. Bundy used a weapon of opportunity obtained at the crime scene and left near another. He left the victims' bodies openly displayed at the death scene, a marked departure from his usual attempts at body disposal. All of these later actions describe the typical behavior of the disorganized killer.

CASE STUDY: 133: MIXED SEXUAL HOMICIDE

Background

Donna Lynn Vetter was a quiet, hard-working woman who had been raised in a rural environment that did not seem to equip her for life in San Antonio, Texas. Vetter used fresh air through open windows and doors instead of the air conditioner in order to save electricity: in her mind, frugality was more of an issue in deciding where she had lived than was the possibility of rape or murder. It was this naive and unsuspecting attitude that became a contributing factor to her death.

Victimology

Vetter worked as a stenographer for the FBI in San Antonio. She had left home for the first time seven months earlier to move closer to her job. She was described as a quiet and hard-working introvert who rarely initiated conversation with fellow employees.

Donna Vetter would have been considered less likely to be targeted as a victim when one considers characteristics that determine victim risk level. Her employment as an FBI stenographer; conservative dress and life-style (she did not frequent bars or nightclubs); total lack of alcohol use, drug use, and criminal history; modest income; and quiet, withdrawn personality all contributed to this low-risk status. In addition, her age and physical state (no handicaps) did not increase her vulnerability.

However, there were two factors that elevated her risk factor. One was the location of her apartment: an industrialized and commercial area of a lower-income, blue-collar neighborhood. The second factor was her trusting attitude and lack of concern for personal safety. She simply would smile at the concerns that fellow employees or apartment security officers voiced over her lack of safety precautions.

On 4 September 1986 at 9:10 P.M., Vetter was observed watching TV and doing leg exercises by a neighbor walking by her open window. At 10:30 P.M., as several other neighbors passed by her apartment, one noticed that the front window screen had been pulled out and notified security officers. Apartment security responded at 10:35 P.M. and found the front door ajar. Upon entering the apartment, they discovered Vetter's nude body lying on the floor and covered with blood.

Crime Scene Indicators

Vetter was found lying on her back on the living room floor. The assault site appeared to be in the kitchen, where the greatest concentration of blood was found. A kitchen knife, a weapon of opportunity, was responsible for her wounds. It was found stuck between chair cushions. She had been dragged from the kitchen through the dining room, leaving a pronounced trail of blood. In the kitchen were her shorts, shirt, bra, and underwear, apparently cut and torn off. Her glasses were under the dining room table. Her car keys were on the table. There were no indications of ransacking in the apartment, and nothing appeared to be missing. The point of entry had been the front window, where the screen was pulled out and a plant was overturned just inside. There were footprints, and palm prints were found on the murder weapon and living room end table.

The primary motive for this attack was rape, but when Vetter offered resistance, the offender responded with violence. Fighting back only heightened the anger and need for retaliation that he usually vented through raping. His inflamed emotional state made the line between rape and murder an easy one to cross.

Initial contact between Vetter and the offender was a blitz style of attack. She was coming out of the bathroom when he hit her in the face, knocking her to the floor in an unconscious state. Apparently, she recovered enough to make it to the kitchen and obtain a knife. The offender grabbed the knife and repeatedly stabbed Vetter, dragged her to the living room, and sexually assaulted her as she lay dying.

The death scene and crime scene were the same, with no attempt to conceal the body. Palm prints, fingerprints, and footprints were left at the scene; all components indicative of the offender's disregard of physical evidence due to the frenzied, unexpected escalation of violence. His inability to establish control over Vetter brought about a deterioration of events that resulted in a more disorganized crime scene.

Forensic Findings

Vetter had sustained blunt-force trauma to the face. In addition, there were three stab wounds to the chest, with one wound penetrating the heart, and stab wounds to the right calf and left upper thigh. There were defensive wounds to three fingers of the left hand; there also was evidence of sexual assault.

A blitz-style attack, common to the retaliatory rapist who wants control of the victim as quickly as possible, was evident. The facial injuries were evidence of the excessive level of force employed by this type of rapist, especially when confronted with a resisting victim.

Investigation

On 24 September 1986 the San Antonio Police Department arrested twenty-two-year-old Karl Hammond for the rape of a 30-year-old San Antonio woman. He was later linked to Donna Vetter's death when palm prints on the outside living room window and living room end table, fingerprints on the murder weapon, and footprints in the apartment all proved to be his.

Hammond was a repeat offender; he had been convicted for the rape of a seventeen-year-old girl five years earlier. He had struck her in the face when she refused him sex, then raped her. He also was arrested for burglary three days after his release on bond for the rape charge. After serving four years, Hammond had been released from the state prison on 23 August 1985 under provisions of a mandatory release program. At the time of his arrest, he was suspected of as many as fifteen other rapes.

Outcome

Hammond was convicted of first-degree murder and given the death penalty. Before his sentencing, he escaped through an unlocked door in the jail but was recaptured within forty-eight hours. He is presently appealing his sentence.

134: SADISTIC MURDER

A sexual sadist is someone who has established "an enduring pattern of sexual arousal in response to sadistic imagery" (Dietz, Hazelwood & Warren 1990, 165). Sexual gratification is obtained from torture involving excessive mental and physical means. The offender derives the greatest satisfaction from the victim's response to torture. Sexually sadistic fantasies in which sexual acts are paired with domination, degradation, and violence are translated into criminal action that results in death.

Defining Characteristics:

Victimology. Sadistic murder victimology has some similarities to the victimology described for organized sexual homicide (Dietz, Hazelwood & Warren 1990). The largest focus group of sexual sadists are white, female adults who are strangers. The victimology of this crime may include males, and multiple offenders have been known to prey on both women and men and may also target children. Nevertheless, exclusive victimization of children is less frequent. Blacks are preyed upon to a much lesser extent. There is an occasional indication of resemblance between a victim and someone of significance in the offender's life.

The victims are chosen through systematic stalking and surveillance. They are approached under a pretext, such as the offender's requesting or offering assistance, asking directions, or impersonating a police officer. A ruse may be employed, such as posing as a talent scout looking for prospective models or actresses and promising them jobs.

Crime Scene Indicators Frequently Noted. There are often multiple crime scenes involved with this type of sexual homicide: the place of initial encounter, the torture/death scene, and/or the body disposal site. The very nature of this crime, sadism expressed through torture, necessitates a secluded or solitary place for the prolonged period of time the offender spends with the victim. This captivity may be from a few hours to as long as six weeks. The offender's residence may be used if it can provide the required seclusion. The offender's vehicle may have been altered for use in abduction and torture: disabled windows and doors, soundproofing, and installed police accessories (Dietz, Hazelwood & Warren 1990).

Gloves are often worn by the offender to avoid leaving fingerprints. Secluded sites are selected well in advance. The offender undertakes his crime with methodical preparation, and the crime scene reflects this. Torture racks or specially equipped torture rooms are constructed. Weapons and torture implements of choice are brought to the scene and removed if the scene is outside.

Restraints are usually present at the crime scene because they are common to this homicide. Sexual bondage, which is the elaborate and excessive use of binding material, unnecessarily neat and symmetrical binding, or binding that enables placing the victim in a variety of positions that enhance the offender's sexual arousal, also is noted (Dietz, Hazelwood & Warren 1990).

The use of customized modes of torture may be evident, especially at the scene of torture and/or death, and include electrical appliances, vise grips, pliers, foreign objects used for insertion, and whips. Sexual arousal occurs most often with the victim's expression of pain and is evidenced by sexual fluids or possibly defecation at the scene.

The body is routinely concealed, especially with the more organized offender, who is prepared with shovels, lime, and/or remote burial sites. Bodies also have been burned. Sometimes inconsistencies are noted, however, as bodies have been left where they will be seen by intimates, have been easily found, or have been disposed of carelessly (Dietz, Hazelwood & Warren 1990). Occasionally, the body may be transported to a location that increases the chance of discovery because the offender wants the excitement derived from the publicity that the body's discovery generates.

Staging. It is possible that there are implications of overkill and/or depersonalization for pragmatic reasons (e.g., to obscure the victim's identity). The offender also may tamper with the crime scene by staging secondary criminal activity (e.g., rape murder, robbery) to veil the primary motive of sadistic murder.

Common Forensic Findings. The offender engages in sex with the victim prior to the victim's death. The most prevalent sexual acts to be forced on victims are as follows (in decreasing order): anal rape, forced fellatio, vaginal rape, and foreign object penetration (Dietz, Hazelwood & Warren 1990). A majority of offenders force their victims to engage in all of these activities. The attack occurs before death because the primary source of pleasure for the sadistic killer is in the pain caused the victim as opposed to the actual sexual act.

The focus of battery is on the sex organs, genitals, and breasts. Sexually sadistic acts may include biting or overkill to areas with sexual association: thighs, buttocks, neck, and abdomen in addition to the breasts and genitals. However, injury can be anywhere that causes suffering.

There is insertion of foreign objects into vaginal and/or anal cavities, often combined with the act of slashing, cutting, or biting the breasts and buttocks (Dietz, Hazelwood & Warren 1990). Evidence of sexual fluids will usually be found in the body orifices or around the body. If partners are involved, they may be evidenced by differing sexual fluids and public hairs. Offenders may also urinate on the victim.

Ligature marks are common, as restraints are used frequently along with blindfolds and gags. Sexual bondage is also prevalent.

The fact that the offender usually spends a long time with the victim is evidenced by varying wound/injury ages or varying stages of healing in injuries inflicted by the offender. Blunt-force trauma from beatings, injuries from painful insertion, biting, whipping, twisting breasts, and burn marks from heat sources and electrical devices are all possible forensic findings.

There are cases where victims were forced to drink or eat feces. Stomach contents would reveal this as well as any variations of it.

The act of killing is often eroticized: death comes in a slow, deliberate manner that is savored by the offender. But because an unconscious or dead victim does not afford the offender the gratification he seeks, great care is taken not to end the victim's life prematurely. In several cases, offenders not only took special measures to keep their victims conscious, but also actually revived near-dead victims in order to cause additional suffering (Dietz, Hazelwood & Warren 1990).

The most common cause of death is by an asphyxial modality in the form of ligature strangulation, manual strangulation, hanging, and suffocation. Gunshot wounds, cutting and stabbing wounds, and blunt-force trauma are other, less frequent forensic findings concerning cause of death (Dietz, Hazelwood & Warren 1990).

Investigative Considerations

The perpetrators of sexually sadistic homicides are predominately white males. Sometimes a partner is involved, either male or female. The offenders may be married while committing the offense, as shown by recent research data: 43 percent of sadistic murderers are married and 50 percent have children (Dietz, Hazelwood & Warren 1990).

The offender is very often involved in an occupation that brings him into contact with the public. He engages in antisocial behavior that may be manifested in arrest records (not necessarily for sex-related offenses) and a history of drug abuse other than alcohol. He is often a police buff who possesses paraphernalia, literature, and weapons collections. The offender is likely to have a well-maintained vehicle because excessive driving is also characteristic of the sexual sadist (Dietz, Hazelwood & Warren 1990). The offender may return to the scene(s) to determine if the body has been discovered or to check on the progress of the investigation.

Search Warrant Suggestions

The following are items, common to sadistic offenders, that should be included in a search warrant:

1. Items realted to sexual or violent themes: pornographic literature, videos, bondage paraphernalia, detective magazines, sexual devices, women's undergarments
2. Gun collections, police uniforms, badges, counterfeit ID, books detailing law enforcement procedures
3. Items in vehicle: modification items to resemble police car (black-wall tires, two-way radios, scanner, whip antenna, flashing red lights, sirens); items for abduction and/or torture (door handles and windows disabled, soundproofing, restraining devices); shovels, lime, and other burial equipment; water; food; extra fuel
4. Torture devices, cameras, recording equipment
5. Items dealing with offenses: written records, manuscripts, diaries,

threatening letters, calendars, sketches, drawings, audio tapes, video-tapes, photographs

6. Personal items belonging to victims: undergarments, shoes, jewelry, wallets, driver's license, other victim ID

CASE STUDY: 134: SADISTIC MURDER

Background

During the last year of his incarceration at California Men's Colony at San Luis Obispo, Roy Lewis Norris met Lawrence Sigmund Bittaker. Both inmates had an extensive criminal history that involved a substantial amount of violent criminal activity. As the relationship developed, the two discovered a topic of mutual interest: dominating, torturing, and raping women. They also shared the attitude that with any future sexual assaults on women, they would leave no witnesses.

Bittaker was released in November 1978 and Norris in January 1979. After their reunion, the duo decided to perpetrate their prison ambitions. The first thing they needed was the proper vehicle to ensure uncomplicated abductions. Bittaker found a 1977 silver General Motors cargo van with a sliding door and no windows on the side, perfect for grabbing their victims with minimal fuss.

Bittaker and Norris felt well prepared after spending the first half of 1979 outfitting the van with a twin-size mattress supported by wood and ply-wood, tools, clothes, and a cooler. They also had carefully selected a remote area in the San Gabriel Mountains above the city of Glendora, California. They found a gated fire road that Bittaker secured with his own lock, added insurance that they would be left undisturbed. In addition, they had picked up more than twenty hitchhikers, not attacking any of them, but simply rehearsing for the right day.

The right day came on 24 June 1979 and at least four other times between June and 31 October 1979. During that time period, Bittaker and Norris were responsible for at least five murders.

Victimology

Lucinda Schaeffer, age sixteen, lived with her grandmother in Torrance, California. She was an attractive teenager who was active in her church, including the senior-high fellowship group. On 24 June 1979 she attended a fellowship meeting at St. Andrews Presbyterian Church in Redondo Beach. She decided to leave early and walked home along the Pacific Coast Highway instead of calling her grandmother for a ride.

Bittaker spotted her. The van pulled alongside her, and Norris asked her if she wanted to go for a ride and smoke some marijuana. She refused and kept on walking, with Norris and Bittaker following at a distance. When they reached a residential area with little traffic, the two men made their move. Bittaker pulled up ahead of her, stopping the van in front of a driveway while Norris waited on the sidewalk as Schaeffer approached. When she reached him, she exchanged a few words with him. Norris then grabbed her and dragged her to the van, threw her inside, and slammed the door. The van squealed away, and Bittaker turned the radio up to mask Cindy Schaeffer's screams. Norris taped her mouth and bound her bands and feet as they drove to the fire road.

Once they arrived, Bittaker and Norris smoked some marijuana while asking Schaeffer questions about her family and boyfriend in Wisconsin. After they became bored with that, Bittaker took a walk while Norris raped her and forced her to perform fellatio. When Bittaker returned, he continued the sexual assault until Norris came back for more.

After they were done, Norris attempted to strangle Schaeffer but lost his nerve when he saw the anguished look in her eyes. Bittaker took over until Schaeffer collapsed on the ground, convulsing and attempting to breathe. Bittaker remarked that it took more to strangle someone than shown on TV; the two men then tightened a coat hanger around her neck with a pair of vise-grip pliers until she was finally still. They wrapped her body with a blue shower curtain so the blood from the hanger cutting into her neck would not get on the van's carpet and dumped her body over the side of a deep canyon.

On 8 July Bittaker and Norris again were stalking victims on the Pacific Coast Highway when they spotted Andrea Joy Hall, age eighteen, hitchhiking. The first attempt to pick her up was unsuccessful because she got into a white convertible, but thinking she would get out sooner or later, they followed her. Around noon, she was let out of the convertible and then picked up by Bittaker while Norris hid under the bed. At Bittaker's urging, Hall obtained a drink from the cooler in the back of the van, at which point Norris made his move to subdue her. Hall's assault followed much like Schaeffer's, with the exception that she was photographed, providing souvenirs for her killers to recall the look of terror on her face. At this point, Bittaker and Norris were becoming comfortable enough with their crime to experiment with torturing their victims, verbally and physically. Hall had an ice pick jabbed into her brain, first through one ear, then the other. She was then strangled and thrown over the cliff.

The next two victims were Jackie Doris Gilliam, age fifteen, and Jacqueline Leah Lamp, age thirteen. The girls had been walking and hitchhiking casually along the road and had stopped for a rest at a bus-stop bench when the van pulled up beside them. They entered the van voluntarily but became uneasy when it turned away from the beach and headed for the mountains. As Lamp attempted to open the van door, Norris struck her over the head with a bat. Bittaker stopped to help Norris subdue the two girls and then headed to San Dimas, California.

Gilliam and Lamp were held for nearly forty-eight hours before they were murdered. Both were tortured, and Norris took approximately twenty-four Polaroid photographs of Gilliam and Bittaker engaged in various sexual acts. She was then stabbed through the ear with an ice pick, manually strangled, and finally struck on the head with a sledgehammer.

Norris claims that Lamp was not sexually assaulted. Before he savagely battered her head with the sledgehammer, Bittaker remarked, "You wanted to stay a virgin, now you can die a virgin." With this torture session, as well with the next one, Bittaker and Norris decided to further preserve their exploits by using a tape recorder.

Shirley Lynette Ledford was last seen hitchhiking on 31 October 1979 around 10:45 P.M. in Sun Valley, California. After Bittaker and Norris picked her up hitchhiking, they enacted the assault differently. Instead of heading for their spot in the mountains, they opted to drive around the streets near San Fernando Valley as they tortured Ledford. She was struck on the elbows repeatedly with a 3-pound sledgehammer. Bittaker decided Ledford was not screaming loud enough to suit him, so he retrieved a pair of pliers and vise grips from his toolbox and pinched her nipples and vagina with them. Ledford was also raped and sodomized. Her torment finally ended with a coat hanger tightened by the vise grips around her neck. Her nude body was dumped on the front lawn of a Sunland residence so the offenders could enjoy the reaction of the news media.

All the victims were targeted because they manifested some common characteristics that suited the preferences of Bittaker and Norris. They all were white females, within a narrow age range, unknown to the offenders, and considered high-risk victims because they were hitchhiking or walking along the highway.

Crime Scene Indicators

The crime scenes of Bittaker and Norris typified organized sadistic murder. They were carefully planned offenses that reflected overall control in conversation and of the victims themselves by the use of restraints. Bittaker derived enjoyment from engaging victims in conversation governed by him. He used the conversation as a means of torture in itself; making victims plead for their lives substantiated his sense of domination.

Their abductions were well planned, beginning with the customizing the offenders did on the van. The weapons, the tools of their assault, were never an issue until capture because the actual crime scene was within the van. At the abduction sites, the only evidence left behind was Schaeffer's shoe.

Bittaker and Norris transported the victims to remote sites that posed little to no risk of interruption or discovery. This ensured the lengthy contact with the victims that was required to fulfill the fantasies and drives that fueled their acts of sadistic murder. Several bodies were transported to a different disposal site from the death scene. With Norris's help, investigators found the broken skeletal remains of Gilliam and Lamp scattered over an area hundreds of feet along the canyon floor. No trace of Schaeffer's or Hall's body was found due to the well-selected disposal sites.

The setting of Ledford's death and assault was still within the realm of the organized, controlled scene, despite the body being left in view with no effort to conceal it. Bittaker's craving for some recognition of his crime was his incentive for this change in MO. There was no staging involved with these homicides.

Forensic Findings

As described above, Lucinda Schaeffer's and Andrea Hall's remains were never found. Partial remains of Gilliam and Lamp, including their battered skulls, were found in the Glendora Mountains. Gilliam still had the ice pick inserted in her right ear.

Shirley Ledford's autopsy revealed death was due to strangulation with a wire ligature around the neck. There was a linear compression mark and soft tissue and petechial hemorrhage around the neck. There was evidence of multiple blunt-force trauma to the face, head, and breasts. Her rectum, the lining inside her rectum, and her vagina had been torn, in part due to the insertion of a pair of pliers by Bittaker. There were bruises on her left elbow, a cut to the right index finger, and a puncture wound to the left hand. The wrists and ankles had ligature marks as well.

Investigation

Bittaker and Norris engaged in other crimes during this time period in addition to the sadistic murders. There were at least three separate incidents: an attempted rape, a rape kidnapping, and an assault with Mace. Photos were found after Bittaker's and Norris's arrests that were indicative of another victim, an unknown white female, who remains unidentified.

One of the victims who was raped and released identified Bittaker and Norris as her assailants. Norris and Bittaker were arrested for charges other than the murder charges in the hope that one or both would fold under interrogation and confess. Norris eventually did, shifting the blame to Bittaker in an attempt to save himself.

The motive for the brutal murders is perhaps best explained by Dr. Ronald Markman, a forensic psychiatrist who examined the offenders. He describes them as being sociopaths who know right from wrong but simply do not care. "They lack the internal prohibitions, or conscience, that keep most of us from giving full expression to our most primitive, and sometimes violent, impulses" (Markman 1989, 268). Dr. Markman stated that by their union, Bittaker and Norris helped each other "fulfill their most savage, primitive potential as sociopaths" (Markman 1989, 268).

Outcome

Roy Norris pleaded guilty to four counts of first-degree murder, one count of second-degree murder, two counts of rape, and one count of robbery. He is scheduled to serve a minimum of thirty years.

Lawrence Bittaker was found guilty of twenty-six counts of murder, rape, kidnapping, and torture on 17 February 1981. It took forty minutes just for the court clerk to read the verdicts. Bittaker received the death penalty.

140:   GROUP CAUSE HOMICIDE

Group cause homicide pertains to two or more people with a common ideology that sanctions an act, committed by one or more of its members, that results in death.

During the initial stages of compiling the *Crime Classification Manual,* the group cause homicide category included occult or satanic murder as one of its subcategories. The defining characteristics of victimology, crime scene, and forensic findings were written based on the abundance of material available on the subject of occult or satanic murder. However, as the committee involved with writing the group cause section began to review the occult/satanic murder category, several committee members raised questions regarding the validity of including this category in the CCM.

The National Center for the Analysis of Violent Crime's definition of true occult/satanic murder is murder committed by two or more individuals who rationally plan the crime and whose *primary* motivation is to fulfill a prescribed satanic ritual calling for the murder. Committee members raised the question of whether occult/satanic murder, as defined above, truly exists aside from the media hype surrounding this subject.

The popularity of occultism/satanism with the mass media has only served to cloud the issue and sometimes interfere with the objective investigation of a crime. The religious beliefs of a law enforcement officer may further complicate the process of objectively investigating an alleged satanic murder. "The law enforcement perspective must focus on the crime and clearly recognize that just because an activity is 'satanic' does not necessarily mean it is a crime or that it is not a legitimate religious practice protected by the First Amendment. Within the personal religious belief system of a law enforcement officer, Christianity may be good and satanism evil. Under the Constitution, however, both are neutral" (Lanning 1989, 7).

The committee agreed with Lanning's position that law enforcement officers need to know something about satanism and the occult to properly evaluate their possible connections to and motivations for criminal activity. They must know when and how beliefs, symbols, and paraphernalia can be used to corroborate criminal activity. The focus must be on the objective investigation. They also agreed that although occult/satanic killings according to the definition given above may have and do occur, the burden of proof is on those who claim that it has occurred (Lanning 1989).

In regard to the occurrence of satanic murder, the NCAVC has attempted to solicit cases from several sources who have made such claims. The analysis of crime scene photos from the few cases the NCAVC did receive failed to support the definition of occult/satanic murder or the defining characteristics of crime scene indicators and forensics derived from satanic crime conference material. Many of the cases exhibited indicators that either the victim and/or offender(s) had some involvement with the occult or satanism. However, the *primary* motive in each case was found to be sex, money, or interpersonal conflicts and not to satisfy the requirements of an occult or satanic ritual. The actual involvement of satanism or the occult in these cases turned out to be secondary, insignificant, or nonexistent. In addition, during legal proceedings, extraneous information about the subject's involvement in satanic/occult activity was more likely to be introduced by the defense to escape criminal responsibility or minimize punishment. Based on this, the authors decided to exclude occult murder from the CCM. If any law enforcement agency feels they have a homicide case that may meet the definition of satanic or occult murder, the NCAVC will welcome the chance to review the crime scene photographs and other case materials. The agency submitting the case should refer to chapter 8 for the list of case materials needed and mailing information.

141: CULT MURDER

A body of adherents with excessive devotion or dedication to ideas, objects, or persons, regarded as unorthodox or spurious and whose primary objectives of sex, power, and/or money are unknown to the general membership, is known as a *cult*. A cult murder pertains to the death of an individual committed by two or more members of the cult.

Defining Characteristics

Victimology. Occasionally, cult murder is the result of members preying on a random victim, but the prevailing casualty of this type of murder tends to be someone who is a member of the cult or on the fringe of membership. Generally, multiple victims are involved.

Crime Scene Indicators Frequently Noted. The crime scene may contain items that are symbolic, in the form of unexplained artifacts or imagery.

The status of the body is dependent on the purpose of the killing. If it is intended to be a widespread message, there generally will be little to no attempt to conceal the body. A death that is intended to intimidate within the smaller circle of the cult very often is concealed through burial. A more organized group usually demonstrates more elaborate body disposal and/or concealment. There may be a prevalence of mass grave sites in the area where a cult is based (e.g., a farm or rural residence). The crime scene usually exhibits evidence of multiple offenders as well as multiple victims, by either a mass killing or a spree killing.

Staging. Staging is not usually present.

Common Forensic Findings. The forensic findings most common to this type of homicide involve wounds from firearms; blunt-force trauma; and sharp, pointed objects. There may be mutilation of the body as well. Multiple weapons may have been used during a single event.

Investigative Consideration

The leaders of destructive cults often are involved with scams and may have criminal histories. However, this may not be the case if the cult is a splinter group of a mainstream, conventional religion. In either case, the leadership displays a masterful ability to attract and manipulate people, exploiting their vulnerability.

The murder may not have any apparent religious overtones or ritualistic qualities. There may be a message after the killing, especially it is intended for the public.

The motive is very often presented to the general assembly of the cult as part of the group belief. The leader's motivation, however, will be a controlling factor: a macho way to justify the homicide, tighten his control of the group, and/or eliminate troublemakers or less devoted followers who threaten his authority.

Search Warrant Suggestions

Search for literature describing cult activities. Search for clothing, objects, candles, and materials specific to cult activity.

CASE STUDY: 141: CULT MURDER

Background

On 3 January 1990 investigators acted on an anonymous tip they had received and began to dig under a muddy barn floor on a farm 25 miles east of Cleveland. The property once had been occupied by a religious cult. Over the next two days, they unearthed five bodies: two appeared to be adult, two were teenagers, and one was a child.

The former tenants were known as the Lundgren Cult after their leader, Jeffrey Lundgren. Lundgren, his wife, his son, and ten members of his group were subsequently charged and arrested over the next few days for the slayings of the family of five.

Victimology

The victims later were discovered to be Dennis Avery, age forty-nine; his wife, Cheryl, age forty-two; and their three daughters: Trina, age fifteen; Rebecca, age thirteen; and Karen, age seven. They had moved to Kirtland around 1987 from Independence, Missouri. Dennis Avery was described as working various low-paying, part-time jobs. "If it wasn't for some people, they would not have had food on their plates," said one Kirtland neighbor. The Averys were described as a quiet, shy family who kept to themselves. They attended services a few times at the local Reorganized Church of Jesus Christ of Latter Day Saints before joining the radical splinter group of Lundgren's followers.

Once the Averys joined Lundgren's cult, they were further isolated, typical of cult practice. Before their disappearance in April of 1989, they moved from Kirtland to a Madison Township home because they were behind in their rent. It is possible the Averys were attempting to recede from the Lundgren cult, which contributed to their being targeted as the victims for a cult sacrifice. A neighbor described the sudden disappearance of the Averys, as well as the rest of the commune, "like the earth opened up and swallowed them."

Crime Scene Indicators

The grave site was an 8-foot-square area underneath the barn of the 15-acre farm. The barn itself was filled with trash piled 4 feet high. Police had to force their way through the rear of the barn because the only ground level entrance was blocked by trash as well as by a 1978 Volvo. Auto title records showed a 1978 Volvo had been registered to Dennis and Cheryl Avery.

On top of the grave site were several photos of the Avery family. The bodies were found in a common grave 4 feet deep. They had been sprinkled with lime and covered with dirt, rocks, and clay. Dennis Avery's body was in a plastic bag. All the bodies were found fully clothed. All the victims were bound hand and foot with duct tape. Their eyes and mouths also were covered with duct tape.

Forensic Findings

All the victims had been killed by gunshot wounds to the chest. Rebecca Avery also had been shot in the head. The murder weapon was a .45-caliber Colt semiautomatic handgun.

Investigation

The Avery family was killed by an execution-style method. This was evidenced by the use of duct tape to bind their hands and feet and cover their eyes and mouth. The number of victims illustrates that cult homicides often involve spree or mass killing. The photographs of the Avery family left on their grave most likely had a ritualistic significance.

To understand the motive for the Avery family murders, one must examine the dynamics of the Lundgren cult. Jeffrey Lundgren was born in Independence, Missouri. He was a member of the Slover Park Reorganized Church until officials transferred him to Kirtland to serve as a guide at the Kirtland temple. He married Alice Keehler in 1970 and lived for a while in a rented home in Macks Creek, Missouri. The tangible beginnings of his deviation from church doctrines began to emerge at this time. For example, after Lundgren moved from his home, his landlord found an entire bedroom floor and closet littered with hard-core pornographic magazines.

It was also during this period, 1986–87, that Lundgren began to use his position as tour guide for the Kirtland temple to proclaim his interpretation of church doctrine and recruit his followers. Lundgren's supervisor began to hear complaints from temple visitors that Lundgren was misrepresenting teachings of the church. In addition to ethical improprieties at the visitors' center, Lundgren was suspected of stealing money. In 1987 he was removed as a tour guide. In January 1988 he was defrocked as a lay minister because his teachings deviated from church doctrine and were considered apostate. Lundgren resigned from the church and had to move from his rent-free home provided by the church. He relocated to the farm 4 miles away.

Lundgren continued to make recruiting trips to Independence, persuading members of the Reorganized church, including Dennis Avery, to join his "family." Lundgren became the personable father and prophet to emotionally troubled men and women made vulnerable by divorce, financial problems, or personal crises. He supported them, provided spiritual guidance, and took them in, giving them a place to belong. He became the guru who led his group to believe that he was the mouthpiece of God.

It was not long before Lundgren's zeal and manipulations allowed him absolute spiritual authority over the group. He matched couples in the commune based on visions he claimed came from God. Paychecks were signed over to him, phone calls were monitored, and when visitors came, he sat in on their conversations.

As group members became accustomed to Lundgren's control, the cult began to evolve into something more ominous than a religious sect. Rumors of paramilitary activity (shots being fired, usage of code names such as Eagle-2 and Talon-2, wearing of fatigues, and marching) began to reach the ears of area officials. An informant told Kirtland police that Lundgren was planning an assault on the Kirtland temple, an assault that included killing Reorganized church leaders and hundreds of people who lived near the church. He felt that the massacre would cleanse the church and pave the way for the second coming of Christ. Several appointed dates for the attack came and went, but Lundgren had a vision that it was not the right time.

Lundgren remained under the observation of the FBI and local police for several years. Finally, on 18 April 1989 FBI agents interviewed Lundgren and eight followers for about three hours because agents had learned that some of the group wanted to leave the cult. No one left, and no arrests were made because no crime had been committed. No one in the group had even a police record.

That night or early the next morning, Lundgren and his followers left Kirtland. The police were getting too close to the grisly events of the preceding day, 17 April.

A cult member who lived with Lundgren until April 1988 made the observation that the Averys were different from the others on the farm. They did not live there, but they visited a lot. They were half believing and half not believing. "They were weak in mind and strength. Everybody was doing one hundred or so push-ups, and Dennis could only do five or ten," according to the cult member.

Surely this lack of commitment on Dennis Avery's part was an affront to the image of divine prophet that Lundgren ascribed to himself. Lundgren's choice of the Avery family as a cult sacrifice stemmed from this threat to his dictatorship. The precipitating factor for the murders arose from the tradition contained in the Book of Mormon concerning the search for the Sword of Laban. Lundgren was planning to lead his followers into the wilderness in search for this sword, but first there had to be a cleansing sacrifice. Dennis Avery and his family were that sacrifice.

Lundgren probably used the story of Laban, who was killed by his own sword, to justify killing the Averys. Avery had bought a .45-caliber handgun for Lundgren two days before he was killed by a .45-caliber handgun. Because the Averys were about to abandon the cult, their death was rationalized by Lundgren's interpretation of the Mormon doctrine of Blood Atonement, which teaches that the penalty for abandoning the faith is the shedding of the sinner's blood. Lundgren could simultaneously satisfy his doctrinal beliefs, soothe his offended authority, and intimidate any other group members who may have been slipping from his control.

On 17 April the Lundgren family, including the Averys, gathered together at the farm for a last meal. When supper had ended, the men excused themselves, with the exception of Dennis Avery. While the women entertained the rest of the Avery family, several men asked Dennis to follow them outside to the barn. As Avery entered the barn, he was hit with a stun gun. He promised his cooperation, probably still unaware of Lundgren's plans for him and his family. His hands, mouth, and eyes were then taped with duct tape, and he was led to the waiting grave. Once Avery was standing inside the hole, Jeffrey Lundgren passed judgment on him for allowing Cheryl Avery to control their family and declared his heart impure. Lundgren then shot Avery in the chest point blank. Then Cheryl Avery was led to the barn, bound with duct tape, and also shot in the chest as she knelt next to her husband's corpse. One by one, the children were carried to the open grave after being bound by the tape and were shot in the chest, with the exception of Rebecca, who also was shot in the head.

Two days later, the group packed up and left. They traveled through several states before finally splitting up around Thanksgiving.

On 7 January 1990 Jeffrey Lundgren, his wife, and his son were arrested outside a motel in National City, California. It is believed they were attempting to place their younger children with relatives in order to flee across the border to Mexico.

Outcome

Jeffrey Lundgren was sentenced to death on five counts of aggravated murder and kidnapping. His son, Damon Lundgren, was found guilty of four counts of aggravated murder. He is awaiting sentencing. The jury has recommended life sentences without parole for twenty years. Alice Lundgren received five consecutive life sentences for conspiracy, complicity, and kidnapping convictions.

142: EXTREMIST MURDER

Extremist murder is killing motivated by ideas based upon a particular political, economic, religious, or social system. This category of homicide includes both the lone offender whose actions are endorsed by the group and the offense involving multiple offenders.

Extremist Typologies

It is a difficult task to classify a homicide involving an extremist group into a single category. Group causes can rarely be isolated to a single typology; there is often a blending of one or more of the motivations described in this section. Classification is based on the predominant motive.

One example, the Hizballah (holy war), has political objectives that serve to further the Islamic religion. One of these objectives is to eliminate all non-Islamic influences and establish a revolutionary Shia Islamic state in Lebanon modeled after Iran. These terrorists use murder in the form of political warfare to achieve political and religious ends.

Right wing groups like the Covenant, Sword, and Arm of the Lord (CSA) combine religious concepts with elements of extreme racism. Fatal attacks upon blacks, Hispanics, and Jews are justified by these hate groups' distortion of Biblical passages, which differs significantly from mainstream religious interpretation.

Extremist-group murder typologies are summarized below.

Political. This type of homicide is motivated by doctrines or philosophies that oppose a current position of government and/or its representatives.

Religious. This is homicide prompted by a fervent devotion or a system of beliefs based on orthodox religious conventions. This type of offense does not include cult or occult killings. Some examples of the mainstream religious groups included in this category are the Islamic, Jewish (Yahwehs), and Christian religions (Catholic, Protestant, Mormon, etc.).

Socioeconomic. This murder results from an intense hostility and aversion toward another individual or group that represents a certain ethnic, social, economic, or religious group. This category includes hate groups, such as the neo-Nazi skinheads, the Ku Klux Klan, the so-called gay-bashers, and the Black Panthers.

Defining Characteristics

Victimology. There are several types of victims targeted in extremist murder. Predominantly, the victim represents the antithesis of the offender's system of beliefs; therefore, victimology depends on this doctrine. If multiple victims are involved, there will be similarities of race, religion, political beliefs, social status, or economic status. Selectivity is apparent in varying degrees. The victim may be a victim of opportunity, a random target who just happened across the path of the offender at the wrong time. Conversely, a victim may be targeted and die as the result of a premeditated, well-planned attack.

Extremist murder victimology also includes the victims that come into conflict with the group's objectives. This type of victim includes the informant, the straying member, or any member who poses a threat to either the leader's control or group integrity.

A third type of victim is the one who is killed due to association with targets of the group. An example of this is the stabbing death of twenty-four-year-old Scott Vollmer by a skinhead, Michael Elrod. Vollmer had brought a black friend to a party when Elrod began shouting racial slurs. Elrod stabbed Vollmer as he tried to intercede on behalf of his black friend.

Crime Scene Indicators Frequently Noted. A group cause extremist murder often will include multiple crime scenes: confrontation site, death scene, and body disposal/burial locale. The calling card of the group (symbols, communiqués, etc.) may be left at the scene.

Crime scene indicators for this category depend on the number of offenders: a lone offender acting on behalf of the group or multiple offenders. Generally speaking, multiple offenders will present the obvious crime scene indicators. There may be evidence of different weapons and ammunition. The victim usually is well controlled. An example of this at the crime scene would be minimal signs of victim escape attempts (i.e., no widespread blood-splatter patterns and trails, overturned furniture, and other signs of struggle). A significant number of victims also may be indicative of multiple offenders.

If there are multiple offenders, the location of the crime scene may be one that is convenient and low risk for the killers. Offender risk is lowered by preplanning and surveillance for both the assault and/or abduction and escape. A group effort allows for a more organized, methodical approach to the killing, especially with an abduction murder. Body disposal will often be more elaborate and low risk when a group effort is involved. As in many individual homicides, the crime scene is best represented by a continuum from the disorganized, sloppy offense to the highly sophisticated, well-organized one. The amount of physical evidence left at the scene and the ease of assault, abduction, and escape will depend on the level of criminal sophistication of the group.

A lone offender also may demonstrate control and organization at the crime scene(s), depending on his or her level of professionalism. However, the number of victims will most likely be limited, and the overall offense usually is not committed with the same ease as one involving multiple offenders.

Staging. Staging to mislead investigators is not present because the homicide is intended to communicate some message on behalf of the group.

Common Forensic Findings. The physical evidence of multiple offenders (fibers, hairs, prints, shoe impressions) may be evident at the crime scene, depending on the level of group organization. There may be evidence of different weaponry (e.g., different caliber firearms or combinations of weapons such as firearms and knives).

The forensics often will reveal the calling card or signature aspect of the group. The following list offers examples of different extremist groups and their preferred method of attack:

Yahwehs: dismemberment, especially decapitation

IRA: bombing

Many left-wing groups: firearms

Skinheads: blunt-force trauma from personal weapons (hands, feet)

Multiple or excessive trauma are other indicators of possible group involvement. The lone offender will mostly likely not involve the signs evident of multiple offenders as described above.

Investigative Considerations

Preoffense behavior may be evident in the planning, surveillance, and selection of the victim. In addition, the ease of escape often will demonstrate this preplanning. An example of this is bombings that use a transmitting device. One offender will trigger the bomb from a car that another offender is driving away from the scene, thus allowing for an escape masked by the confusion of the explosion.

Postincident analysis of any claims and/or communiqués is important to determine authenticity. An investigator should not conclude that the communicating party is the offender without careful examination through such techniques as psycholinguistics.

A postoffense protection conspiracy by the group should be expected. Great caution should always be used when approaching any group meeting places or compounds. The use of booby traps is not an uncommon practice of many extremist groups.

Search Warrant Suggestions

Search warrant suggestions include documentation of offense preplanning and execution stages (e.g., diaries, journals, recordings [audio or videotaped], maps, and photos of the victim). Also useful are any mass media materials pertaining to the group's beliefs and activities as well as to the victim, especially if the murder is a political assassination. Firearms, explosive devices related to the group signature, and evidence of stalking (travel tickets or receipts and/or photos) also should be considered.

CASE STUDY: 142: EXTREMIST MURDER

POLITICAL EXTREMIST MURDER

On 6 November 1973 Marcus Foster, the highly respected black superintendent of the Oakland, California, school system, was leaving an education committee meeting with his deputy, Robert Blackburn. As they exited the building, two gunmen ambushed them, killing Foster and wounding Blackburn. The autopsy on Foster revealed the killers had used bullets filled with cyanide crystals.

A letter sent to a local radio station stated that the Symbionese Liberation Army (SLA) was responsible for the ambush. The letter stated that

Foster and his deputy had been found guilty by a court of the people for "crimes against the children and life of the people." Some of these so-called crimes included a proposal to form a school police unit, the use of identity cards for students, and an effort to coordinate teachers, probation officers, and police to help reduce juvenile crime.

The SLA was founded by a black escaped convict, Donald DeFreeze. Its roots sprang from the black prison population in California. The most famous incident involving the SLA was the kidnapping of Patty Hearst, who later joined the organization and assisted in a bank robbery perpetrated by the SLA.

On 10 January 1974 police arrested Russell Jack Little, age twenty-four, and Michael Remiro, age twenty-seven, near Concord, California. A ballistics report linked a gun in Remiro's possession to Foster's murder. Shortly afterward, a nearby house belonging to another SLA member was set on fire. Police responding to the call found a cache of guns, ammunition, explosives, cyanide, and SLA pamphlets. Police also discovered a list of officials marked for kidnapping and execution.

On 17 May 1974 six members of the SLA were killed in a shootout with police. The FBI arrested Patty Hearst on 18 September 1975, after she had spent sixteen months as a fugitive. Little and Remiro, both admitting their membership in the SLA, were sentenced to life imprisonment for the murder of Marcus Foster and the attempted murder of Robert Blackburn.

RELIGIOUS EXTREMIST MURDER

In 1967 on Chicago's South Side, nine black families under the leadership of Ben Carter formed the Original Hebrew Israelite Nation of Jerusalem. They had developed a theory that they were the true Jews, robbed of their heritage and culture by four centuries of white domination. After many of the members immigrated to Israel and subsequently returned in a few years, a reconstruction of the movement took place from which the Black Hebrews Organization, or Yahwehs, was created.

In 1981 a black male named Hulan Mitchell led the Miami chapter of the group. Mitchell has assumed the name Moses Israel and originally had been a Black Muslim. During this time, a former member, Ashton Green, appeared as guest on a local radio talk show and publicly criticized the Yahwehs. Soon after, Green began receiving death threats. On 13 November 1981 Green's decapitated body (and head) were found in a Dade County field.

On 15 November 1981 police questioned Mildred Banks and Carlton Carey, friends of Green and former Yahweh members. When they returned to their apartment, they were both shot by unknown assailants. Banks's neck also was hacked with a machete-like weapon, but he survived. Carey did not survive the attack. Banks could not identify the assailants.

The original leader of the Yahwehs, Ben Carter, publicly repudiated and castigated the Miami chapter for its alleged involvements in the homicides. In response to this, Moses Israel severed his links with the national leadership and pursued a separate course.

SOCIOECONOMIC EXTREMIST MURDER

On 18 June 1984, the outspoken talk-show host Alan Berg was gunned down as he stepped from his Volkswagen in front of his house. Berg had drawn criticism from many different people representing a spectrum of beliefs and opinions. But the people who seemed the most antagonistic toward him were members of the Ku Klux Klan. He was threatened and hated by them not only for his outspokenness, but also for his Jewish ancestry.

The group found to be responsible for Berg's death was a paramilitary white-supremacist group called the Order. The Order was founded in October 1983 by Robert Mathews, a former member of another white-supremacist group, the Aryan Nations. Mathews was inspired by a novel written by a white supremacist in which the author describes the exploits of a band of self-conceived American patriots turned guerrillas. This group, called the Order, mounted a campaign to overthrow the U.S. government. The brief history of the Order has been full of racketeering, counterfeiting, arson, armed robberies, and murder.

After a lengthy investigation, charges were brought against Order members Jean Craig, David Lane, and Bruce Pierce for civil rights violations in conjunction with the murder. Jean Craig had been responsible for the detailed surveillance that enabled Pierce and Lane to know everything about Berg's routine. Her report on Berg came complete with photographs. Pierce eventually was convicted for the murder of Berg, and Lane was convicted for his part of the murder, driving the getaway car.

142.01: PARAMILITARY EXTREMIST MURDER

Extremist groups often adopt a paramilitary organizational structure and method of operation. Characteristics of a paramilitary extremist group include the wearing of uniforms, the use of training compounds, a hierarchy of leadership based on rank, and an internal code of discipline and conduct. They are highly organized groups and often have an abundance of written materials pertaining to their beliefs and structure.

Defining Characteristics

Victimology. See victimology section in 142.

Crime Scene Indicators Frequently Noted. The crime scene of a paramilitary extremist group is usually highly organized. The use of military tactics and MO will be demonstrated. Knowledge of the group's MO will be important in examining not only the crime scene, but also all elements of the offense.

Staging. There will be no staging because the intent of the killing is to convey a message.

Common Forensic Findings. The forensics of a paramilitary attack generally do not demonstrate overkill. The assault is usually a clean kill, again exhibiting a military style of operation. Firearms and explosives are most frequently the weapons of choice.

Investigative Considerations

The offense will involve selection, surveillance, and even rehearsal. Suspects involved in paramilitary operations often have criminal records. Booby traps are especially a danger when approaching this type of extremist group operation.

Search Warrant Suggestions

See search warrant suggestions in section 142.

142.02: HOSTAGE EXTREMIST MURDER

In hostage extremist murder, a homicide takes place within the context of a hostage or kidnapping situation. The hostage or kidnap situation is perpetrated by an extremist group. See section 129: Hostage Murder and section 104: Kidnap Murder for complete definitions of each situation.

CASE STUDY: 142.02: HOSTAGE EXTREMIST MURDER

Background

On 11 January 1983 Memphis Police Officer R. S. Hester, along with two other patrolmen, responded to a bogus tip about a shoplifting warrant for Lindberg Sanders who resided at 2239 Shannon Street. Upon entering the residence, a group of individuals later described as religious fanatics attacked the three officers in an apparent attempt to capture them. One officer was shot in the face but managed to escape. The second officer was severely beaten about the face and head but also managed to escape.

At 3:15 A.M. on 13 January, members of the Memphis Police Department tactical response team swept into the house through a back door and found Bob Hester dead. The seven offenders who had held him hostage were subsequently killed when they engaged police in a gun battle.

Victimology

Patrolman Hester, age thirty-four, was one month shy of his ten-year anniversary as a Memphis police officer when he was taken hostage. He had worked the North Precinct most of his career. He was hurt once in the line of duty, in 1977 when he was attacked by a man in a pool hall.

Hester had the reputation for making many quality felony arrests, and he had received several commendations. He also was active with the police department athletics program.

Crime Scene Indicators

The crime scene in this case combined the last known hostage location and the place of confrontation with police: both usually contain indicators crucial to any hostage murder. The incident involving Hester never left the confines of the Shannon Street house.

Forensic Findings

The autopsy report for Hester stated that he had suffered numerous injuries caused by blunt-force trauma. Most of the injury was focused on his face and head. His skull was fractured in at least one place. There were numerous scrapes and lacerations on Hester's head and face in addition to bruises on his upper thigh and abdomen near the groin. There were lacerations behind the elbows and below both knees. A blunt instrument also produced two puncture wounds on his right leg. Cause of death was summarized as beaten to death. Hester's time of death was estimated to be between twelve and fourteen hours before the house was stormed. The offenders all died of gunshot wounds to the head and chest.

Investigation

Lindberg Sanders, the leader of the Shannon Street Seven, was described by friends as once having been an easy-going, dependable craftsman. He began to undergo a change in 1973, when he was hospitalized for psychiatric problems. After several more hospitalizations and outpatient treatment, Sanders was diagnosed as a schizophrenic with religious delusions. He stopped working altogether in 1975 and devoted his time to reading the Bible and holding meetings at his Shannon Street home. From these meetings, a small group of followers emerged who adopted Sanders's beliefs and routinely gathered with him to fast, smoke marijuana, and read the Bible. Sanders believed that pork and scavenger fish should not be eaten and water could be consumed only if it was colored. His followers would put mustard, Kool-Aid, or catsup in their water to color it.

At some point, Sanders's doctrine began to take an ominous direction, dictating that police were agents of the devil, were antireligious, and were anti-Christian. The precipitating factor of the Shannon Street siege may have been the fact that Sanders believed the world was due to end that week. His group had congregated four days before the incident and began to fast and pray in preparation for the end. Sanders had expressed his belief that he was gifted with a special immortality, so he expected to survive the end of the world as well as a bullet from a policeman's gun.

The incident actually started with an earlier call on 11 January, when police were told a suspect wanted in a purse snatching was at the Sanders residence. The police talked to Sanders and those gathered with him at his home. The members of the group were upset that the world had not ended when Sanders had predicted. The responding officers left without incident.

At 9:00 P.M. the call was placed for them to return. Hester and the other two officers were met with a barrage of gunfire. The two other officers escaped, although both were wounded. Negotiators tried for the next twenty-four hours to reason with Sanders without success. On 12 January at 11:11 P.M., all the lights in the house were turned out by its occupants. Approximately four hours later the TACT team stormed the house and found Hester already dead.

---

143 GROUP-EXCITEMENT HOMICIDE

A group-excitement homicide involves two or more persons who cause the death of an individual. A death that results from group excitement can be structured or unstructured and has a contagious and spontaneous component.

Defining Characteristics

Victimology. The victim initially may be a targeted individual, and as the chaos and excitement escalates, random persons may become victims. Another variation of this is that the group chooses a victim randomly. There are often multiple victims and possibly surviving victims of the attack.

Crime Scene Indicators Frequently Noted. There are often witnesses to this type of attack, although they may be hesitant to come forward. The attack usually occurs in an open, public place. The weapons used are typically those of opportunity, especially personal weapons (hands, feet). The crime scene is disorganized with no cover-up; the body is left in the open with minimal or no effort of concealment. There are usually signs of multiple offenders (fingerprints, footprints, fibers, semen, etc.)

Staging. There is no staging present.

Common Forensic Findings. There is usually overkill due to bludgeoning and generalized blunt-force trauma. The victim shows multiple wounds from a frenzied assault. There may sexual assault or insertion.

Investigative Consideration

Drugs and alcohol are often used by the offenders. The attack is of short duration, but as previously mentioned, there are often witnesses due to the openness of the crime. Because a loosely structured group with no main leader is involved, the weakness of the group may be exploited.

Search Warrant Suggestions

Search for clothing to obtain hair, blood, and fiber samples. Also search for newspaper clippings reporting the crime.

CASE STUDY: 143: GROUP-EXCITEMENT HOMICIDE

Background

Around dusk on 1 October 1984, Catherine Fuller was taking a shortcut home from the grocery store when she was confronted by a large group of young adults ranging in age from sixteen to twenty-six years old, male and female. What started as a robbery turned into a brutal melee in which the 99-pound woman was savagely beaten to death.

Victimology

Catherine Fuller, age forty-eight, was described as good Samaritan who helped the elderly people in her neighborhood and who always was smiling. She was a small woman, standing only 5 feet tall. David, her husband of fifteen years, described her as strong and feisty despite her small stature. Catherine Fuller had six children, three of whom still lived at home at the time of her death. She was characterized as someone who enjoyed staying at home with her family more than going out.

Crime Scene Indicators

The crime scene of group excitement murder reflects the disorganized, spontaneous nature of the crime. The initial confrontation occurred in a public, open place: an alley less than two blocks from Fuller's home. She had been spotted from across the road by the offenders. They had been smoking marijuana and had decided it was time to rob someone when Fuller walked by. Her small stature probably made her appear an easy target. Several offenders caught up with her and boxed her in, driving her into the alley. She was assaulted and killed in a vacant, litter-strewn garage, and her body was left at the death scene, openly displayed.

Police believe as many as twenty-five to thirty people were involved. There were many witnesses, but due to their fear of the offenders, few would talk to police. The weapons were those of opportunity, a 1-foot pole probably found in the alley and the use of hands and feet. The violence of the assault escalated as the group excitement intensified.

Forensic Findings

Catherine Fuller had suffered extensive blunt-force trauma resulting in massive internal bleeding from being kicked and punched. A 1-foot pole was shoved into her rectum with such force that it tore through her intestines and ruptured her liver. Either the beatings or the internal damage from the pole could have caused death by itself.

Investigation

The group that was involved with the murder was not a structured gang at the time of assault but was more a gathering of bored young people. The attack was not directed by distinctive leadership but started with a suggestion from someone to rob somebody. Not long after the proposition was raised, Catherine Fuller walked by.

It was not clear whether any of the offenders knew the victim. Her identity did not matter because victim selection was motivated by convenience: Fuller was simply a victim of opportunity.

One offender stated that he did not think anyone had planned to do any of the things they did beyond robbing Fuller. But she fought back, and this resulted in an eruption of violence that fed on itself. The offenders were not going to let Fuller make them lose face in front of their peers.

One witness described the attack as having a carnival-like atmosphere, with people shouting, "Let me see," and joining in. Some were shocked, but they did not intervene or tell anyone, probably due to fear of becoming the focus of the attack themselves. One sociologist explained the group dynamics of the attack by saying that everyone wanted to be part of the group; they were swept along with the chaos and excitement, wanting their share of it. Or put more simply in the words of an offender, "Everyone was doing stuff. I wanted to show I could do stuff, too."

Later, several of the offenders jogged past the garage to see if Fuller was still alive. A vendor going into the alley to urinate found the body when he saw blood coming from under the garage door.

Outcome

Ten people were found guilty in the murder of Catherine Fuller. A jury convicted eight of them, and two others pleaded guilty to felony murder. Police believe there are still many more who took part in the kicking and punching that killed Fuller, but they probably will never be brought to justice because of the confusion of the attack and the reluctance of witnesses to come forward.

2

Arson

200: Vandalism-motivated arson
  201: Willful and malicious mischief
  202: Peer/group pressure
  209: Other
210: Excitement-motivated arson
  211: Thrill seeker
  212: Attention seeker
  213: Recognition (hero)
  214: Sexual perversion
  219: Other
220: Revenge-motivated arson
  221: Personal retaliation
  222: Societal retaliation
  223: Institutional retaliation
  224: Group retaliation
  225: Intimidation
  229: Other
230: Crime-concealment-motivated arson
  231: Murder
  232: Suicide
  233: Breaking and entering

234: Embezzlement

235: Larceny

236: Destroying records

239: Other

240: Profit-motivated arson

  241: Fraud

    241.01: Insurance

    241.02: Liquidating property

    241.03: Dissolving business

    241.04: Inventory

  242: Employment

  243: Parcel clearance

  244: Competition

  249: Other

250: Extremist-motivated arson

  251: Terrorism

  252: Discrimination

  253: Riots/civil disturbance

  259: Other

260: Serial arson

  261: Spree arson

  262: Mass arson

Arson statistics in the United States are collected by the National Fire Protection Association (NFPA) and the Federal Bureau of Investigation (FBI) as part of its Uniform Crime Report (UCR). In collecting these statistics, each of these organizations focuses on slightly different aspects of the arson problem. The NFPA's focus is on structure arsons and combines both established arsons and suspicious fires in compiling its statistics. The FBI collects data relating to all types of property, tabulating them under the headings of structures, mobile, and other, but limits this to incidents that definitely have been determined to be arsons. When this difference in the focus of data collection is taken into account, the statistics compiled by both the NFPA and the FBI closely agree.

Unfortunately, a consistent underreporting of the arsons in this country leaves us short of a true picture of the problem. Nearly 13,000 law-enforcement agencies across the country annually report arson statistics to the FBI. The UCR cautions that the reported arsons do not represent the nation's total arson experience. For example, in 1990, 9,043 agencies covering only 72 percent of the United States population submitted reports for all twelve months of the year. Nevertheless, trends can be established.

According to the NFPA, arson is consistently responsible for 13 to 14 percent of all structure fires. FBI statistics indicate the national arson rate averages around 50 per 100,000 population with predictable regional variations. The annual clearance rate for arson averages in the 15 to 16 percent range. According to the 1990 UCR, 38 percent of all arson clearances involved young people under the age of eighteen. Juveniles were the offenders in 40 percent of the city arson clearances. Of the estimated actual arson arrests for 1990, 44 percent were under eighteen years of age and 64 percent under twenty-five. Males comprised 87 percent of all arson arrestees. Seventy-five percent of those arrested were white, 23 percent were black, and the remainder were of other races.

Arson is the willful and malicous burning of property. The criminal act of arson is divided into three elements (DeHaan, 1990):

1. There is a burning of property. This must be shown to the court to be actual destruction, at least in part, not just scorching or sooting (however, some states consider the visible impairment of a surface).
2. The fire is incendiary in origin. Proof must be established by evidence, either through specific forensic findings (e.g., presence of accelerants, incendiary devices) or by expert testimony that *all* possible natural or accidental causes have been considered and eliminated.
3. The fire is proved to be started with malice.

Much of the existing arson research has been conducted from a clinical viewpoint, which provides an academic understanding of the act and/or develops treatment protocols for the offender (Lewis & Yarnell, 1951) but does not, however, address the crime from the perspective of fire service and law enforcement needs. To meet these needs, it has become a primary mission of the NCAVC to conduct arson offender research in order to provide investigative assistance to police and fire agencies in unsolved arson cases (Icove & Estepp, 1987).

Through this research, the NCAVC has recognized that the identification of the offender's motive is a key element in crime analysis. This method of analysis is used by the NCAVC to determine the recognizable personal traits and characteristics exhibited by an unknown offender. Motive can be defined as an inner drive or impulse that is the cause, reason, or incentive that induces or prompts a specific behavior (Rider, 1980).

The NCAVC has reviewed arson research literature and actual arson cases and interviewed incarcerated arsonists across the country. As a result, the following motive classifications consistently appear and have proven most effective in identifying offender characteristics:

1. Revenge
2. Excitement
3. Vandalism

4. Profit
5. Crime Concealment
6. Extremist

ARSON: GENERAL CHARACTERISTICS

DEFINING CHARACTERISTICS

Victimology: Targeted property

- The essential factor that often determines the motive
- Random, opportunistic vs. specific

Crime Scene Indicators Frequently Noted

- *Organized arsonist*
  - Elaborate incendiary devices (electronic timing mechanisms, initiators, etc.)
  - Less physical evidence; if forced entry, more skillful (footprints, fingerprints, etc.)
  - Methodical approach (trailers, multiple sets, excessive accelerant use, etc.)
- *Disorganized arsonist*
  - Materials on hand
  - Matches, cigarettes, more common accelerants (lighter fluid, gasoline)
  - More physical evidence left (handwriting, footprints, fingerprints, etc.)

Forensic findings

- Incendiary devices: components (initiators, timing devices, candles, electronic timers, tape, wires, etc.)
- Accelerants: gasoline, lighter fluid, mixtures (gasoline/kerosene)
- More sophisticated accelerants: diesel/kerosene, water soluble (alcohol)
- Molotov cocktail: glass fragments for fingerprints, cloth for fiber match

SEARCH WARRANT SUGGESTIONS

- Evidence of incendiary devices: packing, components, fireworks, firecrackers, tape for matching with crime scene evidence, how-to books

- Accelerants: clothing, shoes, washcloths, towels from offender cleaning up), carpet, floor mats from vehicle, containers (gasoline cans)
- Molotov cocktail: bottles, cloth for fiber matching, flammable liquids

200: VANDALISM-MOTIVATED ARSON

Vandalism-motivated arson is due to malicious and mischievous motivation that results in destruction or damage. The types of vandalism-motivated arson in this category are willful and malicious mischief (201), peer/group pressure (202), and other (209).

Defining Characteristics

Victimology: Targeted Property. Educational facilities are a common target for arson motivated by vandalism (Icove, 1979). Other properties targeted by the vandal arsonist are residential areas and vegetation (which includes grass, brush, woodland and timber).

Crime Scene Indicators Frequently Noted. Arson by vandalism frequently involves multiple offenders who act spontaneously and impulsively. If multiple offenders are involved, one personality tends to be the leader or instigator of the group. The typical crime scene reflects the spontaneous nature of the offense and is representative of a disorganized crime (Ressler, Burgess & Douglas, 1988). The offenders tend to use materials present at the site and leave physical evidence at the scene (e.g., footprints, fingerprints). Occasionally, flammable liquids are used. The offenders may gain entrance to a secured structure through windows. Evidence will show a mechanical breaking of the glass as opposed to heat breakage. Matchbooks, cigarettes, and spray-paint cans (used for graffiti) often are present. Other signs suggesting vandalism may be present (e.g, writing on chalkboards, materials missing from the scene, and general destruction of property).

Common Forensic Findings. In addition to the common forensic findings, analysis of any flammable liquid used is the main forensic finding. The occasional use of firecrackers or fireworks provides additional evidence for forensic analysis. If the offenders entered the property by breaking a window, glass particles may be present in the clothing of the identified suspects.

Investigative Considerations

The typical offender is a juvenile male who has seven to nine years of formal education. He tends to have a record of poor school performance and does not work. He is single and lives with either one or both parents. Alcohol and drug use generally are not associated with the firesetting. The offender may be already known to the police and may have an arrest record. It also is probable that at least one of the offenders is known to school authorities as being disruptive and having a problem dealing with authority.

The majority of these offenders live less than one mile from the crime scene. Most offenders flee immediately from the scene and do not return. If they do return, they view the fire from a safe and distant vantage point.

To narrow the scope of the investigation and limit the number of suspects, the investigator should solicit the help of school, fire service, and police officials. These officials would be the most likely to come into contact with previous vandalism-motivated activities of the juvenile offender.

Search Warrant Suggestions

- Spray paint cans
- Items from the scene, especially if a school was the target
- Explosive devices: fireworks, firecrackers, packaging, or cartons
- Flammable liquids
- Clothing: evidence of flammable liquid, evidence of glass particles, for witness indentification
- Shoes: footprints, flammable liquid traces

CASE STUDY: 201: WILLFUL AND MALICIOUS MISCHIEF

Background

At 10:37 P.M. on a clear, cool Saturday night in the fall of 1990, a fire was discovered at a junior high school. The fire caused in excess of $250,000 damage to the school's library and an adjacent all-purpose room. As insurance costs were extremely high in the low-income area this school served, coverage was minimal and included large deductibles. The financially strapped school district was unable to repair all the structural damage, let alone replace the books lost in the fire.

Victimology: Targeted Property

The school, built in 1972 to serve grades six through nine, had a history of fires over the years. But none were as large as this latest fire. As with many schools, vandalism was a problem. There were occasional false fire alarms and bomb threats, and graffiti was evident in many areas of the building. Periodically, shop equipment and windows were broken deliberately with rocks. There was also some degree of theft.

Crime Scene Indicators

After interviewing fire fighters, investigators examining the crime scene determined that a library window facing an interior courtyard had been broken. Glass had been removed from the lower edge of the frame, and a sweatshirt was placed over the sill, apparently so that the burglars would not cut themselves. Inside the building, investigators found the origin of the fire in a wastebasket against a wall, beside a photocopy machine. Hundreds of books had been pulled from the shelves and lay in the aisles where they had fallen. By noting the protected floor areas beneath the books, fire fighters confirmed that the books were in that position before the fire began. Smoke damage and fire damage were too extensive to determine if other acts of vandalism took place. The fire was ruled to be arson.

Forensic Findings

No evidence of flammable liquid was found at the scene. It appeared that an open flame was applied to the available material in and around the wastebasket. No footprints were found that could have belonged to the suspects, and if there were any, they were obliterated during the fire-fighting efforts. A fragment of basalt block was found on the floor inside the library, opposite the broken window. The sweatshirt found was of medium size, dark blue in color, and had no lettering. After the sweatshirt was dried and examined carefully (it was soaking wet due to the fire-fighting efforts), black hairs were found inside of it.

Investigation

Because of the type of target, the manner of attack, and the evidence found at the scene, investigators suspected that students might have been responsible for setting the fire. Investigators approached school authorities and asked a vice principal for a list of students she thought capable of the crime. After consulting student counselors, she supplied twenty-three names. Several days later, as investigators were nearly through interviewing those listed, they received a call from the mother of one of the students. She reported that her son had told her that another student had boasted that he and another youth had set the fire. These two students, whose names were on the list provided by school authorities, were interviewed separately confessed to the crime.

Outcome

The boys, both fourteen years old, were turned over to juvenile authorities. Both had been in previous trouble involving minor violations, and one was suspected of involvement in burglaries. They were adjudicated delinquent and remanded to the state youth facility. Their parents could have been liable for fire damage, however, neither had insurance or was able to pay.

210: EXCITEMENT-MOTIVATED ARSON

The excitement-motivated arsonist is prompted to set fires because he craves excitement that is satisfied by firesetting. This offender rarely intends the fire to harm people. The types of arsonists included in this category are thrill seeker (211), attention seeker (212), recognition (213), sexual perversion (214), and other (219).

Defining Characteristics

Victimology: Targeted Property. The type of property targeted by the excitement-motivated arsonist will help determine the motive. Dumpsters, vegetation (grass, brush, woodland, and timber), lumber stacks, construction sites, and residential property are common targets of the excitement firesetter. The offender may select a location that offers a good vantage point from which to safely observe the fire suppression and investigation. In some cases where fires occur inside unoccupied structures, volunteer fire fighters and fire buffs should not be eliminated as possible suspects. Both lone and multiple offenders are common to this type of arson.

Crime Scene Indicators Frequently Noted. The targeted properties are often adjacent to outdoor areas that have a reputation as a hangout or place of frequent parties. The offender often will use materials on hand. In incendiary devices are used, they usually have a time-delay mechanism. Offenders in the eighteen to thirty age group are more prone to use accelerants. Matches and cigarettes are frequently used to ignite vegetation fires.

A small percentage of excitement fires are motivated by sexual perversion (Lewis & Yarnell, 1951). At these crime scenes, the investigator may find ejaculate, fecal deposits, and/or pornographic material (e.g., magazines or pictures). In most cases, this firesetter uses available material and starts small fires.

Common Forensic Findings. In addition to the standard examination of fingerprints, vehicle and bicycle tire tracks, and so on, the forensic analysis that is performed should look for the possible remnants of the components of incendiary devices. If the arsonist is motivated by sexual perversion, ejaculate or fecal material may offer forensic information of value.

Investigative Considerations

The typical excitement arsonist is a juvenile or young adult male with ten or more years of formal education. This offender is generally unemployed, single, and living with one or both parents. His family tends to be from the middle-class to lower-middle-class bracket. In general, this offender is socially inadequate, particularly in heterosexual relationships. Serial offenders are common to this category of firesetters.

The use of drugs or alcohol usually is not found with the youngest offenders, but does occur with older ones. A history of police contact for nuisance offenses is prevalent with the excitement-motivated offender. The older the offender, the longer the record.

The distance that the offender lives from the crime scene can be frequently determined by an analysis of the targets he or she burned. Through target and cluster analysis, the investigator can determine if the offender is mobile (Icove, 1991).

Some excitement-motivated arsonists do not leave once the fire has started. They prefer to mingle with the crowds who have gathered to watch the fire. The offenders who do leave the scene usually return later and observe the damage and activity of their handiwork.

Search Warrant Suggestions

Vehicle:

- Material similar to incendiary devices used: fireworks, containers that components were shipped in, packaging, wires, etc.
- Floor mats, trunk padding, carpeting: residue from accelerants (not conclusive evidence, but indicative)
- Beer cans, matchbooks, cigarettes: to match any brands found at the scene

House:

- Material similar to incendiary devices used: fireworks, containers that components were shipped in, packaging, wires, etc.
- Clothing, shoes: accelerant and soil samples if vegetation fire
- Beer cans, matchbooks, cigarettes: to match any brands found at scene
- Cigarette lighter, especially if subject does not smoke
- Diaries, journals, notes, logs, recordings and maps documenting fires
- Newspaper articles reporting fires
- Souvenirs from the crime scene

CASE STUDY: 212: ATTENTION SEEKER

Background

During the summer months, several junior volunteer fire fighters sat in the fire station of a small city, complaining that no one, least of all their chief, took them seriously. These sixteen- and seventeen-year-olds were thrilled at the chance to ride on the fire engines they had always admired. Yet, they often were stung by the chief's criticism of their performance. As the bored youths sat and talked, they had an idea: if they could set a fire in a vacant house, they would have a chance to show the chief how well they work. Although some of the young volunteers were reluctant, none of them challenged the idea.

Victimology: Targeted Property

Over the span of one year, ten houses were set on fire. The houses were vacant and had been deemed uninhabitable before the fires occurred. Few of these houses were insured.

Crime Scene Indicators

Fire investigators noticed a pattern: all of the fires occurred in a jurisdiction served by the volunteer fire department, were in vacant houses, and were set during night-time hours. All the houses had electricity and other utilities disconnected.

Forensic Findings

The fires were set with available material. Paper products found at the scene, such as newspapers, cardboard, and kindling of all sorts, were used. These materials were gathered, piled somewhere within the building, and then set on fire with a match or cigarette lighter. No traces of flammable liquid were found. Any footprints or tire tracks were obliterated when the youths returned with the fire-suppression equipment. Forcible entry was rarely necessary and was not apparent at the crime scenes.

Investigation

With so many youthful co-conspirators, the truth eventually reached the authorities conducting the investigation. A search conducted during the course of the investigation produced a diary, in which one of the volunteers detailed the times and locations of a few of the fires. The author of the diary implicated himself and other volunteers, who in turn provided investigators with additional names. Subsequently, eleven of the volunteer fire fighters were charged with arson. One defendant was quoted as saying, "It isn't like we wanted to go out and burn down houses to hurt people. The firehouse was like our second home."

Outcome

Since the defendants had no prior criminal records, they ultimately received sentences ranging from probation to juvenile detention time, depending on the extent of their involvement.

220: REVENGE-MOTIVATED ARSON

A revenge-motivated fire is set in retaliation for some injustice, real or imagined, perceived by the offender. This offense may be a well-planned, one-time event compared with the other categories of arson; or the offender may be a serial arsonist taking revenge against society, with little or no pre-planning. Many arson motivations have an element of revenge in addition to the main motive. The types of revenge-motivated arson included in this category are personal retaliation (221), societal retaliation (222), institutional retaliation (e.g., against the government) (223), group retaliation (e.g., against gangs) (224), intimidation (225), and other (229).

Defining Characteristics

Victimology: Targeted Property. As with most of the arson categories, victimology becomes the key factor in determining the motive. This is especially true with the revenge category. The victim of a revenge fire generally has a history of interpersonal or professional conflict with the offender. Examples are conflicts developing from a lover's triangle, a landlord/tenant relationship, or an employer/employee association. Revenge-motivated arson also tends to be an intraracial offense.

The targeted property often varies with the sex of the offender. Female subjects usually target something of significance to the victim, such as a vehicle or personal effects. The ex-lover revenge arsonist frequently burns clothing, bedding, and/or other personal effects. For the revenge arsonist in general, residential property and vehicles are the prime targets. Arsonists who seek revenge against society may exhibit displaced aggression by choosing targets at random. Other offenders retaliate against institutions such as churches, government facilities, and universities or corporations.

Crime Scene Indicators Frequently Noted. The female offender usually burns an area of personal significance, such as the living room sofa or the bedroom. She often starts the fire by using the victim's clothing or other personal effects. If she targets the victim's vehicle, she usually sets fire to the interior passenger compartment.

The male arsonist also may begin with an area of personal significance, but his fire-setting episode is more wide ranging and destructive. He may use an excessive amount of accelerant and sometimes Molotov cocktails.

Common Forensic Findings. The female arsonist's accelerant of choice tends to be flammables that are readily accessible, such as lighter fluid. However, the male in this category is inclined to use excessive amounts of accelerants such as gasoline. If he uses a Molotov cocktail, cloth for fiber comparisons, glass for possible fingerprints, as well as accelerant residue, are important forensic evidence.

Investigative Considerations

The revenge firesetter is predominantly an adult male with ten or more years of formal education. If employed, this offender usually is a blue-collar worker in the lower socioeconomic status. A revenge arsonist typically resides in some type of rental property. Even though this offender tends not to be a loner and has close relationships, the relationships generally are not stable or long term. An exception is the revenge-motivated serial arsonist who is often a loner.

The revenge arsonist most often will have some type of prior law enforcement contact for crimes such as burglary, theft, or vandalism. The use of alcohol with this offense is common. The offender also may use drugs during the crime, but alcohol use is more prevalent. The offender is rarely accompanied to the crime scene and seldom returns once the fire is set. In fact, he wants as much distance between himself and the fire as possible and concentrates on establishing an alibi. The offender usually lives within the affected community. Mobility is a factor with him, so he often uses a vehicle to get to and from the crime scene. This is in contrast to the revenge-motivated serial arsonist who frequently walks to the scene. After the fire, the offender may increase alcohol consumption. He expresses a short-lived sense of relief and satisfaction and an uncaring attitude toward the victim.

Since the revenge fire is a focused attack, the investigator needs to determine who has suffered the most from this fire. Does the victim have a history of conflict with someone? If the victim is a landlord, who has he evicted recently? If the victim did have an evolving conflict with someone, was an escalation of violence apparent?

The investigator is cautioned that documented studies show the event(s) that precipitate the revenge-motivated arson may take place months or even years prior to the fire (Icove & Horbert, 1990). This factor is commonly overlooked. An investigator should be prepared to expand the search if no suspects or viable leads are apparent from the beginning.

Search Warrant Suggestions:

- If accelerants used: shoes, socks, clothing, glass particles in clothing (if break-in)
- Discarded, concealed clothing
- Bottles, flammable liquids, matchbooks
- Cloth (fiber comparison), tape (if device used)
- Objects taken from the scene
- Clothing, shoes if liquid accelerant used (or homicide victim's blood; glass fragments if windows broken during burglary attempt)

CASE STUDY: 221: PERSONAL REVENGE

Background

A private residence located in a metropolitan suburb was the scene of personal-revenge arson. The owner, a male who lived alone in the house, had been away for a few days. When he returned, he found the interior of his house on fire. In trying to extinguish it himself, he discovered that not one but two fires had been set.

Victimology: Targeted Property

One fire was set in the bedroom and another on the living room couch. A closed bedroom door prevented the two fires from burning together. The living room television set was missing.

The owner of the house was homosexual. He often had male visitors and recently before the fire had a male friend living with him.

Crime Scene Indicators Frequently Noted

The fire was suspicious to investigators from the outset. It was obvious that two separate fires had occurred, with the closed bedroom door preventing the fires from communicating. Investigators eliminated all possible accidental causes of the fire, leaving arson as the only possibility. In the bedroom, a large bed was completely consumed by fire, and the wall behind it was damaged. In the living room, a couch had burned completely through the floor to the ground below. Smoke damage was extreme throughout the home.

Forensic Findings

There was no evidence of forced entry. Doors to the house were locked when the owner returned. The fires were accelerated by lighter fluid applied to both the bed and the couch. An open flame, such as a match or cigarette lighter, was used to ignite the flammable materials. The concentration of fire destroyed both items of furniture. On closer examination of the surrounding areas, the bed and couch were determined to be the points of origin.

Investigation

When the victim noticed his television set was missing, he mentioned to police that a twenty-one-year-old male acquaintance who had recently moved out of the house wanted that television set and previously had stolen other property from him. The former roommate was located and, when interviewed, confessed to setting the fires.

The offender stated he had lived in the victim's home for a few months and moved out about one month before the fire. He complained that visitors went through his belongings and spoke negatively about him to others. Further, on one occasion when all of the guests were drinking, one of them took sexual advantage of the offender. Intent upon revenge, the offender returned to the house when he knew the owner was away and gained entry with a key he had kept. While he was removing the television, he thought about the unpleasant sexual incident and became angrier. He obtained some lighter fluid from a nearby convenience store, returned, and set the fires. He had set the couch on fire because that was where the sexual episode had taken place.

Outcome

The offender was convicted and sentenced to prison for an eight-year term.

230:   CRIME CONCEALMENT-MOTIVATED ARSON

In this category, arson is a secondary or collateral criminal activity, perpetrated for the purpose of covering up a primary criminal activity of some nature. The types of crime concealment-motivated arson included in this category are murder (231), suicide (232), breaking and entering (233), embezzlement (234), larceny (235), destroying records (236), and other (239).

Defining Characteristics

Victimology: Targeted Property. The targeted property is dependent on the nature of the concealment. The target may be a business, a residence, or a vehicle.

Crime Scene Indicators Frequently Noted

Murder Concealment. The fire is an attempt to obliterate the fact that a homicide has been committed, destroy forensic evidence of potential lead value, and/or conceal the victim's identity. The investigator should observe the position and location of the victim to determine whether the victim was alive when the fire started, and if so, why the victim could not escape. Victims grouped together should lead one to suspect murder.

The offender commonly uses liquid accelerant. Although the origin of the fire is usually on or near the victims, many of these fires are not adequate to totally consume the body and/or the evidence. The offender tends to act toward the disorganized end of the spectrum (Ressler, Burgess & Douglas, 1988). Correspondingly, the investigator should expect to find more physical evidence than with other arsons. An attack that appears to be personalized suggests a lone offender. More recently, we have learned of the "DNA torch," an offender who, concerned about the detection of unique genetic markers contained in anatomical fluids, uses fire to conceal a homicide that involves a sexual assault.

Burglary Concealment. With an unsophisticated or less experienced burglar, the crime scene often reflects the use of available materials to start the fire and the presence of multiple offenders.

Auto Theft Concealment. In the case of auto theft concealment, the offender will use and/or strip and burn the vehicle to eliminate prints. This crime frequently involves multiple offenders.

Destruction of Records. When arson is used to destroy records, the fire is set in the area where they are contained. In arson-for-profit cases, records are commonly one of several points of fire origin in (Icove, Schroeder & Wherry, 1979).

Common Forensic Findings. With the use of forensics, one should determine if the victim was alive when the fire began and why did he or she not escape. If the victim sustained injuries, determine whether they were a result of the fire or from a deliberate injury, which could have been sufficient to have prevented escape. The victim of a DNA torch will demonstrate a concentrated area of burns around the genitals. In such instances, the investigator should suspect that a sexual assault had occurred.

Investigative Considerations

Alcohol and recreational drug use is common to the crime-concealment-motivated arsonist. The offender can be expected to have a history of police or fire department contacts or arrests.

The offender is most likely a young adult who lives within the surrounding community and is highly mobile—especially someone involved in auto theft. The offender who uses arson to conceal burglary or auto theft is routinely accompanied to the scene by co-conspirators. Almost all offenders in this category leave the crime scene immediately and do not return. Post-offense behavior may include an increase in alcohol and/or drug consumption.

Murder concealment is usually a one-time event and does not involve serial arson. The investigator inquiring into an arson set to destroy records should discover who would benefit from their concealment.

Search Warrant Suggestions

- Refer to category dealing with primary motive
- Gasoline containers
- Clothing, shoes if liquid accelerant used (or if homicide victim's blood)
- Glass fragments if windows broken during burglary attempt
- Burned paper documents

CASE STUDY: 231: MURDER CONCEALMENT

Background

During the early morning hours, a fire department responded to a fire involving a seventy-year-old two-story residence. The fire soon became a three-alarm blaze requiring over an hour and a half to suppress. As firemen sifted through the debris, they discovered a badly burned body in what appeared to be a sitting position on a sofa in the living room. Firemen noted a hole approximately two inches in diameter in the left frontal area of the skull. Suspecting foul play, they notified the police department's homicide team.

Victimology: Targeted Property

The victim was identified as an eighty-six-year-old woman who had lived alone at the residence for thirty-five years. According to one of her three sisters, the victim had not allowed anyone into her home for six or seven years preceding her death. One sister, who lived nearby, delivered the victim's meals to her but never was allowed farther than the front door.

The victim kept large amounts of money hidden away in the many boxes she had stacked around the house. Her reputation of being a miser was common knowledge in her neighborhood. Her sisters told investigators that the victim was afraid of fire and, consequently, never cooked or used candles, did not smoke, and had the heat turned off.

The victim was a feisty woman who had confronted a intruder in the house just two days before her death. She told her sister that during the night she had awakened to see the intruder and threatened to "poke him full of holes" if he did not leave. She then struck him with a broom handle. She never reported the burglary attempt to the police.

Crime Scene Indicators Frequently Noted

The fire investigators quickly determined that arson was the cause of the fire. Common combustibles and furniture upholstery had been ignited with an open flame in the living room. The use of available materials to start a fire is a typical crime scene indicator of the less-sophisticated arsonist. The origin of the fire was on or near the sofa, where the victim's body had been found.

Most murder-concealment fires are not adequate to destroy the corpse. Even in this instance, in which the fire was aided by the large amount of combustible materials in the house (cardboard boxes full of books, magazines, clothing, and other items piled three to four feet deep in some rooms) investigators found an intact body.

Several pieces of fabric and paper with red stains similar to blood were found in the vicinity of the body. In addition, forcible entry had been made through the rear door.

Forensic Findings

The autopsy revealed a concentration of burns around the victim's head. Even though the corpse was badly burned, pathologists were able to locate and accurately identify the multiple trauma, injuries, unrelated to the fire, which had caused her death. The trauma consisted of an irregularly edged hole in the frontal temporal area of the skull and more than one hundred stab wounds over the entire body. Two of these wounds were gaping holes approximately four inches by three inches. It was obvious the fire began postmortem and was intended to conceal the corpse.

Investigation

The police received several phone calls that provided direction to the investigation. In addition, immediately after the fire, a paperboy came forward and told police he had seen two males counting money on a stairway during the morning after the discovery of the fire. As he approached the men, he was warned to keep walking and forget what he had seen. The paperboy had observed dried blood on the back of one of the suspect's hands.

Subsequently, the police arrested three juvenile males. A female was discovered to have picked them up at the scene in her car, but she was not directly involved with the break-in and murder. The offenders were single males living with family members within the surrounding community of the victim. Each of the suspects had lengthy histories of disruptive behavior at school and police records for arrests (including burglary). All three admitted to heavy alcohol and drug use, with a marked post-offense increase in consumption. They did not return to the scene after the fire was set.

Outcome

After the offenders were arrested and interviewed, each admitted his role as a participant in the crime but shifted the major responsibility of the homicide to one of the others. All three were found guilty of first-degree felony murder and arson and were sentenced to a maximum of twenty-six years in prison.

240: PROFIT-MOTIVATED ARSON

Arson for profit is a fire set for the purpose of achieving material gain, either directly or indirectly (Icove, Schroeder, and Wherry, 1979). It is a commercial crime and exhibits the least passion of any of the motivations that generate the crime of arson. The types of profit-motivated arson found in this category are fraud (241)—including fraud to collect insurance (241.01), fraud to liquidate property (241.02), fraud to dissolve business (241.03), fraud to conceal loss or liquidate inventory (241.04), employment (242), parcel clearance (243), competition (244), and other (249).

Defining Characteristics

Victimology: Targeted Property. The property targeted by arson for profit includes residential property, businesses, and modes of transportation (vehicles, boats, etc.).

Crime Scene Indicators. This type of arson usually involves a well-planned and methodical approach. The crime scene demonstrates a more organized style by containing less physical evidence that would identify the offender and more sophisticated incendiary devices (Ressler, Burgess & Douglas, 1988). When a large business is burned, multiple offenders may be involved.

As the complete destruction of the target is intended, an excessive use of accelerant and multiple sets are evident. Accelerant trailers may also be found at the crime scene.

A lack of forced entry is not infrequent in arson-for-profit cases. Use of incendiary devices is more prevalent than the use of available materials. Such devices are often elaborate (e.g., constructed with timing devices, electrical timers, initiators, candles). The remnants of these devices usually can be found at the crime scene.

Items of value are often removed, especially if a residence is the target. For example, the removal of expensive paintings before the fire may be evidenced by the presence of studs to hold the paintings but no residue of frames present after the fire. Investigators may observe substitution of lower-quality furniture and clothing and lack of personal effects, such as family pictures and photo albums. A suggestion for the investigator is to count the clothes hangers, especially in the woman's closet, to see if the subject's claims of lost belongings match what appears at the crime scene. The torching of select areas not consistent with the pattern of an accidental fire should also raise one's suspicion.

The point of origin of the fire can also be a determining factor. As the intent of the offender is usually to totally destroy the target of arson, the selected point of origin is that which is most efficient to establish the desired loss (e.g., in a structure fire, probable multiple points of origin; in a inventory fire, centered on, or restricted to, that portion of the inventory effected.)

Forensic Findings. A common forensic finding with arson for profit is the use of more sophisticated accelerants (water-soluble accelerants such as alcohol), or mixtures (such as gasoline with diesel fuel or kerosene). Because the use of incendiary devices is common with arson for profit, components of these devices (initiators, electrical timers, timing devices, candles, etc.) are additional forensic findings that may assist the investigator.

Investigative Considerations

The typical primary offender in this category is an adult male with ten or more years of formal education; this may vary, however. A secondary offender is the "torch for hire," who most frequently is a male, twenty-five to forty years of age, and usually unemployed. The torch operates as an agent for the primary offender, who contracts the torch's services and is the dominant personality in the total offense.

The typical primary offender for commercial fires may have no police record. The "torch for hire" will likely have a prior arrest record for offenses such as burglary, assault, public intoxication, and possibly even a previous arson arrest.

The offender generally lives more than one mile from the crime scene. Many arsonists for profit are accompanied to the crime scene, and most leave the scene and do not return.

The offender's pre-offense conversations with others may offer indications of premeditation (e.g., a subject planning to burn his business telling workers to remove their personal effects the day before the fire breaks out). A recent change of ownership and/or increase in insurance policy should raise one's suspicion. The investigator should look for any of the following indicators of financial difficulties if arson for profit is suspected:

Business:
- Decreasing revenue
- Increasing production costs
- New technology making current process/equipment inadequate
- Costly lease or rental agreements

- Unprofitable contracts, loss of key customer
- Failure to record depreciation
- Personal expenses paid with corporate funds
- Bounced checks
- Hypothetical assets, liens on assets, over-insured assets
- Inventory levels: removal prior to fire, overstocking caused by overproduction, exaggeration of loss
- Litigation against business or owners
- Bankruptcy proceedings
- Two sets of books maintained
- Prior years losses
- Prior insurance claims
- Duplicate sales invoices
- Alleged renovations
- Property has frequent change of ownership preceding fire
- Use of photocopies instead of original source documents

Personal:

- Bounced checks
- Costly lease or rental agreements
- Large number of overdue bills
- Inability to pay current bills (utilities, telephone, etc.)
- Credit limits imposed by lenders
- Payment of bills by cashier's check, money order
- Alleged renovations
- Sales between related parties
- Often these offenders have negative cash flow, but they maintain appearances of continued financial health

Search Warrant Suggestions

- Check financial records (worksheets, loan records, credit history, accountant's books, bank records, income tax forms, bank deposit tickets, canceled checks, check stubs)
- If evidence of fuel/air explosion (gasoline vapor and ambient air mixture at sufficient temperature) at the scene, check emergency rooms for patients with burn injuries (this type of explosion does not occur in accidental fires).
- Determine condition of utilities (gas, electric) as soon as possible (eliminate gas, the common accidental cause of fires)

CASE STUDY: 241.01: INSURANCE FRAUD

Background

Early one summer morning, the owner of a rural residence drove to a neighbor's home and asked that the fire department be called. He told neighbors that he had discovered a fire in his house, but as his telephone was out of service, he could not report it himself. He then drove back to his burning home.

Witnesses to the fire noticed that the owner was fully dressed at such an early hour and that he appeared very calm, even after the fire had completely destroyed his home. By the time fire units arrived, the fire had totally destroyed his house, and the only thing left standing was the fireplace chimney.

Victimology: Targeted Property

Although the property was purchased only nine months before the fire, there were four trust deeds. The total purchase price was $271,000. The buyer had made a $5,000 cash down-payment to the previous owner, but he never made any further payments. The buyer had obtained a policy insuring the dwelling for $171,000, the contents for $85,000, and $24,000 for additional living expenses in case of fire.

Crime Scene Indicators

When examining the fire scene, arson investigators found burn patterns that indicated a flammable liquid had been used to accelerate the fire throughout the house—patterns inconsistent with an accidental fire.

Forensic Findings

The carpeting that had been located under the washer and dryer was burned in a manner indicating that flammable liquid had flowed underneath the machines. Furthermore, the investigators found burned studs showing that the fire had been hottest near the floor. They concluded that flammable liquid had been distributed in the kitchen, the living room, the two bedrooms, and the den.

Investigation

Shortly after the fire, the owner of the home submitted a claim to the insurance company. The insurance company subsequently paid the owner

$12,000 in advance claims, over $51,000 to the mortgage holders, and nearly $7,000 to clean up the site.

Several of the items listed on the formal sworn claim submitted to the insurance company by the owner were subsequently found in two storage lockers. In one of the storage lockers, deputies found a very expensive automobile that had been reported stolen.

Outcome

The owner was arrested, convicted, and sentenced to eight years in state prison. He was found to have an extensive criminal record, which included previous arson-for-profit schemes, as well as mail fraud and a host of minor offenses stretching throughout his adult life.

250:   EXTREMIST-MOTIVATED ARSON

Extremist-motivated arson is committed to further a social, political, or religious cause. The types of arson in this category are terrorism (251), discrimination (252), riots/civil disturbance (253), and other (259).

Defining Characteristics

Victimology: Targeted Property. Analysis of the targeted property is essential in the determination of the specific motive for extremist arson. The target usually represents the antithesis of the offender's belief. Examples of targets are research laboratories, slaughter houses, and fur stores burned by the animal rights groups; abortion clinics targeted by extremist right-to-life groups; businesses targeted by unions; religious institutions targeted by individuals holding contrasting beliefs; and groups or individuals targeted by political extremist organizations who seek to intimidate or eradicate racial, religious, political, or sexual-oriented opponents.

Crime Scene Indicators Frequently Noted. The crime scene reflects an organized and focused attack by the offender(s). Multiple offenders are common to this arson. These offenders frequently employ incendiary devices, such as Molotov cocktails, which offer both offender and forensic information. Offenders may leave some form of message (e.g., spray-painted symbols or slogans and/or literature supporting their cause) at the crime scene. Symbolic messages often indicate younger offenders. Communiques are sometimes delivered orally or in writing to the media claiming responsibility or attempting to justify the violent act.

When confronting with obvious "overkill" in setting the fire, investigators should be aware of the possibility of extreme concentrations of flammable or combustible materials used to set the fires. Unexploded incendiary devices may be found at the scene.

Common Forensic Findings. The general arson outline at the beginning of this chapter details more common forensic findings. Extremist arsonists often are more sophisticated offenders and may use incendiary devices.

Investigative Considerations

The extremist offender is frequently readily identified with the cause or group in question when friends, family, and other associates are interviewed. The offender may have previous police contact or an arrest record for violations such as trespassing, criminal mischief, or civil rights violations. Post-offense claims should undergo threat assessment examination to determine authenticity.

Search Warrant Suggestions

- Literature, writings, paraphernalia pertaining to a group or cause. Manuals, diagrams if incendiary devise used (how-to books)
- Incendiary devise components, travel records, sales receipts, credit-card statements, bank records indicating purchases
- Flammable materials, liquids, and containers used to transport the accelerants to the scene

---

CASE STUDY: 250: EXTREMIST-MOTIVATED ARSON

Background

On two separate mornings during the summer, fires were set at the same office building. The first fire was caused when someone stuffed paper and matches through the mail slot of the door and ignited them. On this occasion, damage was confined to charring on the door.

Three months later, another fire was set through the same mail slot. This time, gasoline was poured through the opening and ignited. The rapidly spreading fire caused $150,000 damage before it was contained.

Victimology: Targeted Property

The targeted building housed a medical clinic that performed abortions. The clinic's office manager stated that she had encountered a possible suspect prior to the last fire. The suspect, a white female, was a religious, pro-life advocate, who had been dismissed from a pro-life group because of her radical views. She had threatened to kill the office manager and other office employees. On one occasion, she even followed the office manager to her car.

In addition to the $150,000 fire damage, the victims (a partnership) lost over $220,000 in business. The office manager feared the suspect was not only a danger to the community, but also a danger to clinic employees and their families.

Crime Scene Indicators Frequently Noted

The cause of the first fire was readily apparent due to the limited damage. Fire department investigators were able to determine the cause of the second fire by using burn indicators that enabled them to trace the fire to its source at the mail slot.

The fact that the targeted property was an abortion clinic that had received threats and had suffered a previous fire made it a high risk for an attack by an extremist. Studies show that once a commercial establishment is unsuccessfully set on fire, additional arson attempts will be made (Icove, 1979).

Forensic Findings

Use of gasoline accelerant was determined through laboratory analysis of samples of burned material.

Investigation. The police department spoke to the offender immediately after the first fire at the abortion clinic. She denied any involvement, and there was not sufficient evidence to tie her to the arson. However, after the second fire and another confrontation with the police, she confessed.

One year before the fires, the offender took her bicycle into another abortion clinic and was subsequently arrested for trespassing. The charge was later dismissed.

Outcome

The offender was eventually convicted of arson and is serving a sentence in a state prison. She was found to have a history of mental disorders.

260: SERIAL ARSON

Arsonists who set fires repeatedly are referred to as serial firesetters (Lewis & Yarnell, 1951). The NCAVC classifies compulsive firesetting as mass, spree, or serial (Icove & Horbert, 1990).

The *serial* arsonist is involved in three or more separate firesetting episodes, with a characteristic emotional cooling-off period between fires. This period may last days, weeks, or even years. Serial arson is the most serious type of arson due to the apparent random selection of victims and unpredictable gaps between incidents. Furthermore, a serial arsonist may commit a spree of arsons during each firesetting episode. Serial arson is not a separate or distinct motive for setting fires; rather it is a pattern of firesetting frequently encountered in revenge-, excitement-, or extremist-motivated arsons.

Serial arsonists often create a climate of fear in entire communities. Community leaders tend to compound the problem by pressuring law enforcement agencies to identify and quickly apprehend the firesetter. Often, the arsonist evades apprehension for months, while investigators become increasingly frustrated by a lack of experience in handling these baffling cases.

Defining Characteristics

Victimology: Targeted Property. The arsonist usually selects vulnerable targets such as unoccuppied or abandoned property, during nighttime hours. The choice of targets may be random.

Crime Scene Indicators Frequently Noted. This type of arson usually involves a disorganized crime scene; physical evidence is often present. The offender frequently uses available materials found at the scenes and carries the source of ignition with him. Usually, a lone offender is involved.

Common Forensic Findings. Forensic findings of materials found at the crime scene may correspond to the underlying motivation. For example, a large quantity of flammable liquid may indicate a revenge fire or arson for profit. Spray paint samples from an aerosol can might point to vandalism as a motive. A lack of forensic evidence may be indicative of the serial arsonist who uses available material to kindle his fires. Conversely, many wildland serial arsonists use cigarette and match devices.

Investigative Considerations

The typical offender in this category is usually male. His age is generally younger than the single-event arsonist. He tends to be a loner, but a secondary party may have knowledge of his activities. He will tend to be minimally educated and an underachiever. He generally has poor interpersonal relationships and is socially inadequate. Often, he is unemployed, and if he has an employment history, it is erratic and involves little or no skills. Serial arsonists often have a history of substance abuse and a history of police contact/arrests for minor, nuisance offenses.

The offender walks to the scene of the fire and generally lives within one mile of the crime scenes. He is very likely to be familiar with the crimes scenes and could justify his presence in the area.

It is important to analyze the cluster centers of fire activity. The tighter the cluster, the closer to the area of significance to the offender (e.g., residence or place of employment) (Icove, 1991).

A subtype of the serial arsonist is the extremist serial arsonist. Research suggests that this offender is usually well educated and above average in intelligence. He is highly mobile and focuses his attacks on specific targets. He uses sophisticated incendiary devices. The crime scene is organized, and there is little or no physical evidence.

CASE STUDY: 260: SERIAL ARSON

Background

During the summer and fall months, a series of arsons targeting unoccupied dwellings plagued a medium-sized midwestern community. The arsonist's fires became increasingly destructive and life threatening, alarming local residents and overtaxing the resources of law enforcement and fire officials. Based upon a request by local law enforcement for assistance, the NCAVC participated in the case.

Victimology: Targeted Property

The targeted property consisted at first of abandoned dwellings in an area marked for an urban renewal project. The arsonist escalated his fire setting over time to include occupied dwellings when the owners were away. In one later case, a fire was set to a house when the family was sleeping inside.

Crime Scene Indicators

The fires were set to the inside of the abandoned buildings using whatever material was at hand to kindle the fire. Available materials were also used to set fire to the outside porches of occupied dwellings. In more than one case, kerosene or another flammable liquid was used when found at the scene by the offender. On several occasions, footprints were found. With other fires, where little damage was done, matches were found at the origin. Due to the fairly limited geographical area in which the fires occurred, it was apparent the arsonist walked to the scene of the fires. They all took place between 11:00 P.M. and 3:00 A.M.

Forensic Findings

Available material, particularly paper goods such as newsprint or cardboard, which survived fires which did little damage, were examined for fingerprints with limited success. Partial prints were recovered but may not have been those of the offender. Photographs and plaster casts were made of footprints suspected of belonging to the arsonist.

Investigation

Local investigators interviewed scores of potential witnesses and failed to develop any good suspects. Unable to break the case, the police turned to the NCAVC for assistance.

Arson specialists from the NCAVC examined all the case material submitted, which included a spot map, reports, and photographs. The analysis consisted of a target, temporal, and geographical study of the incidents. The conclusions of the analysis suggested the offender was a white male between the ages of 19 and 25, an unemployed loner with an alcohol problem. His apparent undetected movements to and from the crime scenes suggested a familiarity with the neighborhood. The geographic cluster analysis indicated the location of the "centroid" predicting the area in which this offender lived. Psychologically the arsonist was predicted to be an underachiever who did poorly in school and raised in a dysfunctional home in which he still lived with one parent. It was predicted he would have an arrest record with a variety of minor offenses. The police were further directed to look for an individual who was unkempt in appearance and behaved in a disorganized fashion. The police were able to develop a suspect based upon the NCAVC report and investigative suggestions.

Outcome

The arsonist confessed to the police during an initial interview and was convicted of twelve of the twenty-three counts of arson.

261: SPREE ARSON

A *spree* arsonist sets fires at three or more separate locations with no emotional cooling-off period between them. Examples include arsonists in Detroit, Michigan, who roam the city setting numerous fires during its so-called Hell Night, the night before Halloween.

262: MASS ARSON

Mass arson involves one offender who sets three or more fires at the same location during a limited period of time. An example is an offender who sets a fire on each floor of a multi-story building.

3

Rape and Sexual Assault

300: Criminal enterprise rape
  301: Felony rape
    301.01: Primary felony rape
    301.02: Secondary felony rape
310: Personal cause sexual assault
  311: Nuisance offenses
    311.01: Isolated/opportunistic offense
    311.02: Preferential offense
    311.03: Transition offense
    311.04: Preliminary offense
  312: Domestic sexual assault
    312.01: Adult domestic sexual assault
    312.02: Child domestic sexual abuse
  313: Entitlement rape
    313.01: Social acquaintence rape
      313.01.01: Adult
      313.01.02: Adolescent
      313.01.03: Child
    313.02 Subordinate rape
      313.02.01: Adult
      313.02.02: Adolescent

313.02.03: Child

313.03: Power-reassurance rape

313.03.01: Adult

313.03.02: Adolescent

313.03.03: Child

313.04: Exploitative rape

313.04.01: Adult

313.04.02: Adolescent

313.04.03: Child

314: Anger rape

314.01: Gender

314.02: Age

314.02.01: Elderly victim

314.02.02: Child victim

314.03: Racial

314.04: Global

315: Sadistic rape

315.01: Adult

315.02: Adolescent

315.03: Child

316: Child/adolescent pornography

316.01: Closet collector

316.02: Isolated collector

316.03: Cottage collector

317: Historical child/adolescent sex rings

317.01: Solo child sex ring

317.02: Transitional child sex ring

317.03: Syndicated child sex ring

318: Multidimensional sex rings

318.01: Adult survivors sex rings

318.02: Day-care sex rings

318.03: Family/isolated neighborhood sex rings

318.04: Custody/visitation dispute sex rings

319: Abduction rape

319.01: Adult

319.02: Adolescent

319.03: Child

330: Group cause sexual assault
  331: Formal gang sexual assault
    331.01: Single victim
    331.02: Multiple victims
  332: Informal gang sexual assault
    332.01: Single victim
    332.02: Multiple victims
 390: Sexual assault not classified elsewhere

Sexual assault includes criminal offenses in which victims are forced or coerced to participate in sexual activity. Physical violence may or may not be involved. In many offenses involving children, the offender may gain the cooperation of the victim using little or no force. This "seduction" of child victims has no comparable offense when committed against adults.

Definitions of what constitutes rape and sexual assault vary from state to state, resulting in marked differences in the reported frequencies of offense and behavior categories in different samples reported in the literature. Although distinction is made in the literature between rape and sexual assault, for the purposes of this book, the terms are used interchangeably and are not to be construed as a legal definition. Each jurisdiction will apply its own legal definition to an offense.

Classification of entities into homogeneous groups is a fundamental process in all sciences. Because, currently, there are no taxonomic systems for rapists or child molesters that have achieved universal acceptance, we have attempted to integrate components from several typological systems that have been shown to have some empirical utility (Groth 1979; Lanning 1986; Prentky, Cohen & Seghorn 1986; Hazelwood 1987; Knight, Carter & Prentky 1989.) These systems continue to undergo revision (e.g., Knight & Prentky 1990), and we hope to incorporate empirically validated developments into future editions of this manual.

The subtypes described here attempt to capture components judged to be critical across taxonomic systems. Where possible, we have attempted to derive descriptions from published research or from cases drawn from these ongoing research programs. Classifications were made in the following manner. The lengthy clinical files were condensed into research files, which included diagnostic and evaluation information, school and employment reports, police reports and court testimony, parole summaries, probation records, social service notes, past institutional records, and complete records on familial and developmental history. The research files were read and subtyped independently by two senior clinicians familiar with the subject population. When there was disagreement in primary subtype, the raters met to resolve discrepancies and reach a consensus. In the event that discrepancies could not be resolved, a third clinician made an independent rating. If this third judgment failed to promote a consensus of agreement, the case was omitted. This occurred in 8 of 108 cases.

RAPIST CLASSIFICATION

The taxonomic studies on which the following descriptions of convicted rapist types are based on focus on the interaction of sexual and aggressive motivations. Although all rape clearly includes both motivations, for some rapists the need to humiliate and injure through aggression is the most salient feature of the offense, whereas for others the need to achieve sexual dominance is the most salient feature of the offense. In abbreviated fashion, four of the subcategories of rapist follow.

For the *power-reassurance rapist,* the assault is primarily an expression of his rape fantasies. There is usually a history of sexual preoccupation typified by the living out or fantasizing of a variety of perversions, including bizarre masturbatory practices, voyeurism, exhibitionism, obscene telephone calls, cross dressing, and fetishism. There is often high sexual arousal accompanied by a loss of self-control, causing a distorted perception of the victim/offender relationship (for example, the rapist may want the victim to respond in a sexual or erotic manner and may even try to make a date after the assault). The core of his fantasy is that the victim will enjoy the experience and perhaps even fall in love with him. The motivation derives from the rapist's belief that he is so inadequate that no woman in her right mind would voluntarily have sex with him. In sum, this is an individual who is compensating for his acutely felt inadequacies as a male.

For the *exploitative rapist,* sexual behavior is expressed as an impulsive predatory act. The sexual component is less integrated in fantasy life and has far less psychologic meaning to the offender. In other words, the rape is an impulsive act determined more by situation and contact than by conscious fantasy. The assailant can best be described and understood as a man on the prowl for a woman to exploit sexually. The offender's intent is to force the victim to submit sexually, and hence, he is not concerned about the victim's welfare.

For the *anger rapist,* sexual behavior is an expression of anger and rage. Sexuality is in the service of a primary aggressive aim, with the victim representing, in a displaced fashion, the hated individual(s). Although the offense may reflect a cumulative series of experienced or imagined insults from many people, such as family members, wife, or girlfriends, it is important to note that there need not be any historical truth to these perceived injustices. This individual is a misogynist; hence, the aggression may span a wide range from verbal abuse to brutal murder.

For the *sadistic rapist,* sexual behavior is an expression of sexual-aggressive (sadistic) fantasies. It appears as if there is a fusion (i.e., no differentiation) or synergism betweem sexual and aggressive feelings. As sexual arousal increases, aggressive feelings increase; simultaneously, increases in aggressive feelings heighten sexual arousal. Anger is not always apparent, particularly at the outset; the assault may actually begin as a seduction. The anger may begin to emerge as the offender becomes sexually aroused, often resulting in the most bizarre and intense forms of sexual-aggressive violence. Unlike the anger rapist, the sadist's violence is usually directed at parts of the body having sexual significance (breasts, anus, buttocks, genitals, mouth).

CLASSIFICATION BY AGE OF VICTIM

This chapter classifies the victim by age. Victims are divided into three categories. *Adults* are defined as individuals at least eighteen years of age who are almost always pubescent and usually are considered capable of consent under laws proscribing sexual conduct. Some exceptions may include persons who are mentally retarded, brain impaired, or psychotic. *Adolescents* are defined as individuals thirteen to seventeen years of age who are usually pubescent but whose legal status under laws proscribing sexual conduct varies from state to state and even statute to statute within the same jurisdiction. *Children* are defined as individuals twelve years of age or younger who are usually prepubescent and who are considered minors incapable of consent under almost all laws proscribing sexual conduct.

Every attempt should be made to evaluate whether a sexual assault was committed for situational or preferential sexual motives. *Situationally motivated sexual assaults* are those committed to fulfill sexual and other needs without the elements of the offense being necessary for arousal or gratification (e.g., raping a woman because she is available and vulnerable). *Preferentially motivated sexual assaults* are those committed to fulfill sexual and other needs with some elements of the offense being necessary for arousal or gratification (e.g., raping a woman because without an unwilling partner, the offender cannot feel aroused or gratified).

Preferentially motivated sexual offenses usually involve strong patterns of behavior or sexual rituals that are difficult for the offender to change. *Sexual ritual* involves repeatedly engaging in an act or series of acts in a certain manner because of a sexual need. In other words, in order for a person to become sexually aroused and/or gratified, he or she must engage in the act in a certain way. This sexual ritualism can include such things as the physical characteristics, age, or gender of the victim; the particular sequence of acts; the bringing or taking of specific objects; or the use of certain words or phrases.

Sexual ritual is more than the concept of method of operation, or modus operandi, (MO) known to most law enforcement officers. MO is something done by an offender because it works. Sexual ritual is something done by an offender because of a need. Therefore, it is much harder for an offender to change, vary, or adjust the ritual than his MO. Both preferential and situational sex offenders may have an MO, but the preferential offender is more likely to have a sexual ritual.

Attempting to identify both patterns of behavior (MO and ritual) and distinguishing between them is a difficult but worthwhile investigative effort. From an investigative view, the preferential offense often has clear evidence that the offender thought, planned, and went searching for a particular victim. In the situational offense, there is evidence of impulsive, opportunistic, predatory behavior, such as the victim being present or a spur-of-the-moment decision to offend.

It is especially important in child victim sexual assaults to attempt to determine if the child was the victim for preferential or situational reasons. The corroborating evidence, whether there are additional child victims, how to interview a suspect, and so on depend on the type of child molester involved. Situational child molesters do not have a true sexual preference for children but engage in sex with children for varied and sometimes complex reasons ranging from child availability to offender inadequacy.

The preferential child molesters have a definite sexual preference for children. Their sexual fantasies and erotic imagery focus on children. Preferential child molesters almost always have access to children, molest multiple victims, and collect child pornography or child erotica.

A preferential child molester (*pedophile*) might have other psychosexual disorders, personality disorders, or psychosis or may be involved in other types of criminal activity. A pedophile's sexual interest in children might be combined with other sexual deviations (*paraphilias*), which include indecent exposure (*exhibitionism*), obscene phone calls (*scatophilia*), exploitation of animals (*zoophilia*), urination (*urophilia*), defecation (*coprophilia*), binding (*bondage*), baby role playing (*infantilism*), infliction of pain (*sadism, masochism*), real or simulated death (*necrophilia*), and others. The preferential child molester is interested in sexual activity with children that might, in some cases, involve other sexual deviations. A preferential sex offender who is involved in a variety of specific sexual deviations might become a situational child molester by selecting a child victim who is available or vulnerable. The preferential child molester must have (1) a high amount of victim contact and (2) a high level of fixation.

Amount of Victim Contact. A preemptory distinction is made between those offenders who have spent a substantial amount of their time in close proximity to victims (*high contact*) and those offenders who have spent little or no time with victims outside of sexual assaults (*low contact*).

Amount of contact is a behavioral measure of the time spent with victims. It includes both sexual and nonsexual situations but excludes the contact that results from parental responsibilities. The contact distinction must be distinguished from the fixation decision, which attempts to assess the strength of an individual's pedophilic interest.

High Contact. Evidence for high contact includes structured and non-structured involvement with a victim through an occupation or through recreation (e.g., schoolteacher, bus driver, carnival worker, riding stable attendant, newspaper delivery person, scout leader, sports coach, youth group volunteer, baby-sitter). These occupational criteria are only intended to help identify the level of contact for those already determined to be child molesters. Other evidence for high contact may include regular visits by the victim to the offenders's home or the offender acting as an adopted father or big brother. In addition, we assume that repeated sexual (nonincestual) encounters with a victim imply the development of a relationship that goes beyond sexual involvement. For that reason, when there are three or more sexual encounters with the same victim, the offender is coded as having high contact.

Fixation. The *level of fixation* decision attempts to access the strength of an offender's pedophilic interest.

High Fixation. An offender is considered *highly fixated* if any of the following are present:

1. There is evidence of three or more sexual encounters with a victim, and the time period between the first and third encounter was greater than six months. These encounters may be with a single victim over many incidents and should not be limited to charged offenses.
2. There is evidence that the offender has had enduring relationships with the victim (excluding parental contact). This includes sexual and nonsexual contact and professional and nonprofessional contact.
3. The offender has initiated contact with children in numerous situations over his lifetime.

General Forensic Evidence Collections for Rape and Sexual Assault

There are many physical evidence recovery methods and procedures that can be used in investigating sexual assault. These methods and procedures usually will depend on the age and sex of the person on whom they are used, as well as whether this individual is a victim or suspect. The following is essentially a general description of forensic evidence. More detailed information can be found in Hazelwood and Burgess 1987.

Most of the evidence will come from the victim and will fall into the following categories: clothing, human hair (head and pubic), swabbing (vaginal, penile, oral, and anal), vaginal aspirate, oral rinse, nasal mucus, fingernail scrapings, blood, saliva, and miscellaneous debris. Each item must be packaged separately to avoid transfer of evidence from one item to another. Sections of manila-type wrapping paper or sturdy paper bags can be supplied for packaging purposes. Unstained control samples of all the gathering mediums are retained and packaged separately. Rape evidence kits that contain the necessary equipment usually are used by hospital examining staff.

All clothing worn by the victim should be obtained and packaged in a sealed, secure condition. The head-hair region of the victim is combed or brushed for evidence substances. This requires the use of an uncontaminated comb or brush specifically for the head area only. The comb or brush and adhering materials are packaged and sealed. An appropriate amount of hair to represent color, length, and area variation is obtained. Known hairs (hairs from a known source) should be acquired after the head-hair combing/brushing procedure is completed.

The pubic region of the victim also is combed or brushed for evidence materials. An appropriate amount of hair to represent color, length, and area variation is obtained. Hairs should be obtained whenever possible. Known pubic hairs should be acquired after the pubic-hair combing/ brushing procedure is completed.

In the event an individual is observed to have excessive body hair, a separate, uncontaminated comb or brush and appropriate packaging material can be utilized to collect trace evidence (e.g., fibers from clothing) that may be present.

The vaginal, oral, and anal cavities are swabbed to detect the presence of spermatozoa and/or seminal fluid. In addition to vaginal swabbing, aspiration of the vaginal region is accomplished by irrigation with saline solution. Spermatozoa not located through the swabbing procedure may be recovered in this manner. The mouth of the person examined can be rinsed in order to remove spermatozoa not collected via the swabbing procedure. The rinse is expectorated into a tube or vial. A control sample of rinse is retained and packaged separately. Control samples of the irrigation and rinse fluids also are retained and packaged separately.

For male victims, the penis is swabbed to detect the presence of blood or other evidence.

Nasal mucus samples also can be of use. Nasal mucus is acquired by having the individual being examined blow his/her nose on cloth. The mucus may contain spermatozoa that were deposited in the mouth or facial area. An unstained portion of the cloth can function as a control sample.

Using appropriate materials, the area underneath the fingernails is scraped for significant debris, such as hairs, fibers, blood, or tissue. The gathering implement is retained. It is suggested that each hand be scraped individually, and the resulting debris should be packaged separately.

Blood is drawn into a sterile test tube for blood grouping purposes. A minimum of 5 milliliters is recommended, preferably without the inclusion of a chemical anticoagulant or preservative.

Evidence materials that fall into the category of miscellaneous debris are substances not included in the previous categories and can often be observed during the forensic examination. These also should be collected and packaged separately. A section of paper or cloth on which the person can stand while undressing can be supplied. Additionally, a separate piece of paper or cloth can be used to cover the examining table to collect any evidence that is dislodged during the examination.

300: CRIMINAL ENTERPRISE RAPE

Criminal enterprise sexual assault involves sexual coercion, abuse, or assault that is committed for material gain.

301: FELONY RAPE

Sexual assault committed during the commission of a felony, such as breaking and entering or robbery, is considered felony rape. The classification is made as to whether the rape was primary or secondary in intent.

301.01: PRIMARY FELONY RAPE

The intent of primary felony rape is a nonsexual felony (e.g., robbery or breaking and entering). The victim is at the scene of the primary felony and is sexually assaulted as a second offense. If the victim was not present, the felony would still occur.

Defining Characteristics

Victimology. The victim is usually an adult female. Either the victim is employed at the crime scene or the felony occurred in the victim's residence.

Crime Scene Indicators Frequently Noted. Evidence of a breaking and entering, burglary, or robbery (missing property, etc.) is noted in a primary felony rape.

Common Forensic Findings. For common forensic findings, see the general forensic evidence collection for sexual assault as outlined above.

Investigative Considerations

Investigators should look for similar felonies in the area of the crime. These felonies usually have reported similar items stolen and a similar MO. The sexual offense is situationally motivated.

Search Warrant Suggestions

Warrants should be requested for a suspect's residence and car. Suggested items should include clothing to test for blood, hair, and fibers. Investigators should search for the victim's personal possessions reported stolen and for newspaper articles related to similar crimes.

CASE STUDY: 301.01: PRIMARY FELONY RAPE

Background/Victimology

A nineteen-year-old woman and her twenty-year-old boyfriend were awakened at 3:00 A.M. by three men who broke into their motel room. Two of the intruders robbed them of money and jewelry. The third man pulled back the bedcovers and stated, "What do we have here?" He then proceeded to rape the young woman.

The couple were students at a nearby college. After the intruders left the room, the couple dressed, and the boyfriend went to the front desk to return the room key. When asked why he was leaving so early, he reported the robbery. The desk clerk called police.

Crime Scene Indicators

When police inspected the crime scene, they noted blood on the sheets in addition to the disarray of the room. They asked if anything else had occurred during the crime. At that point, the young woman said she had been raped.

Investigation

Further investigation revealed that a next-door occupant had called the front desk around 3:15 A.M. to report hearing a woman screaming. It was also learned that a housekeeper recently had been fired and had taken a master key set. Several robberies had been reported at the motel, but no rapes. In this case, robbery was the primary motive, and when the opportunity presented itself, rape also occurred.

The offender would be classified a power reassurance rapist (see 313.03).

Throughout the rape, he asked many personal sexual questions. The fact that he raped with witnesses, both the boyfriend and his co-defendants, emphasizes the exhibitionistic nature of the act. Also, the rape was situationally motivated.

Forensic Findings

Forensic evidence noted semen present; blood matched the victim's blood.

Outcome

The offenders were never apprehended. A civil suit against the motel resulted in a substantial settlement for the couple.

301.02: SECONDARY FELONY RAPE

The primary intent of the offender in secondary felony rape is sexual assault with a second felony also planned. The nonsexual assault felony would still occur if an adult female were not present.

Defining Characteristics

Victimology. The victim is usually an adult female.

Crime Scene Indicators Frequently Noted. Evidence of breaking and entering or robbery is noted in a secondary felony rape.

Common Forensic Findings. In addition to the general forensic evidence, the forensics report indicates that the offender's primary focus while at the crime scene was the sexual assault, not the robbery. The secondary felony was committed knowing the victim of the sexual assault would be present.

Investigative Considerations

In secondary felony rape, the offender targets the victim/crime scene, and the offender has been in the area before. There will be a history of robberies and rapes in the area. In addition, the sexual offense is preferentially motivated.

Search Warrant Considerations.

See 301.01.

CASE STUDY: 301.02 SECONDARY FELONY RAPE

Background/Victimology

A masked offender confronted a twenty-one-year-old, white, single female in her residence at 5:30 in the morning. He had entered her apartment through an open bathroom window. He put a razor to the victim's throat, forcing her to the ground and threatening her with the razor. He took off her pants and underwear and told her he would cut her if she did not comply. He removed a tampon and threw it in her face. He forced oral sex and then raped her. He robbed the victim and fled the scene.

Offender Characteristics

The offender is a thirty-five-year-old, single, Black Muslim male who states he lives in a racist white society. Although charged with multiple offenses, he feels he did not commit the offenses and believes that the five women he was accused of raping worked for him as prostitutes because he was their pimp.

He is the third oldest of seven children born to parents who divorced when he was eight years old. His father is an engineer; his mother a registered pharmacist and dietician; his siblings hold responsible jobs. The offender has an eleventh-grade education and served one and one-half years in the army.

The offender also could be classified as an anger rapist. His victims included white and black women who were social acquaintances, as well as strangers. His assaults were violent, had a high level of aggression, and were preferentially motivated.

Outcome

The offender was sentenced to fifteen to twenty years for assault with intent to rape, with concurrent sentences for five counts of rape and for armed robbery, assault and battery, assault with intent to murder, and indecent assault and battery.

310   PERSONAL CAUSE SEXUAL ASSAULT

Sexual assault motivated by personal cause is an act ensuing from interpersonal aggression that results in sexual victimization to person(s) who may or may not be known to the offender. These sexual assaults are not primarily motivated by material gain and are not sanctioned by a group. Rather, an underlying emotional conflict or psychological issue propels the offender to commit sexual assault. Although the case may be legally defined as *rape,* the term *sexual assault* is used in this classification to encompass a wide range of forced and pressured sexual activities.

311: NUISANCE OFFENSES

There are four separate categories for this group of nuisance offenses. The offense occurs for sexual gratification. The defining characteristic is that the offense involves no physical contact between victim and offender. Police need to investigate and deal with these offenses given the amount of time and priority they have available.

Offenders in these four categories may be viewed as undesirable individuals, but when they are interviewed with empathy and understanding, the police officer may find that the individuals already have committed serious contact sexual offenses. Spending time with these offenders may have an important payoff in solving other sexual assault crimes.

One question to consider regarding nuisance offenders is whether they are dangerous. It is important to evaluate two points: (1) focus and (2) escalation.

Do these crimes have a focus? Is there a pattern occurring over and over? Anything that indicates there is a pattern, such as the offender calling the same number repeatedly or exposing himself at the same location, should be evaluated carefully. The most important aspect of focus to evaluate is victim focus. Are victims being selected at random, or is a specific individual being targeted?

Is there escalation? Has this individual escalated his behavior from peeping outside to burglarizing an indoor location? Is he progressing to more serious invasive activity over time?

It would be important to investigate the background of the nuisance offender. What did the individual do as a teenager? Is this a sixty-year-old man who has been doing this for years? What else is happening in the individual's life? Does he have a stable life? Did he go to school? Is he working? Is he functioning? Such interview areas help to evaluate the offender.

311.01: ISOLATED/OPPORTUNISTIC OFFENSE

Isolated/opportunistic offenses are isolated incidents of individuals who take an opportunity or something presents itself (e.g., they call someone on the phone and get a wrong number and blurt out an obscenity; or when in a public place after having too much to drink, they urinate as a woman walks by and turn and expose themselves). Another example is an offender who walks down a street and takes advantage of an opportunity to look into a window at something sexually stimulating.

311.02: PREFERENTIAL OFFENSE

Preferential offenses relate to the psychiatric diagnoses termed the *paraphilias*. The acts are the individual's preferred sexual act (e.g., the true voyeur, the exhibitionist, etc.). Sexual gratification is intended from the act. These are the individuals for whom this has been a long-term pattern of compulsive behavior. The individual may have regular routes for window peeping or elaborate procedures covering such behavior, such as walking a dog. In some cases, the offender carries a video camera to record his sexual interest.

The key to this type of case is having the time to discover the evidence, as it is a highly solvable case. What makes this type of case easy to solve are these rigid, ritual patterns of behavior. The offenders return to specific areas over and over for peeping, or they expose themselves in certain places. They repeatedly make obscene phone calls, which makes it easy to trace them. Thus, although the preferential pattern is highly solvable, the demand for solving contact sex offenses takes a higher priority for police departments.

311.03: TRANSITION OFFENSE

The transition offender may be caught in a peeping act, but he is trying to find out if the act is capable of producing sexual gratification. He is exploring his arousal patterns, building confidence, and improving his ability to commit crime. This offender is often a younger individual, such as a teenager who is exploring his sexuality and starts out with peeping. However, this is just an early step in his criminal sexual development. In one case, a serial rapist described this type of early sexual interest. No one had stopped or encountered him at this early point. Although not all nuisance sex offenders progress to more serious offenses, some do.

311.04: PRELIMINARY OFFENSE

A preliminary offender is an individual whose nuisance offense is a preliminary aspect to contact sexual offenses. He may be a fetish burglar who cases a home prior to returning to commit a rape. This noncontact offense is a prelude to other serious sex offenses. For example, the rapist may be a window peeper. The police officer encounters him window peeping prior to his intended future rape at that location. The important point is that any nuisance offense may be a prelude to a contact offense and needs to be evaluated as such.

312: DOMESTIC SEXUAL ASSAULT

Domestic sexual assault is when a family, household member, or former household member sexually assaults another member of the household. This definition includes common-law relationships. The sexual assault may be spontaneous and situational and is triggered by a recent stressful event, real or imagined, perceived by the offender as an injustice. It also may be the result of a cumulative buildup of stress over time.

312.01: ADULT DOMESTIC SEXUAL ASSAULT

In addition to assault of a spouse, the spouse sexual assault category includes sexual assault on a nonmarital companion with whom the offender is living if it appears that he has been in a long-term relationship with the victim.

Defining Characteristics

Victimology. The victim has a familial or common-law relationship with the offender. There is usually a history of prior abuse or conflict with the offender.

Crime Scene Indicators Frequently Noted. Usually, only one crime scene is involved, and it is commonly the victim's and/or offender's residence. The crime scene reflects disorder and the impetuous nature of the assault. The crime scene may also reflect the escalation of violence (e.g., the confrontation starts as an argument, intensifies into hitting or throwing things and culminates in the sexual assault).

Common Forensic Findings. Alcohol or drugs maybe involved. If the sexual assault is preceded by violence, trauma to the face and body may be seen on the victim.

Investigative Considerations

If the crime occurred in the residence, domestic sexual assault should be a consideration. When other family members are contacted, they often describe a history of domestic conflict involving the victim and offender. A history of conflict due to external sources (financial, vocational, alcohol, etc.) are common elements of domestic sexual assault. The offense is usually situational. The offender may have demonstrated aggression in the past as well as a change in attitude after the triggering event.

Search Warrant Suggestions

A search warrant is used for the collection of clothing or a weapon at the offender's residence if different from the victim.

CASE STUDY: 312.01 ADULT DOMESTIC SEXUAL ASSAULT

Background/Victimology

On the evening of 16 April 1990 and again the following morning, Mrs. R. was raped by her estranged husband, Herb. The incident began when Herb called her at work asking to rotate her tires, which she declined. She came home and walked her dog, and Herb appeared. Grabbing her wrist, he ordered her into the house, shut and locked the door, and stated, "This is the end." She was terrified. She testified that he had clenched fists and a menacing look on his face. He forced her into an upstairs bedroom and made her undress. After standing naked for a long period of time, she sat down, at which point Herb became angry, saying he had not told her she could sit down. During this time, Mrs. R. was cold and frightened, and she tried to keep him talking, hoping to out think him. Eventually, he allowed her to dress.

Herb left to get sandwiches, but Mrs. R. was too frightened to leave. The offender returned and ate his sandwich, but Mrs. R. was too scared to eat. Herb then stated he wanted sex. Mrs. R. said no and pleaded with him not to force her. Herb raped her then and in the early morning. Mrs. R. was crying and rigid throughout the rape and did not sleep the remainder of the night. After Herb left in the morning, Mrs. R. called her therapist and lawyer. She moved in with a relative, who accompanied her to work each morning and evening.

Offender Characteristics

Mrs. R. and Herb were married in 1984. Since that time, Herb had a history of several affairs. He had verbally threatened to kill Mrs. R. on several occasions, pushing her around physically and threatening her with guns that he kept in the home. His violence included ripping her clothes and tearing the telephone off the wall. She obtained a restraining order against him, which he defied and which resulted in a legal separation. Despite the restraining order, he continued to threaten her and waited for her at her residence. This behavior resulted in Mrs. R.'s moving six times in a four-month period, because he would discover her whereabouts and continue to stalk her.

Outcome

As part of the divorce action, a civil suit was filed in which rape was part of the extreme cruelty charges. Additional compensation was obtained for the wife as a result of her suffering post-traumatic stress disorder.

312.02: CHILD DOMESTIC SEXUAL ABUSE

The category of child domestic sexual abuse includes sexual assault on any household member under the majority age in the state where the crime is committed.

Defining Characteristics

Victimology. The victim has a familial or common-law relationship with the offender. There is usually a history of prior abuse or conflict with the offender. Other members of the family may also be sexually or physically abused.

Crime Scene Indicators Frequently Noted. Usually only one crime scene is involved, and it is commonly the victim's and/or offender's residence.

Common Forensic Findings. If the sexual assault takes place over a period of time, there maybe evidence of vaginal or anal scarring. However, lack of medical corroboration does not mean the child was not victimized.

Investigative Considerations

Prior abuse of the victim or other members of the household may have been previously reported by other family members or by third parties.

Search Warrant Considerations.

Search warrant considerations are not usually indicated if family member is in residence with the child.

CASE STUDY: 312.02: CHILD DOMESTIC SEXUAL ABUSE

Background/Victimology

Two sisters, ages fifteen and fourteen, were sexually abused multiple times by the live-in boyfriend of their mother. The abuse was reported to the natural father's second wife (stepmother of the two girls).

Each girl was forced to take naps and showers with the abuser. He would rub the girl's breasts and genitals and force oral and vaginal sex. The girls were given beer and liquor and were threatened with physical violence if anyone found out about the abuse. The abuse continued for eight to ten years. Food, clothing, and medical attention were withheld from the children. One of the victims was forced to touch a hot radiator, which caused severe burns to her palms. When the girls reached puberty, the abuser would rip open or unfasten their shirts, exposing their breasts to his male friends who were present.

The abuser had many previous offenses, such as armed robbery, conspiracy, and weapons possession. He also had been charged with arson, but the charge was dropped due to insufficient evidence.

The offender first met the victims when he saw them panhandling on the street; the girls were three or four years old at that time. He then met their mother shortly afterwards, and the relationship began. When the girls visited their natural father and stepmother at age twelve and thirteen, suspicions were raised that the girls were abused and neglected. After the girls moved in with their natural father, they were able to disclose directly the abuse. The case was reported to authorities.

The mother denied any knowledge of the offenses. She stated she was beaten severely many times as well as subjected to severe mental cruelty by the offender. He fathered her two sons, and it was suspected that the boys were both physically and sexually abused by their father. He was reported to have had a series of homosexual relationships. The mother was very concerned that she would be harmed by the abuser if he found out that she was cooperating with the investigation.

Neighbors reported suspected child abuse when the girls were in third and fourth grades. The girls were interviewed by a social worker but denied abuse because of the abuser's threats of harm if they told. The four children were not allowed to take school physical examinations.

The abuser told the girls that their natural father had been abusive to them when they were little children. One girl was told that the birthmark on her back was from a bite from her father. Thus, the girls were frightened when they would visit their father.

One of the girls, when refusing to comply with the sexual acts, had her arm twisted by the offender. Later, she complained of her arm hurting. She was taken to the hospital, where the arm was X-rayed and placed in a cast. Another time, a milk carton was thrown by the offender, and it produced a facial scar on one of the girls.

Crime Scene Indicators

The offenses occurred over an eight- to ten-year period, usually in the home of the abuser. Sometimes he took the girls for a ride, and abuse was reported to occur in his car. The abuse occurred about four times weekly.

Forensic Findings

Hospital and child protective service records were reviewed, and they revealed that child abuse had been suspected several times. However, each time the abuser had an explanation that was plausible enough to avoid being charged.

Outcome

Just prior to trial, the offender plea-bargained the charges. He received five years' probation.

313: ENTITLEMENT RAPE

In an entitlement sexual offense, the offender forces the victim into sexual activity. Issues of power and control are underlying psychological conflicts. Three age groups are identified under each subcategory: child, adolescent, and adult. One of each group is described with a case study.

Classification of sexual assault as either entitlement rape, anger rape, or sadistic rape uses, as the determining criterion, the amount of aggression involved. Evidence for high expressive aggression used to determine the correct classification includes any combination of the following:

1. Injuries greater than minor cuts, scratches, and abrasions
2. Force in excess of that needed to attain victim compliance (e.g., slapping, punching, or kicking when there is no evidence of victim resistance)
3. Specific acts in the offense (e.g., mutilation, burning, stabbing, choking to unconsciousness, biting, kicking, anal penetration, or insertion of foreign objects
4. Desires or attempts to humiliate a victim (derogatory or demeaning remarks, any use of feces or urine, any forcing of a male to observe, or evidence of forced fellatio after sodomy).

313.01: SOCIAL ACQUAINTANCE RAPE

Subcategories of social acquaintance rape include 313.01.01: Adult, 313.01.02: Adolescent, and 313.01.03: Child.

In this offense, there is prior knowledge or relationship between the victim and offender. Often, the relationship is social, and for adults and adolescents, the assault usually occurs on a date. Other relationships include student/teacher or athlete/coach relationships. For child cases, the relationship might include a neighbor or family friend.

Defining Characteristics

Victimology. This type of offense involves low expressive aggression and no severe physical injuries to the victim. It begins with a consenting interpersonal encounter.

Offender Characteristics. It is likely that this offender has good social skills and has not been involved in serious criminal activities. The offense is usually situational for adult victims and preferential for child victims.

CASE STUDY:　313.01: SOCIAL ACQUAINTANCE RAPE

Background/Victimology

Rose had a brief, romantic involvement with Frank approximately two years before the sexual assault, which occurred in 1979, but she had not seen him in the interim. Then, one evening while en route to a friend's house for dinner, she found herself driving by Frank's home, and impulsively she decided to stop to say hello. Frank, who greeted Rose in his bathrobe at the downstairs back door, sent Rose to a nearby liquor store to purchase liquor for him. They had a drink together, and Frank continued to drink after Rose had finished. At first, they talked and reminisced about old times. At some point, Frank rolled and smoked a cigarette he made from a substance that he kept in a jar.

As Frank became increasingly intoxicated, he started to become physically and sexually suggestive. Eventually, he grabbed at Rose, threatened her with an ornamental knife, and burned her with his cigarette, according to Rose's testimony. Frank became even more aggressive, and at various times, slapped, kicked, punched, and pulled Rose into the bedroom, where he raped her three times, both vaginally and orally.

Eventually, Frank fell asleep, and Rose managed to leave the apartment and get to her car, only to discover she had left some belongings inside the apartment. When she reentered the apartment, Frank was on the telephone with his girlfriend with whom he had a date later that evening. The girlfriend hung up, and an enraged Frank became angry and shouted at Rose. As Rose headed toward the back stairs to leave, Frank kicked or pushed her down the stairs, causing her to fall into the window in the door at the bottom of the stairs, where the broken glass cut her deeply.

After some delay, Frank drove Rose to the hospital because she was almost blinded by the blood in her eyes, but only after she promised not to reveal how she was injured. At the hospital, she told hospital personnel that she had fallen down the stairs. After being treated, she was driven by Frank back to his apartment, where she stayed and slept until the next morning, when she drove herself home.

It was not until two days later under the prodding questions of close relatives that Rose revealed the true source of her injuries and the fact that Frank had raped her. She returned to the hospital, where she was examined for rape trauma.

Outcome

Rose pressed criminal charges against Frank immediately, and her attorney filed a civil action within a few weeks of the incident in order to obtain a real-estate attachment against the defendant's holdings, as there was a possibility that he would transfer his property to a relative.

Frank was acquitted of all criminal charges in March 1980.

In the civil suit, the trial court directed a verdict in favor of the third-party defendant, Frank's homeowner's insurer. An appeals court overturned the directed verdict and awarded to Rose, the plaintiff.

313.02: SUBORDINATE RAPE

The subcategories of subordinate rape are 313.02.01: Adult, 313.02.02: Adolescent, and 313.02.03: Child.

The relationship between the victim of subordinate rape and the offender is one of status imbalance. One person has power over another by employment, education, or age. The offender uses this authority relationship to take advantage of the victim.

Defining Characteristics

Victimology. The victim is known to the offender. The offender must be in some authoritative relationship to the victim (e.g., teacher, supervisor, manager or employer, parole officer, therapist, physician, etc.). Typically, there is low expressive aggression, with no severe physical injuries to victim.

Offender Characteristics. The offender uses familiarity to gain access to or trust of the victim. This is often a preferential offense. He often has prior arrests and may make frequent and unexpected moves due to detection.

Common Forensic Findings. The victim should be referred for a sexual assault examination.

Investigative Considerations

Investigators should seek out other subordinates for possible victimization by the offender.

Search Warrant Suggestions

See section 313.01.

CASE STUDY: 313.02.01: SUBORDINATE RAPE, ADULT

Background/Victimology

Five patients, ranging in age from twenty-two to seventy-eight, accused their physician of sexual assault and rape between the fall of 1983 and the fall of 1984. The twenty-two-year-old victim described how the physician who was treating her for what she believed was a cyst on her ovary questioned her about her sex life and molested her with an ungloved hand during a pelvic examination. He asked her if she had an orgasm when having sex and told her that if not, he could show her how. The doctor then leaned against her and rubbed his pelvis against her while examining her breasts. When asked why she waited four months before telling a fellow worker about the assault, the woman testified, "I thought it was in my head that he was doing something wrong."

Another woman, age twenty-three, testified that during three visits to the doctor for stomach pains, the doctor asked her each time "how often I had sex with my boyfriend, if I pleased my boyfriend." On the last visit, the doctor told her to get up from a chair, pressed his pelvis against her stomach, and asked "if I could please him."

A thirty-eight-year-old deaf woman, being treated by the doctor for severe stomach pains, testified that during one visit, the doctor examined her with ungloved hands and asked if she enjoyed oral sex, how often she had sex, and what positions she used. Then he asked "could we go somewhere where nobody knew either of us and let it go from there."

A 79-year-old woman, weeping and in a wheelchair, testified that the doctor wanted to look at a rash on her back and lifted her onto an examining table, where he raped her. Her eighty-four-year-old husband testified that his wife appeared very shaky and upset when she returned home and that he noted blood stains in her underclothes. The additional victims came forward after media coverage of the physician's arrest.

Outcome

The physician was convicted on all charged counts of sexual assault. His appeal of the convictions was denied, and he was sentenced to prison for seven to ten years.

313.02.02: SUBORDINATE RAPE, CHILD

The primary aim of the child subordinate sexual assault is to have sex with a child. Sexual activity with children may range from a few acts to a lifelong pattern. These offenders tend to be self-centered, with little or no concern about the comfort or welfare of the child. The sexual acts are typically phallic (the goal is penetration and achieving orgasm, with the child used as a masturbatory object). The offenses are usually impulsive, with little or no planning; physical injury is absent or minimal. These offenders are usually promiscuous, with many different victims of varying ages. Vulnerable individuals include the sick, the disabled, and the handicapped as well as healthy children in day-care settings.

Defining Characteristics

Victimology. The victim is under the state's age of majority. The child can be either male or female.

Crime Scene Indicators Frequently Noted. There is low expressive aggression (i.e., no more aggression than necessary to secure victim compliance). There is no evidence that aggression or victim fear is an important part of the offense or that it is needed to enhance sexual arousal. There is no attempt to relate to the child or to engage the child in nonsexual activities. These offenders tend to be predatory and exploitative. They will have prior arrests and frequent moves. The offense is usually preferential.

CASE STUDY: 313:02:03: SUBORDINATE RAPE, CHILD

Background/Victimology

A parent became suspicious of her twelve-year-old son's gradual withdrawal from social and sports activities, his reluctance to go to school, and his increasing physical complaints, such as headaches and stomachaches. Further inquiry revealed he was being sexually abused by his seventh-grade teacher.

The district attorney's office began further investigation and learned of several additional boys who were possible victims of this teacher. Confrontation of the teacher led to a confession.

Offender Characteristics

The forty-three-year-old teacher was married and had a ten-year-old daughter. He had been teaching at a prominent, coed, private school for sixteen years. He was a popular teacher with the boys, but girls found him intimidating and critical of them and their work. He clearly favored boys and frequently would take boys individually to his home for tutoring and on vacations.

Outcome

School administrators had knowledge of suspicious sexual activity between the teacher and students but had minimized and not reported it. The school was held liable for failure to report suspected child abuse. The offender was sentenced to five years in prison and was required to pay therapy costs for the boys he had victimized.

313.03: POWER-REASSURANCE RAPE

This category includes the following subcategories: 313.03.01: Adult, 313.03.02: Adolescent, and 313.03.03: Child.

This rapist type is highly sexualized and fantasy-driven. The rape is usually planned/premeditated.

Defining Characteristics

Victimology. The victim is usually unknown to the offender. If known, the victim will be a casual acquaintance, such as someone living in the same neighborhood or working in the same building. There is usually low expressive aggression, with no severe physical injuries to the victim.

Offender Characteristics. The offender often makes some attempt to relate to the victim and assure the victim that he does not intend to injure him or her. The offender generally has had problems as an adolescent or adult. The offense often is planned, at least to the extent of the offender having thought about the assault (e.g., a rehearsed fantasy); these offenders may have other signs of sexual preoccupation and sexually deviant behavior. This type of offender has been descriptively termed a *compensatory or power-reassurance rapist.*

CASE STUDY: 313.03.01: POWER-REASSURANCE RAPE, ADULT

Background/Victimology

Eugene's sexual offense history began in his early twenties (during the time he was married) with exhibitionism. Four years after he began exposing himself, he assaulted two young women. When he grabbed one woman—with his genitals exposed—the other woman slapped him in the face. He released his hold, and the two women ran away.

Two years later, he committed his first rape. While walking along a riverbank, he observed a jogger running toward him. He stopped her by asking a question. After they had conversed for a while, he grabbed her, fondled her breasts, and forced her to remove her clothes. He placed her clothes on the ground and told her to lie on them. While raping her he repeatedly asked her sexual questions. After achieving orgasm, he left.

A second rape occurred about one year later. This offense was similar to the first. He picked up a pedestrian, drove her to a park, and raped her, again asking the victim for assurance that the assault was a pleasurable experience.

Offender Characteristics

Eugene is a thirty-year-old divorced male who came from a relatively large, intact family. His father worked many hours away from home and returned to the house only on weekends. When he was at home, he spent most of his time drinking; however, there is no evidence that he was abusive toward members of the family. Because his mother also worked and consequently was gone much of the time, caretaking and child-rearing responsibilities were assumed by the immigrant paternal grandmother, who spoke almost no English.

Eugene got along poorly with his five brothers and sisters. He stated that he was the family's black sheep. His school-related difficulties began as early as the third grade; his earliest memories are of skipping school and vandalizing deserted buildings. Although clearly of average or above-average intelligence, he repeated several grades and eventually dropped out of school before finishing the tenth grade.

He enlisted in the army and remained in the service for several years, with a record marked by disciplinary hearings. Shortly after discharge from the service, he married.

The marriage lasted two years and produced one child, who died at birth. Although the child allegedly died of natural causes, his wife and in-laws blamed him for the death.

His employment history was as erratic as his school and military history. He worked as a truck driver in construction, in warehouses, as a security guard, for moving companies, and as a mechanic, quitting all jobs he held, typically within two months.

Eugene's childhood, juvenile, and young-adult history of instability, low frustration tolerance, acting out, and delinquent behavior underscores his impulsive life-style. The compensatory nature of his offenses is amply illustrated by his exhibitionism, his attempts to confirm his sexual adequacy, and his attempts to reassure the victim as well as himself.

Outcome

Eugene was convicted of two rape charges and committed to the Massachusetts Treatment Center for an undetermined sentence.

313.03.02: POWER-REASSURANCE RAPE, ADOLESCENT

The primary aim of the offender in an adolescent power-reassurance sexual assault is to develop a relationship with an adolescent. The sexual activities are secondary to the interpersonal intent. The victim is seen as an appropriate social and sexual companion; the offender perceives that the relationship is mutually satisfying and that it benefits the adolescent in some way. The sexual acts usually are limited to fondling, caressing, kissing, frottage, or oral sex performed on the victim. The victim may be known to the offender, and if so, the relationship between the victim and the offender is usually long-term or there have been multiple encounters with the victim. The offenses are usually planned and are not characterized as impulsive. The offenses are not violent, and rarely is there any physical injury to the victim.

CASE STUDY: 313.03.02: POWER-REASSURANCE RAPE, ADOLESCENT

Background/Victimology

Jim's criminal record started in 1973 at the age of twenty-three. His first offense was an attempted rape of an eighteen-year-old woman. The same year, he committed a second, similar offense against a seventeen-year-old woman. In neither case was there physical force, and in neither case did the assault eventuate in rape. In 1974 he raped a nineteen-year-old woman; in 1975 he raped a twenty-three-year-old woman; in 1976 he raped a fifteen-year-old girl. This last rape was the offense for which he was committed.

In every case, his MO was more or less the same. It involved picking up a hitchhiker, brandishing a knife, and threatening harm, but never actually applying more force than needed to gain submission. In fact, in the first two assaults, the victims talked him out of the rape.

The scripted or ritualized aspect of the pattern assaults suggests Jim's compensatory nature. The offender had no long-term history of conduct disorder. The acts themselves had an element of premeditation in that he set out to locate victims on the occasions of the crimes. On several occasions, he expressed interest in dating the victims and, in fact, was apprehended after the last rape when he met his victim for a date the next evening. Jim represents the pure compensatory rapist.

Offender Characteristics

Jim was the first of three sons. His early years were described as reasonably happy ones. However, after being laid off from his job as a machine operator, his father started drinking heavily and became destructive during fits of rage. Jim graduated from high school and worked as a general laborer before joining the military. After a full term in the military, he was again employed as a laborer. At the time of the last rape, he was working as a security guard. He met his wife while in the military, and they were married a short time later. They were divorced after about three years, and Jim was given custody of their three-year-old child.

Outcome

Jim was committed to the Massachusetts Treatment Center in 1978 for an indefinite sentence after having been convicted of kidnapping and rape.

313.04: EXPLOITATIVE RAPE

Subcategories of exploitative rape include 313.04.01: Adult, 313.04.02: Adolescent, and 313.04.03: Child.

In exploitative rape, sometimes called *opportunistic rape*, expressed aggression is generally low and does not exceed what was necessary to force victim compliance. Callous indifference to the victim is evident.

Defining Characteristics

Victimology. The victim may be an adult, adolescent, or child. The victim, either female or male, is often unknown to the offender.

Offender Characteristics. The offender usually has limited formal schooling; a poor job record; and short-term, unstable relationships. The offender is usually very impulsive and has a long record of serious behavior problems or of arrests for criminal offenses, starting in adolescence and throughout most of his adult life. Offenses tend to be highly impulsive, with very little or no planning involved. Alcohol/drug abuse is common.

CASE STUDY: 313.04.01: ADULT EXPLOITATIVE RAPE, HIGH IMPULSE

Background/Victimology

Richard is a thirty-two-year-old single male. His first rape was a twenty-five-year-old woman. He grabbed her around the throat and placed a knife to her neck, forcing her to the basement of a building. The victim was held prisoner and repeatedly raped and sodomized. The offender stole a small amount of money from her purse before allowing her to leave. A second (twenty-seven-year-old) victim was seized on the street and forced into a vacant house, where she was raped and and change was removed from her purse. A third (twenty-five-year-old) victim was seized at knife point on the street, forced to her apartment, and repeatedly raped and sodomized. The victims were blindfolded, and the last one was bound with rope. None of the victims was injured by weapons.

Offender Characteristics

Richard was the third of four brothers. His father was a cab driver who both worked and drank regularly. He was described as a womanizer and was very abusive when intoxicated. His mother was a waitress and a maid. She attended church regularly and appeared to have been devoted to her family. Shortly after the death of a younger sister (age six months), Richard (then two years old) began wandering away from home. By the age of three, he was killing kittens by locking them in an icebox, and by age four, he was removed from a day nursery for fighting. By age six, he was pulling up girls' dresses and exposing himself. He was placed in a foster home the same year and has remained in penal institutions, juvenile detention centers, and foster homes throughout his life. He remained in the fourth grade until his sixteenth birthday, eventually earning his general equivalency diploma while in prison. Richard has a long juvenile and adult criminal record that includes numerous instances of larceny, statutory burglary, breaking and entering, motor vehicle offenses, armed robbery, assault and battery, and rape.

Richard's profile is typical of an exploitative, high-impulse rapist. The assaults were all impulsive, predatory acts. Although there was little gratuitous aggression (compared with the expressive rapist), there was no concern for the victims' fear or discomfort (compared with the compensatory rapist). There is a long history of behavior management problems going back to early childhood, resulting in a low level of adult social, professional, and interpersonal competence. It is this extensive history of acting out concomitant with a low level of social competence that distinguishes this individual from the opportunistic low-impulse rapist (see case study 313.03.01).

Outcome

Richard was committed to the Massachusetts Treatment Center in 1975 for an indefinite sentence after having been convicted of rape, sodomy, armed robbery, breaking and entering, and assault and battery.

314: ANGER RAPE

Sexual assault in the category of anger rape is characterized by high expressive aggression (unprovoked physical and verbal aggression or physical force in excess of that necessary to gain victim compliance must be present). Rage is evident in this offender. He may have manifested behaviors listed for sadistic sexual assault, but these must appear to be punishing actions done in anger, not to increase sexual arousal. The primary motive for the offense is anger and not sexual gratification. When the offender knows the victim, the assault on that victim appears to be the result of the offender's easy access to the victim. These offenses are predominantly impulse driven (e.g., opportunity alone, possibly coupled with impaired judgment due to drugs/alcohol).

314.01: ANGER RAPE, GENDER (WOMEN-HATING)

The category of gender anger rape is reserved for offenders who hate women and express their rage through sexual assault.

Defining Characteristics

Victimology. The victim must be a woman, and high expressive aggression must be present. In addition, there must be clear evidence from the offender's behaviors and/or verbalizations that the primary intent of the rape is to hurt, demean, humiliate, or punish the victim (e.g., calling the victim derogatory names or forcing the victim to engage in acts that are seen by the offender as demeaning or humiliating, such as fellatio).

CASE STUDY: 314.01: ANGER RAPE, GENDER

Background/Victimology

The commitment offense involved a twenty-six-year-old woman who was awakened at 2:00 A.M. when the offender, Randy, put his fist through the glass door of her apartment building. He reached in an unlocked the door as the victim came out into the hallway. He grabbed her around the neck, put a knife to her throat, and dragged her into his car. When in the car, he warned her that if she moved he would "chop her up" with the knife. When they arrived at an abandoned building, he forced her to undress, dance in the nude, and utter obscenities about women while dancing. He grabbed her breasts and buttocks, and he grabbed her hair and slapped her face, all while ordering her to repeat more obscenities about women over and over again. He then sodomized her, performed cunnilingus, forced her to perform fellatio, and finally had intercourse with her. Throughout the assault, he told her to keep swearing, saying he liked to hear it. Eventually, he got back into his car and drove off, leaving the victim to walk 5 miles to the nearest house.

Offender Characteristics

Randy's father died in a car accident when Randy was two years old. Randy's mother was a cocktail waitress and heavy drinker who died of pneumonia at the age of thirty. After his father died, Randy was raised by foster parents. He reports not seeing his mother more than six times a year after that. His relationship with his foster parents was apparently a good one, although his foster father died when Randy was thirteen. His foster mother alone was unable to provide the supervision and guidance he needed, and before long he was getting into trouble with the law.

At age seventeen, Randy left home and moved in with a male companion. He was never married, although at the time of arrest he was engaged. He attended six different primary and secondary schools, eventually dropping out in the eleventh grade at age seventeen. In the five years between leaving high school and his arrest, he held many different jobs, primarily as dishwasher, busboy, cook, and clerk. He had been drinking heavily since he was sixteen and also used amphetamines, cocaine, and marijuana. Although this was his first sexual offense, Randy had a long history of delinquent behavior, including ten prior court appearances for motor vehicle violations, larceny, writing bad checks, and drugs.

This is a typical case of a high-impulse, displaced-anger rapist. The primary aim of the rape was the expression of rage through physically assaulting, degrading, and humiliating the victim. A pattern of chronic acting out began in the offender's early adolescence, reflecting an impulsive life-style. Comments from his psychiatric report suggest that his behavior was frequently unplanned and guided by whim and that there was an exaggerated craving for excitement. Although Randy's impulsiveness did not appear until adolescence, some offenders express an impulsive style as early as childhood.

Outcome

Randy was a twenty-two-year-old single male when committed to the Massachusetts Treatment Center in 1977 for an indefinite sentence. He was convicted of rape, kidnapping, armed robbery, assault with a dangerous weapon, and unnatural acts.

314.02: ANGER RAPE, AGE

The motive of the offender in age anger rape is to seek out victims of a specific age group, usually elderly or young.

314.02.01: ANGER RAPE, ELDERLY VICTIM

The category of elderly victim anger rape is reserved for sexual assault on elderly women. The victim is a woman sixty years of age or older. High expressive aggression must be evident, and the choice of an elderly victim must be intentional on the part of the offender (i.e., not strictly a victim of opportunity).

CASE STUDY: 314.02.01: ANGER RAPE, ELDERLY VICTIM

Background/Victimology

A sixty-five-year-old widow returning from church entered her bedroom and noted that several bureau drawers were open and that jewelry and money were missing. Walking into the den, she was struck by a closed fist to her face. A man grabbed her by the throat and threw her onto a couch. The intruder tore off her clothing, tried to strangle her, and said, "Die, damn you, die." He then sexually assaulted the woman.

Offender Characteristics

The offender, Dan, age twenty-five, came from a broken home and lived until age six with a foster family. His natural mother abandoned the family when Dan was three. When his father remarried, Dan went to live with his father and stepmother. The stepmother was a severe disciplinarian who burned Dan's fingers with a cigarette lighter when she caught him smoking.

Dan ran away from home as often as he could. There were frequent family arguments and beatings because he was a slow learner in school. Dan attended four different grammar schools and four high schools. Part of his high school experience was at a boys' training center, where he was labeled an unruly child. At age fourteen and fifteen, he admitted to being obsessed with thoughts of murdering his stepmother, and he continually thought of different ways to carry out the killing.

Dan enlisted in the army at age nineteen and served six years. He reports receiving approximately twenty reprimands for misconduct during this time. He claims to have become addicted to alcohol and drugs while in the service.

Dan married a woman whose husband had been killed in Vietnam, and the agreement to marry was for the purpose of splitting the extra pay he would receive if married. They never lived together and were divorced ten months later. Dan claimed to be on LSD during his rape offense.

Outcome

Dan pleaded guilty to the crime of rape and was sentenced to a five year term.

314.02.02: ANGER RAPE, CHILD VICTIM

The category of child victim anger rape is reserved for those offenders who express extreme anger at children, with no evidence that the aggression is eroticized (not sadistic); the aggression is rooted in rage or anger at the victim as a child, at the world, at people in general, or at some specific individual. Any physical injury to the child results by accident: due to the clumsiness or ineptness on the part of the offender or because the victim may have been injured during a struggle.

CASE STUDY: 314.02.02: ANGER RAPE, CHILD VICTIM

Background/Victimology

The victim, a nine-year-old boy, lived at a church-operated home for boys. According to Bruce, the sixteen-year-old offender, the two met, talked a bit, and decided to hunt for snakes and fish at a nearby reservoir. As they sat on a dock fishing, Bruce started fondling the boy, becoming sexually aroused. He undid the boy's pants and performed fellatio. He then began to try to take the boy's pants off. The boy resisted as Bruce turned him over on his stomach, preparing to sodomize him. They fell into the water and a struggle ensued. The boy slipped on a rock and hit his head, which rendered him unconscious. Bruce tried to lift the boy but slipped, dropping the boy into the water.

Offender Characteristics

Bruce has a brother two years older than he is. His parents divorced when he was a few months old. The brother, according to Bruce, beat him up daily from the time he was three until he was ten or eleven. When he was five, the mother and two boys moved to live with his maternal grandfather. This was an important relationship for Bruce; however, the grandfather died four years later. Bruce reports that soon after he turned eleven, he was fishing one day when an eighteen-year-old youth approached him and told him about a good fishing spot in the woods. As they proceeded into the forest, the youth forced fellatio and sodomy on Bruce. He claimed he yelled but that it did no good. He felt helpless, and the act was painful.

Upon entering the seventh grade, Bruce tested in the high intelligence range and was advanced two grades. He was socially immature and found it too lonely to be with the older adolescents. He became rebellious and hostile. He spent most of the years between ages twelve and sixteen on his own, in youth detention centers or psychiatric facilities. His juvenile criminal involvement includes sixteen court appearances on forty-three charges, including shoplifting, assault and battery, use of a dangerous weapon, motor vehicle violations and four charges of sexual abuse of juveniles under age fourteen. He maintained that the victims were willing partners of his own age.

Bruce began homosexual activities in early adolescence and moved in with a male partner. However, six months later this adolescent was killed in a car accident, and Bruce attempted suicide by consuming an overdose of aspirin. The assault of the boy at the reservoir happened on the anniversary of his friend's death.

Crime Scene Indicators

The victim's body was found floating in the reservoir. The body wore no trousers. A search of the area revealed shorts with the victim's initials sewn inside.

Forensic Findings

The coroner's examination revealed a laceration 1.5 inches in length and .5 inches in width on the forehead, as well as multiple blows to the head. The victim weighed 45 pounds. Asphyxiation by drowning was noted as possible cause of death.

Outcome

Bruce was sentenced to eighteen to twenty years for manslaughter and eighteen to twenty years concurrent for rape. He was committed to the

Massachusetts Treatment Center as a sexually dangerous person for an indefinite sentence.

314.03: ANGER RAPE, RACIAL

This category is reserved for what appears to be racially motivated sexual assault. Victims are of a different race than the offender.

CASE STUDY: 314.03: ANGER RAPE, RACIAL

Background/Victimology

The offender, Joe, is a twenty-eight-year-old black man who has two offenses: one against a twenty-two-year-old white female and the other against a twenty-seven-year-old white female. Each offense occurred in the presence of the victim's boyfriend. In one instance, the offender approached a couple as they were about to enter their apartment. He came up behind them, forcing his way into the apartment after them. He made the boyfriend stand in the corner of the room facing the wall while he raped the woman. The second offense had a similar MO. During the rapes, Joe would make degrading racial comments to both the victims and their boyfriends.

Offender Characteristics

Joe had a long history of nonsexual crimes, including breaking and entering, larcenies, and motor vehicle offenses. He was bright and charming. He had grown up in an urban inner city. The rapes occurred in the suburbs and in the vicinity of where he worked. His work was low skilled. He had dropped out of high school in the tenth grade. He was never married but had a variety of consenting sexual companions.

Investigation.

Joe was identified by both victims through a lineup. A police artist sketch was used to assist in the offender's apprehension.

Forensic findings.

There were positive forensic findings on each victim through a sexual assault examination.

Outcome

The offender was convicted of all charges of sexual assault and committed to the Massachusetts Treatment Center (MTC). He was judged to be a sexually dangerous person and will stay at the MTC until judged no longer dangerous.

314.04: ANGER RAPE, GLOBAL

The category of global anger rape is reserved for offenders who appear to be angry at the world. This is a high expressive aggression assault, with no evidence of sadism and no evidence that the offender was focally angry at women. They have a history of fighting men.

Defining Characteristics

Victimology. Typically, the victim is unknown to the offender. Usually, there is moderate to severe physical aggression and injury to the victim.

Offender Characteristics. This offender is typically very impulsive and has exhibited behavior problems and encounters with the law beginning in adolescence and into his adult life. The offender generally has few social skills. Often, the offender will have a history of verbal and/or physical assaults against both males and females. The offenses usually are not planned.

CASE STUDY: 314.04: ANGER RAPE, GLOBAL

Background/Victimology

The commitment offense involved a seventeen-year-old woman who was walking along a city street as the offender, Steven, drove by. He stopped his car beside her, stepped out, and asked her where she was going. He did not hear her answer and asked again in an angry manner. She turned to walk away, which made Steven feel as though she was rejecting him and trying to make a fool of him. He punched her in the stomach, grabbed her under her chin, pulled her into his car, and drove away to a secluded area. After he parked the car, he told the victim to get into the back seat. When she refused, he climbed into the back and dragged her over the seat beside him. He undressed her and violently penetrated her. He states that he then withdrew, without having an orgasm, and let her out of the car, threatening to kill her if she made mention of the attack. The victim's description of her assailant led to his apprehension. When he was arrested shortly thereafter, he immediately admitted his guilt.

Offender Characteristics

Steven came from a relatively normal and seemingly unremarkable family. He has an older sister and a younger brother, both of whom appear to be living normal lives. His father was a strict disciplinarian. His mother was a passive, quiet, religious woman who rarely questioned her emotionally detached husband. His father was a twenty-five-year veteran mechanic. Family life was described as stable and uneventful. Steven remained in school through the eighth grade, held a few part-time, unskilled jobs, and joined the military. He received an honorable discharge after less than one year of service.

During the diagnostic interviews subsequent to his trial, he discussed the incident, describing himself as enraged at the time, not sexually excited. He had gone to visit his girlfriend, a "good" girl whom he had been seeing off and on since early adolescence with no sexual activity throughout the courtship. He found her necking on the porch with another man, and he drove from her house in a blind rage. He was partially aware as he drove away that he was going to look for somebody to attack sexually. His anger was global; everything in his path enraged him.

Steven had an active sexual life, but only with women whom he considered to be "bad." These relationships were short-lived, ending when he was directly confronted with their promiscuity. Terminating the relationship always occurred with violence, either in assaults on the women or on the boyfriends that had replaced him.

His late adolescence was marked by the repetitiveness of these experiences. Over and over again, he became involved with promiscuous women who would then prove to be unfaithful. Although he could only permit himself to have intercourse with women known by him to be sexually indiscriminate, he nevertheless maintained the fantasy that they would be faithful to him.

This is an exemplary case of a displaced anger, low-impulse rapist. As one diagnostic report stated, Steven's attitude toward people was tremendously hostile and bordering on rage. His pattern was to jockey for position in a relationship with a woman where he would feel ashamed, foolish, and hurt. He would respond aggressively, at times explosively, and typically at the woman. He created an effective outlet for discharging—and displacing—his rage. There was never any indication that this aggression was eroticized. Finally, there was no evidence of the developmental turbulence, the behavior management problems, and the poor social and interpersonal competence characteristic of high impulsivity.

Outcome

Steven at age twenty-four was committed to the Massachusetts Treatment Center in 1965. He was convicted of rape. Other than the commitment offense, he had no criminal history.

315: SADISTIC RAPE

The level of violence in a sadistic offender's sexual assault must clearly exceed what is necessary to force victim compliance. The offender's sexual arousal is a function of the victim's pain, fear, or discomfort. Behavioral evidence may include acts such as whipping and bondage, violence focused on the erogenous parts of the victim's body (such as burning, cutting, or otherwise mutilating the breasts, anus, buttocks, or genitals), insertion of foreign objects in the vagina or anus, intercourse after the victim is unconscious, and the use of feces/urine within the offense.

Subcategories of sadistic sexual assault are 315.01: Sadistic Rape, Adult, 315.02: Sadistic Rape, Adolescent, and 315.03: Sadistic Rape, Child.

315.01: SADISTIC RAPE, ADULT

Most often in adult sadistic sexual assault there is high expressive aggression, with moderate to severe injury to the victim. Frequently, the offender uses items to inflict pain/injury (cigarettes, knives, sticks, bottles, etc.). In some cases of muted sadism, however, there is clear evidence of eroticized aggression (insertion of foreign objects, bondage, whipping, etc.) without extensive physical injury.

Defining Characteristics

Victimology. Typically, the victim is unknown to the offender.

Offender Characteristics. The offender typically has previous behavior problems, sometimes beginning in adolescence and often worsening in adulthood. As described by Dietz, Hazelwood, and Warren, a sexual sadist is one who has established "an enduring pattern of sexual arousal in response to sadistic imagery" (1990, 165). Sexual gratification is obtained from torture involving excessive mental and physical means. Sexually sadistic fantasies in which sexual acts are paired with domination, degradation, and violence are transmitted into criminal action that results in sexual assault.

Investigative Considerations

The offense usually is at least partially planned and sometimes is planned in detail. Search warrants are needed to look for literature, diaries, recordings, paraphernalia, and writings related to pornography, sadism and the crime.

CASE STUDY: 315.01: SADISTIC RAPE, ADULT

Background/Victimology

On the occasion of his first rape, the offender, Martin, was at an after-school party and assaulted a fourteen-year-old girl. When she refused his advances, he choked her until she passed out. When she regained consciousness, he was still lying beside her. The commitment offense occurred one year later, when Martin, then age nineteen, killed a thirty-year-old woman by manual strangulation. He had met the victim in a bar, and they left together to go to a secluded area to engage in sex. To what extent the decisions leading up to the rape were mutual cannot be determined.

Offender Characteristics

Martin is the sixth oldest of nine siblings. He described his family life as horrible and including emotional and physical abuse. The father was portrayed as the ruler of the household, who made certain that his orders were carried out or else physical abuse would result. His mother, described as passive and obedient, would often collude in the beatings by reporting to his father incidents of punishable behavior. At the age of thirteen, the offender was sent away to a training school for being an habitual truant. his early schooling continued to be sporadic, and he was eventually expelled for a while in the tenth grade. All employment has been menial.

Martin does not have a long history of violent crime. Most of his transgressions involved truancy, lying/cheating, and disruptiveness in school. His criminal record contains mostly alcohol and automobile-related offenses. He has, essentially, two violent crimes: an initial rape attempt that was reduced to assault and battery, and murder.

Outcome

Martin was convicted of second-degree murder and was committed to the Massachusetts Treatment Center in 1976 for an indefinite sentence. In both offenses, the motive was primarily aggressive and muted sadism. He was indiscriminate in terms of age of victim. The first victim was a child, and the second an adult woman. It did not appear, however, that sex was used as a vehicle for venting anger, but that the aggression was antecedent to or concurrent with sexual arousal. His life-style throughout adolescence was characterized by impulsive acting out, and none of his serious crimes had any semblance of premeditation, compulsiveness, or ritualism.

315.02: SADISTIC RAPE, ADOLESCENT

The offender in adolescent sadistic rape is sexually aroused or otherwise derives pleasure from placing the adolescent victim in pain or fear. Sadistic acts may include aggressive sodomy, insertion of foreign objects, and violence focused on the breasts, genitals, or anus. The sexual acts often occur during or after the violence and aggression.

CASE STUDY: 315.02: SADISTIC RAPE, ADOLESCENT

Background/Victimology

The offender, Terry, has no juvenile criminal record. His first offense occurred two years after discharge from the service. The victim was a seventeen-year-old male whom Terry picked up. Terry smacked, punched, and kicked the victim for twenty minutes before forcing the victim to engage in fellatio. When the victim refused to engage in intercourse, Terry pulled out a knife and began stabbing him in the abdomen. Just prior to the stabbing, Terry demanded that the victim masturbate while Terry cut him with the knife. Following the assault, Terry called an ambulance and police. The commitment offense took place about one year later.

Terry picked up a sixteen-year-old male prostitute and drove toward his home. Before reaching his house, they got into an argument. Apparently, Terry had paid the victim in advance for services that the victim decided he did not wish to provide. Terry stabbed the victim fifteen times, penetrating the thorax, heart, and aorta. He then mutilated the body by amputation of the penis. The penis was never found, and there is some suggestion that it may have been ingested.

Offender Characteristics

Terry came from an upper-middle-class, professional home. However, he did not experience a happy childhood. From early childhood into adolescence, he was plagued by night terrors, nightmares, and sleep talking/walking. He bit his fingernails and sucked his thumb until the age of sixteen. He had few, if any, friends and was convinced that other children did not like him. His pathologic shyness kept him in his room through much of his childhood.

His mother felt bad that he was so lonely. When she failed to coax him from his room, she resorted to purchasing expensive toys for him to play with. Terry was sickly much of the time, often febrile, and was described as glassy-eyed. Although the parents described their sons as good and obedient, Terry felt particularly alienated and withdrawn as he became more and more aware of his homosexual feelings.

Upon graduating from high school, he enlisted in the air force. He spent four years in the service, compiling an excellent record that included five commendations for meritorious action. During this time, he also attended college and earned a degree. After discharge from the service, he began the first of a series of jobs in sales. He proved to be a highly successful salesman and was said to be earning in excess of six thousand dollars per month at the time of his arrest. Terry has a long psychiatric history, with depression and alcoholism presenting as primary features.

Outcome

Terry was a twenty-five-year-old single male when he was committed to the Massachusetts Treatment Center in 1982 for an indefinite sentence after having been convicted of second-degree murder and rape. As an adult, Terry led an exemplary life. He had good intepersonal skills and acquired a fair degree of academic and professional competence. He certainly did not lead what could be called an impulsive life-style. He had no criminal record up to the point of his first offense. His two assaults were ritualized, compulsive, and highly sadistic, much along the lines of the classic case of Jack the Ripper.

316: CHILD/ADOLESCENT PORNOGRAPHY

Collectors are persons who collect, maintain, and prize child pornography materials. They may be classified as to whether they are closet collectors, isolated collectors, or cottage collectors.

316.01: CLOSET COLLECTOR

The *closet collector* keeps secret his interest in pornographic pictures of nude children engaged in a range of behaviors and denies involvement with children. There is no acknowledged communication with other collectors. Materials are usually purchased discretely through commercial channels.

The belief system of the closet collector makes him consciously acknowledge that children should not be used sexually by adults.

316.02: ISOLATED COLLECTOR

The *isolated collector* chooses to have sexual activity with one child at a time. He may be involved with his own child, children of neighbors, nephews, nieces, friends' children, or children in his care (such as students). He may seek out children not known to him by traveling to another country.

The isolated collector's organization and use of pornographic materials varies from casual to meticulous. A prominent feature of these collectors is their belief that they are not harming the child victim. They deny that fear, force, or overpowering strategies demand the child's participation, a denial they maintain even when confronted with evidence that the children were frightened, trapped, and forced.

Isolated collectors usually deny their involvement with children. Often they say that the child encouraged their behavior and that they were kind to the child (i.e., not hurting the child physically). Physical assault is held to be the main criterion by which a collector deems behavior toward a child as abusive. The sexual activities and the photography sessions, no matter how degrading, are not viewed as harmful to the child. When very young children are involved, this belief extends to such activities as inserting wooden objects into the child's vagina and anus. These actions are justified, these collectors say, if they are done with patience, skill, and "love."

The level of abuse does not register on a conscious level. On occasion when the sexual activity is addressed, the collector may acknowledge that it is abnormal and that a child may be frightened, but this awareness holds little conscious emotional weight for the isolated collector to stop activities and admit to harmful effects.

316.03: COTTAGE COLLECTOR

The *cottage collector* is a pedophile who sexually exploits children in a group. The financial component of the pornography is noncommercial; that is, large amounts of money are not involved. The intent of the pornography is for the relationships it creates with other pedophile collectors—it is a method of communication. This category represents the largest number of collectors.

The networking of cottage collectors is more pronounced than the first two categories of collectors. In fact, cottage collectors often team up to lead a group of children. Each collector uses the pornography for his own interest.

When confronted, it is not unusual for cottage collectors to represent themselves as concerned about the children involved; it is only the involvement of the judicial system that threatens the well-being of the children, they say. This belief is substantiated by the trauma and anxiety surrounding the initial period of disclosure and is further compounded by the children's finally venting emotions concerning the negative, frightening, and overwhelming aspects of what has happened.

These collectors also suggest they have done more for the child than the child's parents. Again, this is partially substantiated in the case of absent or neglectful parents. The collector holds the parents responsible for the child's participation, in part because he believes the parents know what is going on by allowing their child to be with him.

317: HISTORICAL CHILD/ADOLESCENT SEX RINGS

In historical child/adolescent sex rings, children are used to create obscene materials such as photos, movies, and videos. These materials can be for private use or for commercial activities.

317.01: SOLO CHILD SEX RING

A solo child sex ring involves several children in sexual activities with an adult, usually male, who capitalizes on his legitimate role in the lives of these victims to recruit them into his illegal behavior.

Defining Characteristics

Victimology. The children know each other and are aware of one another's involvement in sexual acts with the adult offender. The children are conditioned or programmed by the adult to provide sexual services in exchange for a variety of psychological, social, monetary, and other rewards. The offender occupies a position of authority and familiarity with the victims.

The organizational structure of the ring includes an adult (and occasionally a secondary partner) who gathers the children together, either from existing formal groups or by creating a new group. In existing formal groups, such as sports teams or scout troops, the children already are organized. An adult who has access to this existing group can recruit a subgroup. Sometimes one child is targeted to bring other children together, or the adult may initiate action to gather the children together. The adults gain access to children because their presence is not questioned; that is, they hold some legitimate power with parents as well as with other people. Sometimes the adult makes it a point to become extra legitimate with the parents. If the parents do not know the adult directly, they usually have enough legitimizing information not to question their child spending time with this adult.

Crime Scene Indicators Frequently Noted. The crime scene is usually the offender's residence, his vehicle, or a group meeting hall. There can be many locations. The pornographic material usually is hidden in the residence of the offender. The most recent crime scene usually will have the camera and other equipment needed to create the pornography, as well as props, collateral material, and goods used to bribe the victims.

Common Forensic Findings. The victimization usually is reported by a third party, and little, if any, forensic evidence is immediately available. To obtain forensic evidence, detailed medical examinations of the victims are recommended. Medical evidence could include anal or vaginal scarring, bruises as well as a history of sexually transmitted disease(s).

Investigative Considerations

The investigator needs to obtain a search warrant for the offender's residence and check telephone and financial records for purchases of materials needed to create the pornography. It is suggested the investigator be sensitive to props and collateral used to bribe the targeted age group. Interviews with the victims should be done carefully by an investigator specially trained in interviewing children.

CASE STUDY: 317.01: SOLO CHILD SEX RING

Victimology/Background

A nine-year-old boy told a friend that a neighbor had invited him into his house to see some new kittens, had pulled his pants down, and had touched his genitals. The friend told his mother, who called other mothers in the neighborhood. One of those mothers told her former husband, who called police.

A twenty-nine-year-old nursing home employee was charged with the indecent assault on a child. The offender and his parents had recently moved into a small, community housing project in which all homes were single units facing a common courtyard. It was learned that five boys, ages six to nine, were involved with the adult; a sixth boy, medically handicapped and greatly favored by the adult, was suspected of also being involved. Of the six families, four children lived with their mothers, the fathers being absent from the home; one boy came from a family with both parents being present; one boy's father was dead. The sexual activity between the adult and the children began the second day following the adult's move into the neighborhood and continued over a six-month period until disclosure.

Offender Characteristics

At the time of these charges, the offender was on probation for sexual offenses involving two brothers, ages twelve and fourteen, who had been taking music lessons from him. The relationship with the brothers became sexual following wrestling matches and after viewing pornography. The offender would show the brothers a picture hanging on his wall or two babies looking into each other's pants and get the children to imitate it.

In addition to classification in the solo child sex rings category, the offender can be considered in the child victim power-reassurance sexual assault category (313.03.03). His primary intent was to establish a relationship with the children, and in that context, to have sex with them.

Outcome

The offender, after pleading guilty to these charges involving the two brothers, was ordered to avail himself of psychiatric treatment, which he did. His psychiatric file stated his progress in treatment; between the two offenses, he was recommended for volunteer work with the boy scouts. The offender was sentenced to ten to twelve years.

317.02: TRANSITIONAL CHILD SEX RING

The transitional child sex ring involves multiple offenders as well as multiple victims. The offenders are known to each other and collect and share victims.

Defining Characteristics

Victimology. In the transitional sex ring, multiple adults are involved sexually with children, and the victims are usually pubescent. The children are tested for their role as prostitutes and thus are high risks for advancing to the syndicated level of ring, although the organizational aspects of the syndicated ring are absent in transitional rings.

It is speculated that children enter these transitional rings by several routes: (1) they may be children initiated into solo sex rings by pedophiles who lose sexual interest in the child as he or she approaches puberty and who may try, through an underground network, to move the vulnerable child into sexual activity with pederasts (those with sexual preferences for pubescent youths); (2) they may be incest victims who have run away from home and who need a peer group for identity and economic support; (3) they may be abused children who come from disorganized families in which parental bonding has been absent and multiple neglect and abuse are present; and (4) they may be missing children who have been abducted or kidnapped and forced into prostitution.

It is difficult to identify clearly this type of ring because its boundaries are blurred and because the child may be propelled quite quickly into prostitution. Typically, the adults in these transitional rings do not sexually interact with each other, but instead have parallel sexual interests and involvements with the adolescents who exchange sex with adults for money, as well as for attention or material goods.

Crime Scene Indicators Frequently Noted. The crime scene can be the offenders' residences, vehicles, a group meeting hall, or a hotel/motel. There are usually many locations. The pornographic material usually is hidden in the residences of the offenders. The most recent crime scene will usually have the camera and other equipment needed to create the pornography as well as props, collateral material, and goods used to bribe the victims.

Common Forensic Findings. The victimization usually is reported by a third party, and little if any forensic evidence is immediately available. To obtain forensic evidence, detailed medical examinations of the victims are recommended. In addition to the general forensic findings described above, there could be anal or vaginal scarring, bruises, and a history of sexually transmitted disease.

Investigative Considerations

The investigator needs to obtain a search warrant for the offenders' residences and check telephone and financial records for purchases of materials needed to create the pornography. It is suggested the investigator be sensitive to props and collateral used to bribe the targeted age group. Interviews with the victims should be carefully done by an investigator specially trained in interviewing children.

CASE STUDY: 317.02: TRANSITIONAL CHILD SEX RING

Background

From December 1977 to December 1978, described by one Boston newspaper for homosexuals as the year of the witch-hunt, Boston was in the spotlight regarding a male youth prostitution ring. Earlier that year, the investigation of a solo child sex ring had led an assistant district attorney and police to uncover a second generation of rings. In the apartment of a man who had an extensive history of convictions for child molesting, investigators found numerous photos of naked youths as well as pornographic films. Sixty-three of the depicted youths were located and interviewed, and thirteen agreed to testify before a grand jury. From this testimony, additional men (many with professional and business credentials) were indicted on counts of rape and abuse of a child, indecent assault, sodomy, and unnatural acts.

By December 1978 the trial of the first defendant, a physician, began. Testimony from four prosecution witnesses revealed the linkages between the two types of rings. According to news reports, the first witness, a man who was serving a fifteen- to twenty-five-year term after pleading guilty to charges derived from the solo child sex ring, admitted to having sexual relations with boys as young as ten during the thirteen years he had rented the apartment. This witness testified that he could be considered a master male pimp and that he became involved in the sex-for-hire operation after meeting one of the other defendants. He said that initially, no money was involved, but after a few months, expenses increased. As a result, the men were charged, and the boys were given five to ten dollars for sexual services.

Newspapers reported that another prosecution witness, an assistant headmaster at a private boys' school, admitted visiting the apartment more than forty to fifty times over a five-year period. He denied being a partner in a scheme to provide boys for hire but admitted to taking friends to the apartment with him and to paying for having sex with the boys.

Victimology

A prosecution witness, a seventeen-year-old youth, testified to being introduced into homosexual acts by the first witness, who had told the boys they could make all the money they wanted. "All we had to do was lie there and let them do what they wanted to us," he said.

Another victim testified that at age twelve he had met the third witness through friends. He received gifts of clothes and money for going to the man's apartment. While there, he would drink beer, smoke marijuana, and watch stag movies. He brought his younger brother to the apartment, and they both had sex with the man. At age fourteen he was "turning tricks" and charging ten dollars for oral sex and twenty dollars for anal sex. At that point, he met the defendant.

Offender Characteristics

The defendant, a pediatrician and psychiatrist, claimed in his defense that he went to the apartment as part of a research study to interview boy prostitutes. He subsequently wrote an article that was submitted to a journal after his indictment and later was published in a sex research journal.

Outcome

The jury, sequestered for the nineteen-day trial, deliberated two and one-half days before reaching a verdict of guilty. The judge sentenced the physician to five years' probation on the condition he undergo psychiatric treatment. Over a year later, the state's board of medicine revoked his license. The other defendants in the ring plea-bargained their charges, and there were no further trials.

317.03: SYNDICATED CHILD SEX RING

In a syndicated child sex ring, there is a well-structured organization that involves the recruitment of children, the production of pornography, the delivery of sexual services, and the establishment of an extensive network of customers.

Defining Characteristics

Victimology. The syndicated ring involves multiple offenders as well as multiple victims. The syndicated child prostitution ring is a well-established commercial enteprise. Identification of additional victims can be made from the pornography obtained with a search warrant.

Crime Scene Indicators Frequently Noted. There can be many locations. There are many levels of material created. Information and details about locations can be obtained from the pornography itself. The most recent location will have all the equipment necessary to create the pornographic material.

Common Forensic Findings. The victimization usually is reported by a third party and little, if any, forensic evidence is immediately available. To obtain forensic evidence, detailed medical examinations of the victims are recommended.

Investigative Considerations

Investigation requires an understanding of the typical operation of a syndicated ring. The organizational components of the syndicated ring include the items of trade, the circulation mechanisms, the supplier of the items, the self-regulating mechanism, the system of trades, and the profit aspect.

Items of Trade. Items of trade include the children, photographs, films, and tapes. The degree of sexual explicitness and activity may vary. For example, photographs range from so-called innocent poses of children in brief attire taken at public parks, swimming pools, arcades, or similar places where children congregate to carefully directed movies portraying child subjects in graphic sexual activities. In the films, the child is often following cues provided by someone standing off-camera. In audio tapes, the children may be heard conversing, with age-appropriate laughter and noises, as well as using language that is highly sexual and suggestive of explicit behaviors.

Circulation Mechanism. Various mechanisms for circulation include the mail (photographs, coded letters), tape cassettes, CB radio, telephone, and beepers. The mail is a major facilitator for circulation of child pornography. Often, a laundering process may be used. For example, buyers send their responses to another country; the mail, received by the overseas forwarding agent, is opened and the cash or checks are placed in a foreign bank account; the order is remailed under a different cover back to the United States. This procedure ensures that the subscriber does not know where the operation originates and that law enforcement has difficulty tracing the operation.

Suppliers. Suppliers of child pornography include pedophiles, professional distributors, and parental figures. Pedophiles with economic resources and community status may organize their own group to have access to children and to cover their illegal intentions, or they may work within the framework of existing youth organizations. The professional distributors include the pornographer, who has access to an illegal photographer, who in turn generally owns a clandestine photo laboratory and film processor. While these photo laboratories can provide services to many illegal operations, they also represent some problems to the professional pornographers, who may find their photographs or films in magazines or adult bookstores without their knowledge and prior to their own distribution. The professional procurers who supply children also provide photographs and films through wholesale distributors and adult bookstores. Another source of professional distribution is photographic processing facilities. A photographic development laboratory often has a storefront business that handles photographic orders, such as holiday pictures, while its mail-order business is advertised in magazines. One such facility had a mail-order division that promised, through its advertisements in adult magazines, confidential photo finishing. These advertisements also were found in periodicals catering to clientele with special sexual interests.

Parental figures who supply children for pornographic and prostitution purposes include natural parents, foster parents, and group-home workers. The supplier may operate a foster home, as in the case of a self-acclaimed clergyman, who by his own estimates sold approximately two hundred thousand photos per year, with an income from this operation in excess of sixty thousand dollars. The technique used by the man was to have older boys engage younger boys in sex acts. If a youth did not submit, he was beaten and abused by an older youth. After the youth submitted, he was photographed in the sexual acts, and the man would then use the boys for his own sexual purposes. In order to ensure secrecy, a pornographer often keeps a blackmail file on each boy.

Self-Regulating Mechanism. Syndicated child pornography operations do not have recourse to law enforcement or civil process for settling disputes that arise in matters of theft or unauthorized duplication of photographs or resources of supply. Thus, a self-regulating mechanism develops for the elimination of members guilty of actions deemed unfair to or against the best interests of the syndicate. Subscribers may be screened carefully through the grade of paper, typewriter keys, number of letters, as well as the sincerity and insistence of the correspondence. Letters are kept as a security measure. Recriminations between the offender and guilty party may become extremely bitter, and support by fellow members in chastising the guilty party is solicited through immediate correspondence. Members of the syndicates are alert to law enforcement efforts against the group in general or with respect to their syndicate in particular.

System of Trade. One rule for trading is that members of the syndicate may assist each other in finding items of interest to other collectors. Through a system of trades, photographs held by syndicate members are traded, and those pictures chosen to be retained are kept by the receiving member.

Profit. The financial profit of child pornography appears to be an individual matter. Some collectors trade items for their personal use, and others trade items for personal as well as commercial purposes. The financial lure of pornography is seen in the actual cost of production and verified in the correspondence of the pornographers. Frequently, collectors who sell photographs actually are selling duplicate copies of items in their collection, thereby having income to purchase additional photographs from other sources.

CASE STUDY: 317.03: SYNDICATED CHILD SEX RING

Background/Victimology

A child sex ring involved ten boys and one girl. In October 1977 information regarding the offender, Paul, was brought to the attention of a West Coast FBI office.

The children involved ranged in age from eight to sixteen. Paul befriended a family with two boys and one girl; both parents worked. The parents grew to trust Paul, and invited him to live in their house, renting out a bedroom to him. Paul kept the refrigerator supplied with food and bought toys and clothes for the children. He drove a Cadillac equipped with a telephone, and he handed out business cards advertising a twenty-four-hour limousine service that he provided with his Cadillac. At one point, Paul made his child prostitutes wear beepers, calling the child he thought would best suit his customer's desires. Paul was constantly trying to recruit more children, and he would pick up runaways and use the children to recruit others. Paul would charge one hundred dollars or more for an hour with one of his child prostitutes, the price depending on the market, the child's age, the length of time with the child, or what the customer was going to do with this child.

Paul never gave any of his child prostitutes money, as he felt this would ruin them. Instead, he provided food and clothing, bought them various toys, and took them to amusement parks, sporting events, movie shows, or roller rinks.

Offender Characteristics

The offender kept a separate apartment in a complex with a swimming pool and tennis courts. He used this apartment as a "crash pad" for many of his child prostitutes, and they used the pool and tennis courts. The older boys were told by Paul to keep the younger ones in line.

Paul was sexually involved with several of his child prostitutes and provided Quaaludes to all of the children. He also had a sizable collection of child pornography, including 8-millimeter films and photographs. Paul was apprehended through identification of his illegal mail activities.

Outcome

Because it was determined that no federal laws applied to Paul's activities, the case was turned over to local police. In November 1977 Paul was convicted on seven felony counts (nineteen felony counts were dismissed), and in May 1978 he was sentenced to thirteen years' imprisonment and was declared a mentally disturbed sex offender.

318: MULTIDIMENSIONAL SEX RINGS

Multidimensional child sex rings can be among the most difficult and complex cases that any law enforcement officer will ever investigate. The investigation of recent allegations from multiple children under the age of six offers major problems. The investigation of two-year-old to twenty-year-old allegations from adult survivors offers additional problems.

Multidimensional child sex rings seem to have four dynamics in common. These dynamics are: (1) multiple young victims, (2) multiple offenders, (3) fear as the controlling tactic, and (4) bizarre and/or ritualistic activity.

318.01: ADULT SURVIVOR SEX RINGS

In adult survivor cases, adults (almost always women) of almost any age are in therapy. They frequently are hypnotized as part of the therapy and often are diagnosed as displaying multiple personality disorder. Gradually, through therapy, the adults reveal childhood victimization that includes multiple victims and offenders, fear as the controlling tactic, and bizarre or ritualistic activities. The multiple offenders often are described as members of a cult or satanic group. Civic leaders, police officers, or individuals wearing police uniforms frequently are described as present during the exploitation. The offenders may still be harassing or threatening the victims. In several cases, women claim to have had babies that were turned over for human sacrifice. The police and FBI are sometimes contacted to conduct an investigation. The therapists may fear for their own safety after they learn the patient's secret.

318.02: DAY-CARE SEX RINGS

In day-care cases, children currently or formerly attending a day-care center gradually describe their victimization at the center and at other locations to which they were taken by the day-care staff. The cases include multiple victims and offenders, fear, and bizarre or ritualistic activity, with a particularly high number of female offenders. Descriptions of strange games, of killing animals, of photographing activities, and of wearing costumes are common.

318.03: FAMILY/ISOLATED NEIGHBORHOOD SEX RINGS

In family/isolated neighborhood cases, children describe their victimization within their family or extended family. The group is often defined by geographic boundary, such as cul-de-sac, apartment building, or isolated rural settings. The stories are similar to those told by day-care setting victims, but with more male offenders. The basic dynamics remain the same, but victims tend to be more than six years of age, and the scenario is more likely to include a custody or visitation dispute.

318.04: CUSTODY/VISITATION DISPUTE SEX RINGS

In custody or visitation dispute cases, the same dynamics as described in the other multidimensional sex rings are often heard. When complicated by the dynamic of a custody dispute in progress, the case can be overwhelming. This is especially true if the disclosing child victims have been taken into hiding by a parent during the custody or visitation dispute. Some of these parents or relatives may even provide authorities with diaries or tapes of their interviews with the children. An accurate evaluation and assessment of a young child held in isolation while being debriefed by a parent is almost impossible. However well-intentioned, these self-appointed investigators severely damage any chance to validate these cases objectively.

319: ABDUCTION RAPE

In an abduction sexual offense, a person is moved forcibly from one location to another. The sexual assault occurs at the second location. Victims may be adult, adolescent, or child.

Abduction by nonfamily members is defined in the *National Incidence Studies of Missing, Abducted, Runaway, and Thrown-away Children* (1989) as the coerced and unauthorized taking of a child into a building, a vehicle, or a distance of more than 20 feet; the detention of a child for a period of more than one hour; or the luring of a child for the purpose of committing a crime. Included in this category are stereotypical kidnappings that require that the victim be missing overnight, be killed, be transported a distance of 50 miles or more, be ransomed, or that the perpetrator evidence an intent to keep the child permanently.

Subcategories for abduction sexual assault include 319.01: Abduction Rape, Adult, 319.02: Abduction Rape, Adolescent, and 319.03: Abduction Rape, Child.

CASE STUDY: 319.01 and 319.03: ADULT AND CHILD ABDUCTION RAPE

Background

In September 1976 Jane was delivering Sunday papers on her paper route. She was accompanied by her mother. At approximately 6:20 A.M., Jane and her mother observed a man, later identified as Simmons, walking down the street toward them. A few moments later, as Jane was standing beside her mother's car, the man approached the car and placed a gun to the mother's head. Simmons then forced Jane to get into the car, and he got in after her.

Simmons told the mother not to say or do anything or he would physically harm her. The mother tried to grab the gun but was unable to do so. Simmons then blindfolded the mother and forced her to operate the car's brake, clutch, and accelerator while he steered the car to a high school parking lot.

Upon arrival at the parking lot, Simmons forcibly removed the mother and daughter from the car and placed them into his 1973 Plymouth, which was parked there. The mother, still blindfolded, had troubled getting into the car. Simmons forced her head against the side of the car, causing a severe injury. After the mother and daughter were in the car, Simmons began driving toward a rural area.

After Simmons stopped his car, he forced the mother to remove her clothing. At this time, Simmons also began talking with the mother about forcing the daughter to watch her perform fellatio on him and about forcing the daughter to have intercourse with him. The mother pleaded with Simmons not to force her daughter to watch the assault take place. Because of her pleadings, Simmons allowed the daughter to get into the back seat of the car. The mother was forced, at gunpoint, to perform fellatio on Simmons. Afterwards, Simmons attempted to rape the mother. He stopped because she was having her menstrual period. The mother begged Simmons repeatedly to leave her daughter alone.

Throughout the assault, the mother was blindfolded with a neckerchief. After the assault on the mother, Simmons put the mother's sweatshirt over her head to act as an additional blindfold and tied her hands behind her back with her jeans. He then opened the car door and pushed the mother from the car, telling her as he drove off that he would not hurt her daughter. The mother then ran to the nearest house where residents notified police.

After the mother was forced from the car, Simmons drove a short distance and again stopped the car. He forced the girl into the front seat. He forced her to perform fellatio on him and then forcibly raped her. Once finished, he drove back toward town and dropped her off in a deserted area. The girl was subsequently picked up by police and transported to a hospital, where she underwent substantial emergency reconstructive surgery. The offender's car was identified by the mother, and Simmons was apprehended at his residence.

Outcome

Simmons was convicted of two counts of kidnapping, one count of attempted rape, three counts of rape, and illegal weapons possession. In a civil suit by the victims against the newspaper company, a settlement was negotiated. There had been two reported rapes and abductions of newspaper-delivery girls on Sundays, and the crimes had not been reported to the newspaper-delivery girls or their parents.

330: GROUP CAUSE SEXUAL ASSAULT

The category of group cause sexual assault is used for multiple (three or more) offenders. When there are two offenders, each should be classified into the personal cause category. Although there clearly are group dynamics (e.g., contagion effects, defusing of responsibility) and social dynamics (e.g., highly developed gang cultures in particular communities or cities) that foster gang rape, the factors that motivate each of the offenders may well be different.

331: FORMAL GANG SEXUAL ASSAULT

A formal gang is characterized by some internal, organizational structure, a name as well as other identifying features (e.g., colors, insignias, pattern of dress, etc.), and some evidence of group cohesiveness (e.g., members owe some allegiance to the gang and gather to participate in a variety of activities). In sum, the gang must have some mission or purpose other than assault.

Subcategories of formal gang sexual assault include 331.01: Formal Gang Sexual Assault, Single Victim, and 331.02: Formal Gang Sexual Assault, Multiple Victims.

CASE STUDY: 331.01: FORMAL GANG SEXUAL ASSAULT, SINGLE VICTIM

Background/Victimology

In 1981 four teenagers went to a rock concert held at a large amphitheater. During intermission, a group of twelve men wearing shirts labeled The Black Disciples entered the amphitheater. The teenagers became frightened of the accumulating noise and decided to leave. As they were exiting to the center aisle, several of the men grabbed one of the couples and threw them to the aisle. The young woman's clothes were ripped off. Five of the men circled her, pulled her up by the hair, and forced oral sex on her. A sixth man then threw her back on the floor and inserted a tire iron into her vagina. Several security guards stopped the assault. The young woman was taken to a nearby hospital.

Offender Characteristics

The offenders were part of a group well known in the city. The six men were arrested and charged with various counts of assault and sexual assault.

Outcome

The six men plea-bargained the offenses as charged. Nine years later, the young woman was awarded a substantial settlement from several agencies represented at the concert.

332: INFORMAL GANG SEXUAL ASSAULT

An informal gang is a very loosely structured group that congregates, typically on the spur of the moment, with a common purpose of marauding or otherwise engaging in antisocial activity. Although the group may have one or more leaders, there is no formal organizational structure. This category also includes all other instances of multiple-offender assault in which there is no evidence that the group constitutes a formal gang.

Subcategories of informal gang sexual assault include 332.01: Informal Gang Sexual Assault, Single Victim, and 332.02: Informal Gang Sexual Assault, Multiple Victims.

CASE STUDY: 332.01: INFORMAL GANG SEXUAL ASSAULT, SINGLE VICTIM

Background/Victimology

Damon and three companions were driving around when one of them (not Damon) suggested that they "grab a girl and have some fun." They picked up a hitchhiker and, while driving, took turns raping her. When it was Damon's turn, he engaged in frottage but did not actually rape her. The victim was raped repeatedly over a period of two hours while in the car. Eventually, they arrived at an abandoned house. The four men, including Damon, raped the victim throughout the night, occasionally waving revolvers in her face to subdue her protests. The following day, they drove back to the victim's home and dropped her off.

Offender Characteristics

Damon is a twenty-one-year-old, single male. Damon's father was a self-educated engineer who was gainfully employed until his premature death from heart failure. Damon described his father as a chronic, heavy drinker who suffered from bouts of deep depression and crying spells that lasted for days. Damon reported that his father was never abusive to anyone in the family. His mother was a college-educated schoolteacher whom Damon described as strict, puritanical, very religious, and a nondrinker. His early years seemed to be stable and reasonably happy.

While in elementary school, Damon was an above average student. His academic performance drifted into the average or satisfactory range during the last two years of high school, coinciding with the death of his father. After the death, the family seemed to fall apart. His mother became seriously ill and, as a result, bedridden. His older brother was incarcerated for assault and battery. Damon dropped out of school in his senior year and enlisted in the service. He was honorably discharged after six months at the discretion of the military. The primary difficulty was Damon's intractable behavior.

Damon's employment history after the service can best be described as good, when he was in the mood. He was perceived by his employers as apathetic, unreliable, and diffident. Overall, Damon's educational, military, and professional track record reflects an evolving picture of social maladjustment, poor interpersonal skills, and a particular disaffection with authority.

Two months after leaving the service, he was arrested for stealing hub caps; the charges were later dropped. This is his only known criminal offense prior to the rape. The rape occurred exactly two years after Damon's discharge from the service.

In this particular case, the offense was clearly exploitative. In fact, the expressed intention, "to grab a girl and have some fun," could not be stated in a more predatory, exploitative way. Damon's childhood and adolescence were not marked by impulsivity. He excelled in school and only began sliding downhill after his father's death. During the last two years prior to the rape, he became increasingly unreliable and belligerent toward authority; however, at the time of the offense, he had no record of any criminal conduct.

Outcome

Damon was committed to the Massachusetts Treatment Center in 1967 for an indefinite sentence after having been convicted of rape, kidnapping, and assault with a dangerous weapon. The remaining defendants were convicted on charges of rape.

390: SEXUAL ASSAULT NOT CLASSIFIED ELSEWHERE

This category is reserved for those assaults that cannot be classified elsewhere.

PART
TWO

Crime Scene Analysis

4

The Detection of Staging and Personation at the Crime Scene

JOHN E. DOUGLAS
CORINNE M. MUNN

Most crime scenes tell a story. The ability of the investigator to perceive the details of this story depends on his or her ability to analyze the crime scene. The crime scene and forensic evidence contain messages that will lead to the answers that the investigator needs to solve the crime. Not only does crime scene analysis require careful observation and scrutiny of each and every one of these messages, it also requires a clear mental image of the total picture formed by these details.

A major part of the process of crime scene analysis depends on the analyst's insight into the dynamics of human behavior. Speech patterns, writing styles, verbal and nonverbal gestures, and other traits and patterns compose human behavior. This combination causes every individual to act, react, function, or perform in a unique and specific way. This individualistic behavior usually remains consistent, whether it concerns keeping house, selecting a wardrobe, or rape and murder.

The commission of a violent crime involves all the same dynamics of normal human behavior. The same forces that influence normal everyday conduct also influence the offender's actions during an offense. The crime scene usually reflects these behavior patterns or gestures. Learning to recognize the crime scene manifestations of this behavior enables an investigator to discover much about the offender. Due to the personalized nature of this behavior, the investigator also has a means to distinguish between different offenders committing the same offense.

There are three manifestations of offender behavior at a crime scene: *modus operandi (MO)*, *personation* (the *signature*), and *staging*. This chapter discusses personation and staging and illustrates them by case example.

THE ASSESSMENT PHASE

One aspect of interpreting the behavior patterns of an offense depends on attention to details. These details often escape notice during the initial phase of protecting and preserving the crime scene. A violent crime may not only emotionally detach the investigator from the offense, but it may also desensitize that investigator to minute clues offered by the crime scene. Another pitfall that obscures these important details is the inability of the investigator to achieve a comfortable distance from the crime. Identification with the victim, perhaps relating the victim to a family member, prevents detachment from the crime, and judgment may become clouded by emotion. (Good-quality crime scene photographs and exhaustive crime scene processing may remedy this in part by providing a more removed and less emotional environment for the investigator.)

The assessment phase of crime analysis should attempt to answer several questions. What was the sequence of events? Was the victim sexually assaulted before or after death? Was mutilation before or after death? Observations like this can offer important insights into an offender's personality. How did the encounter between the offender and victim occur? Did the offender blitz attack the victim, or did he use verbal means (the con) to capture her? Did the offender use ligatures to control the victim? Lastly, any items added to or taken from the crime scene require careful analysis.

As the police investigator makes these assessments of the crime scene, puzzling elements may arise. These details may obscure the underlying motive of the crime. The crime scene also may contain peculiarities that serve no apparent purpose in the perpetration of the crime. The latter of these two crime scene characteristics, personation, is discussed first.

PERSONATION

Most violent crime careers have a quiet, isolated beginning within the offender's imagination. The subject daydreams about raping, torturing, killing, building bombs, setting fires, or any combination of these violent acts. When the offender translates these daydreams into action, his needs compel him to exhibit unusual behavior during the crime

In one National Center for the Analysis of Violent Crime case, police found a twenty-six-year-old white female on the roof of her apartment in New York City. She had died of ligature strangulation. The offender had left her body face up and positioned to resemble a Jewish religious medal. He had carefully removed her earrings and had placed them on either side of her head. He had cut her nipples off and had placed them on her chest. The offender also had inserted her umbrella into the vagina and placed her comb into the pubic hair. He then had placed the victim's nylons around her wrists and ankles. He had scrawled a derogatory message to police on her body using her pen. Finally, he had left a pile of his own feces, covered with her clothing, a few feet from the body. The NCAVC assessed all of this activity as being postmortem. A few inexpensive articles of jewelry were missing, including the Jewish religious medal that resembled the body's positioning.

This crime scene displayed some unusual input by this offender. The perpetration of this crime did not require the positioning of the body, the postmortem mutilation, insertion, removal of items, and use of postmortem ligatures. The significance of this behavior was not readily apparent to the investigator. The act of sexual assault and murder had little to do with most of this offender's behavior at the crime scene. His behavior went far beyond the actions necessary to carry out this offense (the MO) because assault and murder alone would not satisfy his needs.

Unusual behavior by an offender, beyond that necessary to commit the crime, is called *personation*. The offender invests intimate meaning into the crime scene (e.g., by body positioning, mutilation, items removed or left, or other symbolic gestures involving the crime scene). Only the offender knows the meaning of these acts. When a serial offender demonstrates repetitive ritualistic behavior from crime to crime, it is called the *signature*. The signature aspect of a crime is simply repetitive personation.

Undoing represents a form of personation with more obvious meaning. Undoing frequently occurs at the crime scene when there is a close association between the offender and the victim or when the victim represents someone of significance to the offender. The following case exemplifies undoing: A son stabbed his mother to death during a fierce argument. After calming down, the son was hit by the full impact of his actions. First, he changed the victim's bloodied shirt, then placed her body on the couch with the head on a pillow. He covered her with a blanket and folded her hands over her chest so she appeared to be sleeping peacefully. He displayed his remorse by attempting to emotionally undo the murder. Other forms of undoing include the offender washing up, cleaning the body, covering the victim's face, or completely covering the body with something.

STAGING

Staging is when someone purposely alters the crime scene prior to the arrival of police. There are two reasons why someone employs staging: to redirect the investigation away from the most logical suspect or to protect the victim or victim's family.

When a crime is staged, the responsible person is not someone who just happens upon the victim. It is almost always someone who had some kind of association or relationship with the victim. This offender will further attempt to steer the investigation away from him by his conduct when in contact with law enforcement. Thus, investigators should never eliminate a suspect solely on the grounds of that person's overly cooperative or distraught behavior.

The second reason for staging, to protect the victim or victim's family, is employed most frequently with rape-murder crimes or autoerotic fatalities. The offender of a sexual homicide frequently leaves the victim in a degrading position. One can hardly fault the protective staging behavior, but the investigator needs to obtain an accurate description of the body's condition when found and exactly what that person did to alter the crime scene. A good investigator will do this without adding to this person's already distressed condition by reproaches of ruining physical evidence.

This type of staging is also prevalent with autoerotic fatalities.[1] The victim may be removed from the apparatus that caused death (e.g., cut down from a noose or device suspending the body). In one-third of autoerotic fatalities, the victim is nude, and in another one-third, the victim is wearing a costume of some sort (Dietz & Hazelwood 1982). This costume often involves cross dressing, so not only does the person discovering the body have to endure the shock of finding the victim dead, but also the shock of finding the victim in female dress. To prevent further damage to the victim's or family's reputation or to protect other family members, the person discovering the body may redress the victim in men's clothing or dress the nude body. He or she will often stage the accident to look like a suicide, perhaps writing a suicide note. This person may even go as far as staging the scene to appear as a homicide. Nevertheless, scrutiny of forensics, crime scene dynamics, and victimology probably will reveal the true circumstances surrounding death. Evidence of previous autoerotic activities (bondage literature, adult "toys," eye bolts in the ceiling, worn spots from rope on beams, etc.) in the victim's home also will help determine if an autoerotic activity caused death.

Finally, the investigator should discern whether a crime scene is truly disorganized or whether the offender staged it to appear careless and haphazard. This determination not only helps direct the analysis to the underlying motive, but also helps to shape the offender profile. However, the recognition of staging, especially with a shrewd offender, can be difficult. The investigator must scrutinize all factors of the crime if there is reason to believe it has been staged. Forensics, victimology, and minute crime scene details become critical to the detection of staging.

---

[1]Autoerotism is the sexual arousal and/or gratification without a partner.

"RED FLAGS" FOR THE INVESTIGATOR

An offender who stages a crime scene usually makes mistakes because he stages it to look the way he thinks a crime scene should look. While doing this, the offender experiences a great deal of stress and does not have time to fit all the pieces together logically. Inconsistencies will begin appearing at the crime scene, with forensics, and with the overall picture of the offense. These contradictions will often serve as the "red flags" of staging and prevent misguidance of the investigation.

Red Flags at the Crime Scene

The crime scene often will contain these red flags in the form of crime scene inconsistencies. The investigator should scrutinize all crime scene indicators individually, then view them in the context of the whole picture. Several important questions need to be asked during crime scene analysis. First, did the subject take inappropriate items from the crime scene if burglary appears to be the motive? In one case submitted to the NCAVC, a man returning home from work interrupted a burglary in progress. The startled burglars killed him as he attempted to flee. A later inventory revealed the offenders had not stolen anything, but it appeared they had begun taking apart a large stereo and TV unit for removal. Upstairs, they had passed over smaller items (jewelry, coin collections, etc.) of greater worth. With further investigation, police discovered the victim's wife had paid the offenders to stage the burglary and kill her husband. She was having an affair with one of the offenders.

Second, did the point of entry make sense? For example, an offender enters a house by a second-story window despite the presence of easier, less conspicuous entry points.

Third, did the perpetration of this crime pose a high risk to the offender? In other words, did it happen during daylight hours, in a populated area, with obvious signs of occupation at the house (lights on, vehicles in the driveway), and/or involving highly visible entry points?

The following case illustrates some of these points. In a small northeastern city, an unknown intruder attacked a man and his wife one Saturday morning. The offender placed a ladder against the house, climbed up to a second-story window, and entered after removing the screen. This all occurred in a residential area during a time when the neighbors were up and about. Thinking he heard the offender downstairs, the husband followed behind with a gun. He claimed the offender struck him on the head after a struggle. The offender then returned upstairs and killed the wife by manual strangulation. He left the body with the nightgown pulled up around the waist, implying he had sexually assaulted her.

As the detectives processed the crime scene, it was noted that the offender's weight on the ladder had left no impressions in the yard. However, when the police investigator placed one foot on the bottom rung, the ladder left an impression in the ground. In addition, the offender had positioned the ladder backward, with the rungs going in the wrong direction. Many of the rungs could not support even 50 pounds of weight because the wood was rotted. The offender left no foot impressions and no transference of debris from the rungs to the roof, either.

Why didn't the offender choose entrance through a first-story window? This would have decreased the chance of detection from both the occupants and the neighbors. Why burglarize on a Saturday morning in an area full of potential witnesses? Why choose a house obviously occupied, with several vehicles in the driveway? If the criminal intent was homicide, why didn't the intruder seek his intended victim(s) immediately? Instead, he went downstairs first. If he intended to murder, why didn't he come equipped to kill? He never displayed or used a knife, gun, or any weapon. Why did the person posing the greatest threat to the intruder receive only minor injuries? When an investigator analyzes a crime scene demonstrating a great deal of offender activity and no clear motive for this activity, the statements of the victim/witness should be questioned.

Another red flag apparent with many staged domestic murders is the fatal assault of the wife and/or children by an intruder while the husband escapes without injury or with a nonfatal injury. If the offender does not first target the person posing the greatest threat or if that person suffers the least amount of injury, the police investigator should especially examine all other crime scene indicators. In addition, the investigator should scrutinize forensics and victimology (any recent insurance policies on victim?) with particular attention.

Forensic Red Flags

Do the injuries fit the crime? Forensic results that do not fit the crime should cause the investigator to think about staging. The presence of a personal-type assault utilizing a weapon of opportunity when the initial motive for the offense appears to be for material gain should raise suspicion. This type of assault also includes manual or ligature strangulation, facial beating (depersonalization), and excessive trauma beyond that necessary to cause death (overkill).

Sexual and domestic homicides will demonstrate forensic findings of this type: a close-range, personalized assault. The victim (not money or goods) is the *primary* focus on the offender. This type of offender often will attempt to stage a sexual or domestic homicide to appear motivated by criminal enterprise. This does not imply that personal-type assaults never happen during the commission of a property crime, but usually the criminal enterprise offender prefers a quick, clean kill that reduces his time at the scene. Any forensic red flags, after careful analysis, should be placed in context with victimology and crime scene information.

Other discrepancies may arise when the account of a witness/survivor conflicts with forensic findings. In one case, an estranged wife found her husband, a professional golfer, dead in the bathroom tub with the water running. Initially, it appeared as if the golfer slipped in the tub, struck his head on a bathroom fixture, and drowned. However, the autopsy began to raise suspicion. Toxicology reports revealed a high level of Valium in the victim's bloodstream at the time of death. The autopsy also revealed several concentrated areas of injury or impact points on the head, as if the victim had struck his head more than once. Later, investigators learned the wife had been with him the night of his death. The wife later confessed that she had made dinner for her husband and had laced his salad with Valium. After her husband passed out, she let three men she had hired into the house to kill him and make the death look accidental.

Investigators often will find forensic discrepancies when a subject stages a rape murder. The offender frequently positions the victim to infer sexual assault has occurred. An offender who has a close relationship with the victim will often only partially remove the victim's clothing (e.g., pants pulled down, shirt or dress pulled up, etc.). He rarely leaves the victim nude. Despite the body's positioning and the partial removal of clothes, the autopsy demonstrates a lack of sexual assault. (The investigator should remember sexual assault can take many forms: exploratory probing, regressive necrophilia, insertion, etc.) With a staged sexual assault, there is usually no evidence of any sexual activity and an absence of seminal fluids in the body orifices.

Finally, if the investigator suspects a crime has been staged, he or she should look for other signs of close offender association with the victim (e.g., washing up or any other indications of undoing). In addition, when an offender stages a domestic homicide, he frequently plans and maneuvers a third-party discovery of the victim. The case that involved the husband staging his wife's murder to appear as the work of an intruder illustrates this point. Instead of going upstairs to check on his wife and daughter, he called his brother, who lived across the street. The husband stayed downstairs in the kitchen while the brother ran upstairs and discovered the victim. Offenders often will manipulate the victim's discovery by a neighbor or family member or will be conveniently elsewhere when the victim is discovered.

STAGING IN ARSON

Most of the same red flags of staging that apply to a staged homicide also apply to a staged arson. Arson investigation warrants the same attention to crime scene information, targeted property and/or victimology, and forensic findings as a homicide investigation.

When it is suspected that arson has been used for crime concealment, especially a murder, one of the first questions answered should be, Do the forensics fit the crime? One example, a California case, began when a passing motorist saw a mobile home engulfed in flames. He honked his horn to get the neighbors' attention as he pulled in front of the burning home. Face down in the yard, apparently unconscious, was a thirty-four-year-old white male, a resident of the burning home. Upon hearing a female voice calling for help, the motorist and a neighbor attempted to enter the structure, but the heat was too intense. When fire fighters and police arrived, the man who had been unconscious in the yard began to cry out, "My wife is in there. She's asleep in the bedroom!" He attempted to enter the trailer but was held back by fire fighters.

The husband told investigators he had fallen asleep in the living room while watching TV when he was suddenly awakened by fire coming from the bedroom where his wife was sleeping. He had no memory of anything except jumping out the window to escape the burning trailer.

The first inconsistency of his story became evident after his wife's autopsy. She had sustained numerous head wounds, including a skull fracture running from the left cheek to the top of her head. One wound was described as a large gaping hole that seemed to have torn the scalp loose from the skull. Physical evidence within the home could not account for these injuries, the extent of which could have been fatal. The immediate cause of death was asphyxiation and extensive thermal burns over 90 percent of the body, with a secondary cause of compound head injuries.

The crime scene also offered many red flags. The victim's body was found in the living room, not the bedroom. A large amount of blood was found in the living room floor close to the place the husband had been sitting. Bloodstains also were observed on the husband's shirt, pants, and shoes. The most extensive damage by the fire occurred in living room area, particularly around the husband's chair, and not in the back bedroom, where his wife allegedly had been sleeping and the fire supposedly had originated. The husband offered no explanation of his wife's brutal beating. He denied hearing or seeing anything related to the incident. Closer observation of the crime scene made it apparent the fire had been set to conceal the struggle and homicide that had occurred that night between the husband and wife. The husband was subsequently convicted of both arson and second-degree murder and was sentenced to fifteen years to life.

Arson is often employed for the purposes of insurance fraud. The fire may be staged to appear accidental or as arson committed by some party unknown to the apparent victim. The detection of staging often depends heavily on investigation beyond the crime scene indicators. The following example illustrates the investigative leads that uncovered the staging of a crime made to appear as if the offenders were victims of arson.

A couple in their mid sixties were summoned from a short shopping trip with the news that there had been a fire in their $850,000 home. The fire had done minimal damage to all but the second floor and a stairway leading to the third floor, where a gasoline container was found. There were some flammable-liquid burn patterns in the master bedroom, where the most extensive damage was done. The fire fighters had noticed an unusual lack of furniture and personal effects in the spacious home. The couple reported that, indeed, many items were missing from their home and filed a burglary report. It appeared the arson was intended to cover the tracks of a burglar.

Three days later, fire fighters were again summoned to the couple's home. At this time, the house was unoccupied, and the fire was set in the living room. The investigation began to focus on the couple, although they seemed unlikely criminals. (The wife was very active in community organizations, and neither husband nor wife had any criminal record other than a few traffic violations.) However, the missing items were not typical articles targeted by theft. The list included photographs, personal items, paintings of family members, a dresser, and a three-foot safe.

Upon checking the furnishings and clothing still in the house, investigators noted the furniture appeared to be of poor quality and much of the clothing looked secondhand. A real estate agent who had recently listed the house told investigators that the residence previously had contained some nice furnishings, including some expensive looking china.

The case became more solid as investigators began checking local rental truck and storage businesses. They found the suspects had rented a truck several times to move furniture from their home to a storage unit, a newly rented house, and the out-of-state home of the suspects' son. The storage unit and the rented home both were rented under aliases. The house rent was paid in cash, and the suspects unsuccessfully had tried to convince the landlord to turn on the utilities under his name. In addition, a phone call was made by the suspects' daughter at 11:38 A.M. on the morning of the fire to inform a friend that some of his belongings had been destroyed in a fire at her parents' home. However, fire department records show the first fire call concerning that residence was made at 2:08 P.M. Finally, most of the items reported missing or destroyed in the fire were found at either the storage unit, the rented house, or the son's home. The couple was charged and convicted of arson and insurance fraud.

As these cases illustrate, the detection of staging at the arson crime scene often depends on the careful investigation of factors outside the crime scene. These factors include forensics and the alleged victim's background (especially financial status).

CONCLUSIONS

The crime scene of most violent offenses requires a special kind of literacy from the police investigator. This literacy places many demands on the investigator. It requires detachment, a judgment unclouded by emotions. But with too much detachment, the investigator risks insensitivity to the minute, crucial details within the scene. Investigators need to be crime scene diagnosticians. They must understand the dynamics of human behavior displayed at the crime scene. They should be able to recognize the different manifestations of this behavior: the MO, personation, and staging. During the assessment phase, they need to ask the right questions. During the investigative phase, they must then provide the right answers.

No investigator is able to meet all of these demands all of the time. But if investigators approach each crime scene with an awareness of these factors, they will steadily improve their ability to read the true story of each case. Through the development of this literacy, law enforcement will cut short lethal careers and more effectively battle violent crime.

5

Modus Operandi and the Signature Aspects of Violent Crime

JOHN E. DOUGLAS
CORINNE M. MUNN

In September 1989 a Shreveport, Louisiana, man named Nathaniel Code, Jr., stood trial for murder. The jury determined Code had murdered a total of eight people between 1984 and 1987. These homicides involved three different events: one murder in 1984, four in 1985, and three in 1987. Several disparities existed among the three crime scenes. The offender gagged the first victim with a piece of material from the scene, but the last two incidents involved the use of duct tape. The killer stabbed and slashed the first victim, whereas the other two crimes included the additional use of a firearm and ligature strangulation. The victims ranged in age from eight years old to seventy-four years old and included both sexes. All the victims were black. The offender took money from one house but not from the other two (Douglas 1989).

Could one man be linked to all three of these crimes? Would not such differences in *modus operandi* (MO) and *victimology* (characteristics of the victims) eliminate the connection to one offender? MO and victimology alone would have failed to link Code with each of these eight homicides. But Code not only left gags, duct tape, and bodies with gunshot wounds and slashed throats at the crime scenes, he left his calling card. Every crime scene demonstrated this calling card or signature aspect and thus linked Code to the offenses.

No one involved with contemporary law enforcement would dispute our society has an abundance of Nathaniel Codes. The upward spiral of violent crime has required law enforcement to develop new measures. One measure includes the recognition of the serial offender (who often crosses jurisdictional boundaries) through crime analysis. A more effective interagency effort depends on this early recognition. Comprehensive analysis of victimology, crime scene, forensics, and with living victims, verbal and nonverbal offender behavior forms this vital process of linking offenses to one offender.

The MO has great significance when investigators attempt to link cases. An appropriate step of crime analysis and correlation includes connecting cases due to similarities in MO. However, an investigator who rejects an offense as the work of a serial offender solely on the basis of disparities in MO (as in the Code cases) has made a mistake. What causes an offender to use a certain MO? What influences shape a modus operandi? Is it static or dynamic? By answering these questions, one sees the error of attributing too much significance to the MO when linking crimes.

THE MODUS OPERANDI

A novice prowler prepared to enter a house through a basement window to burglarize it. Although the window was closed and locked, the prowler shattered the window and gained access to the house. He had to rush his search for valuables because he feared the breaking window had attracted attention. During a later crime, he burglarized another residence, but this time he brought tools with him to force the lock and keep the noise minimal. This allowed him time to commit the crime and to obtain a more profitable haul.

This example demonstrates that MO is a learned behavior. The offender's actions during the perpetration of a crime form the MO. The offender develops and uses an MO over time because it works, but it also continuously evolves. The modus operandi is very dynamic and malleable. During his criminal career, an offender usually modifies the MO as he gains experience. The burglar refines his breaking and entering techniques to lower his risk of apprehension and to increase his profit. Experience and confidence will reshape an offender's MO. Incarceration usually impacts on the future MO of an offender, especially the career criminal. He refines the MO as he learns from the mistakes that led to his arrest.

The victim's response can also significantly influence the evolution of an MO. If the rapist has problems controlling a victim, he will modify his MO to accommodate resistance. He may bring duct tape or other ligatures, he may use a weapon, or he may blitz-attack the victim and immediately incapacitate her. If such measures are ineffective, he may resort to greater violence or kill the victim. Thus, the MO will evolve to meet the demands of the crime.

THE SIGNATURE ASPECT

The violent, repetitive offender often exhibits another element of criminal behavior during an offense: the signature aspect, or calling card. This criminal conduct goes beyond the actions necessary to perpetrate the crime. It composes a unique and integral part of the offender's behavior while he is committing the offense.

An offender's fantasies often give birth to violent crime. As the offender broods and daydreams, he develops a need to express these violent fantasies. When he finally acts out, some aspect of the crime will demonstrate a unique, personal expression or ritual based on these fantasies. Committing the crime does not satisfy the offender's needs. This insufficiency compels him to go beyond the scope of perpetration and perform his ritual. When the subject displays this ritual at the crime scene, he has left his calling card.

How does the crime scene manifest this calling card, or signature aspect? The subject introduces an aspect of his personality into the scene through this ritual. The crime scene displays this aspect by peculiar crime scene characteristics or unusual offender input during the perpetration of the crime. A rapist demonstrates his signature by engaging in acts of domination, manipulation, or control during the verbal, physical, and/or sexual phase of the assault. Exceptionally vulgar and/or abusive language or scripting represents a verbal signature. When the offender scripts a victim, he dictates a particular verbal response from her (e.g., "Tell me how much you enjoy sex with me" or "Tell me how good I am"). The use of excessive physical force exemplifies another aspect of a subject's signature. One example of signature sexual behavior involves the offender who repeatedly engages in a specific order of sexual activity with different victims.

The core of the offender's ritual will never change. Unlike the MO, it remains a constant and enduring part of the offender. However, signature aspects may evolve (e.g., the lust murderer, who performs greater postmortem mutilation as he progresses from crime to crime). Elements of the original ritual become more fully developed. In addition, the signature does not always show up in every crime because of contingencies that might arise, such as interruptions or an unexpected victim response.

The investigator cannot always identify the signature aspect. Violent offenses often involve high-risk victims or decomposition from outdoor body disposal, both of which interfere with recognition of the signature.

MODUS OPERANDI OR SIGNATURE CRIME?

A rapist entered a residence and captured a woman and her husband. The offender ordered the husband to lie on his stomach on the floor. He then placed a cup and saucer on the husband's back. "If I hear that cup move or hit the floor, your wife dies," he told the husband. He then took the wife into the next room and raped her.

In another situation, a rapist entered a house and ordered the woman to phone her husband and use some ploy to get him home. Once the husband arrived, the offender tied him to a chair and forced him to witness the rape of his wife.

The rapist who used the cup and saucer had developed an effective modus operandi to control the husband. The second rapist, however, had gone beyond the simple commission of rape. The full satisfaction of his fantasies not only required raping the wife, but also humiliating and dominating the husband. His personal needs compelled him to perform this signature aspect of crime.

In Michigan a certain bank robber made the tellers undress during the robbery. In Texas another bank robber also forced the bank employees to undress, but then made them pose in sexually provocative positions as he snapped photographs. Do both these crimes demonstrate a signature aspect? The Michigan robber used a very effective means to increase his escape time (i.e., the tellers dressed before summoning police). When interviewed, these employees offered vague, meager descriptions because their embarrassment had prevented eye contact with the perpetrator. This subject had developed a clever MO. The Texas robber, however, went beyond the required actions to perpetrate his crime successfully. He felt compelled to enact the ritual of posing the tellers and taking pictures, leaving his signature on the crime. The act of robbing the bank did not gratify his psychosexual needs.

LINKING CASES

When investigators attempt to link cases, the modus operandi plays an important role. However, as stated previously, MO should not be the only criterion used to connect crimes, especially with the repeat offender who alters the MO through experience and learning. The first offenses may differ considerably from later offenses. However, the signature aspect remains the same, whether it is the first offense or one committed ten years later. The ritual may evolve, but the theme persists.

The signature aspect also should receive greater consideration than victim similarities (these should not be discounted, however) when investigators attempt to link cases to a serial offender. Physical similarities of victims are often not important, especially when crimes are motivated by anger. The offender expresses his anger through the rituals he engages in, not by attacking a victim who possesses a particular characteristic or trait.

CASES LINKED BY OFFENDER SIGNATURE

Ronnie Shelton: Serial Rapist

Ronnie Shelton, a serial rapist, committed as many as fifty rapes. He was convicted of twenty-eight, receiving a sentence in excess of one thousand years. Both his verbal and sexual assaults manifested his signature. Verbally, he was degrading and exceptionally vulgar. He also would say such things as, "I have seen you with your boyfriend," "I've seen you around," or "You know who I am." Thoughts of Shelton lurking around their neighborhood terrorized the victims (Douglas 1990).

The sexual assault occupied a central position in Shelton's ritual. He would rape the victim vaginally, then withdraw and ejaculate on the victim's stomach or breasts. He would also frequently masturbate over the victim or between her breasts. He often used the victim's clothing to wipe off ejaculate. Shelton forced many of his victims to have oral sex with him and then insisted they swallow the ejaculate. He also would force them to masturbate him manually. The combination of these acts displayed Shelton's signature.

Shelton's MO included entrance to the victim's dwelling through a window or patio facing a wooded area or bushes offering concealment. He wore a ski mask, stocking, or scarf. He convinced the victims he was not there to rape but to rob them ("I just want money"). When he had the victim under control, he would return to the rape mode. The victim would then comply because she had seen his earlier propensity for violence (throwing her to the floor, holding a knife to her throat, etc.). Shelton would use such phrases as "Keep your eyes down," "Cover your eyes," or "Don't look at me and I won't kill you (hurt your kids)." Before he left, he would verbally intimidate the victim with warnings such as "Don't call the police" or "I'll come back and kill you." This latter behavior served the MO, whereas the former sexual actions were his calling card.

Shelton's signature linked him to the twenty-eight sexual assaults. Without the recognition of his calling card with each of these offenses, he may not have been charged and prosecuted to the full extent he deserved.

Serial Arson

Just as the serial killer or rapist develops an MO, so will the arsonist. An arsonist's modus operandi may involve targeting structures of a certain type that offer easy access and escape. The use of certain accelerants and incendiary devices are components of the MO, as is the selection of a specific site to set the fire (i.e., inside or outside).

The signature aspects of an arsonist may be bizarre behavior at the crime scene, such as defecation or urination. He may take certain items from the crime scene (e.g., women's undergarments). The arsonist also may demonstrate his calling card by what he leaves at the crime scene. One firesetter would draw pictures on the walls before setting fires. Specific incendiary mixtures and accelerants may offer peculiarities indicative of a signature aspect (e.g., the unusual combination of kerosine and gasoline).

An investigator should apply the same principles used in detecting the signature aspect of a sexual assault or homicide to arson. The crime scene needs to be analyzed for any offender activity that appears unusual or unnecessary for the successful perpetration of the arson.

UNABOMB: Serial Bomber

Between May 1978 and February 1987, an unknown offender mailed or placed a series of elaborate bombs that targeted university students and faculty, airlines, and other businesses. There has been one fatality, and twenty other victims have been injured in the twelve bombings attributed to UNABOMB.

UNABOMB's modus operandi consisted of the use of pipe bombs, booby-trap mechanisms, and nail, wire-insulated stables, and screws for fragmentation. He used untraceable items, such as common wire, batteries, and several types of tape. As he became more sophisticated, his MO evolved from the use of smokeless powder and match heads to ammonium nitrate and aluminum powder as explosive filler.

UNABOMB had a very distinctive calling card. He frequently carved an unusual marking on a component part. He used lamp cord and other unique parts as part of an initiator. He constructed elaborate and descriptive address labels and wooden boxes or frames to mail the devices. He also handcrafted wood components and bomb housing. The most obvious aspect of UNABOMB's signature was the construction of the bombs. He built electrical components and switching mechanisms that required a considerable amount of time when low-cost, over-the-counter electric components were readily available. The extraordinary (and unnecessary) amount of time required to design, construct, and assemble the bombs demonstrated the ritualistic aspects of this offense, aspects that satisfied the unique needs of this offender. The UNABOMB case remains unsolved.

SERIAL KILLERS AND SIGNATURE CRIME

Steven Pennel

Steven Pennel was a sexual sadist who murdered at least three victims. His MO involved using duct tape and ligatures to control his victims while he tortured them. He used hammer blows to the head to kill them (Douglas 1990).

Pennel's signature could be seen in the nature of the wounds inflicted upon his victims. He targeted the buttocks and breasts, beating and pinching them with tools (hammer and pinching device). The victims were alive during these assaults, as he derived sexual gratification from their response to torture. Autopsy results confirmed this: none of the victims had been sexually assaulted.

The victims also had ligature marks around their necks, although the blunt-force trauma to the head caused death. Pennel enjoyed tightening the ligature to the point of near strangulation. Because he required his victims to be alive and conscious during torture, he did not kill them this way. Strangulation was not Pennel's MO but was part of his ritual, a method to cause the extreme suffering that satisfied his needs.

The violence escalated as Pennel's ritual matured and his fantasies seasoned: the last victim had suffered the greatest amount of antemortem trauma and postmortem mutilation (again Pennel targeted the breasts). The fact that *postmortem* mutilation to the breasts occurred caused some debate as to whether this victim bore Pennel's signature and had been killed by him. Pennel inflicted breast injury on previous victims while they were alive.

There were two reasons why this case could be linked to Pennel. His signature was still very evident with this victim. He had inflicted a great deal of injury to the victim's buttocks *while she was alive*. Therefore, the signature aspect of torturing a live victim was present, but it was evolving. With each victim, the torture became more brutal. As stated above, interference with the ritual due to contingencies arising will alter that ritual. This victim probably died too soon for Pennel to complete his signature.

MO and victimology also served to strengthen the connection between these victims and Pennel. The victims were all high risk: they were prostitutes and/or had a history of drug abuse. They disappeared from the same area, a state highway, and police recovered the bodies within a few miles of each other. Body disposal was similar; Pennel left the bodies in full view, dumped with cold indifference by roadsides. The absence of remorse demonstrated by Pennel's body disposal methods can be considered another aspect of his calling card.

Nathaniel Code

Nathaniel Code, the offender referred to earlier in this chapter, killed eight times on three separate occasions. The first homicide, a twenty-five-year-old black female, occurred 8 August 1984. Code stabbed her nine times in the chest and slashed her throat.

Approximately one year later on 19 July 1985, Code struck again, this time claiming four victims: a fifteen-year-old girl, her mother, and two male friends. Code nearly severed the girl's head from her body. Her mother died from asphyxiation and was draped over the side of the bathtub. Code shot one of the males in the head, leaving him in a middle bedroom. The other male was found in the front bedroom, shot twice in the chest and with his throat slashed.

The last killing took place on 5 August 1987. The victims were Code's grandfather and his two young nephews, ages eight and twelve. The boys died of ligature strangulation. Code stabbed his grandfather five times in the chest and seven times in the back.

The changes of Code's modus operandi, exhibited from case to case, offer an excellent example of the refinement of an MO. With the first murder, a gag had been used from material at the scene. The next time, Code came prepared, bringing duct tape to the scene. It is evident that Code engaged in some type of surveillance activity to obtain information about the victims, especially with the second homicides. He brought a gun to dispose quickly of the greatest threats, the males. The last victims, an elderly man and two children, posed little threat to someone of Code's large physical stature, so Code did not use the gun.

All three cases involved single-family dwellings. The air conditioners and/or TVs were on, drowning out the noise of the intruder as he entered through a door or window. Code quickly gained and maintained control of the multiple victims by separating them into different rooms.

Nathaniel Code had a very distinctive calling card. The injuries suffered by the victims demonstrated one aspect of his signature. Code employed a very bloody method of attack and overkill. He could have simply murdered each of these victims with a single gunshot wound, a clean kill involving very little mess. Instead, Code slaughtered his victims, slashing their throats with a sawing motion, causing deep neck wounds. Although brutal, the attack did not satisfy Code's ritual: all the victims who sustained neck wounds also suffered additional injury, with the exception of the fifteen-year-old girl. One male victim sustained gunshot wounds to the chest, and another multiple stab wounds to the chest. Code wounded nearly all of the victims far beyond what was necessary to cause death (overkill).

This physical violence and bloody overkill satisfied Code's need for domination, control, and manipulation. He positioned all of the victims face down, more evidence of this theme of domination. Code forced the mother to witness her daughter's death as part of this ritual of control, formed from his rage. (Forensics revealed the daughter's blood on the mother's dress.) If the victim's response threatened his sense of domination, Code reacted with anger and the excessive violence that led to overkill.

The last signature aspect of Code's crimes probably best illustrated his unique calling card: the ligature. Code used both an unusual configuration and material. In all three cases, the victims were bound with electrical appliance or telephone cords acquired at the scene. Code could have brought rope or used his duct tape, but the use of these cords satisfied some personal need. He used a handcuff-style configuration, with a loop around each wrist. He also bound the ankles handcuff-style and connected them to the wrists by a lead going through the legs.

The dissimilarities of theses cases involves the MO, *not the signature aspect.* The use of a gun with threatening males present revealed an adaptive offender. At the time of the grandfather's homicide, additional financial stressors affected Code, as evidenced by the theft of money from the grandfather's residence. Three years of living reshaped this offender's behavior at each of the crime scenes. The MO reflected this change, not his calling card.

Physical characteristics, age, even sex do not enhance or diminish the ritual driven by rage. Code's ritual of anger required control and domination of his victims, so victimology was not as important. Code, like Ronnie Shelton, the serial rapist, selected victims he could control, manipulate, and project his anger on.

CONCLUSIONS

Understanding and recognizing the signature aspects of crime have obvious importance. It is vital in the recognition, apprehension, and prosecution of an offender, especially the serial offender.

No one appreciates the importance of recognizing an offender's calling card more than David Vasquez. In 1984 Vasquez pleaded guilty to the murder of a thirty-two-year-old Arlington, Virginia, woman. The woman had been sexually assaulted and died of ligature strangulation. The killer left her lying face down with her hands tied behind her back. He had used unique knots and excessive binding with the ligatures, and a lead came from the wrists to the neck over the left shoulder. The body was openly displayed so that discovery would offer significant shock value.

The offender had spent an excessive amount of time at the crime scene. He had made extensive preparations to bind the victim, allowing him to control her easily. His needs dictated that he move her around the house, exerting total domination over her. It appeared he even had taken her into the bathroom and had made her brush her teeth. None of this behavior was necessary to perpetrate the crime; the offender had felt compelled to act out this ritual.

Vasquez had a very low IQ. His lawyers felt this would make it difficult to prove his innocence, so they convinced him he would probably receive the death sentence if he went to trial. Vasquez opted for life imprisonment and thus pleaded guilty.

In 1987 police discovered the body of a forty-four-year-old woman, nude and face down on her bed, with a rope binding her wrists behind her back. The ligature strand tightly encircled the neck, with a slipknot at the back, continued over her left shoulder down her back, and then wrapped three times around each wrist. Forensics revealed she had died of ligature strangulation and had been sexually assaulted. The offender left the body exposed and openly displayed. He appeared to have spent a considerable amount of time at the scene. This homicide occurred *four blocks* from the 1984 murder.

David Vasquez had been imprisoned for several years when the 1987 murder occurred. The National Center for the Analysis of Violent Crime conducted an exhaustive analysis of these two homicides, a series of sexual assaults, and several other killings that had happened between 1984 and 1987. Eventually, the NCAVC linked these offenses, through analogous signature aspects, to an Arlington, Virginia, subject. Physical evidence later corroborated this connection.

Vasquez was released from confinement after his exoneration because the calling card left at the 1984 homicide was not his. Recognition of the signature aspects of a violent crime not only serves justice and society by curtailing the violent criminal's career, it will help assure that the right person is punished.

CHAPTER 6

Crime Scene Photography

PETER A. SMERICK

T raditionally, photography has been used to document what occurred at a crime scene prior to, during, and after the commission of the offense. Its purpose was to refresh the memories of detectives and witnesses, to show the placement and significance of physical evidence, and to convey to a jury the circumstances of the crime (i.e., the who, what, where, why, and how of the incident). There is, however, another equally important role of crime scene photography. These photographs can be analyzed to determine behavioral and personality traits of the offender (criminal investigative analysis) and aid in the proper classification of violent crime.

American juries are composed of individuals acclimated to television, videotapes, and movies in which there is a beginning, a middle, and an end to a story. Consequently, crime scene photographers should keep this factor in mind and attempt to tell a logical story with their cameras. A police photographer is not just a person pushing a button; he or she is, in fact, an investigator analyzing the scene through the lens as the perpetrator of the crime may have seen it. Therefore, it is essential that the scene is photographed in a logical, organized sequence.

This chapter outlines basic crime scene photography. This information is intended to supplement the investigator's knowledge and to enhance the investigative process through the optimal use of the crime scene photographer and crime scene photographs.

APPLICATIONS OF CRIME SCENE PHOTOGRAPHY WITH CRIMINAL INVESTIGATIVE ANALYSIS

The criminal investigative analyst recognizes that the crime scene often reflects the behavioral characteristics of the offender. Through analysis of these behavior patterns, the investigator may construct a profile that describes critical offender traits. The offender usually is unaware of these behavioral clues because during the offense, his actions are a natural part

FIGURE 6-1

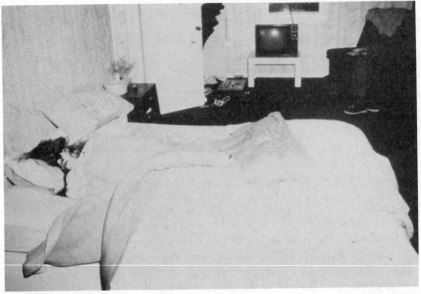

of his personality and, therefore, feel appropriate. Photographs, when properly executed, will capture this information for further analysis and will allow repeated evaluation and critique by investigators. For example, the manner in which a homicide victim's body was covered can sometimes indicate whether the offender was angry at the victim, cared deeply for the victim, showed remorse for what he had done, or was making a statement about who the victim represented (see figure 6–1).

By carefully analyzing crime scene photographs, an investigator may be able to detect signs of a staged crime scene, as exemplified in the following case: A husband claimed to have been attacked by three men while he was asleep on the living room couch. When he regained consciousness, he found his wife and two daughters brutally slain in their bedrooms. Crime scene photographs refuted his story that a violent fight occurred in the living room between four men because of the lack of any significance disturbance of furniture and the absence of significant physical evidence indicative of a struggle (hairs, fibers, bloodstains, shoe impressions). The positioning of furniture and placement of magazines and slippers failed to support this story (see figure 6–2).

Analysis of crime scene photographs also can link cases together because of certain signature aspects of the crime. A signature aspect, as discussed in chapter 5, relates to some psychologically satisfying activity by the offender that does not directly relate to the commission of the crime itself. It could consist of always leaving the body in a particular pose, always binding the victim with rope looped thirteen times, or placement of a certain object on the body. Figure 6–3 illustrates the signature aspect of the murderer's

FIGURE 6-2

FIGURE 6-3

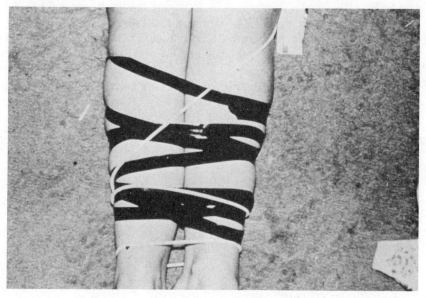

crime scene. Other victims of this offender were tied in this same, specific manner.

TECHNIQUES

The Use of an Autofocusing Camera at the Crime Scene

While each crime scene is unique, there are accepted photographic techniques applicable to all crime scenes. The general procedures for photographing these scenes are well documented. However, there are specialized photographic applications available that enable the photographer to provide the investigator with additional evidence and clues not previously considered.

The introduction of autofocusing cameras with built-in electronic strobes has led to the growing belief that anyone can take crime scene photographs, so the need for a highly trained police photographer is diminished. Although these automatic cameras are suitable for the amateur photographer, they are inadequate for recording blood splatter, invisible bloodstains, or latent bite mark or shoe print evidence. For these situations, a professional 35mm single lens reflex camera (with interchangeable lenses) or, ideally, a larger film format camera is required in the hands of a knowledgeable police photographer. (Instant picture cameras, such as the Polaroid camera, should not be used to document a crime scene because of the lack of sufficient sharpness in the print and the absence of a negative from which enlargements can be made.)

This is not to say that autofocusing cameras are useless for law enforcement. In fact, they can assist the investigator greatly if employed in a timely manner. One of the basic principles of crime scene processing is the preservation of the scene for the investigator. Usually, a uniformed patrol officer is the first to arrive at a crime scene. The officer is instructed to aid the victim, protect the scene, and make notes and observations. A conflict frequently occurs between patrol officers dedicated to protecting the scene and emergency medical personnel dedicated to preserving life, not crime scenes. Although this conflict may never be satisfactorily resolved, the officer could provide an invaluable service by photographing the uncontaminated scene with an autofocusing camera before medical personnel arrive.

Photographic Procedures at the Crime Scene

In general, the photographer will take long-range, medium-range, and close-up photographs, beginning with the exterior of the location. Figure 6–4 illustrates a typical long-range crime scene photograph. Many photographers believe that photographing the exterior of the building where the

FIGURE 6-4

crime occurred is the extent of long-range photography. In reality, a series of photographs should be taken showing the building in relationship to the rest of the neighborhood. Figures 6–5 and 6–6 illustrate a long-range crime scene photograph showing the victim's home in relationship to the neighborhood.

There are no requirements that prescribe precise distances for long-range, medium-range, or close-up photographs. There also are no rules that state that photographs have to be taken in the previously mentioned sequence. For instance, if a shoe print is observed on a dew-covered step, close-up photographs of the impression should be taken before it evaporates, and long-range photographs can be taken at a more convenient time.

Crowds gathering around a crime scene should always be photographed because occasionally the offender returns to observe police at work. These photographs also are useful in identifying possible eyewitnesses. In addition, photographs should be taken of vehicles parked in the area, especially their license plates, because the killer may have fled the scene on foot and may return for his vehicle after police depart. A photographic record offers the best proof that the vehicle was at the scene of the crime. If only a written notation is made, there is always the possibility that the license plate number has been copied incorrectly.

If there have been a series of similar violent crimes committed in a neighborhood, aerial photographs should be taken to show the relationship of the crime scenes to one another. Analysts will use the aerial photographs (and maps) to develop a cluster analysis and try to ascertain where the

FIGURE 6-5

FIGURE 6-6

FIGURE 6-7

offender lives in relationship to the crime scenes. Figure 6–7 is an aerial photograph of a crime scene that shows the analyst the environment in which the crime or crimes occurred.

The first photograph taken at a crime scene should not be of the scene itself. Instead, a card or sheet of paper containing the title of the case (if known), address of the crime scene, date, and name of the photographer should be photographed first. In this way, if the film is ever misfiled or misplaced, the first negative contains identification data.

Once this is recorded, the photographer proceeds to photograph the exterior of the scene as previously described. The photographer should be careful not to photograph accidentally fellow police officers who may not be involved directly in the investigation. Although some detectives insist on directing the photographer as to every photograph to take, most experienced police photographers are knowledgeable enough to cover the site without direction. They should be directed only when evidence is discovered during the search.

Most photographers covering outdoor crime scenes scrutinize the ground for shoe prints, tire prints, and trace evidence. One technique that has proven useful for search teams is to have all team members wear identical shoes in which an *X* or other unique mark is placed in the heel and sole. If the photographer spots an impression like this, he or she knows it belongs to a team member and not a suspect. Some teams go one step further and insist that team members wear white cotton jumpsuits so that fibers from their street clothes do not contaminate the scene. (White cotton fibers are so prevalent that they rarely are considered valuable as physical evidence).

All doorways to crime scenes should be photographed to prove or disprove signs of a forced entry. (A forced entry indicates the killer may have been a stranger to the victim.) At the entrance to a scene, care should be exercised so that latent shoe impressions are not accidentally destroyed by police or ambulance personnel. The photographer should point a flashlight at an oblique angle to the surface and skim its light along the floor to detect these impressions in dust or waxed surfaces. If the impressions are in dust, there are electrostatic dustlift impressions kits available to recover this evidence. Once the dust impressions are transferred to the plastic lifting sheet, they should be photographed immediately because they can be erased by careless handling. Fingerprints may not be found at a crime scene for a number of reasons, but there is no feasible way for an offender to eliminate every shoe impression he or she has made. Figure 6–8 is a shoe impression showing points of identification.

For most crime scene situations, the camera should be held at eye level from a standing position. This ensures the viewer will be observing the scene as the photographer/investigator did. A relatively fast color negative film (ISO 200) will enable flash photographs to be taken using the recommended shutter speed and a small lens opening (f/11 or f/16). A small lens opening guarantees that the majority of the scene will be in acceptably sharp focus, especially if the photographer focuses at a point one-third to

FIGURE 6-8

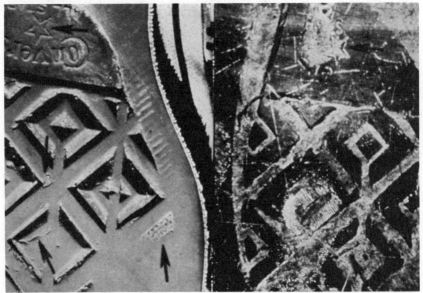

one-half into the scene. (If the focus point is on an object in the background, items in the foreground may be out of focus).

In figure 6–9, understanding depth of field enables a professional law enforcement photographer to produce sharp photographs at a crime scene. Foreground and background contain considerable detail. Use of a moderate wide-angle lens (35mm) enables an average size room (10 feet by 12 feet) to be covered in four photographs, one from each corner.

Light exposure is important. Figure 6–10 illustrates an improper exposure. The light meter reads the light areas (brick front, wood facade) and the dark area (storm door) and attempts to provide exposure for an average scene. Consequently, the door is underexposed, and the analyst cannot detect any pry marks on the lock.

Rarely will a telephoto or zoom lens be utilized for an indoor crime scene, but use of a macro lens is common, especially for close-ups of physical evidence. When using a macro lens, the photographer should mount the camera on a tripod to ensure that the film plane is parallel to the object being photographed, thus reducing distortion. One photograph should be taken with a measuring device, and one without. It is important that the measuring device be the same distance from the film plane as the piece of evidence; otherwise, the evidence or the scale could be out of focus. A photograph is a two-dimensional reproduction of a three-dimensional scene, and distortion can occur. However, measuring scales will accurately depict size and distance relationships of objects at the scene. Figure 6–11

FIGURE 6-9

FIGURE 6-10

shows macro photography. Macro photography can prove a sheet of paper toweling found at a crime scene once was attached to a roll of paper toweling in a suspect's dwelling, because of the randomly produced paper tears and pattern match.

Photographic Perspectives of the Crime Scene

There are certain photographic views that emphasize different aspects of a crime scene. The photographer should consider each of the following as he or she approaches the scene: (1) the location of the crime, (2) the nature and results of the crime, (3) the physical evidence at the scene, and (4) the follow-up activities.

The location photographs should depict the environment surrounding the overall crime scene area, not just where the crime scene tape is

FIGURE 6-11

stretched. Aerial and neighborhood photographs, possible surveillance sites of the offender while he was casing the victim's home, viewpoints of potential witnesses, and the indoor/outdoor photographs of the dwelling are examples of this idea.

The nature and results photographs depict each aspect of the offender's activities and interaction with the victim at the crime scene. If an offender commits several offenses during one incident, each offense should be photographed individually. For example, a rape incident begins with a breaking-and-entering offense, develops into vandalism, and culminates with the rape of the victim, who confronted the intruder. The crime scene photographer should photograph the point of forced entry, thus depicting the breaking-and-entering offense. Next, he or she should photograph the property destroyed during the act of vandalism. Finally, the indicators of sexual assault, such as semen and the victim's torn clothing strewn on the floor, are recorded. Thus, the nature and results of each portion of the crime are depicted in a sequential fashion.

Nature and results photographs also may assist the investigator to determine whether an incident was a homicide, a suicide or an accident. For example, a victim is discovered in bed with a bullet entrance wound to his head. Photographs may show if it was possible for the victim to have held the weapon at the angle that caused the fatal wound.

Sometimes, nature and results photographs help to determine the motive for a crime when none is readily apparent. A wealthy widow living alone in a luxury condominium was found strangled to death in her living room. There were no signs of a forced entry, no defensive wounds on the body, and no evidence of sexual assault. Expensive jewelry, credit cards, and a large sum of money were found, and there were no signs of ransacking. Theft was the actual motive for the crime, but this was not discovered until investigators analyzed the crime scene photographs. The victim collected valuable Chinese art, especially jade figurines. On one shelf were nine statues where there should have been ten. When the offender stole the one statue he wanted, he rearranged the remaining figurines to make it appear that nothing was missing. However, he failed to consider that the victim was not a good housekeeper and that dust had collected on the shelf. There were ten dust-free areas on the shelf, but only nine objects.

Of great importance is the recording of physical evidence taken from and left behind at the crime scene, for it will enable a connection to be made

FIGURE 6-12

between the offender and the crime. The location of fingerprints, hairs and fibers, blood splatter, and so on has to be well documented for investigators to reconstruct the crime. Photographing blood splatter on walls is particularly difficult because the reflection of light off the wall creates "hot spots," which obliterate the evidence. The photographer should either use available light, bounce flash, or diffused light when attempting to photograph blood droplets. Figure 6–12 illustrates blood splatter photographed at an angle that mades the blood splatter interpretation difficult. Figure 6–13 illustrates that blood splatter should be photographed with the lens parallel to the stain.

The follow-up photographs represent a final stage of the crime scene investigation. After the crime scene search is completed, additional photographs of the scene should be taken prior to its release. In one instance, a defendant challenged a search warrant in court by declaring that the officers were on a "fishing expedition" and had cleaned out his apartment.

FIGURE 6-13

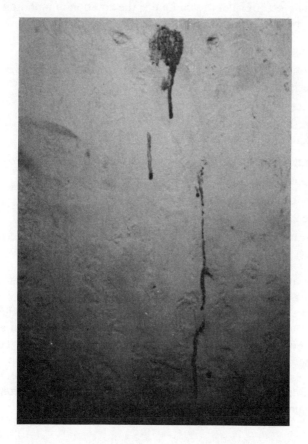

Follow-up photographs of the crime scene after the search clearly showed the judge that the defendant was lying.

Follow-up photographs also include those taken of a suspect to show lacerations, contusions, bruises, cuts, and wounds. These photographs also are required of the victim in rape investigations. When there is a possibility of a false rape allegation, these photographs may support the victim's story by showing that self-infliction of her injuries was impossible. Follow-up photographs also are taken of a homicide victim during the autopsy. If it is suspected that the offender bit the victim, but bite marks are not readily apparent, the victim may be photographed using ultraviolet light. This technique will enhance the damage to soft tissue under the skin and can even be utilized several days after the incident occurred.

The Photographic Log

Because of the number and variety of photographs normally taken at a crime scene, there must be a procedure for documenting the photographic effort. The most prevalent technique is the creation of a photographic log, which normally consists of the following:

1. Name of the photographer
2. Date and time
3. Specific location of the crime
4. Description of the photographic scene
5. Type of camera
6. Type of film
7. Light source (available light, electronic strobe)
8. Camera-to-subject distance for each photograph
9. Environmental conditions
10. Focal length of lens
11. Shutter speed
12. Lens opening

The accumulation of this information will enable the photographer to answer questions in the courtroom regarding photographic coverage of the crime scene. All original negatives are to be retained, regardless of their quality or subject matter. Even if ten exposures are made on a thirty-six-exposure role of film, it is preferred that the film be removed from the camera and a fresh roll inserted when photographing another scene. The photographer should also prepare a rough photographic sketch with the photographic log, depicting his or her approximate location when the exposure was made.

Crime Scene Photography in the Courtroom

No matter how extensive the photographic effort, the photographs must stand the test of legal admissibility: (1) accurate representations, (2) distortion free, (3) relevant to the matter under investigation, and (4) unbiased. A critical aspect of admissibility relates to the probative versus the prejudicial value. If a photograph is deemed to be gruesome and designed to excite the emotions of the juror, it made be deemed prejudicial and eliminated by the judge. The photographer, however, can only use good judgment and common sense at a crime scene and cannot be reluctant to take a photograph because a judge may find it repulsive.

Photographic distortion may be so prominent that the accuracy and reliability of the photographs are questioned. There are several categories of photographic distortion to consider:

Incorrect point of view. Just by looking through the viewfinder, the photographer can crop out or overemphasize certain aspects of a crime scene and create a false illusion of what actually occurred.

Perspective. Perspective refers to distance and size relationships in a photograph. By using a wide-angle lens and attempting to photograph the relationship of a revolver to a deceased person, the photographer can create an impression that the weapon was too far away from the victim to have been used in a suicide. Conversely, using a telephoto lens would create an illusion that the weapon was extremely close to the victim, and thus, the victim was capable of holding the weapon. These illusions occur most frequently when the camera lens is relatively close to the object being photographed. In most instances, this problem can be reduced by including measuring devices or even grids at a crime scene. Figure 6–14 illustrates perspective. Where a photographer stands to take a photograph is important. At first glance, the victim may have committed suicide. Figure 6–15 illustrates another viewpoint. The presence of another weapon and a bloody shoe print suggests the apparent suicide may have been a homicide.

Tone problems. These problems relate to lighting conditions, film exposure, and chemical development. If black-and-white film is used to photograph a crime scene, it is possible that red blood on a green carpet will not be seen because the colors will reproduce as the same shade of gray on the photographic gray scale. To correct this situation, the photographer would be required to use a color filter (either red or green) so that the blood will appear as a different shade of gray than the green carpet.

When color photography is utilized, it is imperative that the lab technician print the negatives correctly, for it is possible to make a brass cartridge case found at a crime scene appear silver in the photograph. In court, a sharp defense attorney may claim that investigators switched evidence to

FIGURE 6-14

FIGURE 6-15

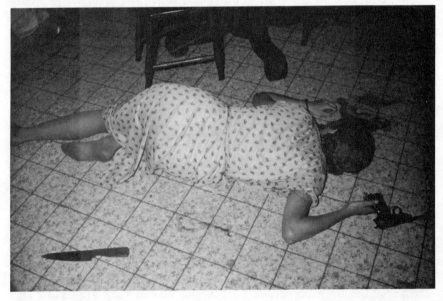

support their case. It is the responsibility of the investigator to ensure that the color crime scene photographs are printed accurately.

To contend with the photographic distortion question, the crime scene photographer needs to authenticate the accuracy of the photographs in court. If, for some reason, the photographer is not available to testify, it may be necessary for a detective who witnessed the taking of the photographs to authenticate them.

It should be emphasized that it is not necessary to have the crime scene photographer qualified as an expert in photography in court. In fact, the photographer should refrain from claiming to be an expert because it would enable the defense attorney to question his or her knowledge in extremely technical areas (e.g., the physics of light, chemical formulas, etc.).

Although photographers should not be qualified as experts, they certainly can testify as to their photographic training, knowledge, and experience. Photographers should be familiar with the principles of photography, camera, lens, film selection, lighting conditions, and darkroom techniques. On a practical level, every photographer must be aware of these aspects of photography, but technical knowledge alone will not automatically produce a competent crime scene photographer.

Conclusions

Photographing a scene involves an understanding of all aspects of photography and eliminating mistakes due to poor composition, poor focus adjustment, and incorrect exposure. Unlike a fashion photographer, who has the luxury of time, unlimited film, and tightly controlled conditions, the crime scene photographer normally has only one opportunity to record the scene accurately. The crime scene photographer also needs to analyze the scene from the viewpoint of the investigator, who is trying to reconstruct the crime, while thinking like the perpetrator and asking why the crime occurred in a particular fashion.

CRIME SCENE PHOTOGRAPHY BY CRIME CATEGORY

Homicide: Victim, Suspect

If the victim died from a gunshot wound and the weapon is found near the body, a frequent question is whether it is a homicide or suicide. One method of determining if the victim fired the weapon is to spray his or her hands, especially the palm, trigger finger, and thumb area, with a chemical, 8-hydroxyquinoline, a trace metal detector. Photograph these areas using ultraviolet light and black-and-white film. If the victim cocked the hammer, the impression of the hammer may appear on the thumb. There have been instances where the weapon's inscribed logo appeared on the shooter's hand. One word of caution, however: 8-hydroxyquinoline is considered carcinogenic and should be handled with care.

Although it is common procedure to swab the victim's/suspect's hands for gunshot residue, this technique is not always successful. However, research has disclosed that gunshot residue can be inhaled through nasal passages, and close-up photography of the person's nose may detect these particles. Swabbings would be taken of the nasal passages afterward.

In one unusual case, an estranged husband surprised his wife in bed with her lover. To document the affair for divorce court, he had brought along a friend with a camera. However, the situation escalated into violence, and the husband shot and killed the couple with a semiautomatic pistol. The incident was photographed. The husband claimed self-defense in that the victims lunged at him, causing the weapon to discharge accidentally. The Special Photographic Unit of the FBI laboratory used photogrammetry when analyzing the photographs. (Photogrammentry utilizes mathematical formulas to correct perspective distortions in photographs, enabling relatively accurate measurements to be obtained.) It was determined that the victims were at least 6 feet away from the gun when it went off and were in no position to wrestle the weapon from the offender as he had alleged.

The neck, ankles, and wrists of the victim should be photographed close up to detect signs of bondage. If tape was used, there may be adhesive residue present.

If the victim's nude body is located away from his or her residence, photograph the bottom of the feet for signs of trace material from the offender's environment.

Homicide: Crime Scene

Bloodstain pattern analysis/interpretation is dependent upon quality photography to demonstrate its findings. The photograph attempts to reconstruct the events of an incident with regard to the movement of persons, weapons, and blood with the greatest possible accuracy. This type of analysis is based on the premise that blood will produce the same patterns in the laboratory setting as at the crime scene when subjected to similar actions and circumstances. If the pattern occupies a small area at the scene, a macro lens should be used to record the pattern, and a scale should always be visible.

A problem arises when a club-like weapon is used to kill the victim and there are multiple patterns of blood on the ceiling. Because the droplets of blood are minute, it may be impossible to show the complete pattern in one photograph. Consequently, the ceiling should be photographed in sections, similar to the technique used to photograph tire impressions. A large format camera, such as the old fashioned Speed Graphic, is preferred because of the image size it provides. Of paramount importance is keeping the camera (and film plane) parallel to the pattern. Lighting is also critical because the ceiling will reflect light from the electronic strobe, creating hot spots that obliterate the pattern.

In indoor crime scenes where the body has been removed by the offender and an effort has been made to clean the scene, bloodstains may not be visible. In this situation, lab technicians can saturate the scene with Luminol, a fine spray that can provide chemical indications for the presence of blood. Luminol can reveal patterns of trace bloodstaining in drag marks, shoe/foot impressions, and occasionally the outline of a body. Although Luminol is relatively easy and safe to use, is noncorrosive, nonstaining, and generally nondestructive for blood, it does have disadvantages. Luminol will react with certain vegetable peroxidases, chemicals, and metals and is not completely specific for blood. Luminol is not recommended for outdoor crime scenes.

However, its greatest drawback is that it has to be applied in darkness. When Luminol reacts with blood, it produces light in the form of blue-white luminescence that normally is reproduced on film through a time exposure (fifteen to sixty seconds). The resulting photograph will show the luminescence only and not the object it appeared on. Consequently, another photograph (with strobe) has to be taken of the object to show its location. Another approach is to use electronic strobe exclusively, but only if the amount of light leaving the unit is greatly restricted through the use of filters, which softens the light considerably and does not override the luminescence.

Ultraviolet light can be used to detect and photograph urine and other bodily fluids not visible at a crime scene. In one case, the decomposing body of a male was discovered in the alley between two tenement buildings. However, the investigator believed that the victim was killed in a vacant apartment and the body tossed into the alley by the offender several days later. Ultraviolet-light photography recorded the outline of a body in the apartment because decomposing body fluids seeped into the hardwood floor.

Another unusual application of ultraviolet-light photography was discovered by police photographers in Great Britain. During a kidnapping investigation, the victim's body was discovered in her automobile, which had been set on fire by the offender. Investigators wanted to determine if the victim's vehicle had been concealed in the suspect's garage. In darkness, the photographer illuminated the concrete floor with ultraviolet light, and four distinct tire impressions became visible. Because the victim's vehicle had tires bearing four different tread designs, it was proven photographically that her vehicle had been stored in the suspect's garage.

This technique appears to work best on concrete that has been poured within the past six months, and the vehicle has to have remained for several days in one spot. Because tires contain oils, if the car is stationery for a period of time, the hydrocarbons will bleed into the concrete, leaving an impression. This technique would have failed, however, if the offender's car had possessed the same wheel base and dimensions, as his tire impressions would have obliterated the victim's tire impressions. This technique will not work with macadam (blacktop) surfaces because they contain their own oils. It should be noted that ultraviolet-light photography can be time-consuming, as unlike conventional daylight or strobe photography, the photographer has to use a trial-and-error method to determine the correct film exposure, and it could take several hours or longer to record the image satisfactorily.

Figure 6–16 illustrates the inside of a victim's boot photographed with black-and-white film and strobe lighting. Figure 6–17 is the same boot photographed using ultraviolet light and black-and-white film; it revealed a previously invisible service number and identifying data. *Care should be exercised at all times when using short-wave ultraviolet light because it can be potentially harmful to the eyes.*

Occasionally, it is important for the investigator to determine who shot first. For example, a narcotics officer may be walking up a driveway to interview a narcotics suspect in his home. For some unknown reason, the suspect draws a weapon and points it at the officer through the living room window. Shots are exchanged, and the suspect is killed. The victim's girlfriend claims the detective drew his weapon, fired first, and her boyfriend shot back in self-defense. By photographing the radial cracks in glass, this question can be resolved. Figure 6–18 is a photograph of a chart depicting

FIGURE 6-16

FIGURE 6-17

FIGURE 6-18

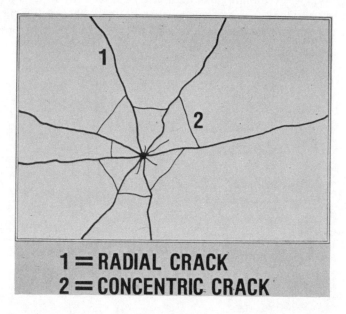

1 = RADIAL CRACK
2 = CONCENTRIC CRACK

radial and concentric cracks in glass. When the first bullet entered the glass, cracks emanated from the bullet hole. When the second bullet penetrated the glass, additional radial cracks were formed; however, they are of a shorter length because they stop when encountering the previous cracks. Figure 6–19 is a photograph of a chart depicting how a radial crack will stop once it encounters another crack. Thus, a sequence of shots can be determined by analyzing the length of these cracks. In addition, by stretching a string from the bullet holes, investigators can photographically determine where both individuals were positioned at the time of the shooting.

Other Types of Homicides

In death due to asphyxia as a result of hanging, doubt sometimes exists as to whether the occurrence was murder, suicide, accidental death, and/or autoerotic death. Photograph the original position of the body to help in determining the manner of death. An overall view of the body and rope should be taken at torso level and at foot level. Show the height of the body above the ground; a murderer usually tries to raise the body completely, while the suicide victim frequently never gets his or her feet off the ground and is sometimes found in a sitting or half-prone position. Photograph objects, such as a chair or box, that may have been kicked out from under the deceased. If there is suspicion that the death was autoerotic in nature, photograph any cushioning material placed between the rope and the victim's neck, and look for an escape mechanism that either malfunctioned or was in a position that the victim could not reach in time before losing

FIGURE 6-19

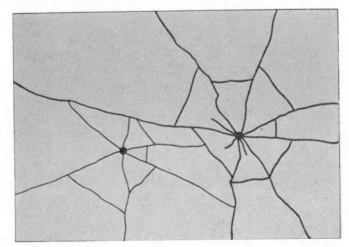

consciousness. Frequently, mirrors and erotic literature will be found adjacent to the body.

In drowning cases, the question to be answered is whether the victim died from drowning or whether he or she was thrown into the water after dying from another cause. Photograph with color film the entire body to depict discoloration, any foam around the mouth, position of the mouth (open or closed), damage to the teeth as a result of a blow, any wounds, bruises, or evidence of bindings. Cuts or tears to clothing could indicate a struggle between the offender and victim.

In death by stabbing cases, the number, nature, and location of the stab wounds in the victim's body are routinely photographed. However, the victim's clothing also should be photographed with backlighting to determine if the stab wounds in the body coincide with the corresponding holes in the clothing. Some of these stab wounds may be jagged, indicating the victim was still struggling with the assailant, while the remainder are smoother cuts, which may indicate the victim was dead or dying and unable to move. The number and location of postmortem stab wounds would be of significance to the analyst. Figure 6–20 illustrates how the number, location, and configuration of stab wounds in a shirt can be compared with stab wounds in a victim to help determine how many wounds were antemortem or postmortem.

FIGURE 6-20

Arson: Crime Scene, Victim, Evidence

The photography of a fire scene can last several days. It normally begins as soon as possible to show the fire in progress in order to help establish the following:

1. Point of origin or points of origin
2. Direction, speed, and spread of the fire
3. Nature of the burning material as indicated by the color of the smoke and flame in addition to the size of the flames (Remember, however, that although the color of smoke and flame is subject to interpretation, it could indicate if an accelerant was used.)
4. Progressive stages of the fire as determined by changes in color of the smoke and flames
5. Positioning of all windows and doors for signs of a forced entry or whether the offender closed the drapes for concealment
6. People observing the fire and fire fighters at work

After the fire has been extinguished, photographs should be taken of the building's exterior from all sides, including an aerial view, if possible, with particular attention devoted to the areas affected by the burning. Photographically examine broken windows and doors to determine if the offender's clothing may have snagged as he or she entered the dwelling, thus leaving fiber evidence. Shoe print evidence also may be present.

After the interior has been deemed safe to enter, the photographer systematically will record the scene prior to the sifting of debris by investigators. As the scene in all probability will be blackened and charred, the photographer must ensure that the photographs are not underexposed. (Expect to increase exposure by two f-stops more exposure than for a normal scene.)

A fire scene is unlike a homicide crime scene, where the photographer may have an opportunity to record the crime scene before it is disturbed. If the fire does not alter the scene dramatically, the water sprayed on the fire and the movement of fire fighters will. However, the investigative photographer should still look for evidence of arson (e.g., wires, clocks, timers, candles, matchbooks, lighters, trailers from accelerants, excelsior, flammable liquids and their containers, etc.). Figure 6–21 is a close-up photograph of a match and matchbook in an arson case. Torn edges and fibers from the paper can sometimes verify that a match found at a crime scene originated from one matchbook.

The photographer should also be alert for staging at an arson-for-profit crime scene. Certain items may be arranged in a certain manner to ensure they are destroyed by the fire, while other items are removed. For instance, if an expensive art collection was allegedly destroyed at a fire, determine on what walls they were displayed. Although the paintings may

FIGURE 6-21

have been destroyed, the metal brads holding the frames together, the wire on the frame, and the metal bracket and nail should all be found at the base of the wall. If not, the paintings may have been removed prior to the fire. If expensive clothing was destroyed in a closet, look for metal hangers on the floor. In some cases, it is also possible to show the positioning of wooden furniture at a fire scene because of the location of the metal studs on the feet of the furniture's legs left behind.

The photographer should also be alert for evidence of tampering of fire alarm or sprinkler systems, unusual adjustments to gas or electrical heating systems, open doors that should have been closed, and fire doors forced open. In one case, a movie theater featuring adult entertainment caught fire, and dozens of patrons died. As the fire was being extinguished, the owner of the building arrived and expressed grief at the loss of life and offered his complete cooperation to authorities. He speculated that faulty wiring may have caused the fire, and subsequent investigation verified his statement. However, the theater owner had an ulterior motive for cooperating with authorities. While assisting the investigators, he found an opportunity to remove discreetly the padlocks he had previously placed on exit doors, which prevented many of the victims from escaping. Fortunately, these doors were among the first areas documented on film, and the photographs proved that the doors had been secured at the time of the fire.

As previously mentioned, special attention is devoted to the burned areas, especially the points of origin, accelerant trailers, path of the fire, charring, or so-called alligator patterns on burned wood. As investigators discover physical evidence, the evidence is photographed at the scene. If physical evidence is found bearing writing or markings concealed by charring, these objects can be photographed in the laboratory using infrared film in order to decipher the writing.

The location and position of the bodies, manner of dress, signs of violence, underside of the body, and the surface the body was lying on should all be photographed. In a hotel casino fire, the bodies of scores of patrons were discovered near an exit. Photographs depicted a scene where the patrons apparently panicked when they could not open an exit door (it opened inward instead of outward). They were not in immediate danger until someone tossed an object through a window, which allowed a rush of air into the room, feeding the fire, which quickly destroyed the victims.

Sexual Crimes of Violence: Victim Suspect, Crime Scene

During a rape investigation, the purpose of crime scene photography is to record any signs of struggle at the scene where the attack occurred and any indications of the victim's efforts to resist the attack. The locale itself may be important to show that the screams of the victim could not be heard or to illustrate the fact that the locale was an unlikely place for normal social contact. The photographs also may depict the reasons why the offender chose certain locations to attack his victims based upon his personality traits (i.e., the rapist with an inadequate pesonality who wants to reassure his masculinity may attack the victim at her apartment in a surprise style of attack, while an assailant who hates women and is a loner may utilize a blitz style of attack along a heavily wooded path).

Signs of offender activity prior to, during, and after the attack could reveal information regarding his criminal sophistication. Photographs could record method of entry to a dwelling and a planned escape route (an unlocked door). Other signs of criminal sophistication could include disabling of the telephone; removal from the crime scene of bed linen or other items of clothing that may contain the offender's bodily fluids, hairs, and fibers; and bondage material the offender brought to the scene.

Photographs could also depict the offender's economic status based on items removed from the dwelling (i.e., money, jewelry, credit cards, television sets, etc.) and the degree of familiarity he may have had with the residence. (A rapist may burglarize the victim's apartment months before he returns to commit the rape.)

One problem encountered at many rape crime scenes, however, is the fact that the victim may have cleaned herself and the rape site prior to the arrival of police. Consequently, crime scene photography will not be as useful as in other criminal cases.

Earlier in this chapter, the importance of photographing the bodies of the rape victim and the suspect was discussed, with emphasis placed on bite marks, scratches, bruises, and so on. However, there are two categories of sex offenders for which photography of the suspect can be instrumental in positively identifying the offender, not just recording injuries. The two categories include serial sexual sadists and sexual exploiters of children. Both of these offenders have been known to photograph themselves with their victims while engaged in sexual activities. However, the offenders usually cover their faces or crop the photograph so their faces are not seen by the camera. They can still be identified, however, through birthmarks, wrinkles, moles, pimples, freckles, and other features that appear in a random fashion on their bodies. Figure 6–22 is a photograph taken by a

FIGURE 6-22

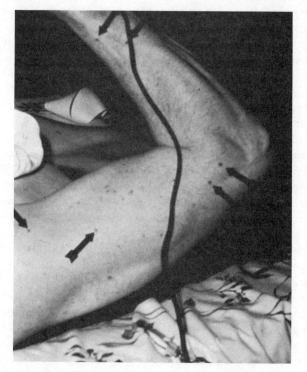

serial rapist holding a camera cable release as he attempted to photograph himself and his victim. Although his face was not visible, he was identified through freckle patterns on his arms.

The photographer must study all of the photographs taken by the offender and select those with the sharpest resolution or detail depicting the assailant. The offender is then posed in the same manner as he was observed with his victim and photographed using the same type of film (color or black-and-white) under similar lighting conditions (electronic strobe, photofloods, available light). A side-by-side photographic comparison is then conducted, and the identification (or nonidentification) effected. Although a court order may be required in order to photograph the assailant in the nude, it is well worth the effort if he can be photographically linked to the crime.

In child pornography/rape cases, the victim may be observed only from the rear, making identification difficult. Although the investigator may know the identity of the victim, it is recommended that the victim not be photographed in the nude even if the child's parents grant approval. It is believed the child victim has suffered enough by having an adult photograph him or her in a compromising position without subjecting the child to the same embarrassment by having a parent or law enforcement officer take additional photographs. Instead, it is recommended that the investigator ask the parents for any photographs previously taken of the child in the bathtub or wearing a swimming suit.

Frequently in child sexual abuse cases, the parents do not initially contact police when they believe their child has been abused. Instead, they call the day-care center or baby-sitter, demanding an explanation regarding their child's claim of abuse. By the time police are notified, the offender has removed all photographs, slides, and videotapes from his residence or place of employment, and when a search warrant is executed, no photographic evidence is discovered.

Rarely will these photographs, slides, or videotapes be destroyed by the offender because they represent a trophy or souvenir of his conquest. In one case, an informant led investigators to a secret cache of sexually explicit photographs depicting children. When confronted with the evidence, the suspect admitted the photographs were his but said that he had received them in the mail from another collector of erotica.

One of the photographs depicted two small girls performing a sex act in a chair. After analyzing the background in the photograph, the photographer took a series of photographs of the offender's pine-paneled recreation room. It was demonstrated in court that the photographs of the girls were taken in the recreation room because of the placement and configuration of knotholes in the paneling. Figure 6–23 illustrates how the identification of knotholes in the pine paneling proved that obscene photographs of a child were taken in the suspect's dwelling.

FIGURE 6-23

Videotaping Crime Scenes

The videotaping of crime scenes has become common practice in many jurisdictions. However, it should never become a substitute for still photography. Regardless of the system used, videotape does not provide the sharpness or resolution of photographs, and it is virtually impossible to observe fine detail on evidence left at a scene. Common errors committed by video-camera operators include panning the camera rapidly horizontally and vertically, walking while videotaping, which creates a bobbing effect for the viewer, poor focusing and overuse of the zoom feature of the camera, and improper lighting of the scene. Nevertheless, videotaping, like still photography, can greatly assist the investigator and criminal investigative analyst if used properly and professionally.

Prior to videotaping a crime scene, the operator should script a plan of action so that the viewer is walked through the crime scene. As in still photography, there has to be a beginning, middle, and end to the story, depicted in a logical manner. The operator should describe on tape what is observed through the viewfinder but should not be definitive unless he or she knows for certain that, for instance, the stain observed is really a bloodstain. In those situations, it is appropriate to state that "the stain appears to be a bloodstain."

If there is to be a running verbal narrative describing the scene, it is imperative that no other investigators or technicians be heard on tape. Through discovery, the defense attorney will have access to the unedited tape, and it can be embarrassing to the investigators if inappropriate comments were made and recorded.

It is also suggested that crime scene investigators and evidence technicians not be videotaped, as they may employ crime scene processing techniques that differ from those advocated by the department or textbooks. Based upon investigative experience, many investigators will legitimately employ methods that have been successful for them in the past. Unfortunately, a defense attorney may attempt to discredit the investigator by showing that he or she failed to follow agency policy.

7

Prescriptive Interviewing

Interfacing the Interview/ Interrogation with Crime Classification

GREGORY M. COOPER

T he defendant's own confession is probably the most probative and damaging evidence that can be admitted against him.

—Justice Byron White, *Bruton* v. *U.S.*

In determining and isolating the guilt of an offender, there is no evidence more incriminating, damaging, and conclusive than a voluntary confession. Although the underlying thrust of an interrogation is to explore and resolve issues, the successful interview of a culpable offender culminates when the pernicious truth is surrendered in a confession.

All of the physical evidence and eyewitness testimony combined is still not worth as much as the criminal's own self-incriminating words, "I did it." The admissible confession proves guilt independently. It requires no authentication, no chain of custody, no scientific examination, no opinion testimony, no inferences, and no interpretation.

THE PROSECUTION'S ARSENAL

The Eyewitness

Eyewitness testimony is undeniably vital to a successful prosecution; however, it is often characterized by weakness. The witness may have problems seeing or hearing and describing what occurred. Additionally, the witness may have a subtle reason to maliciously misrepresent the facts or alter them by unintentional or even targeted prejudice. The witness may be afraid to get involved and consequently becomes reluctant. Inconveniently before trial, witnesses may alter their accounts, become forgetful, move out of the state, or even die.

It is a well-known phenomenon that two eyewitness accounts of the same incident can differ significantly. Research has substantially illustrated this effect:

> The data of experimental psychology now establishes quite securely that no two individuals observe any complex occurrence in quite the same manner; that the ability of different individuals to retain and recall observations differ; that the elements which are retained and recalled are influenced by past experience and attitudes; and that the ability of various individuals to express what they have observed, retained, and recall vary greatly. There is no wholly reliable witness since the observations of all witnesses are faulty in some degree and some situations. (Loevinger 1980, x)

Although an eyewitness account greatly authenticates an occurrence, it should not be overestimated. The effects of time, the limits of human perception and recollection, bias, prejudice, greed, and all human emotions influence perception.

Physical Evidence

Physical evidence is also imperfect. Questions can be raised about the method of collection, preservation, analysis, and introduction of evidence. All too numerous times, strong cases have been jeopardized and lost due to evidentiary error. Still an integral part of the effective prosecution, the strength of physical evidence is enhanced when combined with the complete prosecutorial arsenal.

Plea Bargaining

In some cases, law enforcement officers may take offense even at the suggestion of associating an efficiency and value factor to the application of justice. Nevertheless, plea bargaining must be accepted unconditionally as a negotiable leverage, especially considering the monumental costs of the American justice system and the effective use of tax dollars.

At a seminar on trial advocacy, a distinguished federal judge stated: "Law is not a search for truth. The whole objective is to achieve the highest quality of justice in the least amount of time at the lowest possible cost" (Kestler 1982, 4). The following legal professional opinion supports this philosophy while stating that "the ultimate strategic objective of questioning techniques is not to win at trial, rather it is to force an early settlement of the case on favorable terms." Furthermore,

> a favorable settlement is more desirable than trial despite the strengths and righteousness of the cause, because it eliminates the uncertainties and vicissitudes as well as the expense of litigation. In the vast majority of cases, the successful advocate is not the one who ultimately prevails at the appellate level, or perhaps the Supreme Court of the United States, but rather is the advocate who quickly demonstrates to an opponent that further costly resistance is unreasonable and that a just result for both parties can best be achieved at the settlement table. (Kestler 1982, 6)

Plea bargaining is an extremely difficult approach to accept, for example, when forced to negotiate a settlement between first-degree or second-degree homicide. Even worse is a descent to manslaughter, especially when the investigation suggests a more serious charge. Some prosecutive weakness effectively targeted by the defense may release the offender from being prosecuted to the full extent of the law. And even more tragic, the offender may escape any form of judicial justice whatsoever. However, a plea-bargaining agreement can and should be sustained as an effective antidote when there is insufficient evidence to support the maximum charge and accompanying penalties.

THE CONFESSION: THE BEST WEAPON

> Admissions of guilt are essential to society's compelling interest in finding, convicting, and punishing those who violate the laws.
> —Moran v. *Burbine*

Surpassing all other forms of evidence and reinforcing their support of the truth, the confession remains unique. Unquestionably, the confession will prompt immediate deliberation of both the advantages and disadvantages of a trial or plea-bargaining alternative. If a trial is warranted, a voluntary, admissible confession is undeniably paramount in considering the totality of the evidentiary presentation. The admissible confession will strengthen the integrity of the both the eyewitness account and the physical evidence while fueling the synergistic effect of the prosecutive arsenal.

Confession Described

A legal description of a confession is contained in the following case proceedings: "An accused person knowingly makes an acknowledgement that he or she committed or participated in the commission of the criminal act. This acknowledgement must be broad enough to comprehend every essential element necessary to make a case against the defendant" (*James* v. *State* 1952). According to this legal description, a confession should consist of (1) acknowledgement of the commission of or participation in a criminal act and (2) the acknowledgement must be sufficiently comprehensive to include every element of the criminal act as defined by statute. A review of burden of proof and the criminal act requirements and their implications allows investigators to understand and implement the confession as described above.

Burden of Proof

Criminal investigators assume the prosecution's responsibility to prove guilt beyond a reasonable doubt. This includes the requirement of proving each element of the offense for which the accused is charged. There is no prosecution without the presentation of proof. And the proof initially is discovered, organized, assessed, and finally presented to the prosecution by the investigator. A successful prosecution, securing a conviction, is the fruit of a productive, meticulous, and intensive investigation. If the prosecution fails to prove all of the elements of a crime beyond a reasonable doubt, the verdict dictates the accused guilty of a lesser crime: "Failure of the prosecution to gather and introduce sufficient evidence to meet this burden will result in an acquittal or, at least, the reduction of a more serious crime to a less serious one" (Klotter 1990, 18).

Criminal Act Requirements

Actus Reus. Before a person can be convicted and punished for a crime, the prosecution must present evidence that one person (acting as a principle, accessory, or accomplice) committed a criminal act as defined by statute. Each element of the crime prescribed by law must be present in the offender's actions to duly constitute a criminal offense. This principle is referred to as *actus reus*. It is the first condition required to label an act a crime (Klotter 1990).

Mens Rea. The formula for committing a crime is incomplete without the evidence of criminal intent. The actus reus must be combined with the criminal state of mind *mens rea* to constitute a crime. If the defense can show that the defendant's mind was innocent, then a crime has not been committed.

Criminal intent must accompany the criminal act, except as otherwise provided by statute. Criminal intent also can be satisfied if the act is accompanied by such negligent and reckless conduct as to be regarded by the law as the equivalent to criminal intent (Klotter 1990, 18). This concept may be expressed in the following formula: criminal act (actus reus) + criminal intent(mens rea) = criminal conviction (Klotter 1990, 30–43).

Causation

The criminal conviction formula incorporates (through logically deductive reasoning) the existence of a causal relationship between conduct and results. In other words, for "one to be guilty of a crime, his act or omission must have been the proximate cause thereof" (Klotter 1990, 41). There is usually little or no difficulty in showing causal relationship. In summation, the prosecution must show the following:

1. A specific party/parties participated
2. Criminal acts as constituted by law were committed
3. The presence of a criminal state of mind
4. The conduct was the proximate cause of the crime

What does the criminal act requirement (actus reus, mens rea, and causation) have to do with the confession? What is the relationship between the confession and the prosecution's burden of proof responsibility?

Recall the previous legal description of the confession. The confession requires: (1) acknowledgement and (2) comprehensive culpability of each required element to constitute a crime.

Regretfully, interviews are concluded prematurely for many reasons, sometimes unknowingly. While devoting a concentrated effort to the first criteria (participation in the criminal act), the interviewer mistakenly overlooks the pivotal third criteria (criminal intent). Although the offender's acknowledgements may satisfy the actus reus and causation provisions of the criminal act requirements, the admission alone is insufficient to expose every essential element as described in *James* v. *State*.

The offender's admission may reveal his participation in a criminal act (actus reus) and that his conduct was the direct cause of the crime (causation). The act, although interrelated, is only a reflection of his character. However, it does not fully reveal his character or criminal state of mind, and it is imperative that this be displayed. The interview provides the investigator a chance to extract and unravel the offender's thought process and reveal his or her criminal state of mind.

Criminal Intent

To comprehensively understand the criminal act, the investigator must unravel the criminal mind. This issue is especially significant when a crime is classified by various degrees of seriousness depending on the defendant's state of mind (i.e., accidental vs. intentional). Not only must the confession reflect that the defendant did something bad, but also it must show that he had a bad intent. This distinction is especially useful for the prosecution when it is essential to determine the level of seriousness of the crime and its associated degree of punishment. Moreover, it may also be considered when assessing the predictability of the defendant's propensity toward violence and potential for recidivism.

The confession provides the psychological environment for the offender to reenact the crime. It sets the stage for him to relive his behavioral role (actus reus) and display his psychological role (mens rea). The well-prepared interviewer can write the script for the final scene as the offender recounts each phase of the crime. The interviewer can preview the offense by allowing the offender to escort him or her through every scene until the full panorama of events is related. The interviewer assumes the role of a scribe while urging the offender to return mentally to the crime and dictate his every act, precipitating thoughts, emotions, and feelings. The defendant's own explanation of his state of mind will uncover his criminal intent.

Criminal intent can effectively be articulated and demonstrated by building the state of mind portion of the confession from the foundation of three basic questions:

1. Did the offender premeditate?
2. Did the offender deliberate?
3. Did the offender harbor malice aforethought?

These three questions provide the framework to formulate queries that solicit the defendant's thoughts, behavior (including habits), and feelings that he or she experienced before, during, and after the crime.

The interviewer should not restrict the review of the defendant's history but should probe as far back as possible. Furthermore, if the content of the confession clearly illustrates the defendant's willful misconduct, it will reject any alleged impaired understanding by the offender of his criminal behavior. This renders the diminished capacity or insanity defense implausible.

It is emphasized that there is no short-cut approach to producing an all-inclusive confession. But when considering the consequences of failing to solve a capital crime, expediency should never be an issue.

The investigative tool in the following section is presented to supplement law enforcement's efforts in achieving successful results during the interview. It will also serve to elevate the interviewer's awareness of proactive steps that can be applied to increase interview effectiveness. Enhanced interview skills and techniques are especially fitting in light of the following court decision:

On 3 December 1990 in *Minnick* v. *Mississippi*, the U.S. Supreme Court ruled 6 to 2 precluding law enforcement officials from reengaging a suspect after the suspect has requested an attorney. The court stated that "when counsel is requested, interrogation must cease, and officials may not re-initiate interrogation without counsel present, whether or not the accused has consulted with his attorney." Consequently, it is best to assume that law enforcement has *one* opportunity to interview a defendant. Therefore, the interviewer will serve the public's best interest with an exhaustive preparation. As such, if the interview does not terminate with the confession, neither will it be unresolved with a burden of regrets.

Prescriptive Interviewing

I have no data yet. It is a capital mistake to theorize before one has data. Insensibly one begins to twist facts to suit theories, instead of theories to suit facts.

—Arthur Conan Doyle, *A Scandal in Bohemia*

Preparation—Essential to Success

The vital link to a successful interview is preparation. Preparation establishes the foundation for developing a successful approach in the interview setting. Preparation includes four steps.

Data Collection. First, a comprehensive and meticulous data collection system must be implemented to reconstruct each phase of a capital crime. Each criminal offense consists of fundamental elements that must be present to conform to specific criminal code requirements. Data collection is a principal factor in determining that those requirements have been met as prescribed by law.

Assessment. Secondly, assessing the relevancy of the data to the crime is required. It is necessary to judge objectively the value of the data collected to determine if they apply to the elements of the crime (i.e., Does the information contribute to the criminal act requirements?).

Analysis. Thirdly, analysis of the data is imperative to complete the preparatory process. Law enforcement must do more than merely *see* that each criminal element is intact. Professionalism requires that we organize and dissect the information, thereby *observing* the complex web of interrelated components of the crime. For example, I may see a set of stairs before me. However, I observe that there are exactly sixteen steps covered with a distinctive color and quality of carpet. Additionally, the carpet is soiled and cluttered with specific toys and items of clothing, suggesting the presence of children of corresponding ages. The condition of the carpet and disarray of clothing and toys may also suggest the housecleaning habits of the owners and even infer an economic and social stratum. It is during this phase of preparation that meaning and substance are assigned to the (criminal) act and the actor. Armed with this enhanced understanding, the investigator proceeds to the fourth step.

Theorizing. Theorizing assumes the challenges of identifying the motivation underlying the criminal thought process and of reconstructing the crime. Theorizing attempts to crystallize mentally the interwoven thread or current of thought that the criminal mind uses to justify the crime and general behavior.

Consequently, this sometimes laborious preparatory process will elevate the interviewer's ability to empathize successfully with the offender's state of mind and prompt a better understanding of his or her thoughts and rationalization.

The preparatory phase of the interview is preeminent in conducting a successful interview. There is no substitute for this principle, and it should never be sacrificed for convenience or expediency. Granted, depending on the grievous nature of the crime, varying degrees of effort will be applied. However, especially with capital crimes, success will be tantamount to preparation.

Crime Classification

Crime classification integrates all preparatory steps of the interview. It is the precursor to humanizing the offender and revealing his thought process. It includes the accumulation and assimilation of data compiled during the investigative phase for the purpose of conducting a criminal investigative analysis. To formulate a profile of the criminal personality, a criminal investigative analyst will review and analyze area photos, maps, sketches, crime scene photos, victimology, and all incident-related reports. The analyst also examines autopsy and forensic findings, initial and follow-up reports, and newspaper clippings. A close examination of this data will begin to reveal behavioral characteristics of the offender, thereby exposing major personality traits.

Criminal Investigative Analysis

The process applied by a criminal investigative analyst in developing an offender's personality characteristics is similar to the process of a forensic pathologist. The forensic pathologist identifies the elements surrounding the cause and method of death by examining closely the physical evidence through an autopsy. The criminal investigative analyst examines all referred reports and documents and conducts a behavioral autopsy. This process may suggest the cause/motive of the crime and may offer implications about the offender's personality as suggested by the method he or she selected to commit the crime. The offender's behavior patterns unmask an undercurrent of emotional deficiencies and needs. An improved understanding or insight of these emotional deficiencies and needs can provide a solid foundation for the interviewer. This foundation will support the strategic construction of tailored approaches and appeals to prevail upon the offender.

Consider, for example, the advantage held by an interviewer having knowledge of the following personality characteristics generated through a criminal analysis of a disorganized lust murderer:

- Of average intelligence and a high school or college dropout
- Probably unemployed or blue-collar, unskilled occupation
- Financially dependant upon domineering female
- Previous criminal record of assault-related offense
- Probable voyeuristic activities
- Probable pornography interest and collection
- Alcohol/drugs exhibited in his behavior
- Keen sense of fantasy
- Inability to carry out preplanned activities
- Difficulty in maintaining personal relationships with female for extended time
- Need to dominate and control relationships
- Sexually inexperienced
- Sexually inadequate
- Never married or brief, combative marital relationship
- Sadistic tendencies
- Controlled aggression, but rage or hatred of women present
- Confused thought process
- Feels justified in his murderous behavior, while feeling no remorse or guilt
- Defiant of authority
- Low self-esteem
- Frustration from lack of direction/control of life
- Combustible temper
- Impulsive
- Deep anxiety

While considering the foregoing characteristics in concert with investigative activities confirming some of the biographical and descriptive information provided, an interviewer can begin to visualize this offender. The interviewer may recognize and exploit certain personality characteristics and associated emotional deficiencies. In pondering the offender's behavior, thought processes, and aligned emotions, the interviewer now is better prepared to design various approaches to conform to the offender's personality.

Although traditional and canned approaches have worked in the past, they must not be overestimated. The interviewer must step into the foreign territory of the offender. If the offender decides to cooperate, it will be because he can justify his decision from his perspective. There is only one frame of reference that is important in the offender's decision-making process—his own. And if the interviewer successfully influences the offender to conform, it is because an alliance was forged in the offender's territory. The offender must be able to visualize the personal advantage in complying. The interviewer must develop the ability to speak the language of the offender in order to extract the best evidence—the confession.

The criminal investigative analysis process permits the diagnosis of offender emotional strengths and weakness and general behavioral characteristics. Having been briefed with this information, the interviewer is better prepared to prescribe effectively the interview approaches that are customized to the offender's perspective. Such prescriptions may include identifying the following:

1. Who should conduct the interview
2. Where the interview should take place
3. What type of environment is best suited for the particular approach or approaches used
4. How the approach or appeal should be constructed
5. What emotional appeals are most likely to be effective

The offender has been preparing his responses to conceal his guilt from the moment he committed the crime and probably before. He will use every tactic available to counter and dismantle every offensive attack. To know the offender is the best strategy, but it takes time, commitment, and effort. Although prescriptive interviewing is not a panacea for the challenges in obtaining confessions, it is still one more high-precision instrument to be used in swaying the balance of justice in society's favor. A prescriptive interview will enhance law enforcement's efforts to persuade serious capital offenders to escort us under the water into the caverns of their minds, to surrender their secrets, and to expose their culpability. The successful use of this method will help both promote the cause of justice and deter effects of recidivism.

8

The Investigative Support Unit's Role in Assisting Law Enforcement

CORINNE M. MUNN

The National Center for the Analysis of Violent Crime began as a pilot project in 1984, funded by the National Institute of Justice. The center is now completely funded by the FBI. The NCAVC functions as a law enforcement-oriented behavioral science and data processing center. It combines research, instruction, and investigative support for the purpose of providing expertise to any legitimate law enforcement agency confronted with unusual, bizarre, and/or repetitive violent crime.

The NCAVC is staffed by crime analysts, psychologists, sociologists, criminologists, political scientists, and police specialists who bring a multidisciplinary approach to a wide variety of problems facing contemporary law enforcement. Three separate units constitute the NCAVC: the Behavioral Science Services Unit (BSSU), the Special Operations and Research Unit (SOARU), and the Investigative Support Unit (ISU).

The NCAVC conducts special educational and training activities that include courses, seminars, symposia, and conferences. Both the BSSU and ISU are involved with the ten-month police fellowship program in criminal investigative analysis. Research activities include studies of serial and violent crimes, such as homicide, rape, sexual sadism, child abduction, arson, threats, assassin personality, computer crime, and counterintelligence matters. The SOARU is responsible for all FBI training in crisis management and negotiation, major case management, special events management, special weapons and tactics (SWAT), observer/sniper operations (OBS), and tactical air operations (TAO).

The ISU provides many investigative services at no cost to federal, state, county, and city law enforcement through the Criminal Investigative

Analysis Program (CIAP), the Violent Criminal Apprehension Program (VICAP), and Arson and Bombing Investigative Services (ABIS). The ISU also offers all of these services at no cost to foreign law enforcement agencies. This chapter discusses the services available to law enforcement through the ISU. In addition, it describes how law enforcement agencies may employ these services.

CRIMINAL INVESTIGATIVE ANALYSIS PROGRAM

The FBI defines *criminal investigative analysis* as an investigative process that identifies the major personality and behavioral characteristics of the offender based on the crimes he or she has committed. This process involves a behavioral approach to the offense from a *law enforcement perspective,* as opposed to a mental health viewpoint. This law enforcement perspective focuses on the identification and apprehension of the offender, while the mental health viewpoint centers on diagnosis and treatment. The process generally involves seven steps:

1. Evaluation of the criminal act itself
2. Comprehensive evaluation of the specifics of the crime scene(s)
3. Comprehensive analysis of the victim
4. Evaluation of preliminary police reports
5. Evaluation of the medical examiner's autopsy protocol
6. Development of the profile, with critical offender characteristics
7. Investigative suggestions predicated on construction of the profile

The process used by the person preparing an analysis is quite similar to that used by clinicians to make a diagnosis and treatment plan: data are collected and assessed, the situation is reconstructed, hypotheses are formulated, a profile is developed and tested, and the results are reported back. Criminal investigative analysis unfortunately does not provide the identity of the offender, but it does indicate the type of person most likely to have committed a crime having certain unique characteristics.

The effectiveness of criminal investigative analysis is limited by the accuracy, completeness, and quality of material received from the submitting agency. A thorough and comprehensive victimology is essential to the process. The victimology report (the victim's personality, life-style, and history) usually has great bearing on the analysis. The FBI Special Agents who are criminal investigative analysts try to evaluate why this victim was attacked and if the victim was known to the offender. They also attempt to gauge the victim's risk level (i.e, how this person's life-style, personality, etc. may have increased [or decreased] his or her chance of becoming a victim of a violent crime). The victimology also gives the analysts an idea of how much risk the offender took by approaching this victim.

A thorough written and pictorial description of the crime scene through

8-inch by 10-inch color photographs and a crime scene synopsis is essential for an optimum criminal investigative analysis. Forensic information is also critical to this process. Because of the great variance in medical examiner standards, this information may not always be as specific and accurate as it should. These inadequacies may greatly hamper and diminish the effectiveness of the overall analysis. The autopsy report should include (if possible) toxicology and serology results, autopsy photographs, photographs of the cleansed wounds, estimated time of death, type of weapon, and suspected sequence of attack. The ISU has a forensic pathologist consultant who is available if any medical examiner, prosecuting attorney, or investigator needs to discuss a case.

By submitting as much of the required information as possible, the criminal investigative analyst may subsequently provide numerous services to the investigating officer. The profile, while not replacing a thorough and well-planned investigation, narrows the scope of an investigation. It provides the detective with another investigative weapon for solving violent crime.

Behavioral assessments are another service offered by the CIAP. The criminal investigative analyst does this type of assessment when an investigator has a known suspect or suspects. By evaluating a suspect, the agent analyst provides an assessment that may reject or confirm for the investigator that he or she has the right suspect in mind.

Other applications of criminal investigative analysis are investigative/ interrogation strategies, search warrant suggestions, prosecution strategies, and jury selection guidance. Criminal investigative analysts also examine equivocal death cases and render opinions as to whether the death was a homicide, suicide, or accident. In some cases, agents provide on-site assistance to law enforcement agencies involved with major violent crime investigations. They may also testify as expert witnesses about the process of criminal investigative analysis. This service has proven especially effective in the prosecution of serial offenders by linking them to their crimes and for exposing offenders who have staged a crime.

Criminal investigative analysis also has proven effective in building profiles of rapists. Through careful interview of the rape victim about the rapist's behavior, ISU personnel may be able to build a profile of the offender. The sexual, physical, and verbal behavior of a rapist reflects the offender's overall personality and underlying motive for the assault. By examining this behavior, the analyst may be able to determine what type of person is responsible for the offense.

Criminal investigative analysis has been especially useful in investigating sexual homicides because many of these crimes appear motiveless and thus offer few clues about the killer's identity. In murders that result from jealousy or a family quarrel or that take place during the commission of a felony, the readily identifiable motive generally provides vital information about the killer. Because many sexual homicides fail to provide this information, the investigator can supplement conventional investigative techniques with criminal investigative analysis to help identify the perpetrator.

Services of the CIAP are extended to the law enforcement community through the FBI field offices. Law enforcement agencies wishing to make use of these services should contact the NCAVC coordinator in the nearest FBI field office. The coordinator determines whether the case is appropriate for the service requested and ensures that all needed materials are provided to the criminal investigative analysts. Some coordinators have received advanced training and may prepare an analysis or profile, which is then forwarded to the CIAP for review prior to being released to the requesting agency. Foreign law enforcement agencies should contact the FBI legal attaché nearest them. Cases are prioritized according to their type, nature, and sensitivity.

ARSON AND BOMBING INVESTIGATIVE SERVICES

The Arson and Bombing Investigative Services (ABIS) subunit has the primary responsibility of providing assistance in arson, bombing, terrorism, and related crimes submitted to the NCAVC by federal, state, local, and foreign law enforcement agencies. Like the CIAP, the ABIS provides profiles, investigative strategies, interview/interrogation recommendations, onsite crime scene assessments, and courtroom testimony. The ABIS crime analysts use the same process and principles as the criminal investigative analysts. They examine the offender's behavioral patterns reflected in the crime scene and targeted property and/or victimology, and from these behavioral clues, they construct a profile that describes critical offender traits.

The ABIS maintains for the NCAVC the Arson Information Management System (AIMS) Project, which detects the temporal and geographic patterns found in serial arson and bombing incidents. The results of the AIMS program are incorporated into the criminal investigative analyses.

Requests for crime analysis will be considered from any legitimate fire or law enforcement agency having the responsibility for fire investigation. The following information is needed to perform an analysis:

1. Summary reports on each incident, including date, time, cause, and geographic location
2. A map of the jurisdiction showing the location of each incident
3. The name and address of the contact for the submitting agency

VIOLENT CRIMINAL APPREHENSION PROGRAM

The Violent Criminal Apprehension Program (VICAP) was conceived during the 1982 and 1983 federally funded meetings of the National Task Force on Missing and Abducted Children and Serial Murder Tracking and Prevention. It became operational in 1985 and now receives VICAP Crime Analysis Reports from the United States, Canada, and other countries in an effort to link homicides committed by serial violent offenders. The investigative agencies involved are then notified so they may coordinate investigations and pool their resources to hasten the identification and apprehension of the offender.

VICAP functions as a nationwide data information center designed to collect, collate, and analyze specific crimes of violence. Currently, cases that meet one of the three following criteria are accepted by VICAP:

1. Solved or unsolved homicides or attempts, especially those that involve an abduction, that are (a) apparently random, motiveless, or sexually oriented or (b) known or suspected to be part of a series
2. Missing persons, where the circumstances indicate a strong possibility of foul play and the victim is still missing
3. Unidentified dead bodies where the manner of death is known or suspected to be homicide

It is important that cases in which the offender has been arrested or identified are still submitted to VICAP so that unsolved cases in the VICAP system can be evaluated for possible linkage to known offenders.

By analyzing case-related information submitted by law enforcement agencies, the VICAP staff determines if similar patterns or characteristics exist among the individual cases in the VICAP system. The identification of similar patterns is made by analyzing MO, victimology, physical evidence, suspect description, and suspect behavior before, during, and after the crime.

The VICAP Crime Analysis Report (see appendix D), released in July 1986, is both shorter and simpler than its prototype. Most of the pages to be completed are checklists that can be answered in fifteen to twenty minutes. VICAP is attempting to have the report distributed to and stocked by every law enforcement agency in the country. Law enforcement agencies may obtain VICAP forms from their nearest FBI field office or resident agency or may write or call VICAP directly.

INVESTIGATIVE SUPPORT UNIT INFORMATION

ISU
NCAVC
FBI Academy
Quantico, VA 22135
(703)640-6131
(800)634-4097

APPENDIX
A

Hiding Places
A Search Warrant Aid

This list is intended to be an aid to investigations and searches. As previously discussed, serial rapists and sexual exploiters of children frequently retain souvenirs and trophies of their conquests, such as photographs, jewelry, and items of clothing, and may also maintain a diary of their activities. These items have to be concealed not only from law enforcement officers, but also from family members who may not be aware of the offender's activities.

The following list has been compiled by investigators from federal, state, and local law enforcement agencies. These concealment locations have been used by drug dealers and users, intelligence operatives, organized crime members, illegal gambling figures, and sex offenders, to name a few. Although this list is intended to be comprehensive, there undoubtedly will be other hiding places discovered by investigators. It is requested that investigators with knowledge of additional concealment sites not listed here advise the Investigative Support Unit, Training Division, FBI Academy, Quantico, Virginia, 22135.

HOMES

Living Areas

Behind walls
Behind baseboards and moldings
Built inside room dividers
Wall and ceiling light fixtures
Behind wall and electrical outlets

Inside hollow doors (removable top)
Inside transom over doorway
Door knobs

Behind pictures
Behind mirrors
Behind posters
Hem of drapes and curtains
Hung behind curtains
Inside hollow curtain rods
Rolled up in window shades

Behind acoustical ceiling tiles
Above false ceiling
Under carpets
Under throw rugs

Electric baseboard heaters
Removable air conditioning and heating registers
False bottom on radiator covers
Inside heating and air conditioning ducts
Spring-loaded shelving inside vertical ventilation ducts

Inside chimneys
Chimney clean out

Furniture Articles

Furniture upholstery
Hidden drawers in tables
Under or inside the cushion of a hassock

Base of lamp
Miniature chess board

Inside transistor radio
Inside TV and radio sets
Inside TV tube
Inside color TV antenna
Base of rabbit-ear antenna

Inside telephone base and handle
Under number plate of phone
Pay telephone coin return

Clock
Flower pots and window box

Holy Bible (hollow cover)
Magazines and books
Inside door chimes and doorbell
Inside stairway posts

Inside and behind vacuum cleaner bags
Inside handle of vacuum cleaners

Ironing board cover
Ironing board legs
Clothespin bag
Inside string mop

Flashlights—rolled around batteries
Hollowed-out flashlight batteries

Shoe polish container and equipment

Musical instruments and cases
Art kits

Typewriter and covers
Inside letters
Hollowed-out pad of paper
35mm film cans

Mixed with tobacco
Sealed cigarette package

Dog collars
Pet box
Bottom of dog-food bag
In bird cage
Inside rabbit hutch

Attic and Basement Areas

Attic insulation

Furnace
Fuel of oil heaters

Conduit from fuse box
Inside abandoned plumbing

Toolbox
Seams of field cots and hollow cap of cot legs
Inside hollow legs of outdoor aluminum furniture

Inside tube and barrel of air rifle
Inside patch trap of antique rifle

Inside Christmas decorations
In surfboards

Bedroom Areas

Mattresses
Hidden box in mattress frame
Bedposts
Pillowcases
False-bottom baby carriage and cribs

False floors of closets
Inside closet hanging rods
Closet clothing—waistbands, pens, sleeves, hatbands, shoes, gloves

Taped to hatboxes
Inside and under wigs
Footlockers
Hollow cane
Dolls
Jewelry box

Bathroom

Under tub
Behind leg of bathtub
Shower nozzle head
Inside shower curtain rod
Behind plumbing inspection doors

Under washbowl, sink
Rolled inside cardboard tube of toilet paper or behind the toilet paper
sheets
Inside toilet tank
Inside hollow handle of toilet-bowl brush

Clothes hamper
Behind and inside medicine cabinets
Razor blade slot disposal
Razor blade dispenser
Shaving brush handle
In toothpaste tubes
In electric toothbrush holder
Hair dryer
Talcum and cold-cream containers
In prescription bottles
Bromo Seltzer
Within sanitary napkins and in box
Douche bags

Kitchen

Range hoods and filters
Stovepipes
Under burning element of stove top
Bottom half of double broiler
In stove insulation and stove exhausts and drip pans

Behind kick plates of kitchen cabinets

Underneath sink
Sink traps
Inside garbage disposal
Under lip ring of plastic trash cans
Garbage bags

Behind wall phones

Rolled inside the cardboard tube of paper towels or rolled between the paper sheets

Toaster crumb tray
Inside knife handles
Inside plastic rolling pin
Inside deep-well fryers

All kitchen canisters and containers
Pots, pans, bowls, with false bottoms while containing food

Inside fake beer or soda cans
Fruit containers in refrigerator

Baked bread, cookies, brownies, and candy bars
In eggs
Tea bags

Refrigerator underneath fruits, vegetables, meat, taped under door, motor compartment, ice tray

Outside

Mailbox
Under corner mailbox

Tree
Hollowed-out tree

Under fence-post tops

Rain gutters and drain spouts

Under tile steps
In clothesline pipe
Dog houses
Hanging out window

Rice paper
Flash paper

AUTOMOBILES

Dashboard Area

In and over sun visors
Ornamental objects on dashboard
Instrument panel
Inside dash knobs
Cigarette lighters
Ashtray—in and under
Fuse box

False radio
Radio speaker grill
Glove compartments—top of compartment or trap

Heater
Vents (air and heater)

Interior

Under brake and gas pedals
Shift knobs
Inside console between bucket seats

Upholstery
Inside seats
Under seats
Backseats

Under rugs
Floorboard

Dome lights
Inside light sockets

Inside or behind arm rests
Taped to rolled down window

Compartment under floor of older Volkswagen cars
Behind Volkswagen battery box

Trunk Area

Trunk
Inside trunk lids
False bottom of trunk beds

Spare tire—treads and well
Service station travel kits

Picnic jug in trunk
Inside flashlights

Engine Area

Insulation under hood
Air filter
Carburetor
Hollow batteries
Hollow voltage regulator

False heater hoses—heater
Inside oil cap
Windshield washer well
Inside horn

Exterior

Taped behind bumper
Behind license plate
Under chrome
Inside and behind headlights and taillights

Antenna base

Hub caps
Under tire air-value caps

Inside tubing on roof rack
Inside auto surfboard rack

Convertible tops

Underside

Rocker panels
Underside of fender
Attached to frame
Tied to axle
False dual muffler
Tail pipe
On top of gas tank (suspended or concealed in compartment)
Magnetic key case (Hide-A-Key)

Miscellaneous

Taxicab roof light

Motorcycle taillights
Inside motorcycle handlebar tubing

ON PERSON

Head

Processed hair, hair buns, and wigs

Ears
Battery box of hearing aid
Taped behind ears
Hearing-aid glasses
Inside artificial eye
Nose
Mouth
False caps on teeth
Under false teeth
Swallowed with string attached to teeth

Torso and Limbs

Under Band-Aids and bandages
False limbs
Casts
Taped under breast
Foreskin of penis
Vagina
Rectum
Cheeks of buttocks
Between toes and taped to feet

Underclothing

Brassiere
Jock straps
Pinned to shorts
In corsets
In male girdle
Money belts
In swimming trunks

Outer Clothing

Women's hair barrette
Hatband
Label of jackets and coats
Behind collar and collar stays
Tied knot of tie

Tie pins, clasps, and cuff links
Lining of clothing
False buttons
Military cap insignia, lapel, and shoulder patches
Behind campaign ribbon and uniform brass
Under insulation in motorcycle helmet

Belt buckles
Slit belts or zippered belts
Waistbands
Inside fly trap of trousers
Pockets
Handkerchiefs
Pants cuffs
Socks and shoes

Jewelry

Earrings
Inside neck and wrist lockets, bracelets, and charms
Inside and back of watch and other jewelry
Inside identification bracelets
Rings

Handbag and Pocket Articles

Inside pens
Fountain pens
Cigarette lighters
Cigarette packs
Cigarette filters
Tobacco tins and pouches
In stem of pipe

Eyeglasses case
Contact lens case
Lipstick tube
Compact
Inhalers
Pill vials
In addressed envelopes

In gum sticks
35 mm film cans
Wallet
Lining of change purse

Miscellaneous

Inside sanitary napkins or tampons
Inside feces bag
Baby diapers
Hollow end of cane or umbrella handle
Inside hollowed-out crutches
Liners of luggage
Canteens
Thermos jugs

B

Indicators of Financial Difficulty

This appendix presents indicators that a business and/or subject is or was experiencing financial problems. The presence of one or more of these indicators is not conclusive proof that financial problems do exist; such proof requires further examination and documentation by the investigator. These are simply areas or indicators to give the investigator direction if a motive of financial profit is suspected with an arson or homicide.

BUSINESS

Decreasing revenue

Increasing production costs (labor, overhead, etc.)

New technology makes current process/equipment inadequate

Increased competition (new products, new competition)

Costly lease or rental agreements

Unprofitable contracts, loss of key customers

Failure to record depreciation

Excessive spoilage or defects

Double payment of bills

Numerous bank accounts

Low or overdraft cash balance

Large or frequent currency transactions

Increased borrowing

Personal expenses paid with corporate funds

Bounced checks

Hypothetical assets, liens on assets, overinsured assets

Inventory levels: removal prior to fire, overstocking caused by overproduction, exaggeration of loss, slow-moving items, obsolete items

Large or numerous overdue accounts payable

Inability to pay current bills (utilities, payroll, etc.)

Litigation against business or owners

Delinquent loan payments

Loans to/from officers/employees

Credit limits imposed by lender, suppliers

Frequent COD purchases

Payment of bills by cashier's checks, certified checks, money orders

Delinquent or tardy tax deposits

Bankruptcy proceedings

Two sets of books maintained

Prior years losses

Prior insurance claims

Duplicate sales invoices

Alleged renovations

Property has frequent change of ownership preceding fire

Use of photocopies instead of original source documents

PERSONAL

Bounced checks

Costly lease or rental agreements

Inability to pay current bills (utilities, telephone, etc.)

Credit limits imposed by lenders

Payment of bills by cashier's check, money order

C

Witness Typologies

RELUCTANT WITNESS

The reluctant witness is hesitant and reserved, finding it difficult to talk freely. This reluctance is due to a natural restraint, which is part of the witness's personality. It may also be due to apathy ("not my business").

INTIMIDATED WITNESS

The intimidated witness is apprehensive of involvement with law enforcement due to fear of retaliation for his or her cooperation, specifically from the offender(s) or generally from other criminal or antisocial individuals.

INVENTIVE WITNESS

The inventive witness embellishes or creates details when interviewed. This is not necessarily due to an intent to mislead but from an inability to differentiate between an active imagination and reality, and/or the need to be important.

DISTRAUGHT WITNESS

The distraught witness is in a condition of extreme emotional distress due to his or her involvement directly as a witness to an offense or indirectly because of a relationship with the victim or the targeted property (arson).

HOSTILE WITNESS

The hostile witness is purposefully antagonistic and/or noncompliant or deliberately invents facts to mislead law enforcement. This may due to culpability, a relationship with the offender (e.g., protective reaction), or a pervasive animosity towards law enforcement.

FRAUDULENT WITNESS

The fraudulent witness comes forward as a witness, yet has no first-hand knowledge of the offense (attention seeker).

VICAP Crime Analysis Report

VIOLENT CRIMINAL APPREHENSION PROGRAM

HOW TO COMPLETE THE VICAP CRIME ANALYSIS REPORT FORM

VICAP SUBMISSION CRITERIA

The VICAP Crime Analysis Report form has been designed to collect information regarding the following types of crimes whether or not the offender has been arrested or identified:

(1) Solved or unsolved homicides or attempts, especially those that involve an abduction; are apparently random, motiveless, or sexually oriented; or are known or suspected to be part of a series.

(2) Missing person, where the circumstances indicate a strong possibility of foul play and the victim is still missing.

(3) Unidentified dead bodies, where the manner of death is known or suspected to be homicide.

Cases where the offender has been arrested or identified should be submitted so unsolved cases in the VICAP system can be linked to known offenders.

INSTRUCTIONS

- Use black ink or pencil. Legibly print all written responses.

- Unless stated otherwise, check as many boxes as apply for each item.

- If in doubt about how to respond to a given item, be guided by your experience and good judgment. Proof beyond a reasonable doubt is not required, but do not guess either.

  If there are details of the case that you feel are important but that do not fit well into the items provided in the VICAP Crime Analysis Report, describe them in the narrative.

- If you wish to supplement or correct information previously reported to VICAP, submit a new VICAP Crime Analysis Report but complete only Items 1 through 18, 27 and 36 plus the Item(s) you wish to supplement or correct. You need not resubmit unchanged items.

- For advice or assistance regarding this report or its completion, call VICAP at **(703) 640-6131.**

- If you are submitting this VICAP Crime Analysis Report in conjunction with a request for a criminal personality profile evaluation, you **must** contact the **CRIMINAL PROFILE COORDINATOR** assigned to the FBI Field Division in your area. The **CRIMINAL PROFILE COORDINATOR** is charged with the responsibility of assisting you with your request for a criminal personality profile and will advise you of additional materials that must be submitted in order to evaluate your case properly. He/she will review the materials and will submit the entire profile package to the National Center for the Analysis of Violent Crime on your behalf. *Do not submit Criminal Personality Profiling case materials directly to VICAP.* Only the VICAP Crime Analysis Report should be submitted directly to VICAP.

- *Multiple victims & multiple offenders*

  If your incident has **MULTIPLE VICTIMS,** you must complete a separate VICAP Crime Analysis Report form for each victim. Offender information need not be duplicated.

  If your incident has **MULTIPLE OFFENDERS,** submit only one complete VICAP Crime Analysis Report per victim; xerox and attach additional offender page(s) (Items 55 through 84) to each Report as needed.

Examples:

1) For two (2) victims and one (1) offender, you must complete two (2) VICAP Crime Analysis Report forms (one for each victim). Do not duplicate the Offender information (Items 55 through 84) in the second Report.

2) For two (2) victims and two (2) offenders, you must complete two (2) VICAP Crime Analysis Report forms. Victim #1 and offender #1 would go on the first Report form and victim #2 and offender #2 would go on the second Report form.

3) For one (1) victim and two (2) offenders, you must complete one (1) VICAP Crime Analysis Report form. The victim and offender #1 would be reported in the body of the VICAP Crime Analysis Report form, and offender #2 would be reported by copying an additional offender page (Items 55 through 84), completing it, and attaching it to the VICAP Crime Analysis Report.

● Before submitting the VICAP Crime Analysis Report, make a copy for your records.

● Mail all VICAP Crime Analysis Reports, Supplements, and/or Corrections to:
VICAP
National Center for the Analysis of Violent Crime
FBI Academy
Quantico, VA 22135.

● Enclosing Crime Scene Photographs with the VICAP Crime Analysis Report will assist the VICAP staff in the evaluation of the case.

A VICAP Case Number will be assigned to your case when it is processed and will be provided to you as soon as possible. The VICAP Case Number should be referenced in any subsequent correspondence or telephone communications with VICAP regarding the case.

● The Narrative Summary is intended to provide VICAP Analysts with a general overview of the case. Minute details of the investigation need not be provided here; the VICAP Crime Analysis Report will capture most of the detail necessary to complete the analysis. A person unfamiliar with your case, however, should have at least a general idea of what happened after reading your brief narrative.

Examples:

1) The partially decomposed body of an adult female was discovered in a wooded area of a state park, one-quarter mile from a major state highway. There are indications of sexual assault. Victim died of gunshot wounds. It appears that the victim was not killed at the body recovery site. The victim's whereabouts prior to her death have not been established.

2) Female juvenile was last seen at school. Investigation indicates that she was possibly abducted at or near the school while en route home. The victim has not returned nor has her body been recovered. Investigation indicates that it is unlikely that the victim is a runaway or that she disappeared of her own accord. This case is strikingly similar to one that occurred approximately 8 months ago in the same vicinity.

3) The reported offender entered a locked single-family residence occupied by a man, his wife, and 2 infant children. While the offender was gathering property in the residence, the husband confronted the offender. The husband was shot immediately and died. The wife responded after hearing the gunshot and was physically restrained by the offender. The offender hit her repeatedly with his fists, forced her to commit oral sex, and raped her repeatedly. The wife survived the attack. The children were not assaulted. The offender left the residence, and a vehicle was heard to leave the area. Offender arrested during the commission of a burglary in the same neighborhood one week later.

TABLE OF CONTENTS

I.   ADMINISTRATION

CASE ADMINISTRATION

FOR VICAP USE ONLY

1. **VICAP Case Number:** _____   2. **FBI Case Number:** _____

3. **FBI OO:** _____   4. **VICAP Assignment:** _____

5. Reporting Agency: _____

6. Address: _____   7. City: _____

8. County: _____   9. State: _____   10. ZIP: _____

11. Reporting Agency's ORI Number: _____

12. Reporting Agency's Case Number: _____

13. NCIC Number If Victim Is 1) Missing or 2) an Unidentified Dead Body: _____

14. Investigator's Name: _____

15. Investigator's Phone Number: _____ - _____ - _____

16. VICAP Crime Analysis Report Type:

    1 ☐ Original Submission of This Case

    2 ☐ Supplement to Previously Submitted Information

    3 ☐ Correction of Previously Submitted Information

17. Investigating Agency's Case Status:

    1 ☐ Open (active investigation)   4 ☐ Cleared by Arrest

    2 ☐ Suspended (inactive investigation)   5 ☐ Exceptionally Cleared (by UCR
                                                   definition)
    3 ☐ Open —— Arrest Warrent Issued

CRIME CLASSIFICATION

18. This VICAP Crime Analysis Report Pertains to the Following Type Case (check one only):

    1 ☐ Murder or Attempted Murder —— Victim Identified (go to Item 19)

    2 ☐ Unidentified Dead Body Where Manner of Death Is Known or Suspected to Be
         Homicide (go to Item 19)

    3 ☐ Kidnapping or Missing Person with Evidence of Foul Play (victim still missing)
         (go to Item 20)

19. Based on Your Experience and the Results of the Investigation of This Case, Do You
    Believe This Offender Has Killed Before?

    1 ☐ Yes (explain in Narrative Summary)   99 ☐ Unable to Determine

    2 ☐ No

20. There Is an Indication That This Case Is Related to Organized Drug Trafficking:

    1 ☐ Yes   2 ☐ No   99 ☐ Unable to Determine

DATE AND TIME PARAMETERS

21. Today's Date: ____/____/____/
                    (mo) (da) (yr)

		Date	Military Time	Exact	Approximate
22. Victim Last Seen:		____/____/____/ (mo) (da) (yr)	_____	☐	☐
23. Death or Major Assault:		____/____/____/ (mo) (da) (yr)	_____	☐	☐
24. Victim or Body Found		____/____/____/ (mo) (da) (yr)	_____	☐	☐

II. VICTIM INFORMATION

25. This Is Victim _____ of _____ Victim(s) in This Incident.
    (number)   (total)

26. Status of This Victim:
    1 ☐ Deceased (as result of this incident)
    2 ☐ Survivor of Attack
    3 ☐ Missing

VICTIM IDENTIFICATION

27. Name: _____
           (last, first, middle)

28. Alias(es) (including maiden name and prior married names):
    _____
    _____

29. Resident City: _____   30. State: _____   31. ZIP: _____

32. Social Security Number: _____–____–_____   33. FBI Number: _____

PHYSICAL DESCRIPTION

34. Sex:
    1 ☐ Male   2 ☐ Female   99 ☐ Unknown

35. Race:
    1 ☐ Black   3 ☐ Hispanic   5   ☐ Other
    2 ☐ Caucasian   4 ☐ Oriental/Asian   99 ☐ Unknown

36. Date of Birth: ___/ ___/ ___
                   (mo) / (da) / (yr)
    99 ☐ Unknown

37. Age (or best estimate) at Time of Incident: _____
    99 ☐ Unknown   (years)

38. Height (or best estimate): _____ feet _____ inches
    99 ☐ Unknown

39. Approximate Weight: _____ lbs.
    99 ☐ Unknown

40. Build (check one only):
    1 ☐ Small (thin)   3   ☐ Large (stocky)
    2 ☐ Medium (average)   99 ☐ Unknown

41. Hair Length (check one only):
    1 ☐ Bald or Shaved   4   ☐ Shoulder Length
    2 ☐ Shorter Than Collar Length 5   ☐ Longer Than Shoulder Length
    3 ☐ Collar Length   99 ☐ Unknown

42. Hair Shade (check one only):
    1 ☐ Light   3   ☐ Neither 1 or 2 Above
    2 ☐ Dark   99 ☐ Unknown

43. Predominant Hair Color (check one only):
    1 ☐ Gray and/or White   5   ☐ Black
    2 ☐ Blond   6   ☐ Other
    3 ☐ Red   99 ☐ Unknown
    4 ☐ Brown

If your victim is either a missing person or an unidentified dead body, respond to Items 44 through 48. Otherwise, go to Item 49.

44. **Abnormalities of Teeth:**
    - 1 ☐ None
    - 2 ☐ Braces
    - 3 ☐ Broken or Chipped
    - 4 ☐ Crooked
    - 5 ☐ Decayed
    - 6 ☐ Noticeable Gaps
    - 7 ☐ Some or All Missing
    - 8 ☐ Stained
    - 9 ☐ Other (describe): _____ _____
    - 99 ☐ Unknown

45. **Glasses or Corrective Lenses Normally Worn by or Associated with Victim:**
    - 1 ☐ None
    - 2 ☐ Prescription
    - 3 ☐ Contacts
    - 4 ☐ Bifocals
    - 5 ☐ Plastic Frame
    - 6 ☐ Metal Frame
    - 7 ☐ Rimless
    - 8 ☐ Other (describe): _____ _____
    - 99 ☐ Unknown

SCARS AND/OR BIRTHMARKS

46. **Location of Noticeable Scars or Birthmarks (not tattoos):**
    - 1 ☐ None
    - 2 ☐ Face, Head, or Neck
    - 3 ☐ Arm(s) or Hand(s)
    - 4 ☐ Torso
    - 5 ☐ Buttocks
    - 6 ☐ Feet or Leg(s)
    - 7 ☐ Other (describe): _____ _____
    - 99 ☐ Unknown

TATTOOS

47. **Tattoo Locations:**
    - 1 ☐ None
    - 2 ☐ Face, Head, or Neck
    - 3 ☐ Arm(s) or Hand(s)
    - 4 ☐ Torso
    - 5 ☐ Buttocks
    - 6 ☐ Feet or Leg(s)
    - 7 ☐ Other (describe): _____ _____
    - 99 ☐ Unknown

48. **Tattoo Designs:**
    - 1 ☐ Initials or Words
    - 2 ☐ Number(s)
    - 3 ☐ Picture(s) or Design(s)
    - 4 ☐ Other (specify): _____ _____
    - 99 ☐ Unknown

OUTSTANDING PHYSICAL FEATURES

49. **Did the Victim Have Outstanding Physical Features (crossed eyes, noticeable limp, physical deformity, etc.)?** (Do not repeat information reported in Items 44 through 48, above.)
    - 1 ☐ Yes (describe): _____
    - 2 ☐ No
    - 99 ☐ Unknown

CLOTHING OF VICTIM

50. **Generally Preferred Clothing Style** (this item deals with general style of dress typically preferred by the victim, not a detailed clothing description):
    - 1 ☐ Business Suit
    - 2 ☐ Casual
    - 3 ☐ Gaudy or Garish
    - 4 ☐ Sport or Athletic
    - 5 ☐ Western Wear
    - 6 ☐ Work Clothes or Uniform
    - 88 ☐ Other (describe): _____ _____
    - 99 ☐ Unknown

51. **Generally Preferred *Predominant* Color Tone of Clothing** (check one only):
    - 1 ☐ Whites
    - 2 ☐ Yellows
    - 3 ☐ Greens
    - 4 ☐ Blues
    - 5 ☐ Purples/Violets
    - 6 ☐ Reds/Oranges
    - 7 ☐ Browns/Tans
    - 8 ☐ Grays/Blacks

52. **If This Victim Is a Missing Person or Unidentified Dead, Give a Detailed Description of Clothing:**

    _____
    _____

MISCELLANEOUS

53. **Victim's Residence (check one only):**
    - 1 ☐ Single-Family Dwelling
    - 2 ☐ Multi-Family Dwelling
    - 3 ☐ Temporary or Transient Housing
    - 4 ☐ Motor Vehicle
    - 5 ☐ Street
    - 99 ☐ Unknown

54. **Current Occupation(s): 1)** _____

    2) _____

III.   OFFENDER INFORMATION

OFFENDER DEFINED. As used in this VICAP Crime Analysis Report, "offender" includes arrestees, perpetrators, or persons the investigator has reasonable cause to believe are responsible for the commission of the crime.

OFFENDER STATUS

55. This Is Offender _____ of _____ Offender(s) in This Incident.
      (number)   (total)

56. The Offender Is (check one only):
     1 ☐ Unknown——Not Seen (go to Item 85)
     2 ☐ Unknown——Seen
     3 ☐ Identified (named)——Not in Custody
     4 ☐ In Custody
     5 ☐ Deceased

OFFENDER IDENTIFICATION

57. Name: _____
            (last, first, middle)

58. Alias(es) (including maiden name and prior married names):

_____

_____

59. Resident City: _____ 60. State: _____ 61. ZIP: _____

62. Social Security Number: _____—_____—_____ 63. FBI Number: _____

PHYSICAL DESCRIPTION

64. Sex:
     1 ☐ Male   2 ☐ Female   99 ☐ Unknown

65. Race:
     1 ☐ Black   3 ☐ Hispanic   5   ☐ Other
     2 ☐ Caucasian   4 ☐ Oriental/Asian   99 ☐ Unknown

66. Date of Birth: _____/_____/_____
                   (mo) / (da) / (yr)
     99 ☐ Unknown

67. Age (or best estimate) at Time of Incident: _____
     99 ☐ Unknown   (years)

68. Height (or best estimate): _____ feet _____ inches (to _____ feet _____ inches)
     99 ☐ Unknown

69. Build (check one only):
     1 ☐ Small (thin)   3   ☐ Large (stocky)
     2 ☐ Medium (average)   99 ☐ Unknown

70. Hair Length (check one only):
     1 ☐ Bald or Shaved   4   ☐ Shoulder Length
     2 ☐ Shorter Than Collar Length   5   ☐ Longer Than Shoulder Length
     3 ☐ Collar Length   99 ☐ Unknown

71. Hair Shade (check one only):
     1 ☐ Light   3   ☐ Neither 1 or 2 Above
     2 ☐ Dark   99 ☐ Unknown

72. Predominant Hair Color (check one only):
     1 ☐ Gray and/or White   5   ☐ Black
     2 ☐ Blond   6   ☐ Other
     3 ☐ Red   99 ☐ Unknown
     4 ☐ Brown

73. Was Wearing Glasses:
    1 ☐ Yes   2 ☐ No   99 ☐ Unknown

74. Facial Hair (check all that apply):
    1 ☐ None   3 ☐ Beard   99 ☐ Unknown
    2 ☐ Mustache   4 ☐ Other

75. Appeared Generally Well Groomed:
    1 ☐ Yes   2 ☐ No   99 ☐ Unknown

76. Offender Wore a Disguise or Mask:
    1 ☐ Yes   2 ☐ No   99 ☐ Unknown

SCARS AND/OR BIRTHMARKS

77. Noticeable Scars or Birthmarks (not tattoos):
    1 ☐ Yes   2 ☐ No   99 ☐ Unknown

TATTOOS

78. Noticeable Tattoos:
    1 ☐ Yes   2 ☐ No   99 ☐ Unknown

OUTSTANDING PHYSICAL FEATURES

79. Other Outstanding Physical Features of the Offender Not Reported Above (crossed eyes, noticeable limp, physical deformity, etc.):

    1 ☐ Yes (describe): _____
    2 ☐ No
    99 ☐ Unknown

IV.   IDENTIFIED OFFENDER INFORMATION

If you have an offender in custody or identified in this case, complete Items 80 through 84. Otherwise, go to Item 85.

OFFENDER BACKGROUND

80. Cities and States of Residence during Last 5 Years (exclude current city of residence):

    1) _____   3) _____

    2) _____   4) _____

81. List the States the Offender Has Visited during Last 5 Years (attach separate sheet if necessary):

    1) _____   3) _____

    2) _____   4) _____

82. Foreign Countries Lived or Traveled in:

    1) _____   3) _____

    2) _____   4) _____

PROPERTY OF OTHERS

83. Offender Was in Possession of Property of Others (check all that apply):
    1 ☐ Body Parts   4 ☐ Jewelry
    2 ☐ Clothing   5 ☐ Photo(s)
    3 ☐ Credit Card(s), Checks, or other   88 ☐ Other (specify): _____
        I.D.   _____

OFFENDER'S ADMISSIONS

84. Offender Admits Other Similar Crime(s) of Violence:
    1 ☐ Yes (attach details)   2 ☐ No

V.   VEHICLE DESCRIPTION

85. Is a Vehicle Known to Have Been Used in This Incident?
     1 ☐ Yes   2 ☐ No or Unknown (go to Item 96)

     NOTE: Complete vehicle information if 1) a vehicle was used by the offender in this
     incident; or 2) this is a missing person case *and* the vehicle is missing; or 3) this is an
     unidentified dead case *and* the vehicle has been connected with the victim; or 4) the
     vehicle is in any way significantly involved in this incident.

86. Did the Vehicle Belong to, or Was It under the Civil Control of, the Victim?

     1 ☐ Yes   2 ☐ No

87. The Vehicle Would Normally Be Described as Being:
     1 ☐ Exceptionally Well Maintained ("sharp")   3 ☐ Neither 1 or 2 Above
     2 ☐ Not Generally Well Kept ("beat-up")   99 ☐ Unknown

88. The Vehicle Would Normally Be Described as Being:
     1 ☐ Newer/Late Model   3 ☐ Neither 1 or 2 Above
     2 ☐ Older Model   99 ☐ Unknown

89. License Number: _____ 90. License State: _____

91. Vehicle Year: _____ 92. Make: _____ 93. Model: _____

94. Body Style:
     1 ☐ Passenger Car   6 ☐ Motorcycle
     2 ☐ Van   88 ☐ Other (specify): _____
     3 ☐ Pick-up Truck   _____
     4 ☐ "Jeep" Type (i.e., Bronco, Blazer, etc.) 99 ☐ Unknown
     5 ☐ Tractor-Trailer

95. Color: _____   _____
             (top)   (bottom)

VI.   OFFENSE M. O.

96. The Victim or a Witness Reported That the Offender's Approach to Victim Was:
     1 ☐ No Living Victim or Person Witnessed the Offender's Approach to Victim
          (go to Item 100)
     2 ☐ By Deception or Con: Openly, with Subterfuge or Ploy (e.g., offers assistance or requests
          direction) (go to Item 97 and then go to Item 100)
     3 ☐ By Surprise: Lay in Wait or Stepped from Concealment
          (go to Item 98 and then go to Item 100)
     4 ☐ By "Blitz": Direct and Immediate Physical Assault (go to Item 99)

97. If the Offender Initiated Contact with the Victim by Means of Deception, Indicate the Type of
     Deception Below:
     1 ☐ Posed as Authority Figure   7 ☐ Asked for or Offered Assistance
     2 ☐ Posed as Business Person   8 ☐ Caused or Staged Traffic Accident
     3 ☐ Asked Victim to Model or Pose for   9 ☐ Phony Police Traffic Stop
          Photos   10 ☐ Solicitation for Sex
     4 ☐ Offered Job, Money, Treats, or Toys   11 ☐ Offered Ride or Transportation
     5 ☐ Implied Family Emergency or Illness   12 ☐ Other Deception
     6 ☐ Wanted to Show (something)

98. If the Offender Initiated Contact with the Victim by Means of Surprise, Indicate the Type of
     Surprise Below:
     1 ☐ Lay in Wait——Out of Doors   4 ☐ Victim Sleeping
     2 ☐ Lay in Wait——In Building   5 ☐ Other Surprise
     3 ☐ Lay in Wait——In Vehicle

99. If the Offender Initiated Contact with the Victim by Direct and Immediate Physical Assault, Indicate the Type of Direct and Immediate Physical Assault Below:

1 ☐ Immediately and Physically Over-powered Victim (picked up, carried away, etc.)

2 ☐ Hit Victim with Hand, Fist, or Clubbing Weapon

3 ☐ Choked Victim
4 ☐ Stabbed Victim
5 ☐ Shot Victim
6 ☐ Other Direct Assault

EXACT GEOGRAPHIC LOCATION

100. Last Known Location of Identified Victim or Location of Unidentified Dead Body Recovery Site:

a. ☐ City of (if within incorporated city, town, etc.)

_____

b. ☐ County of (if not within incorporated city, town, etc.)

_____

c. State: _____ d. ZIP: _____

LOCATION OF EVENTS

BODY RECOVERY SITE

101. Description of General Area of the Body Recovery Site (check one only):

1 ☐ Rural
2 ☐ Suburban
3 ☐ Urban
99 ☐ Unknown

102. The Neighborhood of the Body Recovery Site Is *Predominantly* (check one only):

1 ☐ Business, Industrial, or Commercial
2 ☐ Farm or Agricultural
3 ☐ Residential
4 ☐ Uninhabited or Wilderness
99 ☐ Unknown

103. The Body Recovery Site Was (check as many as apply):

1 ☐ Any Residence
2 ☐ At or Near a School or Playground
3 ☐ In a Retail Shopping District
4 ☐ On a Public Street
5 ☐ In a Vice Area
6 ☐ A Densely Wooded Area
7 ☐ In an Open Field
8 ☐ In a Vehicle
9 ☐ On Public Transportation
88 ☐ Other (specify): _____
_____
99 ☐ Unknown

104. The Body Recovery Site Was Victim's Residence:

1 ☐ Yes   2 ☐ No   99 ☐ Unknown

105. The Body Recovery Site Was Victim's Work Place:

1 ☐ Yes   2 ☐ No   99 ☐ Unknown

106. Potential Witnesses at the Time the Offender Left the Body at the Body Recovery Site:

1 ☐ Other People Were Present in the Immediate Area
2 ☐ Area Was Essentially Deserted
99 ☐ Unknown

MURDER OR MAJOR ASSAULT SITE

107. Was the Murder or Major Assault Site the Same as the Body Recovery Site?

1 ☐ Yes (go to Item 113)   2 ☐ No or Unknown

108. Description of General Area of Murder or Major Assault Site (check one only):

1 ☐ Rural
2 ☐ Suburban
3 ☐ Urban
99 ☐ Unknown

109. The Neighborhood of Murder or Major Assault Site Is *Predominantly* (check one only):

1 ☐ Business, Industrial, or Commercial
2 ☐ Farm or Agricultural
3 ☐ Residential
4 ☐ Uninhabited or Wilderness
99 ☐ Unknown

110. The Murder or Major Assault Site Was (check as many as apply):

1 ☐ Any Residence
2 ☐ At or Near a School or Playground
3 ☐ In a Retail Shopping District
4 ☐ On a Public Street
5 ☐ In a Vice Area
6 ☐ A Densely Wooded Area
7 ☐ In an Open Field
8 ☐ In a Vehicle
9 ☐ On Public Transportation
88 ☐ Other (specify): _____
_____
99 ☐ Unknown

111. The Murder or Major Assault Site Was Victim's Residence:
     1 ☐ Yes   2 ☐ No   99 ☐ Unknown

112. The Murder or Major Assault Site Was Victim's Work Place:
     1 ☐ Yes   2 ☐ No   99 ☐ Unknown

113. Potential Witnesses at the Time of the Murder or Major Assault:
     1 ☐ Other People Were Present in the   2 ☐ Area Was Essentially Deserted
        Immediate Area   99 ☐ Unknown

SITE OF OFFENDER'S INITIAL CONTACT WITH VICTIM

114. Was the Site of the Offender's Initial Contact with the Victim the Same as the Murder or Major Assault Site?
     1 ☐ Yes (go to Item 120)   2 ☐ No or Unknown

115. Description of General Area of Initial Offender-Victim Contact (check one only):
     1 ☐ Rural   3 ☐ Urban
     2 ☐ Suburban   99 ☐ Unknown

116. The Neighborhood of Initial Offender-Victim Contact Is *Predominantly* (check one only):
     1 ☐ Business, Industrial, or Commercial   4 ☐ Uninhabited or Wilderness
     2 ☐ Farm or Agricultural   99 ☐ Unknown
     3 ☐ Residential

117. The Initial Offender-Victim Contact Was (check as many as apply):
     1 ☐ Any Residence   7 ☐ In an Open Field
     2 ☐ At or Near a School or Playground   8 ☐ In a Vehicle
     3 ☐ In a Retail Shopping District   9 ☐ On Public Transportation
     4 ☐ On a Public Street   88 ☐ Other (specify): _____
     5 ☐ In a Vice Area   _____
     6 ☐ A Densely Wooded Area   99 ☐ Unknown

118. Initial Offender-Victim Contact Was Victim's Residence:
     1 ☐ Yes   2 ☐ No   99 ☐ Unknown

119. Initial Offender-Victim Contact Was Victim's Work Place:
     1 ☐ Yes   2 ☐ No   99 ☐ Unknown

120. Potential Witnesses at the Time of the Initial Offender-Victim Contact:
     1 ☐ Other People Were Present in the   2 ☐ Area Was Essentially Deserted
        Immediate Area   99 ☐ Unknown

VICTIM'S LAST KNOWN LOCATION

121. Was the Site of the Victim's Last Known Location the Same as the Site of the Initial Contact between the Victim and Offender?
     1 ☐ Yes (go to Item 127)   2 ☐ No or Unknown

122. Description of General Area of Victim's Last Known Location (check one only):
     1 ☐ Rural   3 ☐ Urban
     2 ☐ Suburban   99 ☐ Unknown

123. The Neighborhood of Victim's Last Known Location Was *Predominantly* (check one only):
     1 ☐ Business, Industrial, or Commercial   4 ☐ Uninhabited or Wilderness
     2 ☐ Farm or Agricultural   99 ☐ Unknown
     3 ☐ Residential

124. The Victim's Last Known Location Was (check as many as apply):
     1 ☐ Any Residence   7 ☐ In an Open Field
     2 ☐ At or Near a School or Playground   8 ☐ In a Vehicle
     3 ☐ In a Retail Shopping District   9 ☐ On Public Transportation
     4 ☐ On a Public Street   88 ☐ Other (specify): _____
     5 ☐ In a Vice Area   _____
     6 ☐ A Densely Wooded Area   99 ☐ Unknown

125. The Victim's Last Known Location Was Victim's Residence:
    1 ☐ Yes   2 ☐ No   99 ☐ Unknown

126. The Victim's Last Known Location Was Victim's Work Place:
    1 ☐ Yes   2 ☐ No   99 ☐ Unknown

EVENTS AT ASSAULT SITE

127. There Is Evidence That the Offender Disabled the Telephone, Other Utilities, or Security Devices:
    1 ☐ Yes   2 ☐ No   99 ☐ Unknown

128. The Property at the Crime Scene(s) Was Ransacked, Vandalized, or Burned:
    1 ☐ Yes   2 ☐ No   99 ☐ Unknown

129. There Are Indications That the Offender Took Steps to Obliterate or Destroy Evidence at the Scene:
    1 ☐ Yes   2 ☐ No   99 ☐ Unknown

OFFENDER'S WRITING OR CARVING ON BODY OF VICTIM

130. Writing or Carving on Body:
    1 ☐ Yes (describe): _____   2 ☐ No

131. Instrument Used to Write or Carve on Body:
    1 ☐ Knife or Other Sharp Instrument   4 ☐ Writing Instrument (pen, etc.)
    2 ☐ Blood   88 ☐ Other (specify): _____
    3 ☐ Lipstick   _____

OFFENDER'S WRITING OR DRAWING AT THE CRIME SCENE

132. Writing or Drawing at Crime Scene(s):
    1 ☐ Yes (describe): _____   2 ☐ No

133. Instrument Used to Write or Draw at Crime Scene(s):
    1 ☐ Knife or Other Sharp Instrument   4 ☐ Writing Instrument (pen, etc.)
    2 ☐ Blood   88 ☐ Other (specify): _____
    3 ☐ Lipstick   _____

SYMBOLIC ARTIFACTS AT CRIME SCENE

134. Was There Evidence to Suggest a Deliberate or Unusual Ritual/Act/Thing Had Been Performed on, with, or near the Victim (such as an orderly formation of rocks, burnt candles, dead animals, defecation, etc.)?
    1 ☐ Yes (describe): _____   2 ☐ No
    _____   99 ☐ Unknown

OFFENDER'S COMMUNICATIONS

Item 135 deals with communications initiated by the offender with respect to the crime. Examples would be: an offender sending a letter or tape recording to the police or media claiming responsibility for the crime; a ransom note; or a suspicious communication received by the victim prior to the crime. (This item does not refer to conversation between the offender and victim during commission of the crime.)

135. Was There Any Communication from the Offender Before or After the Crime?
    1 ☐ Yes (enclose a copy or synopsis   2 ☐ No
        of the communication)   99 ☐ Unknown

VII. CONDITION OF VICTIM WHEN FOUND

136. There Is Reason to Believe the Offender Moved the Body from the Area of the Death Site to the Area of the Body Recovery Site:
1 ☐ Yes   2 ☐ No   3 ☐ Unable to Determine

137. Evidence Suggests the Offender Disposed of the Body in the Following Manner:
1 ☐ Openly Displayed or Otherwise Placed to Insure Discovery
2 ☐ Concealed, Hidden, or Otherwise Placed in Order to Prevent Discovery
3 ☐ With an Apparent Lack of Concern as to Whether or Not the Body Was Discovered
99 ☐ Unable to Determine

138. It Appears the Body of the Victim Was *Intentionally* Placed in an Unnatural or Unusual Position *after Death* Had Occurred (e.g., staged or posed):
1 ☐ Yes   2 ☐ No   3 ☐ Unable to Determine

139. Body Was Discovered...
1 ☐ Buried
2 ☐ Covered
3 ☐ In a Body of Water (stream, lake, river, etc.)
4 ☐ In a Building
5 ☐ In a Container (e.g., dumpster, box refrigerator)
6 ☐ In a Vehicle
7 ☐ Scattered (body parts)
8 ☐ None of the Above

140. If the Body Was Discovered in Water, Was It Weighted?
1 ☐ Yes —— With What? _____   2 ☐ No

141. Was the Victim Bound?
1 ☐ Yes   2 ☐ No

142. Article(s) Used to Bind or Restrain the Victim or the Body:
1 ☐ An Article of Clothing
2 ☐ Tape
3 ☐ Cordage (e.g., rope, string, twine, wire, leather thong, etc.)
4 ☐ Chain
5 ☐ Handcuffs or Thumbcuffs
88 ☐ Other (specify): _____
_____

143. The Evidence Suggests That the Restraining Device(s) Was (check one only):
1 ☐ Brought to the Scene by the Offender
2 ☐ An Article Found at the Scene by the Offender
3 ☐ Both 1 and 2 Above
99 ☐ Unknown

144. Parts of Body Bound (check as many as apply):
1 ☐ Hands or Arms
2 ☐ Feet, Ankle(s), or Legs
3 ☐ Neck
4 ☐ Arms Bound to Torso
5 ☐ Hands and Ankle(s) Bound Together
88 ☐ Other (specify): _____
_____

145. The Bindings on the Victim Were Excessive (much more than necessary to control victim's movements):
1 ☐ Yes   2 ☐ No   3 ☐ Unable to Determine

146. The Body Was Tied to Another Object:
1 ☐ Yes   2 ☐ No

147. Was a Gag Placed in or on the Victim's Mouth?
1 ☐ Yes (describe):_____
_____
2 ☐ No
99 ☐ Unknown

148. Was a Blindfold Placed on or over the Victim's Eyes?
1 ☐ Yes (describe):_____
_____
2 ☐ No
99 ☐ Unknown

149. Was Victim's Entire Face Covered?
1 ☐ Yes —— With What? _____
_____
2 ☐ No
99 ☐ Unknown

150. Clothing on Victim When Found:
- 1 ☐ Fully Dressed
- 2 ☐ Partially Undressed
- 3 ☐ Nude
- 88 ☐ Other (specify): _____

151. There Is Evidence the Victim Was Re-dressed by Offender:
- 1 ☐ Yes
- 2 ☐ No
- 3 ☐ Unable to Determine

152. There Is Evidence to Suggest That Any or All of the Victim's Clothing had been *Ripped* or *Torn*:
- 1 ☐ Yes
- 2 ☐ No
- 3 ☐ Unable to Determine

153. There Is Evidence to Suggest That Any or All of the Victim's Clothing had been *Cut* from the Body:
- 1 ☐ Yes
- 2 ☐ No
- 3 ☐ Unable to Determine

154. Items of the Victim's Clothing Were Missing from the Body Recovery Site:
- 1 ☐ Yes (identify): _____
- _____
- 2 ☐ No
- 99 ☐ Unknown

155. Victim's Clothing (not on the body) Recovered at the Body Recovery Site Was:
- 1 ☐ Piled Neatly
- 2 ☐ Scattered
- 3 ☐ Hidden
- 4 ☐ Not Applicable

156. Based on the Investigation, There Is Evidence to Suggest That the Offender Took Small Personal Items (other than clothing) From the Victim (these items may or may not be valuable, e.g., photos, driver's license, real or costume jewelry, etc.):
- 1 ☐ Yes (specify): _____
- _____
- 2 ☐ No
- 99 ☐ Unknown

VIII. CAUSE OF DEATH AND/OR TRAUMA

If victim is a survivor, go to Item 158.

157. Medical Examiner's or Coroner's Officially Listed Cause of Death:
- 1 ☐ Gunshot Wound(s)
- 2 ☐ Stab Wound(s)
- 3 ☐ Cutting or Incise Wound(s)
- 4 ☐ Blunt Force Injury
- 5 ☐ Strangulation —— Manual, Ligature, Undetermined (circle one)
- 6 ☐ Smothering
- 7 ☐ Airway Occlusion —— Internal
- 8 ☐ Torso Compression
- 9 ☐ Hanging
- 10 ☐ Drowning
- 11 ☐ Burns —— Fire
- 12 ☐ Burns —— Chemical
- 13 ☐ Burns —— Scalding
- 14 ☐ Hypothermia or Exposure
- 15 ☐ Malnutrition or Dehydration
- 16 ☐ Electrocution
- 17 ☐ Crushing Injury
- 18 ☐ Explosive Trauma
- 19 ☐ Undetermined
- 88 ☐ Other (specify): _____
- _____

158. *Major* Trauma Location(s) (check as many as apply):
- 1 ☐ Head / Face / Neck
- 2 ☐ Arm(s) / Hand(s)
- 3 ☐ Torso
- 4 ☐ Leg(s) / Feet
- 5 ☐ Breast(s)
- 6 ☐ Buttocks
- 7 ☐ Genitalia
- 8 ☐ Anus
- 88 ☐ Other (specify): _____
- _____
- 99 ☐ Unable to Determine

159. Extent of *Blunt Force* Injury:
- 1 ☐ None
- 2 ☐ Minimal (minor bruising only, possibly caused by offender's slapping to control the victim)
- 3 ☐ Moderate (injury inflicted which in itself could not have caused death)
- 4 ☐ Severe (injury which in itself could have caused death, whether it was the cause of death or not)
- 5 ☐ Extreme (injury inflicted beyond that necessary for death. Overkill)

160. Estimated Number of Stab Wounds: _____

161. Estimated Number of Cutting Wounds: _____

162. Number of Entry Gunshot Wounds: _____

163. Range of Gunfire:
    1 ☐ Not Applicable
    2 ☐ Distant (no stippling / tattooing)
    3 ☐ Intermediate (stippling / tattooing)

    4 ☐ Close (powder residue / tattooing)
    5 ☐ Contact

BITE MARKS ON VICTIM

164. Bite Marks Were Identified on the Victim's Body:
    1 ☐ Yes

    2 ☐ No (go to Item 166)

165. Location of Bite Marks:
    1 ☐ Face
    2 ☐ Neck
    3 ☐ Abdomen
    4 ☐ Breast(s)
    5 ☐ Buttocks

    6   ☐ Groin
    7   ☐ Genitalia
    8   ☐ Thigh(s)
    88 ☐ Other (specify): _____
    _____

ELEMENTS OF TORTURE OR UNUSUAL ASSAULT

166. There Is Evidence to Suggest That the Offender Disfigured the Body of the Victim in Order to Delay or Hinder Identification of the Victim (burned body; removed and took hands, feet, head; etc.):
    1 ☐ Yes

    2 ☐ No

167. Elements of Unusual or Additional Assault upon Victim:
    1 ☐ None
    2 ☐ Victim Whipped
    3 ☐ Burns on Victim
    4 ☐ Victim Run Over by Vehicle
    5 ☐ Evidence of Cannibalism / Vampirism

    6   ☐ Offender Explored, Probed, or
          Mutilated Cavities or Wounds
          of Victim
    88 ☐ Other (specify): _____
    _____

168. Body Parts Removed by Offender:
    1 ☐ None (go to Item 170)
    2 ☐ Head
    3 ☐ Scalp
    4 ☐ Face
    5 ☐ Teeth
    6 ☐ Eye(s)
    7 ☐ Ear(s)
    8 ☐ Nose
    9 ☐ Hand(s)

    10 ☐ Arm(s)
    11 ☐ Leg(s)
    12 ☐ Breast(s)
    13 ☐ Nipple(s)
    14 ☐ Anus
    15 ☐ Genitalia
    16 ☐ Internal Organs
    88 ☐ Other (specify): _____
    _____

169. Dismemberment Method:
    1 ☐ Bitten Off
    2 ☐ Cut —— Skilled/Surgical
    3 ☐ Cut —— Unskilled/Rough-Cut
    4 ☐ Hacked / Chopped Off

    5   ☐ Sawed Off
    88 ☐ Other (specify): _____
    _____

SEXUAL ASSAULT

170. Is There Evidence of an Assault to Any of the Victim's Sexual Organs or Body Cavities?
    1 ☐ Yes   2 ☐ No (go to Item 178)   3 ☐ Unable to Determine

171. Type Sexual Assault, or Attempt (check all that apply):
    1 ☐ Vaginal
    2 ☐ Anal
    3 ☐ Victim Performed Oral Sex on Offender
    4 ☐ Offender Performed Oral Sex on Victim

    88 ☐ Other (describe): _____
    _____
    99 ☐ Unable to Determine

172. Semen Identification In a Body Cavity of the Victim:
   1 ☐ No   3 ☐ In Anus   5 ☐ Unable to Determine
   2 ☐ In Vagina   4 ☐ In Mouth

173. Evidence of Other Ejaculation:
   1 ☐ No   3 ☐ Elsewhere at the Scene
   2 ☐ On Body of Victim   4 ☐ Unable to Determine

174. There Is Evidence to Suggest Postmortem Sexual Assault:
   1 ☐ Yes   2 ☐ No   3 ☐ Unable to Determine

175. Is There Evidence of Sexual Insertion of Foreign Object(s) (other than the penis) into the Victim's Body?
   1 ☐ Yes   2 ☐ No (go to Item 178)

176. Evidence of Sexual Insertion of Foreign Object(s) *Still in Body* When First Discovered (e.g., rocks, twigs, knife, clothing):

   (object)   (object)

   1 ☐ Vagina _____   4 ☐ Mouth _____
   2 ☐ Penis _____   88 ☐ Other _____
   3 ☐ Anus _____

177. There Is Evidence of Sexual Insertion of Foreign Object(s) into Victim's Body, but the Object Was *Not In The Body* When the Body Was First Discovered:
   1 ☐ Yes —— _____ into _____
                    (describe object)   (body cavity)
   2 ☐ No
   3 ☐ Unable to Determine

IX.   FORENSIC EVIDENCE

WEAPONS

178. Weapons Used by Offender in This Assault:
   1 ☐ None   5 ☐ Ligature
   2 ☐ Firearm   6 ☐ Hands or Feet
   3 ☐ Stabbing or Cutting Weapon 88 ☐ Other Weapon (describe): _____
   4 ☐ Bludgeon or Club   _____

179. Assault Weapon(s) Used by Offender:
   1 ☐ Weapon of Opportunity (offender finds weapon at or near scene)
   2 ☐ Weapon of Choice (offender preselects weapon and brings to scene)
   3 ☐ Both 1 and 2 Above
   99 ☐ Unknown

180. Recovery of Assault Weapon(s) (check as many as apply):
   1 ☐ Not Recovered   3 ☐ Recovered Elsewhere —— Where? ____
   2 ☐ Recovered At Scene   _____

181. Type Firearm Used:
   1 ☐ Handgun   88 ☐ Other (specify): _____
   2 ☐ Rifle   _____
   3 ☐ Shotgun   99 ☐ Unknown

182. Caliber or Gauge of Firearm(s) Used: _____

183. Number of Grooves and Direction of Twist of Recovered Bullet or Firearm: _____

184. Size of Shotgun Shell Pellets Recovered or Used: _____

BLOOD

185. What Is the Offender's Blood Type?
   1 ☐ A   3 ☐ AB   99 ☐ Unknown
   2 ☐ B   4 ☐ O

186. What Is the Rh Factor of the Offender's Blood?
   1 ☐ Positive   2 ☐ Negative   99 ☐ Unknown

X.   REQUEST FOR PROFILE

187. Is This VICAP Crime Analysis Report Being Submitted in Conjunction with a Request for a Criminal Profile Evaluation?

    1   ☐ Yes (see note below)   2   ☐ No

NOTE: If this VICAP Crime Analysis Report is being submitted in conjunction with a request for a Criminal Personality Profile evaluation, you must contact the CRIMINAL PROFILE COOR-DINATOR assigned to the FBI Field Division in your area. The CRIMINAL PROFILE COORDINATOR is charged with the responsibility of assisting you with your request for a criminal personality profile and will advise you of additional materials that must be submitted in order to properly evaluate your case. He/she will review the materials and will submit the entire profile package to the National Center for the Analysis of Violent Crime on your behalf. Do not submit Criminal Profiling case materials directly to VICAP. Only the VICAP Crime Analysis Report should be submitted directly to VICAP.

XI.   OTHER RELATED CASES

188. Are You Aware of Any Other Cases Which May Be Related to This One or In Which This Offender May Have Been Involved?

    1   ☐ Yes (provide details below)   2   ☐ No

If Yes, List the Agency Name, State, Case Number, Investigator, and Phone Number of the Investigating Agency:

Agency Name	State	Case No.	Investigator	Phone No.

XII. NARRATIVE SUMMARY

189. Give a BRIEF Narrative Summary of This Case So the Reader Will Have a General Overview
of the Case, the Details, the Most Unusual Characteristics, and the Sequence of Events. Also
Include Any Details of This Case You Feel Are Important, But That Have Not Previously
Been Addressed (see examples of Narrative Summaries in the Instructions):

Glossary

ACCELERANT Something, usually a flammable liquid, that is used to increase the spread of the fire.

ACTUS REUS Criminal act. One of the three conditions the prosecution must satisfy before convicting and punishing someone of a crime. Actus reus deals with the criminal act itself. In order for an act to be considered a crime, each and every element of the crime, as defined by statute, must be present in the offender's action.

AUTOEROTICISM Sexual arousal and/or gratification without a partner.

BLITZ An ambush style of attack in which the victim is suddenly overpowered or immediately killed, as with a gun. The victim is frequently attacked from behind. This intense and violent attack catches the victim completely off guard.

BODY OF FIRE An intense mass of flame often accompanied by heavy smoke under pressure, indicating the heart of a major fire. Usually referred to as *large body fire*.

BOILOVER Overflow of flammable liquid from a container due to heat from a fire or due to the excessive application of water, which agitates and floats burning liquid over the top of the container.

BUILDING OF ORIGIN The building in which an extensive or spreading fire is understood to have started.

BUILDUP Increase or acceleration of fire or heat after the arrival of fire fighters.

CAUSATION The offender's actions produced results that are defined as criminal (e.g., when a homicide results from the offender having stabbed the victim in the heart, the offender's actions were directly related to the victim's death). Part of the criminal act requirements.

COMBUSTIBLE A material that will ignite and burn when sufficient heat is applied. Technically, a material that when heated will give off vapors that in the presence of oxygen (air) may be oxidized and consumed by fire.

COMBUSTIBLE LIQUID A liquid having a flash point at or above 100 degrees Fahrenheit.

CONVECTION Heat transfer by a circulating medium, either gas or liquid (e.g., air heated by conduction circulates and transfers heat to distant objects in the room).

CRIMINAL ACT REQUIREMENTS The requirements that must be satisfied by the prosecution to obtain a conviction. The criminal act requirements consists of actus reus, causation, and mens rea.

DEFENSIVE WOUNDS A wound, usually on the fingers, hands, or forearms of the victim of an attack, sustained while trying to grasp a weapon or ward off the assailant. The nature of the wound depends on the weapons used for assault.

DEPERSONALIZATION Actions taken by the offender to obscure the identity of the victim. These actions may take the form of either antemortem or postmortem mutilation. Through excessive facial battery, the offender attempts to dehumanize the victim because he or she represents or resembles a person who has caused him psychological distress. Subtle acts of depersonalization may involve covering the victim's face with a towel, pillow, or clothing or placing the victim face down.

DISORGANIZED Classification of an offender based on criminal investigative analysis from which an offender profile may be constructed. The disorganized offender usually commits a spontaneous, impulsive offense, under stress, in his own geographic area. Therefore, he often knows the victim, at least by sight. He most often uses a weapon of opportunity and a blitz assault, so conversation and the use of restraints are minimal. Sexual acts occur postmortem. The crime scene is random and sloppy with evidence and/or the weapon present. The body is left in view at the death scene.

DNA TORCH Arson used to conceal the evidence of a sexual assault/homicide and evidenced by gasoline applied to the genital areas.

EROTOMANIA Idealized, romantic love by one person toward another person usually of higher status, such as a famous person or a superior at work. This love is based more on spiritual union than sexual attraction. The subject believes the object of his or her affections has mutual feelings of love. Efforts to contact the person focused on by the erotomaniac include letters, gifts, telephone calls, and visits. Stalking and surveillance are common to the erotomaniac who comes in conflict with law enforcement.

EXCESSIVE HEAT Temperatures generally in excess of 300 degrees Fahrenheit, which tend to vaporize exposed fuels and enable fires to spread, the one abnormal part of the fire triangle.

FLAMMABLE LIQUIDS Liquids that readily ignite and burn at temperatures below 200 degrees Fahrenheit. Sometimes classified into high flash-point and low flash-point liquids in terms of whether they flash above or below 100 degrees Fahrenheit.

HOMICIDE-TO-BE A barricade situation in which clear threats are made to victims, but no substantive demands are made on a third party. These victims are primary targets of the offender and are not being used as bargaining chips for money, freedom, and so on.

HOSTAGE A person held at a location known to authorities and threatened by a subject to force the fulfillment of substantive demands made on a third party. In a hostage situation, the victim clearly is being threatened by the subject and the threats are used to influence someone else, usually law enforcement officials.

IMPROVEMENT FIRES Fires set to a target of value other than structures, vegetations, or vehicles (e.g., lumber stacks, fence-post piles).

INCENDIARY A fire that is set deliberately.

KIDNAPPING The seizure, detainment, or removal of a person by unlawful force or fraud—often with a demand of ransom. The victim has been taken by possibly unknown subject(s) and is detained at a location *unknown* to authorities. In contrast, a hostage situation involves a person being held at a location *known* to authorities.

MENS REA Criminal intent. One of three conditions of the criminal act requirements. The offender must demonstrate a criminal state of mind, recklessness, or negligence with the commission of a criminal act.

MISSION ORIENTED An offender who is focused on a self-imposed task without a regard to the consequences of his or her actions. This task usually involves killing an individual(s). A mission-oriented offender usually is unconcerned about escape or even survival once the offense is accomplished. This offender often opts for the conclusion of his or her mission to be "suicide" by police.

MIXED A crime scene that demonstrates elements of both organized and disorganized offender activity. More than one offender, unexpected victim response, unanticipated events (e.g., interruptions), youthfulness, alcohol/drug use, and external stressors all produce a mixed crime scene.

MODUS OPERANDI (MO) The actions taken by an offender to perpetrate the offense successfully. MO is a learned behavior that evolves as the offender becomes more sophisticated and confident.

MONIKER A personal name or nickname.

NECROPHILIA (INSERTIONAL) Substitution for actual sexual intercourse by an offender through insertion of foreign objects into the victim's orifices. The insertion becomes a sexual act through the offender's fantasy. This act commonly is seen with the disorganized offender. It is often mistaken for an act of mutilation when it is actually sexual substitution.

NONCOMBUSTIBLE Material when in the form it is used will not ignite and burn when subjected to fire or is not subject to serious flame spread (e.g., unprotected steel frame or metal).

OPEN FLAME A visible flame, as opposed to a glowing combustion that has no visible flames.

OPPORTUNITY (WEAPON) Weapon accorded offender by the surroundings in which the offense occurs (e.g., a rock or stick [outdoors], piece of the victim's clothing [ligature], or knife [indoors]). A weapon of opportunity, after being used, frequently is left at the crime scene.

ORGANIZED Classification of an offender based on criminal investigative analysis from which an offender profile may be constructed. The organized offender is mobile, usually due to ownership of a well-maintained vehicle. He uses a verbal means, or con, to capture the victim, rather than physical force. The victim is often a targeted stranger, selected by the offender due to his personal criteria. Restraints commonly are used to maintain control of the victim. Aggressive and sexual acts occur antemortem and perimortem. The weapon is one of choice, brought to the offense by the offender. The body is often transported from the death scene and concealed. The multiple crime scenes often involved reflect the offender's well-planned, methodical approach and overall control. The weapon and other elements of physical evidence are absent.

OVERKILL Excessive trauma or injury beyond that necessary to cause death.

PARAMILITARY A style of operation that is characterized by the wearing of uniforms, the use of training compounds, a hierarchy of leadership based on rank, and an internal code of discipline and conduct. Paramilitary organizations tend to be highly organized and demonstrate military tactics during the commission of crimes.

PERSONAL WEAPONS The use of hands and feet as weapons to produce blunt-force trauma during an attack.

PERSONATION Ritualistic actions by the offender at the crime scene that have significance only to the offender. The offender often invests intimate meaning into the scene in the form of body positioning, mutilation, items left, or other symbolic gestures involving the crime scene.

PROTECTED AREA The clean or unburned area left by stock, furniture, contents, and similar materials covering shelves, floors, or other combustible materials.

PSEUDOHOSTAGE A person is held against his or her will, but there are no threats directed toward the victim and no substantive demands are made on a third party.

PSYCHOLOGICAL AUTOPSY A review of investigative findings and the performance and evaluation of a series of structured interviews conducted by a psychiatrist or trained psychologist with close friends, acquaintances, and relatives of a deceased person in order to determine his or her psychological makeup during life. This information may be of assistance in determining if suicide was consistent with the victim's apparent state of mind.

RUNNING FIRE An outside fire spreading rapidly with a well-defined front.

SEAT OF FIRE Area where the main body of fire is located as determined by the outward movement of heat and gases and where the fire is most deeply recorded.

SELECTIVE RECALL Uncharacteristically detailed memory of a suspect when asked to relate his or her whereabouts and actions during the offense in question. The subject usually will have a precise, airtight alibi, sometimes supported by receipts, witness, and so on for the time period the offense was committed but will not demonstrate as precise a recall for periods of time preceding and following the offense.

SET Incendiary fire, or the point of origin of an incendiary fire.

SEXUAL SADISM An offender who has established "an enduring pattern of sexual arousal in response to sadistic imagery" (Dietz, Hazelwood & Warren 1990, 165). Sexual gratification is obtained from the victim's response to mental and physical torture.

SIGNATURE Repetitive ritualistic behavior by the serial offender, usually displayed at every crime scene and having nothing to do with the perpetration of the crime. Repetitive personation.

SMOKE EXPLOSION An explosion of heated smoke and gases pent up in a burning building. Explosion occurs when air is admitted. In a building where the fire has gained headway, the self-ignition temperature of solid materials (450–800 degrees Fahrenheit) may be present. All that is needed is the introduction of air containing more oxygen to produce combustion so rapid as to have the appearance of an explosion.

SOUVENIRS/TROPHIES Items taken from the crime scene by the offender to commemorate the offense. Souvenirs/trophies are often inexpensive items belonging to the victim (e.g., costume jewelry, photos, driver's license, clothing, etc.). Souvenirs/trophies allow the offender to continue to fantasize and relive the events of the crime. They also serve as a commemoration of the offender's successful perpetration of the offense.

STAGING Alteration of the crime scene prior to the arrival of police either by the offender to redirect the investigation away from the most logical suspect or by family or friends of the victim to protect the victim or victim's family.

STAKEOUT A victim who is selected simply because he or she crossed the path of the offender while he was staking out an area in search of a victim. A more opportunistic victim than the stalked victim.

STALKER A predator who stalks and selects a victim based on a specific criterion of the victim. With a serial offender who stalks his victims, the investigator would expect to see victim similarities (e.g., occupation, hair color, age, build, etc.).

TARGET, PRIMARY The focus of the offender's attack due to the offender's obvious or hidden rationale. This victim is the reason the offender is there.

TARGET, SECONDARY A victim because of association with the primary target. Secondary targets may become victims because of the inability of the offender to strike at the primary target.

TORCH A professional firesetter.

TRAILERS Any combustible or flammable material used to spread the fire(s) from one point or area to another. Materials chosen, if completely burned, will leave little ash or telltale residue.

UNDOING Actions by an offender who has a close association with the victim and tries symbolically to undo a homicide (e.g., washing the victim, placing a pillow under the victim's head and covering the body with a blanket, the offender washing up, etc.). Undoing should not be confused with depersonalization: undoing is usually based on an attitude of caring and remorse, while depersonalization is a hostile act.

VICTIM Person who becomes the focus of the offender's attack by crossing the offender's path when the offender views the circumstances (lack of witnesses, time of day, victim vulnerability, etc.) as favorable to commit the crime. The offender's state of mind may influence his perception of the risk involved. Alcohol, drugs, feelings of stress, and impulsiveness, among other factors, may influence the offender to take more risks to commit the crime.

VICTIMOLOGY A complete history of the victim, including life-style, personality traits, employment, and so on.

References

Ault, R. L. 1986. NCAVC's research and development program. *FBI Law Enforcement Bulletin* 55 (12):6–8.

Boring, E. G. 1957. *A history of experimental psychology.* 2d ed. New York: Appleton-Century Crofts.

Bromberg, W. 1965. *Crime and the mind: A psychiatric analysis of crime and punishment.* New York: Macmillan.

Bruton V. United States 391 U.S. 123 (1968). In *Criminal interrogation,* R. Devallis. Sacramento: Custom Publishing, 1987.

Carter, D. L., R. A. Prentky, and A. W. Burgess. 1986. Victim response strategies in sexual assault. *Journal of Interpersonal Violence* 1 (1):73–96.

Cohen, M. L., T. Seghorn, and W. Calmas. 1969. Sociometric study of sex offenders. *Journal of Abnormal Psychology* 74:249–55.

Cohen, M. L., et al. 1971. The psychology of rapists. *Seminars in Psychiatry* 3:307–27.

Criminal victimization in the United States, 1988. A national crime survey report. Washington, D.C.: Government Printing Office.

DeHaan, J. D. 1990. *Kirk's fire investigation.* Englewood Cliffs, N.J.: Prentice Hall.

Dietz, P. E., and R. R. Hazelwood. 1982. Atypical autoerotic fatalities. *Medicine and Law* 1:301–19.

Dietz, P. E., R. R. Hazelwood, and J. Warren. 1990. The sexually sadistic criminal and his offenses. *Bulletin of the American Academy of Psychiatry and the Law* 18 (2):163–78.

Douglas, J. E., R. K. Ressler, A. W. Burgess, and C. R. Hartman. 1986. Criminal profiling from crime scene analysis. *Behavioral Sciences and the Law* 4(4): 401–421.

Douglas, J. E., 1989. Expert witness testimony. *State of Delaware* v. *Steven B. Pennel.*

Douglas, J. E. 1990. Expert witness testimony. *State of Louisiana* v. *Nathaniel Code.*

Douglas, J. E. 1990. Expert witness testimony. *State of Ohio* v. *Ronnie Shelton.*

Doyle, A. C. [1892] 1975. A scandal in Bohemia. In *The Adventures of Sherlock Holmes,* A. C. Doyle. London: George Newnes; New York, A & W Visual Library, 5.

Geberth, V. J. 1981. Psychological profiling. *Law and Order,* 46–49.

Glueck, B. 1918. 608 admissions to sing sing. *Mental Hygiene* 2:85.

Goddard, H. H. 1914. *Feeblemindness, its cause and consequences.* New York: Macmillan.

Goring, C. 1913. *The English convict.* London: H. M. Stationary Office.

Groth, A. N. 1979. *Men who rape.* New York: Plenum.

Harmon, R. B., R. Rosner, and M. Wiederlight. 1985. Women and arson: A demographic study. *Journal of Forensic Sciences* 30 (2): 467–77.

Hazelwood, R. B. 1987. Analyzing the rape and profiling the offender. In *Practical aspects of rape investigation,* ed. R. R. Hazelwood and A. W. Burgess. New York: Elsevier.

Hazelwood, R. R., and A. W. Burgess. 1987. *Practical Aspect of Rape Investigation.* New York: Elsevier.

Hazelwood, R. R., and J. E. Douglas. 1980. The lust murderer. *FBI Law Enforcement Bulletin:* 49(3) 18–22.

Helgason, J. Angel of death. *Dayton Daily News,* 28 October 1990.

Icove, D. J. 1979. Principles of incendiary crime analysis. Ph.D. dissertation, University of Tennessee.

Icove, D. J., and M. H. Estepp. 1987. Motive-based offender profiles of arson and fire-related crimes. *FBI Law Enforcement Bulletin* 56 (April), Washington, D.C.

Icove, D. J., and P. R. Horbert. 1990. Serial arsonists: An introduction. *Police Chief* 57 (12):46–49.

Icove, D. J., J. D. Schroeder, and V. B. Wherry. 1979. Combating arson-for-profit. Columbus, OH: Battelle Press.

James V. State 86 Georgia App. 282, 71, S.E. 2d 568 (1952).

Kestler, J. L. 1982. *Questioning techniques and tactics.* Colorado Springs: Shepards/ McGraw-Hill.

Kinder, G. 1982. *Victim: The other side of murder.* New York: Delacorte Press.

Klotter, J. C. 1990. *Criminal law.* New York: Anderson.

Knight, R. A., Carter, D. L., and Prentky, R. A. 1989. A system for the classification of child molesters: Reliability and applications. *Journal of Interpersonal Violence* 4: 3–23.

Knight, R. A., and R. A. Prentky. 1990. Classifying sexual offenders: The development and corroboration of taxonomic models. In *Handbook of sexual assault,* ed. W. L. Marshall, D. R. Laws, and H. E. Barbaree. New York: Plenum.

Knight, R. A., R. Rosenberg, and B. A. Schneider. 1985. Classification of sexual offenders: Perspectives, methods, and validation. In *Rape and sexual assault,* ed. A. W. Burgess. New York: Garland.

Lanning, K. V. 1986. *Child molesters: A behavioral analysis.* National Center for Missing & Exploited Children, Washington, D.C.

Lanning, K. V. 1989. Satanic, occult, ritualistic crime: A law enforcement perspective. *Police Chief,* October, 1–11.

Lentz, H. M. 1988. Assassinations and executions: An encyclopedia of political violence, 1865–1986. Jefferson, North Carolina: McFarland.

Lewis, N. D., and H. Yarnell. 1951. Pathological firesetting (pyromania). In *Nervous and mental diseases monograph 82.* New York: Coolidge Foundation.

Lindesmith, A. R., and H. W. Dunham. 1941. Some principles of criminal typology. *Social Forces* 19: 307–14.

Loevinger, L. 1980. Preface. In *Law and psychology in conflict,* J. Marshall. New York: Bobbs-Merrill.

Luke, J. L. 1988. The role of forensic pathology in criminal profiling. In *Sexual homicide,* ed. R. Ressler, A. Burgess, and J. Douglas. Lexington, Mass.: Lexington Books.

Markman D. and D. Bosco. 1989. *Alone with the devil: And other famous cases of a courtroom psychiatrist.* Garden City, N.Y.: Doubleday.

Megargee, E. I. 1982. Psychological determinants and correlates of criminal violence. In *Criminal violence,* ed. M. E. Wolfgang and N. A. Weiner. Beverly Hills: Sage Publications.

Megargee, E. I., and M. J. Bohn. 1979. *Classifying criminal offenders: A new system based on the MMPI.* London: Sage Publications.

Minnick V. Mississippi 111 S.Ct. 486 (1990).

Moinar, G., L. Keitner, and B. T. Harwood. 1984. Comparison of partner and solo arsonists. *Journal of Forensic Sciences* 29 (2):574–83.

Moore, K., and D. Reed. 1988. *Deadly medicine.* New York: St. Martin's Press.

Moran V. Burbine 89 LEd 2d 410 (1968). In *Criminal interrogation,* R. Devallis. Sacramento: Custom Publishing, 1987.

Moreau, D. 1987. Concepts of physical evidence in sexual assault investigations. In *Practical rape investigation: A multidisciplinary approach,* ed. R. Hazelwood and A. W. Burgess. New York: Elsevier.

Mosby medical-nursing dictionary. 1987. Louis: Mosby.

National incidence studies of missing, abducted, runaway, and thrown-away children. 1989. Final report. U.S. Department of Justice, Office of Juvenile Justice and Delinquency Prevention.

O'Brien, D. 1989. *Murder in Little Egypt.* New York: Morrow.

Overholser, W. 1935. The Briggs Law of Massachusetts: A review and an appraisal. *Journal of Criminal Law and Criminology* 25:862–68.

Prentky, R. A., M. L. Cohen, and T. K. Seghorn. 1985. Development of a rational taxonomy for the classification of sexual offenders: Rapists. *Bulletin of the American Academy of Psychiatry and the Law* 13:39–70.

Rennie, Y. 1977. *The search for criminal man: The dangerous offender project.* Lexington, Mass.: Lexington Books.

Ressler, R., A. Burgess, and J. Douglas. 1988. *Sexual homicide: Patterns and motives.* Lexington, Mass.: Lexington Books.

Rider, A. O. 1980. The firesetter: A psychological profile. *FBI Law Enforcement Bulletin* 49: 6–8.

Roebuck, J. B. 1967. *Criminal typology.* 2d ed. Springfield, Ill.: Charles C. Thomas.

Rossi, D. 1982. Crime scene behavioral analysis: Another tool for the law enforcement investigator. *Police Chief:* 152–55.

Seghorn, T., and M. L. Cohen. 1980. The psychology of the rape assailant. In *Modern legal medicine, psychiatry, and forensic sciences,* ed. W. Curran, A. L. McGary, and C. Petty. Philadelphia: F. A. Davis.

Sifakas, C. 1981. *Encyclopedia of American crime* New York: Facts on File.

Uniform Crime Reports. 1976–89. *Crime in the United States.* Washington, D.C.: Government Printing Office.

United Press International. 27 March 1981, 6 May 1983, 2 February 1984, 15–16 February 1985, 11 February 1986, 7 December 1986.

Van Zandt, C. R. 1990. *Kidnapping or hostage situation.* Quantico, Va.: FBI Academy.

Vorpagel, R. E. 1982. Painting psychological profiles: Charlantanism, charisma, or a new science? *Police Chief,* 156–59.

Vreeland, R. G., and M. B. Waller. 1978. The psychology of firesetting: A review and appraisal. National Bureau of Standards, grant no. 7-9021.

Wilson, C., and D. Seaman. 1985. *Encyclopedia of modern murder, 1962–1982.* New York: Putnam.

Yorker, B. C. 1988. Nurses accused of murder. *American Journal of Nursing* 11.

Index

About the Editors, Chapter Authors, and Classification Committee Chairs

John E. Douglas

Supervisory Special Agent John E. Douglas, Ed. D., entered on duty with the FBI in 1970 and received investigative experience in Detroit and Milwaukee from 1970 to 77. He is assigned to the National Center for the Analysis of Violent Crime and serves as unit chief of the FBI's Investigative Support Unit. As unit chief, Douglas supervises the bureau's Violent Criminal Apprehension Program, the Criminal Investigative Analysis Program, and the Arson and Bombing Investigative Services Program.

Douglas has been a consultant to law enforcement agencies throughout the United States, Canada, Puerto Rico, England, Australia, Central America, and Italy. He has provided consultation and guidance in over 5,000 cases involving both violent crime and white-collar crime investigations. Included in these cases were the Atlanta child murders; the Columbus stranglings; Chicago's Tylenol case; Buffalo's .22-Caliber Killer; Gainesville, Florida's Co-ed Murders; Seattle's Green River murders; New York's Son of Sam Killer; Wichita's BTK Strangler, and many others.

Over the past twenty years, Douglas has interviewed more than 150 violent offenders, including Charles Manson and his "Family" members, Richard Speck, David Berkowitz, Gary Heidnik, Monte Rissel, Edmund Kemper, James Earl Ray, Arthur Bremmer, Sarah Jane Moore, Joseph Paul Franklin and Joseph Fischer, to name a few.

Douglas has a doctorate degree in education, has published over twenty articles in professional magazines and journals, and is co author of a book entitled *Sexual Homicide: Patterns and Motives*. He has appeared on numerous television programs, including "Prime Time Live," "60 Minutes" "Hard Copy," "NOVA," "Inside Edition," "Top Cop," and a public broadcasting program called "The New Explorers."

Ann W. Burgess

Ann Wolbert Burgess, R.N., D.N.Sc., is the van Ameringen Professor of Psychiatric Mental Health Nursing at the University of Pennsylvania School of Nursing. With Lynda Lytle Holmstrom, she founded one of the first hospital-based crisis intervention programs for rape victims, located at Boston City Hospital, in 1972. She served as chair of the first advisory council to the National Center for the Prevention and Control of Rape of the National Institute of Mental Health, 1976–80. She was a member of the 1984 U.S. Attorney General's Task Force on Family Violence and on the planning committee for the Surgeon General's Symposium on Violence in October 1985, and she served on the National Institute of Health National Advisory Council for the Center for Nursing Research, 1986–88. Currently, she is a member of the Adolescent Health Advisory Panel to the Congress of the United States Office of Technology Assessment.

Burgess had been principal investigator of research projects on the use of children in pornography; heart attack victims and their return to work; sexual homicide and patterns of crime scenes; possible linkages between sexual abuse and exploitation of children, juvenile delinquency, and criminal behavior; and children as witnesses in child sexual abuse trials and currently is principal investigator on the project, "AIDS, Ethics, and Sexual Assault." She has written six textbooks in the fields of psychiatric nursing and crisis intervention; coauthored over ninety articles in the field of rape victimology; and coauthored or edited texts on rape, child and adolescent sexual assault, child pornography and sex rings, adolescent runaways, autoerotic fatalities, and sexual homicide.

Allen G. Burgess

Allen G. Burgess is associate professor in the College of Business, Northeastern University, Boston. He received his B.S.E.E. from Massachusetts Institute of Technology and his M.B.A and D.B.A from Boston University.

Burgess's background has been in the computer industry for over twenty-five years. Through his faculty appointment, he teaches operations management and management in high tech industry, and he provides consulting services in a variety of areas. His most recent assignments have been technology assessment for commercial feasibility of a file-server system for personal computers, specific requirements for high-performance graphics boards for personal computers, evaluation of a new scanner technology, a perception study of the computer-aided engineering market, and development of a specialized data base system for engineering work stations.

Robert K. Ressler

Robert K. Ressler, M.S., is a criminologist in private practice and the associate director of Forensic Behavioral Services, a Virginia-based organization dedicated to training, consultation, and expert witness testimony. He is a twenty-year veteran of the FBI, spending sixteen years in the FBI's Behavioral Science Unit and during this time innovated many of the programs that led to the formation of the FBI's National Center for the Analysis of Violent Crime. Ressler became the first program manager of the FBI's Violent Criminal Apprehension Program.

Ressler's academic affiliations include instructor of criminology while at the FBI Academy, adjunct faculty member at the University of Virginia and the University of Pennsylvania, and adjunct assistant professor at Michigan State University's School of Criminal Justice. He is a clinical assistant professor in psychiatry in Georgetown University's program on psychiatry and law.

Ressler is a member of the International Association of Forensic Sciences, the American Academy of Forensic Sciences, the Academy of Criminal Justice Sciences, the American Society of Criminology, the International Association of Chiefs of Police, the International Homicide Investigators Association, and other professional organizations. He originated the FBI's first research program of violent criminal offenders, interviewing and collecting data on thirty-six serial and sexual killers, resulting in the book, *Sexual Homicide: Patterns and Motives*. He has testified as an expert witness in criminal cases and has lectured at and consulted with law enforcement agencies, universities, and professional organizations throughout the United States and abroad in the areas of criminology, criminal psychology, criminal personality profiling, and hostage negotiation.

Ressler has thirty-four years of service with the U.S. Army, ten years of which was active duty during the Vietnam era, and is a military police and criminal investigation officer currently assigned in a reserve capacity to the U.S. Army CID command headquarters in Washington, D.C. He holds the rank of colonel in the U.S. Army Reserves.

Gregory M. Cooper

Special Agent Gregory M. Cooper graduated from Brigham Young University with a bachelor of arts degree and a master's degree in public administration in 1982. In 1982 he became the chief of police of Delta City, Utah, during a growth transition created by the construction of the Intermountain Power Project.

Cooper entered on duty as Special Agent with the FBI in April 1985. He has served in various investigative and supervisory capacities in the Seattle and Los Angeles field divisions. His responsibilities included conducting police interview/ interrogation instruction for the Washington Police Officer's Standards and Training Academy and serving as the FBI field coordinator for the National Center for the Analysis of Violent Crime, which includes the Criminal Investigative Analysis and Violent Criminal Apprehension Programs.

In August 1990 Cooper was assigned to the Investigative Support Unit of the NCAVC at the FBI Academy in Quantico as a criminal investigative analyst. His responsibilities include the supervision of Special Agent field coordinators located in the FBI's Northwest regional offices.

Cooper has been involved throughout the United States as a consultant in hundreds of cases involving homicides, rapes, child abduction and molestation, arson and bombings, and threat analysis. He also is involved in the ongoing research at the NCAVC and specifically in the development of prescriptive interview methods.

Robert R. Hazelwood

Robert R. Hazelwood is a supervisory Special Agent of the FBI. He is a faculty member of the FBI Academy's Behavioral Science Unit and an adjunct faculty member of the University of Virginia. He received his undergraduate degree from Sam Houston State College and earned his master's degree from Nova University. Hazelwood also attended a one-year fellowship program in forensic medicine at the Armed Forces Institute of Pathology. Prior to entering the FBI in 1971, he served eleven years in the U.S. Army's Military Police Corps, attaining the rank of major.

Hazelwood is coauthor of *Autoerotic Fatalities* (1983) and *Practical Aspects of Rape Investigation: A Multidisciplinary Approach* (1987). He has lectured extensively on criminal sexuality throughout the United States, Europe, Canada, and the Caribbean. He has been consulted throughout North America in the investigation of sexual assaults and homicides.

David J. Icove

David J. Icove is presently the program manager for the National Center for the Analysis of Violent Crime's Arson and Bombing Investigative Services Subunit at the FBI Academy in Quantico. Prior to his employment with the FBI, Icove established and supervised the city of Knoxville (Tennessee) Arson Task Force. He previously had served as an investigator with the arson bureaus of the Tennessee and Ohio state fire marshals' offices.

Icove currently oversees the FBI's Arson Information Management System project, which serves as a computer-assisted investigative tool used in the criminal investigative analysis (profiling) of serial incendiary crimes, such as arsons and bombings. A frequent lecturer to federal, state, and local law enforcement agencies on computer-assisted incendiary crime investigations, Icove has B.S. and M.S. degrees in electrical engineering, a B.S. degree in fire protection engineering, and Ph.D. in engineering science. Icove is a registered professional engineer in the states of Tennessee and Virginia.

Kenneth V. Lanning

Supervisory Special Agent Kenneth V. Lanning is assigned to the Behavioral Science Instruction and Research Unit at the FBI Academy in Quantico. He obtained his B.A. degree from Manhattan College in the Bronx, New York, and his M.S. degree from California Lutheran College in Thousand Oaks, California. He entered on duty with the FBI in 1970 and has been involved in studying the criminal aspects of deviant sexual behavior since 1973. He has specialized in the study of sexual victimization of children since 1981.

Lanning has made presentations before the National Conference on Sexual Victimization of Children, the National Conference on Child Abuse and Neglect, and the National Conference on Missing and Exploited Children. He has testified before the U.S. Attorney General's Task Force on Family Violence, the President's Task Force on Victims of Crime, and the U.S. Attorney General's Commission on Pornography. He also has testified before the U.S. Senate and the House of Representatives and as an expert witness in state and federal court.

Lanning has published articles in the *FBI Law Enforcement Bulletin* and is a contributing author to Ann Wolbert Burgess's *Child Pornography and Sex Rings*. He has authored a monograph, "Child Molesters: A Behavioral Analysis for Law Enforcement," which has been widely distributed by the National Center for Missing and Exploited Children. Lanning has lectured before and trained thousands of police officers and criminal justice professionals.

Gregg O. McCrary

Gregg O. McCrary received a bachelor's degree from Ithaca College, Ithaca, New York, in 1967 and entered on duty as a Special Agent with the

FBI in 1969. Upon completion of FBI training McCrary was assigned to the Detroit division, working in the area of criminal investigations.

Following that assignment, McCrary was transferred to New York City, where he served for six years. His primary investigative responsibilities were in the fields of organized crime investigations and foreign counterintelligence. In 1976 he was transferred to the Buffalo field division, where he continued to investigate organized crime and drug-related activities. He also served as a police instructor and SWAT team member/leader and worked in various undercover capacities. McCrary has continued his formal education at the graduate level in the fields of criminal justice (Long Island University), education (University of Virginia), and psychology (Marymount University).

McCrary has been associated with the National Center for the Analysis of Violent Crime since 1985. His current assignment as a supervisory Special Agent at the FBI Academy at Quantico involves working as a consultant in the investigation and prosecution of such crimes as homicides, arsons, bombings, political corruption, sexual assault, child abduction/molestation, kidnappings, extortions, organized criminal activities, foreign counterintelligence, and terrorism.

He has consulted on hundreds of cases throughout the United States, Canada, Central America, Australia, England, and China. He has provided expert witness testimony before select senate committees on violence in Massachusetts and New York State.

Corinne M. Munn

Corinne M. Munn, R.N., B.S., graduated from Alfred University in Alfred, New York with an associate degree in nursing. She has ten years of experience working as an intensive care unit nurse. She became involved with the *Crime Classification Manual* when she was assigned to the Investigative Support Unit at the FBI Academy at Quantico through an internship sponsored jointly by the FBI and the University of Virginia. Munn served as project coordinator and research associate. She completed a bachelor of science degree in chemistry at Stetson University in Florida.

Judson M. Ray

Special Agent Judson M. Ray received his undergraduate degree from Columbus College, Columbus, Georgia, in 1974 and earned his M.E. degree, with an emphasis in counseling and psychological services, from Georgia State University, Atlanta, in 1978. He also earned an M.S. degree with a concentration in police administration from Troy State University, Montgomery, Alabama, in 1977. Ray was admitted to the doctoral program and pursued doctoral studies in the adult education program at Auburn University, Auburn, Alabama, between 1977 and 1979.

SA Ray served a tour in Vietnam during 1966–67. Following completion of his military commitment, Ray joined the Metropolitan Police Department, Washington, D.C., and served for a period of thirteen months as a patrolman. He then relocated to Columbus, Georgia, where he became a member of the Columbus Police Department. During his ten-year training, he rose to the rank of director of the training division. During this time, Ray held an assistant professorship with Troy State University and became the chairman of criminal justice programs there. He served on numerous state committees on standards, education, and training for police officers in the state of Georgia.

Ray completed his formal FBI training in July 1980 and was assigned to the Atlanta field division, where in addition to criminal assignments, he was a member of the special task force for the investigation of missing and murdered children in Atlanta. Following that assignment, he was transferred to the Charlotte division and was assigned to the Raleigh/Durham resident agency, where he served as a relief supervisor.

Ray joined the FBI Academy's Behavioral Science Unit in 1984 and currently specializes in research and criminal personality profiling. He has conducted hundreds of case analyses and has given expert testimony in both state and federal trials.

Peter A. Smerick

Peter A. Smerick has a B.A. degree in political science from Penn State University and an M.E. degree from the University of Virginia in the field of instructional technology. He served in Vietnam as a U.S. Army combat photography officer in 1966 and at Fort Bragg, North Carolina, in army intelligence in 1967. He was appointed as a Special Agent for the Naval Investigative Service, U.S. Naval Intelligence, in 1967 and was responsible for investigative photographic operations in the Fourth Naval District, Philadelphia.

In 1970 Smerick became a Special Agent for the FBI and served in the Portland, Los Angeles, and New York divisions as the crime scene/surveillance photography coordinator participating in organized crime, foreign counterintelligence, and major criminal investigations. In 1976 he was assigned to the FBI laboratory and was certified as an expert in the fields of forensic photography and questioned document examinations. In 1985 he was reassigned to the FBI Academy as an instructor in forensic science and as an expert in crime scene investigations. In 1988 he was transferred to the training division as a criminal investigative analyst for the National Center for the Analysis of Violent Crime.

James A. Wright

Supervisory Special Agent James A. Wright has been with the FBI for over twenty years and served in the FBI's Chicago and Washington, D.C., field offices, where he was assigned to personal crimes squads and investigated bank robberies, extortions, kidnappings, homicides, and threats and assaults against public officials, most notably the attempted assassination of President Ronald Reagan. He was a counselor for the 123d session of the FBI National Academy.

Wright received a B.S. degree in the administration of justice from American University and is currently a master's candidate in public administration at Virginia Commonwealth University.

Wright was assigned in October 1984 to the FBI training division's Behavioral Science Investigative Support Unit, a part of the National Center for the Analysis of Violent Crime, as a criminal investigative analyst. He currently serves as the program manager of the Criminal Investigative Analysis Program. He has provided instruction and consulted in several hundred violent crimes throughout the United States, Canada, the Caribbean, Central America, and Southeast Asia.